THE MEDIEVAL CAS
ENGLAND AND W

THE MEDIEVAL CASTLE IN ENGLAND AND WALES

A social and political history

N. J. G. POUNDS

CAMBRIDGE
UNIVERSITY PRESS

Published by the Press Syndicate of the University of Cambridge
The Pitt Building, Trumpington Street, Cambridge CB2 1RP
40 West 20th Street, New York NY 10011–4211, USA
10 Stamford Road, Oakleigh, Melbourne 3166, Australia

First published 1990
First paperback edition 1994

Printed in Great Britain at the University Press, Cambridge

British Library cataloguing in publication data

Pounds, Norman J. G. (Norman John Greville)
The medieval castle in England and Wales: a social and
political history.
1. England. Castles, history
1. Title
942

Library of Congress cataloguing in publication data

Pounds, Norman John Greville.
The medieval castle in England and Wales: a social and
political history/ N. J. G. Pounds
p.   cm.
1. Castles – England – History. 2. Castles – Wales – History.
3. England – Social conditions – Medieval period, 1066–1485. 4. Great
Britain – Politics and government – 1066–1485. 5. Wales – History – To
1536. 1. Title.
DA660.P68   1990
942 – dc20   89–77363 CIP

ISBN 0 521 38349 8 hardback
ISBN 0 521 45828 5 paperback

CONTENTS

v

ILLUSTRATIONS

Northbld

Cumb

Durh

Westm

Yorks

Lancs

Chesh

Derby

Notts

Lincs

Staffs

Leic

Norf

Shrop

Warw

Northts

Beds

Hunts

Cambs

Suff

Heref

Worcs

Oxon

Bucks

Herts

Ess

Glouc

Berks

Mddx

Wilts

Surr

Kent

Som

Hants

Suss

Dev

Dors

Cornw

0   50   100km

PREFACE

The field work on which this book is in part based was begun more than fifty years ago when the author set out to visit the majority of castle sites in Britain. The library work, which has proved to be more important than scaling walls and measuring mottes, was largely accomplished in the vast collections of the United States, and the author is deeply grateful to Indiana University for the help and encouragement which it has continuously afforded.

He is also deeply grateful to his close friends John Charlton and Leslie Wayper, who have read the manuscript and have given him the benefit of their great knowledge and expertise, and to Anthony Emery and Pauline Fenley who have read and criticised individual chapters. He wishes also to thank Professor Sir James Holt for his encouragement, and friends who have discussed many points with him, including Beatrice Claire, Jonathan Coad, Charles Coulson, Peter Curnow, Brian Davison, Derek Renn, Andrew Saunders, Peter Spufford, Michael Thompson and others. For opinions expressed, when they differ from theirs, he is alone responsible.

All county references are to the administrative system as it was before the 'reforms' of 1974. In the Middle Ages there was neither county nor sheriff of Avon or Humberside, and that is sufficient reason to ignore these anachronisms. The map facing shows the administrative divisions used in this book.

The author is grateful to the following for permission to reproduce manuscripts (see p. vi) in their care: the Master and Fellows of Corpus Christi College, Cambridge; the Provost and Fellows of Eton College, and the Trustees of the British Library.

Cambridge
July 1990

ABBREVIATIONS

AASRP	Associated Architectural Societies' Reports and Papers
AmHR	*American Historical Review* (Bloomington, Ind.)
A-N St	*Anglo-Norman Studies* (Woodbridge)
Ant	*Antiquity* (Cambridge)
Ant Jl	*The Antiquaries Journal* (London)
Arch	*Archaeologia* (London)
Arch Ael	*Archaeologia Aeliana* (Newcastle-upon-Tyne)
Arch Camb	*Archaeologia Cambrensis* (Cardiff)
Arch Cant	*Archaeologia Cantiana*
Arch Jl	*Archaeological Journal* (London)
A-S C	Anglo-Saxon Chronicle
Barnet S Bull	*Barnet and District Historical Society, Bulletin*
Battle Conf	*Proceedings of the Battle Conference on Anglo-Norman Studies* (Ipswich)
BBOAJ	*The Berkshire, Buckinghamshire and Oxfordshire Archaeological Journal*
Bd Celt St	Board of Celtic Studies
Bd Celt St	*Board of Celtic Studies, Bulletin*
BE	*Buildings of England* (Harmondsworth)
Beds Arch Jl	*Bedfordshire Archaeological Journal* (Luton)
Beds HRS	Bedfordshire Historical Records Society (Bedford)
Beds Mag	*Bedfordshire Magazine* (Luton)
Beds Rec Soc	Bedfordshire Record Society
Berks A J	*Berkshire Archaeological Journal* (Reading)
BIHR	*Bulletin of the Institute of Historical Research*
Bl Pr Reg	*Black Prince's Register*
Bonn Jb	*Bonner Jahrbücher*
Brist R S	Bristol Record Society (Bristol)
Brit Acad	British Academy (London)
Brych	*Brycheiniog* (Brecon)
Bull J R Lib	*Bulletin of the John Rylands Library* (Manchester)

Bull Soc Ant Norm	*Bulletin de la Société des Antiquaires de Normandie* (Caen)
Cal Anc Corr, Wales	Calendar of Ancient Correspondence, Wales
Cal State PD	Calendar of State Papers, Domestic
Camb Law Jl	*Cambridge Law Journal* (Cambridge)
Camb Med Hist	*Cambridge Medieval History* (Cambridge)
Camd Misc	Camden Miscellany, Royal Historical Society (London)
Camd Soc	Camden Society, Royal Historical Society (London)
CBA	Council for British Archaeology (London)
CCR	Calendar of Close Rolls
C Chart R	Calendar of Charter Rolls
C Docts Fr	Calendar of Documents in France
C Docts Scotl	Calendar of Documents Relating to Scotland (Edinburgh)
Cered	*Ceredigion* (Aberystwyth)
C Fine R	Calendar of Fine Rolls
Chât Gaill	*Château Gaillard* (Caen)
Cheth Soc	Chetham Society (Manchester)
C Inq Misc	Calendar of Inquisitions Miscellaneous
C Inq pm	Calendar of Inquisitions post mortem
Class Hist Fr	*Classiques de l'Histoire de France*
C Lib R	Calendar of Liberate Rolls
C Mem R	Calendar of Memoranda Rolls
Colln de Textes	Collection de Textes
Col Top Gen	*Collectanea Topographica et Genealogica* (London)
Cornw Arch	*Cornwall Archaeology* (Truro)
CPR	Calendar of Patent Rolls
CUL	Cambridge University Library
Cur Arch	*Current Archaeology* (London)
Cur Reg R	Curia Regis Rolls
CWAAS	Cumberland and Westmorland Antiquarian and Archaeological Society
CWAS Rec Ser	Cumberland and Westmorland Archaeological Society Record Series (Kendal)
Cym Rec Soc	Cymmrodorion Record Society
DB	Domesday Book, Record Commission
D C Rec Soc	Devon and Cornwall Record Society (Exeter)
Dugd Soc Occ Pap	Dugdale Society Occasional Papers (Birmingham)
E Angl A R	East Anglian Archaeological Reports (Norwich)
EcHR	*Economic History Review* (London)
Econ H	*Economic History* (London)

EHR	*English Historical Review*
Ess Jl	*Essex Journal*
Flint HS	Flintshire Historical Society
Geog	*Geography*
Harv Law Rv	*Harvard Law Review* (Cambridge, Mass.)
Hist	*History*
HMSO	Her (His) Majesty's Stationery Office
JBAA	*Journal of the British Archaeological Association*
J Ches/NW AS	*Journal of the Cheshire and North Wales Archaeological Society*
Jew H S	Jewish Historical Society
JlDerbAS	*Journal of the Derbyshire Archaeological Society* (Derby)
Jl Med Hist	*Journal of Medieval History* (Amsterdam)
Jl Warbg Inst	*Journal of the Warburg Institute* (London)
KW	*The History of the Kings Works*, HMSO
L and P Hen VIII	*Letters and Papers of Henry VIII*, HMSO
Law Qt Rv	*Law Quarterly Review*
L&C Rec Soc	Lancashire and Cheshire Record Society
LeicAHS	Leicestershire Archaeological and Historical Society (Leicester)
Lincs AHA	Lincolnshire Archaeological and Historical Society (Lincoln)
Lincs RS	Lincolnshire Record Society (Lincoln)
Med Arch	*Medieval Archaeology* (London)
MGH	*Monumenta Germaniae Historica* (Berlin)
Midl H	*Midland History* (Birmingham)
Montg Collns	*Montgomery Collections* (Welshpool)
Morg	*Morgannwg* (Cardiff)
NID	Naval Intelligence Division
Norf Arch	*Norfolk Archaeology* (Norwich)
Norf RS	Norfolk Record Society (Norwich)
North H	*Northern History* (Leeds)
Northts R S	Northamptonshire Record Society (Northampton)
Nottm Med St	*Nottingham Medieval Studies* (Nottingham)
Oxon	*Oxoniensia* (Oxford)
P & P	*Past & Present* (London)
Pap BSR	Papers of the British School in Rome
Plac Quo War	*Placita Quo Warranto*, Record Commission, 1818
PP	Parliamentary Papers (Westminster)
Pr Am Phil Soc	*Proceedings of the American Philosophical Society* (Philadelphia, Penn.)
Pr Brit Acad	*Proceedings of the British Academy* (London)

Pr Camb AS	*Proceedings of the Cambridge Antiquarian Society* (Cambridge)
Pr Dev AS	*Proceedings of the Devon Archaeological Society* (Exeter)
PRO	Public Record Office, London
Proc SAS	*Proceedings of the Society of Antiquaries of Scotland* (Edinburgh)
Pr R Art S	*Proceedings of the Royal Artillery Society*
PRS	Pipe Roll Society
Pr Som AS	*Proceedings of the Somerset Archaeological Society* (Taunton)
Pr Suff I A	*Proceedings of the Suffolk Institute of Archaeology* (Ipswich)
RAI	Royal Archaeological Institute (London)
R B Exch	*Red Book of the Exchequer*, Rolls Series
RCAM(S)	Royal Commission on Ancient Monuments for Scotland (Edinburgh)
RCAHM(W)	Royal Commission on Ancient and Historical Monuments in Wales (Cardiff)
RCHM	Royal Commission on Historical Monuments for England (London)
Rec Com	Record Commission
Regesta	*Regesta Regum Anglicanorum* (London)
Res Repts Soc Ant	Research Reports, Society of Antiquaries
RS	Rolls Series
Rot Cur Regis	Rotuli Curiae Regis, Record Commission
Rot Hundr	Rotuli Hundredorum, Record Commission
Rot Lit Claus	Rotuli Literarum Clausarum, Record Commission
Rot Lit Pat	Rotuli Literarum Patentarum, Record Commission
Rot Parl	Rotuli Parliamentorum, Record Commission
RPAS Lincs	Reports and Papers of the Architectural Societies of Lincolnshire, Yorkshire, Northamptonshire and Leicestershire
RP Ass Arch S	Reports and Papers of the Associated Architectural Societies
Rv Belge PH	*Revue Belge de Philologie et d'Histoire*
Sci Am	*Scientific American* (New York)
Seld Soc	Selden Society (London)
Settimane	*Settimane di Studio del Centro Italiano di Studi sull'alto Medioevo* (Spoleto)
S Midl Arch	*South Midlands Archaeology*
Soc Cymm	Society of Cymmrodorion
Soc Med Arch	Society for Medieval Archaeology

Som Dors NQ	*Somerset and Dorset Notes and Queries*
South H	*Southern History* (Southampton)
Spec	*Speculum* (Boston, Mass.)
Staffs Collns	*Staffordshire Collections*
Surr Arch Collns	*Surrey Archaeological Collections*
Surt Soc	Surtees Society
Suss Arch Collns	*Sussex Archaeological Collections*
Suss Rec Soc	Sussex Record Society
SW Mon Rec Soc	South Wales and Monmouthshire Record Society
Tijd Kon Ned Aards	*Tijdschrift van het Koninklijk Nederlandsch Aardrijkskundig Genootschap* (Amsterdam)
TrBGAS	*Transactions of the Bristol and Gloucestershire Archaeological Society*
TrCWAAS	*Transactions of the Cumberland and Westmorland Antiquarian and Archaeological Society* (Kendal)
Tr Cymm	*Transactions of the Honourable Society of Cymmrodorion*
Tr Denb HS	*Transactions of the Denbighshire Historical Society*
Tr Dev A	*Transactions of the Devonshire Association* (Exeter)
Tr Dugd Soc	*Transactions of the Dugdale Society*
Tr Ess AS	*Transactions of the Essex Archaeological Society*
TrHSLC	*Transactions of the Historical Society of Lancashire and Cheshire*
Tr Leic AS	*Transactions of the Leicestershire Archaeological Society* (Leicester)
Tr Lond Mddlx AS	*Transactions of the London and Middlesex Archaeological Society* (London)
Tr Newb FC	*Transactions of the Newbury Field Club* (Newbury)
TrRHS	*Transactions of the Royal Historical Society* (London)
Tr S Cymmr	*Transactions of the Honourable Society of Cymmrodorion* (London)
Tr Shrop AS	*Transactions of the Shropshire Archaeological Society*
TrStAHAAS	*Transactions of the St Albans and Hertfordshire Architectural and Archaeological Society*
Tr Thor Soc	*Transactions of the Thoroton Society*
Tr Woolh FC	*Transactions of the Woolhope Natural History and Field Club*
Tr Worcs AS	*Transactions of the Worcestershire Archaeological Society* (Worcester)
Ulst Jl A	*Ulster Journal of Archaeology*
Univ Lond Hist Ser	University of London Historical Series (London)
VAG Newsl	*Vernacular Architecture Group Newsletter*
V and A	Victoria and Albert Museum, London

VCH	Victoria County History (London)
WAM	*Wiltshire Archaeological Magazine*
Welsh H Rv	*Welsh Historical Review*
Wilts Rec Soc	Wiltshire Record Society
Worcs Arch Soc	Worcestershire Archaeological Society
Y Cymm	*Y Cymmrodor*
Yorks AJ	*Yorkshire Archaeological Journal*
Yorks A & T Jl	*Yorkshire Archaeological and Topographical Journal*

PART I

The first century of English feudalism

CHAPTER 1

Castles of the Conquest

Munitiones enim quas castella Galli nuncupant Anglicis provinciis paucissime
fuerant, et ob hoc Angli licet bellicosi fuerunt et audaces ad resistendum tamen
inimicis extiterant debiliores   Ordericus Vitalis, IV, ii, 184

On the morning of 28 September 1066, William, Duke of Normandy, landed,
together with a small force of knights and men-at-arms, near the ruined Roman fort
of Anderida, on the Sussex coast. It was a dangerous mission on which he had
embarked. He was setting out to conquer a country with a force of no more than
5,000 men. His first act after coming ashore, so we are told by William of Poitiers,
was to enclose a corner of the Anderida fort and convert it into a castle.[1] He then
moved eastwards along the coast to Hastings, which, unlike Pevensey, had the
advantage of a small harbour. Here, on the cliff above the sea, he compelled
conscripted Saxon labourers to build another castle, vividly portrayed in the Bayeux
Tapestry. And it was here, within reach of the sea and his ships, that he awaited the
arrival from the North of King Harold and his army.[2]

The events of the next month call for no retelling. After his victory on the field of
Battle, William continued to linger near the coast, as if unwilling to advance into the
interior of an unknown and hostile country. He moved along the coast to Dover,
where the remains of another Roman fort still crowned the cliffs. There he again
built a castle.[3] Having thus created a strong base, to which he could if necessary
retreat, he set out for London. His force made its way by Canterbury and Rochester,
both exhibiting still the remains of their Roman walls, and so to the south bank of
the Thames, opposite the city of London, which he had to occupy if he was ever to
command this land. But the river crossing proved too difficult, and he decided to
approach the city only after a long swing to the west and north. His route must have
taken him close to Windsor before he crossed the river at Wallingford.[4] From here
he struck north-east, along the Icknield Way, and then turned south, through one of
the gaps which ease the passage of the Chiltern Hills, towards London. At
Berkhamsted he was met by the Anglo-Saxon leaders. They submitted and swore
fealty, and the road to London lay open. On Christmas Day in the following
December he assumed the crown of King Edward in the Confessor's own abbey
church of Westminster.

But England was not a tightly centralised state, and to occupy its largest city was
by no means to control the country. Peoples in the South-west and the North had

1.1 The building of the motte of Hastings Castle, after the Bayeux Tapestry. For the church tower to the right (see p. 233).

played no role in resisting the invasion. They had not suffered defeat at the hands of Duke William and were not prepared to submit. The resistance which broke out, first in Devon and then in the North, was not rebellion, but rather a refusal to submit to alien rule. At the same time William was faced with disloyalty among those who had followed him and had fought with him at Hastings. It was the prospect of land and loot that had attracted many of them, and their grievances, inevitable in these circumstances, led to the first revolt amongst the continental followers of Duke William. Eustace of Boulogne, who had not been one of William's Norman vassals, attacked the castle which had just been built at Dover. He failed and returned to his lands in northern France.

William's rule was also threatened from without. A Danish invasion of northern England had been foiled by Harold, but the threat of further attack continued. In the early years of the reign a Danish fleet was hovering off the east coast, and its presence offers a reason for the building of the great keep at Colchester, as well as a second castle at York. There was even an unsuccessful invasion from Ireland but it was on the Welsh and Scottish borders that, in the long term, the greatest danger lay.

There had long been unrest where the Welsh valleys opened towards the English plain. Even before the death of Edward the Confessor a small number of castles had been built in Herefordshire to contain the threat. After the Conquest 'palatinates' were established throughout the March of Wales in an attempt to secure a more

4

organised and coherent defence. The situation was no less serious along the Scottish border. Here there was no clearcut boundary, either political or ethnic, between the kingdom of England and that of Scotland. Beyond York there lay a kind of frontier within which neither side held effective control.[5] The situation was made worse by the fact that the apparent Anglo-Saxon heir to the Confessor, Edward the Ætheling, had sought refuge with the King of the Scots.

Lastly, it must be remembered that King William was also Duke of Normandy, that this was his primary interest, and that he had of necessity to spend considerable periods of time on the other side of the Channel. It is, indeed, surprising that the Norman state was able to survive the dangers which beset it. That it was able to do so was due, at least in part, to two considerations: the creation through grants of land of a class of men with a vested interest in the Norman settlement, and, secondly, the introduction of the castle as a fortified home and military base.

The nature of the Norman settlement is revealed in Domesday Book. Scarcely any of the Anglo-Saxon holders of land, with the exception of the institutions of the church, remained in 1086. Their possessions had been allocated to the followers of William. It has been estimated, on the basis of the Domesday record, that about 20 per cent of the land was retained in the hands of the king; that about half passed to the lay baronage, and that the rest was in the possession of the church.[6] Change was entirely at the top. The agrarian substructure of the land remained untouched by the Conquest.

The men whom William had to reward were relatively few. Only about eighty of them received estates worth more than £100 a year, and less than a hundred lands to the value of from £10 to £100. 'A body of less than 200 men could have been known personally, even intimately, to the king–duke.'[7] Most of these men possessed estates which were fragmented, parcels of land being found over wide areas of the country. This was not due to the deliberate policy of preventing any great concentration of power, but rather to the ways in which lands came into the king's hands and were allocated to his followers. He inherited no register of landowners and lands. His campaigning must have given him a broad familiarity with the land, but in bestowing it upon his followers he could have been guided only by the tenurial system which he had inherited. The lands of one or more thegns, wherever they may have lain – and of this the king probably had no precise knowledge – were granted to a particular Norman baron. It might even be inferred that it was for the latter to go and find out where these were.

This scattering of estates was intensified by marriage and inheritance, by grants of land and division among heiresses. It nevertheless had an important social and constitutional significance. It diminished the *local* power and importance of a baron, but intensified his perception of the country as a whole.

As a general rule these grants of land were coupled with the obligation on the part of the recipient, to serve the king. The tenant undertook to follow him with a prescribed number of knights for a certain period in each year. How these knights were recruited and maintained was in all probability left for the tenant to determine.

This contractual relationship goes back to the early years of the Conquest. It may have been entered into orally. The baron knew what he owed the king, and the king knew what was due to him. No charter was needed. The allocation of lands and the imposition of knight-service must have been a slow and piecemeal process, as, indeed, was the Conquest itself.[8] Dr Chew has argued that the system of ecclesiastical military service had been imposed on episcopal sees and monastic houses, which mainly lay in the south-east, by 1070.[9] Le Patourel suggests[10] that the feudal organisation of the south-east, up to, in all probability, the line of the Jurassic uplands, took place in 1066–70, and that of the Midlands, as far north perhaps as Chester and York was accomplished by 1080. The subjugation of the North, beyond Lancaster and the Tees valley, was in the main the work of the Conqueror's son and successor, William Rufus.[11]

The second innovation which did much to ensure the eventual triumph of Duke William was the castle. A castle is best defined as the fortified and defensible home of a member of the feudal nobility. It became, on the one hand, a centre from which an estate could be administered and, on the other, a strong point from which territory could be controlled and invasion checked. In royal castles, built and maintained by the king himself, the balance between these functions was different. Few were, in any normal sense, the homes of the ruler, though on occasion he stayed at many in the course of his travels. Their function was primarily administrative and military.

The castles which the Conqueror established during the Hastings campaign were not the first to be built in this country. As an institution the castle had originated possibly as early as the ninth century under the late Carolingians.[12] This was encouraged by the breakdown of centralised authority. In Normandy castles became numerous during the minority of Duke William and they figure prominently in the Bayeux Tapestry. It is not surprising that the Norman favourites of Edward the Confessor introduced the castle to England. There were probably few. One lay north of London and has been somewhat unconvincingly identified with Clavering in Essex. The others appear to have been in Herefordshire, where Edward established his Norman friends in the belief that they would be able to stem the attacks of the Welsh.[13] There is reason to believe that Richard's Castle belonged to the Norman, Richard son of Scrob, and that Osbern Pentecost also held a castle in these parts, tentatively identified with Ewyas Harold, which was *re*fortified after the Conquest.[14] Only one pre-Conquest castle can be identified with reasonable certainty, that which Earl Ralph established in Hereford itself.

Castle-building by the Confessor's Norman favourites was on too small a scale to have restrained the Welsh; enough only to anger the Saxons. On the return of Earl Godwin in 1051, we are told, 'some fled west to Pentecost's castle; some north to Robert's castle'.[15] The castles themselves appear to have been abandoned by the 'Frenchmen', and it is unlikely that any were occupied when Duke William landed on the Sussex coast.

The course of the Conquest was marked by the construction of castles, without which the conquered territory could not have been held. The initial invasion was marked by the building of castles at Pevensey and Hastings, and, in some sort, at Dover. The Conqueror's route to London came within a few years to be studded with them: Canterbury, Rochester, Windsor, Wallingford, Berkhamsted, and the campaigns of the next ten years were accompanied by intensive castle-building. The western campaign of 1068 led to the capture of Exeter, where the king 'chose a spot within the walls where a castle was to be built, and left Baldwin of Meules . . . and other leading knights to complete . . . the castle and remain as garrison'.[16] The surviving gatehouse tower must have formed part of Baldwin's work.[17]

This was followed in 1068–9 by a northern campaign. A castle was built at Warwick and entrusted to Roger of Beaumont, and another at Nottingham, which the king left in the charge of William Peverel. York Castle was built and then held against the local people by William Malet.[18] King William relieved it and, to ensure the security of the city, built a second castle on the other side of the Ouse. The first of his castles is today represented by the mound which supports Clifford's Tower, and the second by the long-abandoned motte known as Baile Hill.[19]

On his return from his first expedition to York the king ordered castles to be built at Lincoln, Huntingdon and Cambridge. In the meanwhile a great castle had been begun within the south-eastern angle of the rampart of the city of London in order, in the words of William of Poitiers, to protect the king from the fickleness of a large and wild (*ferus*) population.[20] This was the Tower of London, whose restraining influence on the urban population was reinforced by others built later in the western quarter of the city.[21]

In the year following the building of the second castle at York, castles were established at Chester and Stafford. Then, following the suppression of Hereward's revolt, one was built within the precinct of the Benedictine abbey of Ely.[22] Durham Castle was founded in the course of a campaign against the Scots, and was entrusted to the bishop for his security against invaders.[23] Castles were built by the king or with his knowledge and consent at Winchester, Wallingford, Oxford, Gloucester, Colchester, Norwich, Worcester and Shrewsbury,[24] and possibly even at Cardiff.[25] Most royal castles were built within the decaying ramparts of a Roman or Anglo-Saxon town, but some, like Corfe, Rockingham and Windsor, were in open country but on sites eminently suitable for defence.

It is impossible to exaggerate the role of castles in the Norman conquest of this country.[26] Their significance was underlined by Ordericus Vitalis: 'the king rode into all the remote parts of his kingdom', he wrote, 'and fortified strategic sites against enemy attack. For the fortifications, called castles by the Normans, were scarcely known in the English provinces, and so, the English, in spite of their courage and love of fighting, could put up only a weak resistence to their enemies.'[27] Ordericus was broadly correct. The castle became the instrument whereby the Conqueror fastened his grip on England. But he was helped by another innovation, the use of the horse in warfare. The Saxons used horses for riding and transport. King Harold had horses on his march southward to meet Duke William at Hastings, but when he got there his men fought on foot. The Normans, on the other hand,

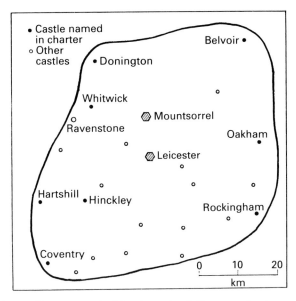

1.2 The 'demilitarised' zone organised by the earls of Chester and Leicester (see pp. 8–9).

brought horses with them from Normandy; and in battle they were used to overwhelm the Saxons. The horse lifted the knight above the humble foot-soldier and gave him both a military and a psychological advantage. In the present context, however, the significance of the horse lay in the fact that it transformed the castle from a means of passive defence into an instrument for controlling the surrounding area.[28] The Pipe Rolls record payments to mounted men, both knights and servants, garrisoning royal castles during the disturbances of 1172–3[29] and the chronicles often mention sallies by horsemen against unsuspecting besiegers.[30] It is evident that a garrison could in this way dominate a large area and this must have been the principal function of castles: to form fixed points *from* which territory could be controlled. Florence of Worcester recorded that in 1140 the men of Malmesbury Castle 'exhausted the whole neighbourhood by their ravages'.[31] In the wars of Stephen's reign there were few skirmishes and no pitched battles. Instead, wrote William of Malmesbury, 'there were many castles all over England, each defending its own district or, to be more truthful, plundering it'.[32] When Robert FitzHerbert gained possession of Devizes Castle in Wiltshire, 'he did not hesitate to boast that by means of that castle he would gain possession of the whole district from Winchester to London'.[33] His claim was exaggerated, but there can be no doubt that he could command a very considerable area. Warfare consisted essentially of attempts by each side to seize or build castles within the territory of the other and to use them to scour the surrounding countryside, always retreating to the walls of a castle whenever threatened by a superior force.[34]

Nowhere is this demonstrated more clearly than in a treaty negotiated in the closing years of Stephen's reign between Ranulf de Gernons, earl of Chester, and his rival, Robert de Beaumont, earl of Leicester.[35] Ranulf de Gernons, in addition to his lands in Cheshire, held Lincoln Castle and lands in Nottinghamshire and Leicestershire. Beaumont's lands lay in the East Midlands and centred on his castle of Leicester. The possessions of the two were intermixed, and each was being devastated by the raids of the other. The intent of the treaty was to sort out this tangle, put an end to the feuding and limit the number of castles which could be used in this way. Ranulf de Gernons first granted to the Earl of Leicester the castle of Mountsorrel, which lay exasperatingly close to Leicester itself. Then the two agreed that neither 'ought to build any new castle between Hinckley and Coventry, nor between Hinckley and Harsthill, nor between Coventry and Donington, nor between Donington and Leicester, nor at Gotham nor at Kinoulton nor nearer [to Leicester?], nor between Kinoulton and Belvoir, nor between Belvoir and Oakham, nor between Oakham and Rockingham nor nearer, except with the common consent of both'.[36]

In this way a 'demilitarised' zone was established, covering some 2,000 square km.[37] It was agreed to exclude castles of others within this zone. That of Ravenstone, which appears to have been a minor irritant to both parties, was to be destroyed, and 'if anyone shall build a castle in the aforesaid places or within the aforesaid limits, each shall aid the other without ill will until the castle shall be destroyed'.[38] Leicester Castle again became the focus of civil strife in 1173, when it was held against the king, and knights from the castle plundered as far afield as Nottingham and Northampton.[39]

The view, expressed here, that the castle and the mounted knight were vital to the Norman conquest and settlement of England has met with significant criticism. H. G. Richardson, whose views are sometimes perverse but always stimulating, has argued that the baronial castle of the Normans 'cannot have differed greatly from the English noble's *burh*',[40] and that they were 'militarily ineffective'. This is surely to misunderstand the ways in which the Normans used their castles.

The castles which the Norman kings and their leading barons established throughout the length and breadth of this land were the bases from which territory was controlled. But the castle was also defensive, giving protection to its family and household in troubled times. There can be little doubt but that many of those built during the first century of English feudalism were intended to serve only this latter purpose. They were too small to provide quarters for a troop of mounted soldiers, and their lords too poor to have been able to support them. Many, perhaps a majority of the unchronicled earthwork castles of this age, were no more than lightly protected homesteads. They were abandoned when no longer needed for protection, and their narrow quarters were replaced by other more comfortable and commodious accommodation (see pp. 21–2, 256). It is important to realise that the England of the years following the Conquest was not a peaceful realm, where the rule of law was enforced and the king's writ ran everywhere. It was, by contrast, 'violent, bloody and disorderly . . . we must think . . . of fearful men seeking to control a rebellious land under the threat of hostile invasion, men ruthless and

9

rapacious, driven by repressions and barbarous cruelties, conquerors in many ways inferior to the conquered'.[41]

It would probably be a profitable exercise to determine who at the time of Domesday held manors in which the smaller earthwork castles were located. Documentary sources occasionally throw light on these simple castles. In the 1140s Bishop Alexander of Lincoln confirmed a grant to the abbot and brethren of Newhouse (Newsham) of the capital messuage of Peter of Goxhill, together with 'the court where his castle had been' – *cum curia ubi castellum suum fuit*.[42] The castle, of which no trace remains, had clearly been abandoned and a house built nearby.

A similar document of the early twelfth century records the grant to the Cistercian house of Meaux, near Hull, of a mill on the river Hull together with land. It lay in the manor of Cottingham, whose lord, Robert de Stuteville, was an important landholder. But what makes this charter important is that the gift was accompanied by that of a wooden castle, from the materials of which various monastic offices were to be built: *castellum etiam ligneum unde edificatae sunt pistrinum* [mill], *stabulum* [stable] *et aliae monasterii officinae*.[43] There is evidence in Cottingham of a moated enclosure which may have been Stuteville's demolished castle.[44] Yet another small castle, abandoned at an early date, was that presumed to have been built by Ernulf de Hesdin at Ruislip in Middlesex.[45] It would appear to have passed out of use even earlier than those at Goxhill and Cottingham, for in 1096 the site was given to the monks of the Normandy abbey of Bec. Here, however, insubstantial traces of the castle survived until overwhelmed by the westward spread of London, and show it to have been a mound with a small bailey. The manor of Goltho in Lincolnshire provides a final example of a small, ephemeral castle of the early years of the Conquest, but here the evidence is almost wholly archaeological. The site was granted to the Bishop of Durham, who subinfeudated it to one Nigel who built, perhaps by 1080, a very small mound and bailey castle. In the early or middle years of the twelfth century Goltho, united with Kyme and other manors in the region, became the head of a small barony. The course of events at Goltho was the opposite of what might have been expected. The motte was partially levelled to turn the bailey into a raised platform on which was built an aisled hall and related domestic offices.[46] A weak castle had been turned into a rather grand manor house, suitable for the conduct of the affairs of the complex of estates which made up the honour. Glasbury (Radnorshire) may be yet another motte castle abandoned at a very early date. Its remains are slight indeed. The manor in which it lay was, like Ruislip, given to the church of Lanthony at Gloucester early in the twelfth century by Earl Miles of Hereford.[47] It would have been most unlikely that the castle would have been retained.

Goxhill and Ruislip, Cottingham and Goltho can have had very little military or strategic importance. They were no more than well-protected and incommodious homes, and were abandoned at an early date.

There are hundreds of such castles, undocumented and unexcavated. It has become almost the custom to dismiss them as 'castles of the Anarchy'. Many were just that,[48] but it is at least likely that a great many of these small and simple castles were the work of the first decades of the Conquest. That, for many of the new landholders, was their time of greatest anxiety and fear, when their grip on the land was still insecure. Is it not likely that castles, built hurriedly under the first or second William, were abandoned during the quieter times of Henry I?

This suggests that a very broad distinction should be drawn between those castles which were built by the king and his greater barons, and those put up by lesser folk for their personal protection. Difficult as it may sometimes be to assign a particular castle to one category or the other, the contrast between them is an important one. Most belonged to the second group. Their importance was merely local, and their existence was of no conceivable interest either to the king or to those who surveyed the land for Domesday Book. There was a world of difference between a small, unchronicled motte and the great mounds with their dependent baileys thrown up by a de Ferrers or a de Clare. The two belong to different species, the humbler bearing a close relationship to the burh of the Saxon thegn.

Mottes and keeps

In the last analysis, a fortification built to provide such protection could assume one of only two possible forms. It might be a tower or, secondly, a space enclosed by bank, wall or ditch, or some combination of the two. In fact, tower and bailey might be combined in a variety of ways. The Anglo-Saxon thegn protected himself with a bank and a palisade with protected *burhgeat* (see pp. 14, 223). Normanists are unanimous in saying that this was not a castle. A ringwork, or roughly circular bank and ditch, has been excavated at Penmaen, in Glamorgan.[49] The bank would have been strengthened by a palisade, and in the gap by which one gained entrance were the postholes of a massive timber gatehouse. Normanists would claim this as a castle. It may have been larger in scale than the thegn's burh, but in *form* it was similar. Translate the structures from wood to masonry, and we have the twelfth-century castle of Rougemont, Exeter, or the original bailey of Ludlow or Newark castles.

The problem is one of confusion between *form* and *function*. In terms of *form* some early Norman castles cannot have differed in any significant respect from the thegn's burh, but in *function* there was a radical difference between them. The burh was little more than a well-protected home; the true castle was the defended focus of feudal administration. A change in function is not necessarily accompanied by a development in form. Given the natural human resistance to change, especially if change costs money or necessitates effort, there is every reason to expect an older form to continue in use and to be gradually altered and adapted as might be thought necessary.

But the early castle in Britain took the form of a mound or motte far more frequently than it did of a ringwork. It is true that the Bayeux Tapestry, in representing four completed castles, shows them as steep-sided, flat-topped mounds, their summits supporting a tower-like house girt with a palisade and

1.3 The motte of the castle of Rennes (Brittany), showing the wooden tower and palisade on its summit. After the Bayeux Tapestry.

reached by ladder from the counterscarp of the surrounding ditch. This is the classic motte castle as presented to us by Ella Armitage[50] and J. H. Round.[51] They assumed that the mound was of one build and that the lord lived in the 'house' on its summit. Below the motte was usually a bailey or court, in which the lord stabled his horses, housed his retainers and stored his supplies. But too few mottes have been sectioned for us to be sure how regularly this classic model was adopted.

Reality may have been somewhat different. The excavation of a number of mottes has shown that they are not always the primary feature of a castle. They were sometimes the culmination of a complex development. It would, indeed, be very strange if it were otherwise. They were not, after all, taken from an eleventh- or twelfth-century equivalent of a pattern book. Forty years ago, in 1949, Brian Hope-Taylor began the excavation of a motte at Abinger in Surrey.[52] The castle itself was almost certainly erected during the Anarchy. It was quickly abandoned, and its historical importance was slight. Its summit, which stood twenty feet above the surrounding ground, was pitted with massive postholes, which, it was postulated, supported a raised structure which could have served as a lookout, a fighting platform or living space. That the lower stage of this wooden tower lay open is

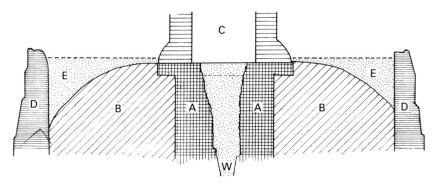

1.4 Section through the motte of Farnham Castle. The motte (B) itself contains a hollow masonry core, at the bottom of which was a well (W). This originally supported a tower (C). The motte was later encased by a masonry wall (D) and its surface levelled up (E). Based on M. W. Thompson, *Med. Arch.* 4 (1960), 81–94.

confirmed by the picture of Dinan Castle, in the Bayeux Tapestry. It was, in Hope-Taylor's words, 'a sort of box on stilts'. Further excavation showed that this stilted tower was the second on the site; that there had been another embedded in the motte, which had been dismantled or had rotted.

That the Abinger structure was not an isolated case is apparent from a carving in Westminster Hall in which a man is shown chopping at one of the supporting pillars.[53] Further evidence adduced by Hope-Taylor comes from Denmark, where the supporting stilts of a wooden tower ran down through the motte until they rested on stone pads on the natural ground surface.

Ten years after the excavation of the motte at Abinger, Kent began to examine the motte at South Mimms, Hertfordshire, reputedly that built by Geoffrey de Mandeville about 1141 (see p. 30).[54] The motte itself stood 10 to 12 feet high. Its diameter at the base was about 110 feet and, at its flattened summit, about 65 feet. Excavation revealed around the base of the motte a low bank of flint. Within was evidence for a wooden tower, about 35 feet square, which rose *through* the motte and reached above its summit. Most curious of all was its entrance by a tunnel through the lowest levels of the motte.[55]

At South Mimms, as at Abinger, the tower appears to have been the primary feature, with the earth of the motte heaped around it. There is practical reason for packing rock and earth against the lower stages of the tower. In the absence of very deep postholes, the only way to make the structure stable was to surround it with earth, to supply which an annular ditch would have been dug.

Only excavation could show how many mottes have concealed within them the wooden skeleton of a tower, but there are masonry towers, among them those at Totnes,[56] Lydford[57] and Farnham[58] castles, which penetrate the motte on which they appear to stand, and reach bedrock. In the case of Farnham (Figure 1.4) the buried tower, which was of masonry and about 12 metres square, was widened at the top to about 16 metres square to support a wooden tower.[59] In the meanwhile, a parallel line of development can be traced. A bank and ditch have been a means of protecting a home or a community since the earliest times. Davison has emphasised that not only a majority of the early castles in Normandy but also many Norman castles in this country conformed more or less to this plan.[60] One has to think only of the vast banks which enclosed Castle Acre, Castle Camps, Castle Rising or Castle Hedingham. In each a great masonry tower, or keep, was built free-standing within the rounded enclosure.

By contrast Aldingham, on the coast of the Furness district in modern Cumbria, began as a small rounded enclosure, some 40 metres in diameter, with banks rising about 3 metres.[61] The next stage in its development was to fill in the ringwork to form a low motte. A similar course of development has been shown at Goltho, in Lincolnshire, and at Rumney (Glamorgan).[62]

But why, it may be asked, was there a desire to raise the level of a ringwork and convert it into some kind of a platform? A study of early settlement sites in the Lower Rhineland has shown that these embraced not only an inner court, or *Hauptburg*, but also a dependent court or *Vorburg*, and that the level of the former was in some instances progressively raised.[63] Many of the motte-like structures in this region were raised on lowlying and marshy ground. The amount by which their level was increased does not seem adequate, at least from Müller-Wille's catalogue, to have added much to their defensive potential, but it would have made the site drier.[64]

Closely similar in origin are the *terpen*, or settlement mounds, found very widely in the lowlying and more westerly parts of the Netherlands. Over 500 can be traced in Friesland alone.[65] Their purpose was to lift the settlement above the water-table and protect it from flood. Their similarity to large mottes is apparent, though they had no feudal or military connotation. The period – the early Middle Ages – when most of these settlements were formed was characterised by a sea-level lower in relation to the land than in modern times. The relative rise in sea-level then became more marked, and settlements were progressively raised to escape the water.

It was a motley assemblage that followed Duke William to England, drawn not only from Normandy and Anjou, but also from Flanders and the Low Countries. Many cultural traditions impinged on England, and it is not improbable, in Davison's words, that a merging took place 'of a Rhenish–Low Countries tradition of low dwelling-mounds with attached forecourts and a Norman–Angevin tradition of defence through height'.[66] There is a long tradition of defensive bank and ditch. For the wooden tower, mounted on stilts, we need look no further than any Roman camp. Alcock has shown that in pre-Conquest Wales the petty lords 'created a demand for fortified residences whose defences differed from those of the Norman castles . . . in degree rather than in kind'.[67] And the burh of the Saxon thegn with its *burhgeat* can also be fitted into this cultural spectrum. There were 'rings' in early Cornwall, and in Ireland raths or 'ringforts' can be numbered in their thousands, each in origin the home of an aristocratic member of the Irish society.[68] Many of them, like some ringworks in England, have been filled in and converted to platforms or mounds.[69]

It is difficult to interpret these 'raised' *raths* as the consequence of a rising water level; more likely they 'represent the transformation of an indigenous settlement form (*rath*) into an imitation of the imported Anglo–Norman mottes', from which they are sometimes extraordinarily difficult to distinguish in the field. If this is so, we have yet another example of the conflation of different cultural traditions.

It is clear that in *some* motte castles the tower which the motte appears to support was in fact the primary feature and that the mound was built as much for structural as for military reasons. In this context M. W. Thompson has suggested[70] a sequence which runs from a wooden tower supported on stilts, and partially buried in its motte, to a masonry tower, as at Lydford, against which earth had been piled, completely masking features which the original builders had intended to leave exposed.[71]

When did the motte, from being a secondary feature to improve the stability of a wooden tower, become primary? When did the builders begin by building a motte and *then* crown it with palisade and tower-house? The answer must await the sectioning of many more early mottes than have been excavated at present to see how they were put together. Nevertheless, Davison made a pertinent observation when he noted a change in the kind of castle built by the Conqueror about the time of his northern campaign in 1068.[72] Hitherto, he wrote, his castles had been enclosures, with or without a tower. Thereafter, they were mostly characterised by massive mottes, too large to be regarded merely as secondary to towers of wood or stone. The cultural traditions which have been outlined above came together to give what is regarded as the typical castle of the Conquest, a simple, even elegant motte and dependent bailey, the functions of each clearly differentiated. But simplicity in human structures, no less than in human institutions, wrote Maitland, 'is the outcome of technical subtlety; it is the goal not the starting point. As we go backwards the familiar outlines become blurred; the ideas become fluid, and instead of the simple we find the indefinite'.[73] The castle of the post-Conquest period, no less than the legal institutions of which Maitland wrote, hides behind its apparent simplicity and uniformity a multitude of cultural strands which had been brought together at this time and place. Imported cultural traditions were always open to modification by local circumstance. Construction was influenced by local terrain and geology, by labour and materials, and by the random wishes and whims of an infinite number of people.

It was stated earlier that defensive works have always conformed to one of two patterns: the fenced enclosure and the tower. The enclosure could, and frequently did, stand alone; the tower demanded some sort of appendage, where horses could be stabled and cattle held during an emergency. It may be questioned whether a motte could be inhabited for long without such provision. As a general rule, however, baileys – crescentic, square, oblong, elongated – were constructed against

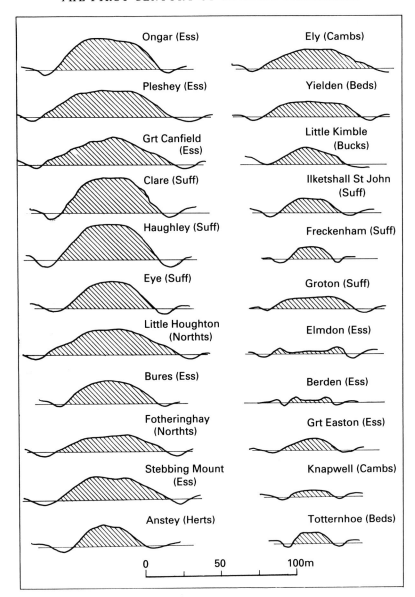

1.5 Sections through a sample of mottes in East Anglia and the East Midlands.

the ditch which surrounded the motte. Sometimes the bailey proved to be too small and a second, even a third, was added. Most often the bank which enclosed the bailey rose no more than two metres above the ground level, but this, accompanied by a ditch and a palisade, would have proved an effective deterrent to all except a large force with a siege train.

The accepted view is that the bailey was added to the motte. This may or may not have been so in all castles. There are numerous instances of a motte being added to a pre-existing enclosure. At Castle Neroche, in Somerset, a motte was added to the corner of a much earlier hillfort.[74] At Burgh (Suffolk) and Carisbrooke (Isle of Wight), a motte was raised in the angle of a Roman fort. At Tomen y Mur a Roman fort was made to serve as bailey to a motte raised within it,[75] and at Caerleon and Usk (Monmouth) a motte was built against a Roman rampart. In other instances the motte was thrown up within a ringwork which may have antedated it by only a few years.

In only a few instances has the bailey of an earthwork castle been adequately excavated, but among them are Hen Domen (Montgomery)[76] and Launceston (Cornwall).[77] In both there is evidence for a dense occupation, with 'houses' of indeterminate use spread more or less irregularly over their area. Not until these internal structures had been rebuilt in masonry can one begin to identify their purpose. By this time many – perhaps a majority – of mottes with attached baileys had been abandoned.

Both motte and bailey varied greatly in size, depending in the main on the needs and resources of those who built them. Their construction must also have been dependent in some degree on the nature of the site. A correlation of motte castles with relief and geological structure shows a high proportion on low ground and in areas of clay or alluvial soil[78] (see pp. 69–70). In hilly areas there was often no need to raise a motte; natural hillocks could be cut and scarped to serve this purpose.

The illustration of the building of Hastings Castle in the Bayeux Tapestry serves as a reminder that the great earthworks were raised by the labour of local people. The Anglo-Saxon chronicler tells that they were 'cruelly oppressed . . . with castle-works'.[79] The chief reason for the long-continued use of earthworks was not only that they could be constructed relatively quickly – sometimes in a few weeks – but that they called for little *skilled* labour. Nevertheless, mottes were often more than simple heaps of earth. Their military value depended on the steepness of their banks, and angles of up to 40° would have been difficult to maintain in unconsolidated material. The Bayeux Tapestry shows a stratification in the Hastings motte and this kind of construction also appears elsewhere. Indeed, it seems that the most carefully constructed mottes consisted of a ring bank – a kind of incipient ringwork – the interior of which was gradually filled in and raised to the required level. There is evidence also that a motte was sometimes clad with wooden boards or stone slabs to prevent soil wash and make it more difficult to climb.

On three of the four completed mottes shown on the Bayeux Tapestry the summit is reached by a flying bridge which rises from the counterscarp of the ditch. This is confirmed by the familiar account, given in the *Acta Sanctorum*, of how the bridge which rose to the motte at Merchem, in Flanders, collapsed under the weight of the crowd which followed the Bishop of Therouanne to his 'house' on the summit.[80] Further evidence, if it were needed, is found in the wooden bridge abutments and timber supports which have in a few instances been excavated.[81] It is evident, however, that in most English cases the flying bridge was replaced by steps cut into the motte.

A large motte represented an immense labour, but converting its dimensions into man-days is fraught with great difficulty. There is no evidence for any payment for the work, and it is improbable that money changed hands. They were by and large made with forced labour. Furthermore, all are in some measure degraded. In some cases their shape has been preserved by the masonry erected on their summits, but the rounded shapes of most mottes are evidence of the degree of erosion that has taken place.

It is relatively easy to estimate the labour that has been expended on banks and ditches. In most instances the ditch did not penetrate deeply into the solid geology (see pp. 69–70) and the 'throw' of the labourer was not great. In the nineteenth century it was estimated that a soldier, equipped with simple entrenching tools, should be able to shift about 15 cubic feet of soil in an hour. But after about three hours' work this figure would decline, and a day's work would not be much over 80 cubic feet, and might be appreciably less in wet or resistant material.[82] The medieval labourer was equipped with little more than a wooden shovel tipped with iron. Picks are mentioned in later building accounts but it may be questioned whether their use was general at this early date.

The military manual assumed that the maximum throw was 12 feet horizontally and 4 feet vertically. A castle bank which kept within these limits would not have been very effective, and there must have been some form of transport between the digger and the motte or bank. This would have the effect of multiplying the labour requirement by a factor of at least three. A hand-barrow is most likely to have been used, calling for two men to carry it. Furthermore, as the earthwork increased in height, so would the labour required to move each cubic foot. The result is that with the growing size of the earthworks the labour inputs must increase exponentially.

It is difficult to analyse the labour requirements of bailey defences, because ditches have largely been filled and banks eroded. Where the former have been sectioned they are generally found to be much deeper – 10 feet and more – than any superficial examination might suggest. One can often measure the area of the bailey but any estimate of the volume of earth shifted in order to create it must err on the low side. Figure 1.5 represents cross-sections through a number of mottes in the East Midlands and East Anglia. Whatever allowance is made for erosion it remains a fact that the largest, at Pleshey, Chipping Ongar and Clare, contain from twenty to forty times the volume of material found in the smaller, and this, given the exponential relationship, must represent a more than proportional increase in the labour employed. Of course there are factors which cannot be allowed for in so simple an equation: variation in water-table, the resistance of the rock, and the fact that a motte might have been the product of several campaigns spread over a number of years.

The distribution of motte castles in the East Midlands and East Anglia is shown in Figure 1.6. For a significant number no measurable remains survive, and in several others the earthworks were subordinate to massive tower keeps. The map shows very approximately the number of man-days needed to build the motte in question.

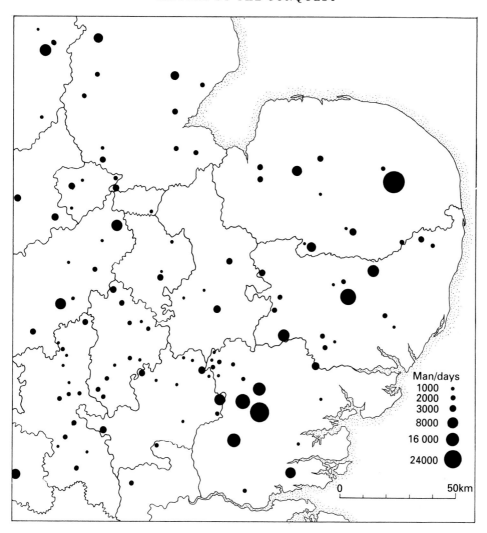

Man/days
1000 •
2000 •
3000 ●
8000 ●
16 000 ●
24000 ●

0   50km

1.6 Mottes in East Anglia and the East Midlands, according to computed labour inputs. The size symbol represents estimated time taken to build the motte. Most are degraded and they must at one time have been larger than at present.

A feature of the map is the considerable number of large mottes in East Anglia, and the close net of small mottes to the north of London (see pp. 52–3).

More significant is the fact that the castles with very large mottes and, as a general rule, extensive baileys can be identified with either the king or his more richly endowed and powerful barons. By contrast, it is difficult to link the small mottes and ringworks with any known baronial family. In a few instances they can be related to an undertenant who did knight-service, but of the origin of most we know absolutely nothing.

By the later years of the twelfth century many of the motte castles that had been built during the previous century were abandoned, and, in a few that continued to be inhabited and used, masonry was slowly replacing the wooden towers and palisades. This was, however, a very slow process. The few new castles that were built were, almost without exception, of stone, but in the older, wooden defences lingered on till the end of the thirteenth century and even later. In motte castles masonry most often took the form of a ring-wall around the flattened summit. The tower which stood within was sometimes rebuilt in stone (as at Launceston), but just as often the domestic apartments were built against the perimeter wall as at Restormel. The shell-keep, as this ring-wall is commonly called, ceased gradually to be the focus of life within the castle, as the lord and his household sought more commodious and comfortable quarters in the bailey.

As the Normans spread across this land, building castles to protect themselves and secure their conquests, speed was essential. Castles had to be built in a minimum of time, and the chronicles make it clear that many rose within the span of weeks or months. The Norman instinct was, probably, to build a tower and to surround it with a protected court.[83] The tower was at first of wood, and this restricted its size and, in particular, its height, though the motte gave it greater strength, and raised it above the level of its surroundings. In Normandy such towers had been built of masonry. They were incomparably stronger and more durable than those of wood. They would not burn, and they could be built large enough to accommodate hall, chapel, private chambers and a large storage space.[84] The great tower-keeps are amongst the most impressive monuments erected by the Normans in either Normandy or Britain. But in the heat of the Conquest they were not practicable.

In the first place construction was slow; Renn has shown from small changes in the style and quality of the masonry, how little could be accomplished in a season. The keep of Scarborough Castle occupied ten seasons; that at Newcastle-upon-Tyne eight, and the great keep at Dover, despite the immense expenditure on it by Henry II, no less than nine years. In general, a keep could be raised by ten to twelve feet in a year. Small keeps were built more quickly, but none could possibly have been erected within a season, and this is what the events of the years following the Conquest called for.

Further constraints were the lack of military engineers and masons and a shortage of building materials. The Anglo-Saxon tradition of church building continued into the Norman period. There was a great deal of monastic building, but comparatively little of this activity carried over into military construction. Lastly, there was the question of cost. Unskilled labour could be conscripted for raising earthworks and for felling and carting timber. But a tower-keep called for skilled craftsmen, and these had to be paid. Most keeps belong to the second half of the twelfth century. They were built by the king, and their cost was recorded in the Pipe Rolls, and they were not cheap.[85] The costs could not have been significantly different a century earlier. The costs of even a medium-sized tower-keep greatly exceeded the annual value of the lands, as recorded in Domesday, of the greatest barons in the land. This alone would have precluded the adoption of the tower-keep except by the richest of them.

A further consideration was that baronial lands were fragmented (see p. 5). This necessitated building more than a single castle. Whether Odo of Bayeux, who had castles at Rochester and Deddington (Oxfordshire), or Richard FitzGilbert at Tonbridge and Clare, would have acted differently if their lands had been consolidated one cannot know. It is nevertheless clear that almost all the tower-keeps built, or at least begun before the Anarchy, were either royal or were located in critically sensitive parts of the country. They were evidently the product of quite abnormal circumstances, which alone could have justified the exceptional expenditure.

Watching over the unruly citizens of London was doubtless such a circumstance, and a keep, the present Tower of London, was begun if not finished before the death of the Conqueror.[86] Another early keep was built at Colchester.[87] It closely resembles the Tower and was begun about 1076, after a Danish raid on the east coast. It was built to the height of one storey, but was raised a further two floors some twenty-five years later.[88]

Few other early keeps can be securely dated. Renn has argued for an early date for the keep at Canterbury,[89] and there is a possibility that those at Chepstow and Monmouth, as well as the idiosyncratic keep at Pevensey, date from the years of the Conquest.[90] A few more can be dated from the early years of the twelfth century: Norwich, Castle Rising, Ogmore (Glamorgan), and Gloucester. At Castle Acre (Norfolk) a rather elaborate manor house, within a modest bank and ditch, was modified and extended to become a tower-keep of massive proportions, and its bank strengthened to become a very impressive ringwork.[91] It is clear that a great keep called not only for the most careful planning but also for immense resources and a period of up to ten years for its construction. At some time in the twelfth century gate-towers, built to command the entrance, began to be converted into tower-keeps, as at Ludlow and Richmond.

In the second half of the twelfth century an important change took place in the ways in which castles were built. There is no documented example of the building of a motte in England after the accession of Henry II, though there are cases in Wales and the Marches. In Ireland, the events of the latter part of the century replicated those in England a hundred years earlier. A large part of the island was overrun by Anglo-Norman invaders who secured their conquests, as their forebears had done in England, by the rapid construction of earthworks. But in England the age of the earthwork castle was over, and for a generation or two the tower-keep reigned supreme.

The motte castle was almost indestructible, but in those which continued to be used beyond the twelfth century the buildings on the mound seem to have been neglected in favour of those in the bailey. In a few instances the motte was removed or greatly reduced in size. At Bramber a motte which lay in the *middle* of the bailey was reduced enough to fill the ditch around it. The first castle at Newcastle-upon-

Tyne was a motte, which appears to have been superseded by the tower-keep built by Henry II.[92] At Gloucester a very tall tower-keep, shown in a marginal drawing in a copy of Geoffrey of Monmouth, replaced a motte,[93] while at Kenilworth, the great keep, known as the Clinton Tower, was probably built over and encapsulated a small motte. At both Berkeley and Farnham the motte was cut back at its base and wholly revetted by a wall producing an elevated but extensive platform.[94] Other examples could be cited of the ways, more or less ingenious, by which builders sought to overcome the inconveniences of the motte. All these changes reflect a trend, not so much towards greater military strength, though that was not ignored, as towards greater domesticity. The castle was becoming less a fortress and more a home and administrative centre.

Armitage has commented on the vagueness of the nomenclature used by medieval writers.[95] The words were of course Latin or its romance derivatives. A number of terms: *castrum*, *oppidum*, *municipium* were used almost interchangeably and their precise meaning has often to be judged by the context.[96] But there were, nevertheless, certain words which acquired a definite connotation. The term *mota* indicated a 'motte', which is its Gallicised form. At Worcester there was a *castellum . . . cum motta*, and a charter granted *motam Hereford cum toto castello*. That the term *mota* ceased to be used regularly in charters is probably due to the fact that it ceased to be a particularly important part of the castle.

The term *castellum*, however, calls for discussion. Its classical meaning was a fortified enclosure, and it was given to the forts which the Romans established throughout their empire. This is the meaning which it retained through the Middle Ages. The *castella* at Worcester and Hereford were the baileys which lay below the *motae*. More important is the association of the word *castellum* with *turris*.[97] The charter of King Stephen to Geoffrey de Mandeville granted him *turris Londoniae cum castello quod ei subest*.[98] There are several other charters which associate *castellum* with *turris*. Henry I granted to Eudo his steward *civitatem de Colecestra et turrim et castellum* and Miles of Gloucester gave to the monks of Lanthony the oblations of those who kept the *turris et castellum* of Gloucester.[99]

The *turris* continued to be distinguished from the *castellum*. Jordan of Fantosme's rhyming chronicle of the Scottish invasion of 1173–4 promised the Scots lordship *en chastel e en tur*, and when the Scottish king came to Carlisle he found *le chastel e la tur* too well provisioned and strongly defended for him to take.[100] Changes in the design of castles later made the expression less appropriate, but Chaucer could still include in his *House of Fame* of about 1384

> Both castel and the tower
> And eek the halle, and every bower.[101]

The connotation of *turris* is thus apparent. It was the large, free-standing keep. The *castellum* was the bailey by which it was surrounded and without which it could not be permanently inhabited and used.

The contradistinction which is thus made between *mota* and *turris* on the one

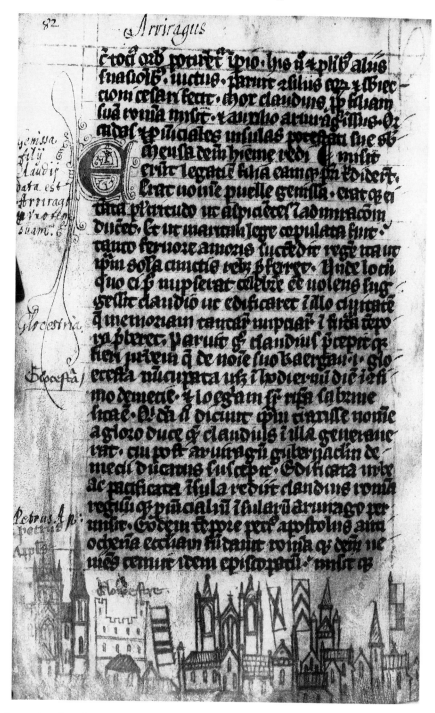

1 The medieval skyline of the city of Gloucester. On the left is St Peter's Abbey, and next to it the tower-keep of Gloucester Castle, which replaced the earlier motte.

hand and *castellum* on the other was a fundamental one in the early decades of English feudalism. It marked the gulf which lay between the lord and his body of retainers, servants and underlings. Both *mota* and *turris*, motte and tower, raised him above them. He was protected from them by thick walls or steep slopes. He could withdraw into his keep, where he could defend himself. Even after mottes and tower-keeps had ceased to be built, the structure of the greater castles continued to symbolise the social stratification of medieval society (see pp. 272–5).

Yet this apposition of lord and dependant does not express the full range of social relations which was demonstrated in the castle. It may be an expression of conflict between two classes, but the castle also represented an antagonism between the local community and those who lived beyond its compass. It was a place of refuge for the former and of defence against the latter. This is demonstrated by the extent of many baileys.

How often do we find a castle with a bailey or even two or more baileys of quite exceptional size? Such an extended rampart could not have been watched, least of all defended by the handful of retainers who were normally to be found about the place. It was an area to which the local community could retreat and which it could *help* to defend. The Northumbrian castle of Dunstanburgh, though much later in date, was a vast pound covering more than ten acres, and serving, in the words of a sixteenth-century writer, as 'a great refuge to the inhabitants of those parts, if enemies came to annoy them'.[102]

The presence of a parish church within a bailey demonstrates, not only that the lord endowed and was at one time the patron of the church, but that the local population frequented the castle, and some no doubt had permanent homes within it. Castle Camps, high on the chalk of south-eastern Cambridgeshire, may serve as an example.[103] Here a large ringwork was built by an early member of the de Vere family. At first a small bailey was created to the north-west, and this, its ditch partially filled, was replaced by a very much larger bailey which enclosed the parish church (Figure 9.1). Within the latter are building platforms which have not yet been excavated but are suggestive of a small village being there.

At Therfield (Hertfordshire) the village defences, consisting of a bank and palisade, were integrated with a motte-and-bailey castle, probably during the period of the Anarchy.[104] At Pirton, ten miles to the west, a village enclosure has a motte-castle, possibly unfinished, on its eastern edge.[105] Another example is Longtown or Ewyas Lacy Castle. Here, on the edge of the Black Mountains, is a motte supporting a round tower-keep, with no less than three baileys which together made up a rectangle of about 125 by 110 m.[106] The more easterly bailey, which covered more than half of the total area, was occupied by the village of Longtown.

All over Britain one finds examples of early castles whose outer bailey contained a church and cottages. It matters little whether one defines this as part of the castle or as a village enclosure appended to a castle. It demonstrates a physical dependence of the community on the protection which the castle was able to provide and also the reliance of the castle on the manpower of the village.

It has been pointed out that, whereas a number of mottes have been excavated, little progress has been made in the excavation of baileys. The stripping of a bailey would be, as a general rule, a far bigger task than dissecting a motte. The excavation at Hen Domen, not a motte-and-bailey of any great size, has already occupied over twenty seasons, and is still far from complete.[107] It demonstrates how formidable is the task. Hen Domen may perhaps be taken as typical of motte-and-bailey castles in which the primitive wooden defences were never replaced by masonry. Around the perimeter was an earthen bank, supporting a palisade and wooden fighting platform. Within was a tight cluster of buildings, all timber framed with their supporting posts driven firmly into the ground. The castle was inhabited for a period of at least two centuries, and during this time timbers decayed and houses were rebuilt.[108] They would have included a hall, kitchen, granary and accommodation for those who lived there, and there is evidence for the existence of a chapel. Given the nature of castle warfare one would have expected to find stabling for horses, but this does not yet seem to have been uncovered. There was little plan in the layout of the buildings, but the site may not have been altogether inelegant. Postholes do not tell how the walls and gables were decorated. Barker thinks that they may have been given a plaster rendering and perhaps coloured, and exposed timbers in gables and around doors may have been carved in the fashion familiar in contemporary churches.[109] And the space between buildings was probably roughly paved with cobbles taken from the river.

One cannot say how many people lived within the castle. It lay in the exposed Middle March against Wales and, as Domesday shows, it was endowed with a small castlery or area set aside for its support (Figure 2.5). A small permanent garrison, supplemented in time of emergency from the region to the east, is what one might expect. Doubtless families lived here, and some probably cultivated the surrounding fields, which show evidence of ridge-and-furrow. Though no luxury articles have been found, life would not have been altogether comfortless by the standards of the twelfth century.

CHAPTER 2

The castle in politics and war

quod castrum illud bene muniatur et salvo et secure custodiatur, ne pro defectu
municionis vel custodie regi inde periculum possit iminere   *Close Rolls*, 1261

The castle came earlier to the north-west of continental Europe than to Great
Britain. In Normandy the homes of the landowning classes began to be put into a
defensible condition from some time in the tenth century, when western Europe was
threatened with invasion from both north and south.[1] Two phases in this process
have been distinguished. In the first only the great men of the land – counts, bishops
and officers of state – fortified their homes. Then, as central authority weakened and
disorder increased, the practice spread downwards to the lower members of the
feudal nobility. Nevertheless, the private as distinct from the ducal castle was still
something of a rarity at the beginning of the eleventh century.

The minority of Duke William, 1035 to 1047, was marked by the more
widespread building of castles. William of Jumièges reported the erection by the
nobles of *tutissimas . . . munitiones*,[2] as conditions analogous to those of the later
Anarchy in England began to develop. But in 1047 Duke William attained his
majority and at once set about restoring some sort of order, and in the process
destroyed many of the castles that had been built during his minority.[3] Thereafter he
succeeded in maintaining some degree of control over the erection of castles in his
duchy.

That Duke William's barons in Normandy possessed castles on the eve of the
conquest of England is apparent both from documentary records and from
archaeological remains.[4] But possession of a fortified home may not be characteristic
of the lesser nobles. The holders of fiefs were legion, but 'fief and castle were two
quite different things'.[5] Few of those who followed Duke William to England could
have possessed a castle back home in Normandy. Possession of a castle, except near
the exposed frontiers of the duchy, seems to have been restricted to the greater
barons.

In 1091 the practices which had developed under Duke William were codified as
the *Consuetudines et iusticie Normanniae*.[6] The fourth clause deals with the right of
the baron to build a castle:

Nulli licuit in Normannia fossatum facere in planam terram nisi tale quod de fundo potuisset
terram iactare superius sine scabello,[7] et ibi non licuit facere palicium nisi in una regula et

illud sine propugnaculis et alatoriis. Et in rupe vel in insula nulli licuit facere fortitudinem, et nulli licuit in Normannia castellum facere, et nulli licuit in Normannia fortitudinem castelli sui vetare domino Normannie et ipse eam in manu sua voluit habere.[8]

The text is clear: no new castles might be built and existing castles could be taken over by the duke should he wish. At the same time, the authors of the text found it difficult to define a castle and to distinguish it from a lightly protected homestead. Where natural protection had been sought, as on an island or rock, the building was indubitably a castle, but when did an earthen bank and ditch cease to be merely a protection for farm animals and become a defensive work? The difference was expressed in terms of the work involved in creating it. If earth could be thrown onto the bank from the bottom of the ditch *sine scabello*, then the work did not qualify as a castle. Similarly, when did a fence become a fortification? When projecting towers and a fighting platform were added.[9]

Royal control of castle-building

The policy of King William and his sons in England was ambivalent. In the first place he was determined that the feudal anarchy that had characterised his early years should not recur. He built castles himself, but would have preferred his barons not to have followed his example. On the other hand, castles were necessary both to hold the conquered land and to protect it from invasion. Not only had he to condone castle-building by his barons, but he was obliged to entrust them with some of the castles that he had himself built.

It would have been difficult at any time for the ruler to retain control over castles in which he had placed subordinates, and in the troubled years following the Conquest almost impossible. Both Warwick and Worcester castles became hereditary in the families which were entrusted with their guardianship.[10] At Exeter, where Baldwin de Meules had been left in charge of the royal castle,[11] his descendant, Baldwin de Redvers, attempted to take possession of it 'unjustly', wrote the author of the *Gesta Stephani*, 'since the king had a reasonable claim to the guardianship of the castle which had always been a royal possession'.[12]

There is no evidence that William and his successors ever gave formal authority for the building of baronial castles. They condoned their construction as a matter of necessity, watched the activities of their occupants, and took them back into their own hands whenever such a course seemed desirable. The case of Tickhill Castle (Nottinghamshire) is particularly illuminating. It had been built by Roger de Busli, but did not pass to Roger's son along with the rest of the Busli inheritance. Instead, Rufus appears to have entrusted it to Robert of Bellême, in whose loyalty he placed a quite unjustified trust. The test came in the course of the revolt by Robert of Bellême and others against Henry I, in support of the latter's elder brother, Robert Curthose. Whereas the castles of the rebels, at Arundel and Bridgnorth, were held against the king until their lord, Robert of Bellême, himself authorised their

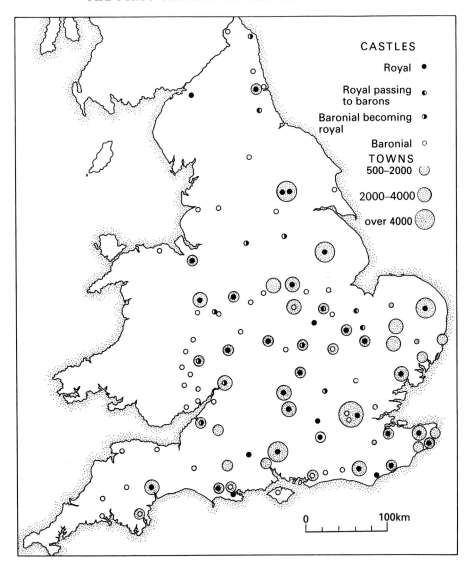

2.1 Royal and baronial castles about 1100. The size of towns is taken from H. C. Darby, *Domesday England*, Cambridge, 1977, pp. 289–98. Towns with an estimated population of less than 500 have been omitted.

surrender, at Tickhill there was no resistance to the king. Its garrison 'welcomed the king as their liege lord and opened their gates to him'.[13] The ingenious explanation offered by Mrs Chibnall is that Rufus had taken possession of a strategically important baronial castle and had merely entrusted it to Robert of Bellême as castellan.[14] In a conflict of loyalties, preference would naturally be given to the king, and so the castle was not defended against him.

This seems to have been in line with contemporary thinking. Comparatively few of William's barons had the resources to build, equip and man a castle of the size and strength of Arundel or Tickhill. But when they did so they always faced the possibility that it would pass temporarily or permanently into the possession of the crown.

The Laws of Henry I, a codification of English legal practice comparable with the *Consuetudines* of Normandy, established the rights of the king over private castles.[15] Along with taxation, and the security of the realm, the king had jurisdiction over *castellatio trium scannorum*. The precise meaning of this expression is unclear. That it defines the limit of what can be regarded as a castle, like the comparable clause in the Norman *Consuetudines*, seems probable. Liebermann interprets it as a fortification with three earthen banks,[16] but many even of the strongest castles were not so defended at this time.[17] A later clause, in listing the offences which would put a man in the king's mercy, includes *castellatio sine licencia*. Here the meaning is clear: a castle might not be built without royal authority. However we interpret the laws of Henry I, we see in them an attempt to differentiate between a small and private enclosure, successor to the thegn's burh, and a larger structure which could pose a threat to the security of the realm.

That this royal control over castle-building was acknowledged in theory if not always observed in practice, is implicit in the chronicles and charters of the period. Henry I was a strong enough ruler for the problem of illicit castles to have been of only minor importance. His successor, Stephen, had no such authority. Unlicensed castles began to appear, but even he, on his return from the South-west in 1135, 'demolished a great many unlicensed castles'.[18] The affair of the castles of the bishops of Lincoln and Salisbury gave renewed importance to the question of control over private castles. The bishops' castles at Newark, Devizes, Sherborne and Wolvesey were of no small size and significance. Stephen demanded their surrender, and the anonymous author of the *Gesta Stephani*, who always portrayed the king in the best possible light, claimed that the barons demanded 'the restitution to Caesar of castles and those things that belong to Caesar'.[19] Even William of Malmesbury, whose standpoint was certainly not anticlerical, admitted that it might be contrary to canon law for the bishops to cling on to their castles.[20] The Archbishop of Rouen, called in to adjudicate, gave it as his judgment that 'even granted that it is right for [the bishops] to have castles, yet certainly, as it is a time of suspicion, all the chief men, in accordance with the custom of other peoples, ought to hand over the keys of their fortifications to the disposal of the king, whose duty it is to fight for the peace of all'.[21]

Whether or not the first three Norman kings had given formal permission for baronial castles – and in the majority of cases they almost certainly had not – they none the less claimed an overriding right to pre-empt them, to place them in the charge of their own servants and to garrison them with their own troops. This right, though not stated in the *Leges Henrici Primi*, was generally acknowledged in France. Rufus, for example, demanded that certain baronial castles in Normandy should be placed in his hands, and appears to have been obeyed.[22]

There are cases of the king encouraging a baron to erect or extend a castle.[23] William of Poitiers claims that the Conqueror distributed rich fiefs amongst his followers who, in return, were expected to build castles to defend them.[24] The number of barons with the resources to establish a strong castle was limited. The king could have known them all and it is possible that he consulted with them on the matter of castle-building. Henry I, for example, gave custody of Rochester Castle to Archbishop William of Corbeil and his successors, at the same time authorising them 'to make in the same castle a fort or tower, as they pleased, and have guard of it'.[25] The result was the great tower-keep.

Even more expressive of royal control over castle-building is the fact that Geoffrey de Mandeville, one of the more powerful and turbulent of the barons of the age of Stephen, thought it prudent to seek permission to build a castle on his lands to the north of London. Stephen's charter granted *ut possit firmare quoddam castellum ubicumque voluerit in terra sua*.[26] That Geoffrey acted upon this licence is apparent, but the location of the resulting castle is uncertain. It has been claimed that the motte-and-bailey at South Mimms, a manor which he held, was the fortress in question,[27] but a case can also be made for it being Saffron Walden, which had a castle more in keeping with the aspirations of de Mandeville. The fact is that when Stephen's fortunes began to wane, the resourceful Geoffrey turned to his rival, Matilda, and, perhaps retrospectively, obtained from her a similar licence.[28]

The multiplication of unlicensed castles was a feature of the Anarchy, but 'it is evident from these charters that the crown struggled hard against the abdication of its right to control the building of castles, and that even when reduced to sore straits, both Stephen and the Empress made this privilege the subject of special and limited grant'.[29] Stephen succeeded at least in preserving intact the doctrine of royal control. It was for Stephen's successor, Henry of Anjou, son of the Empress Matilda, to use this prerogative to the full.

It was generally agreed that the evils of the Anarchy were due primarily to the unrestricted building of castles. The nature of castle warfare was such that the existence of one predatory castle forced neighbouring lords and communities also to build defences. The war itself ground to a stalemate and ended in compromise. In November 1153, Stephen and Duke Henry met at Winchester and agreed on the succession to the throne. Duke Henry was to succeed on Stephen's death and, for the rest, there was to be a return, as far as practicable, to the conditions which existed at the death of Henry I. Above all, the two principals addressed themselves to the question of castles built during the previous two decades. In the words of the contemporary Robert of Torigny 'those castles which had come into being since the death of [Henry I] – their number was said to be more than 1,115 – were to be destroyed'.[30]

This figure, which has received wide currency, was, of course, grossly excessive, though the clusters of earthwork castles which had emerged to the north of London might well have suggested that their total ran to many hundreds. In fact, the number of illicit castles had begun to decline even before the accord of Winchester. Many had been hastily built and were as quickly destroyed. If their palisades and wooden towers had not been burned when they were last captured, they would have rotted into the soil. By 1154 there were in all probability few illicit castles to be torn down. That at Cirencester had already been destroyed. The castle of Malmesbury, built within the precinct of the abbey, was removed, and it was forbidden to rebuild it. In the words of William of Newburgh, 'castles melted away like wax before a flame'.[31] Those built by Henry of Blois on the episcopal estates of Winchester were destroyed, as at Merdon and Downton, or reduced to innocuous proportions, as at Farnham and Bishop's Waltham.[32] Several, prominent during the wars, literally disappeared from the pages of history: Faringdon, Harptree, Bampton, South Cerney.

It was part of the agreement that land and castles should be restored to the families which had held them at the death of Henry I. It proved difficult to achieve such a settlement.[33] Stephen was accused of favouring those who had supported him, but some of the more important castles, among them Oxford, Winchester, Windsor and the Tower, were none the less entrusted to constables who, it was supposed, would carry out impartially the terms of the accord. But when, in October 1154, Stephen died and his nephew ascended the throne, there were still powerful barons ready to hold their castles against the new king.

A number of castles which, before the 'troubles', had been in the hands of the king were taken back, among them Bolsover, Newcastle-under-Lyme, Northampton, Nottingham, Peverel (Peak) and Stafford, all of which had been held by Ranulf de Gernons, earl of Chester. Others, to which the king's claim was at best unclear, were none the less occupied. These included Scarborough, which had been built by William d'Aumâle during or just before the Anarchy; Wallingford, which had been held for Matilda throughout the years of civil strife; Devizes and Sherborne, which had been built by the Bishop of Sarum, and Hereford, taken from the heirs of Earl Roger of Hereford. A group of important castles, including Norwich and Pevensey, had been held by Stephen's son, William of Boulogne. The king assumed possession of them, as he also did of the de Warenne castles in Sussex, East Anglia and Yorkshire. Most of these baronial castles were to remain in the possession of the crown. There was uncertainty, however, over the ownership of some castles, and Henry II had to be assured by a jury that Mountsorrel Castle was his.[34]

It is impossible to say how many castles were demolished in fulfilment of the terms of the Treaty of Winchester. In many cases demolition was unnecessary. Wooden castles were already decaying, but there is evidence for the physical destruction of a number in the early years of Henry's reign. Painter cites twenty-one instances, and there would certainly have been more.[35] In any event, one may well question the extent of destruction. In a number of instances it appears to have been little more than token, and could have been repaired with little trouble if the castle were again needed. It must have borne a certain resemblance to the *Demontage* of

German industry at the end of the Second World War. That the great earthworks were ineradicable is clear from the motte which survives at Thetford and from the very considerable remains at Huntingdon, Groby and Weston Turville.

A case in point is Bennington Castle, in Hertfordshire, which consisted of a small tower-keep of flint rubble, built on a rather low motte.[36] Its destruction was ordered, and the Pipe Rolls record the purchase of one hundred picks for its demolition in 1176-7.[37] This might suggest a fairly thorough job of demolition, if it were not for the fact that the castle was repaired, garrisoned and again *destructa* in 1212.[38] There are other instances of the resurrection of castles after they had been ineffectually destroyed, among them the Bigod castles of Bungay and Framlingham, the de Mandeville castles of Pleshey and Saffron Walden; Leicester, Dudley, Saltwood and Tutbury.[39] On the other hand, at Kinnard's Ferry, Adam Painel was fined two marks for not demolishing adequately his motte castle.[40]

Twenty years later, in 1173, the king was faced with the most serious rebellion of his reign. Leading barons, stung by his attempts to undermine their authority and stimulated by Louis VII of France, broke into rebellion in both Normandy and England. The revolt coincided with a Scottish invasion, but was ill timed and poorly co-ordinated. The castles of the rebels were taken and several were demolished. The king seized the occasion to take into his own possession important castles including Bristol, Chichester and Kenilworth, which were to remain in his hands or those of his nominees.

Three of the chronicles of this period record that the king went so far as to take *all* castles into his own hands.[41] He may well have claimed the right to do this, but it is very doubtful whether he did, or, indeed, could have exercised this right. There is no echo of such an act in the sheriffs' accounts as enrolled in the Pipe Rolls, and, it might be added, the cost of such an undertaking in both money and manpower would have been beyond the king's means. Nevertheless, the events of the first two decades of his reign were a triumphant assertion of his right both to license the building of castles and also to occupy private castles whenever he thought this desirable.[42] Itinerant justices, following the terms of the Assize of Northampton of 1176, went about the country to ensure that castles ordered to be destroyed were in fact 'utterly demolished and those due for destruction are razed to the ground'.[43] This, in the words of Warren, 'was more than an act of reprisal or even of security. A castle was a symbol of authority, as well as a centre of government of a great fief. Its enforced destruction was a public demonstration of the frailty of his power, and the mound, denuded of its fortification, became a symbol of the rebel's humiliation'.[44]

The destruction and confiscation of baronial castles under Henry II marked a change in the balance of feudal power. One cannot be sure of the true number of castles, but there is evidence for there being 274 *active* castles in 1154. Of these only forty-nine were in the hands of the king.[45] The policy of Henry II and of his younger son, John, not only reduced the tally of baronial castles but almost doubled the number of royal ones. In 1214 there were, according to estimates made by R. A.

Brown, ninety-two royal and 179 baronial castles. This change was achieved, not only by confiscation and destruction, but also by construction on a large scale.

Palatinates and Rapes

The ambivalence of the Norman kings and of their successors towards the building of castles is nowhere more clearly seen than in their policies in the more exposed and insecure parts of their realm. In much of England the estates of any one baron were scattered. That this arose from the accident of conquest rather than from deliberate policy seems clear. It can, however, be no accident that in areas where the danger of attack or invasion was greatest the baronies which the king created were more or less compact. William might well have regarded the south coast, together with the Welsh and Scottish borders, as the most vulnerable parts of his realm. Of these, the coast of south-east England was the most threatened. Had he not himself made an unopposed landing on these shores? Here he installed a small group of powerful and trusted barons, each in undisputed control of a substantial area. This is most apparent in Sussex. The county was divided into five units or *Rapes*, each entrusted to a single baron and centring in a particular castle. A century and a half ago Sir Henry Ellis claimed that the Sussex Rapes 'were military districts for the supply of the castles which existed in each'.[46] And modern opinion has seen little reason to modify his judgment.

There were, eventually, six Rapes (Figure 2.2), though the most westerly, that of Chichester, did not acquire a precise identity until the twelfth century.[47] For the others – Arundel, Bramber, Lewes, Pevensey and Hastings – there is evidence both for their creation and for the building of a castle before the time of Domesday. The castles of Hastings and Pevensey were indeed founded in the course of Duke William's opening campaign. The others followed shortly afterwards.[48] Bramber Castle had been built by 1073 on land which was released from payment of geld; was this, one may ask, a case of tax concession in return for the construction of a castle by William de Braose to whom the Rape had been entrusted?[49] Lewes Castle also predated Domesday Book, in which it received only an oblique reference.[50] It was the subject of an exchange between the king and William de Warenne, of which details are obscure but which may not have been unrelated to the strategic value of the site. Arundel Castle was built by Roger of Montgomery, to whom the Conqueror had given the Rapes of Arundel and Chichester.[51]

The Rape of Chichester raises a different problem. Its central-place was the Roman city of *Noviomagus* to which the cathedral of the diocese of Sussex had been transferred about 1075. It is in just such cities that William established most of his castles, but there is no evidence that he did so here. Nevertheless, a motte castle was raised within the northern perimeter of the city, presumably by Roger de Montgomery. But, with the disintegration of the Montgomery inheritance after 1104, the Chichester part of it became detached and, with its castle, passed to

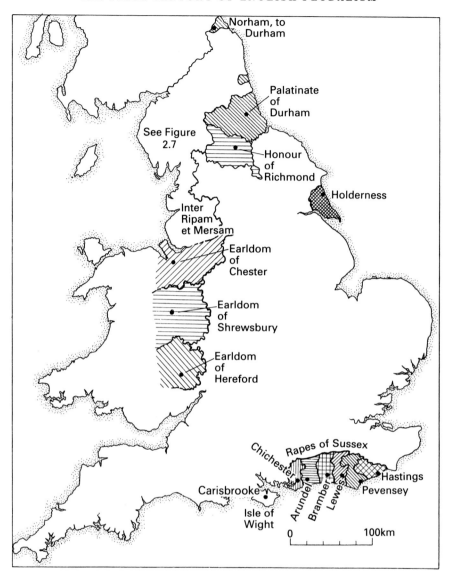

2.2 The 'palatinates' and compact lordships of late eleventh-century England. The extent of the Honour of Richmond is based on *Early Yorkshire Charters*, ed. C. T. Clay, vol. v; that of Holderness on B. English, *The Lords of Holderness*, Oxford, 1979.

d'Aubigny before reverting to the crown. The Rape and castle of Chichester were of less importance than the others. The castle was partially destroyed by Prince Louis of France in 1216, and was later abandoned and its site given to the Greyfriars, whose unfinished church still stands there.

To the west of the Sussex Rapes, the Isle of Wight not only constituted a compact territory but guarded the approaches to the most sheltered harbours on this coast. William is presumed to have built Carisbrooke, the only castle on the island, but his son, Henry I, granted it, together with the lordship of the island, to Baldwin de Redvers, whose family continued to hold it until Isabella de Fortibus sold it to Edward I.[52]

In Kent there were no clearcut territorial divisions such as we find in Sussex. Nevertheless, a small group of great land-holders controlled much of the county. Among them was the king himself, who never relinquished possession of Dover and Canterbury castles. Odo of Bayeux, the Conqueror's half-brother, received Rochester, and Hugh de Montford the coastal district near Hythe and Saltwood.[53] Thus, from eastern Kent to the Isle of Wight, the Conqueror established a successful, though not wholly consistent system of control, the essence of which was a series of castleries, each supporting a centrally placed stronghold.

Only along the Welsh Border and in northern England do concentrations of feudal power, like those found along the south coast again occur. William must have been well aware of the problems which existed along the ill-defined boundary with Wales. In the previous generation Gruffydd ap Llewelyn of North Wales had overrun the more southerly Welsh kingdoms and threatened the borders of England. Three years before the Norman invasion, Gruffydd was killed, and the state which he had put together began to break up into its component tribal areas.[54] The Normans were not to know that the danger from Wales had subsided, and they guarded themselves against it by creating three liberties which together stretched from the mouth of the Dee in the north to the Severn estuary. It is usual to refer to these three earldoms as 'palatinates'. A palatinate is a territory within which royal powers had been delegated to a local prince. The three Border earls had compact lordships, but their authority was less than palatine, and their common titles 'rest on tradition and on local patriotism, not on the record evidence'.[55]

In the north, Hugh d'Avranches was established as Earl of Chester, with jurisdiction over an area which conformed roughly with the county of Cheshire. On the west, however, it was not restricted, and he was free to press into Wales as he wished. William himself founded Chester Castle against the southern wall of the Roman city but seems at once to have left it to Earl Hugh, in whose family both castle and earldom remained until late in the twelfth century.

Shropshire, directly to the south, was no less exposed, and here Roger of Montgomery, who already possessed the Rape of Arundel, became earl.[56] He made the castle of Shrewsbury his seat, and destroyed fifty-one houses in building it. He was succeeded in his English estates by his son, Hugh, and then by his elder son, Robert de Bellême, a turbulent figure who participated in rebellions against both

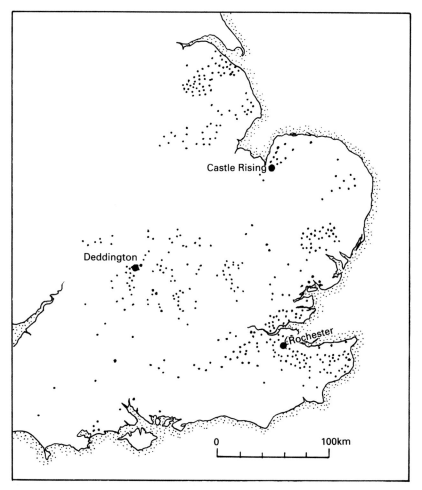

2.3 The lands of Odo of Bayeux, as recorded in Domesday Book, after R. J. Ivens, *Oxoniensia*,
49 (1984), 101–19. Rochester and Deddington castles were the centres of his largest clusters of
estates. It is uncertain whether he had a castle at Castle Rising.

Rufus and Henry I. Amongst his alleged offences was the illicit fortification of the
castle of Bridgnorth. His defeat and humiliation in 1102 was accompanied by the loss
of his lands and titles. The castles of Shrewsbury and Bridgnorth escheated to the
crown.

The southern March, centring in Hereford, was entrusted to William FitzOsbern,
who was also prominent in the defence of the south coast.[57] The *caput* of his earldom
was Hereford Castle, but his authority extended widely. He founded Chepstow
Castle beyond the river Wye, and seems to have exercised some jurisdiction in both
Worcestershire and Gloucestershire.[58] He died in 1071, and much of his land and
eventually his title passed to the family of Miles, hereditary sheriff and castellan of
Gloucester. Control over Worcestershire passed to Urse d'Abitot, whose

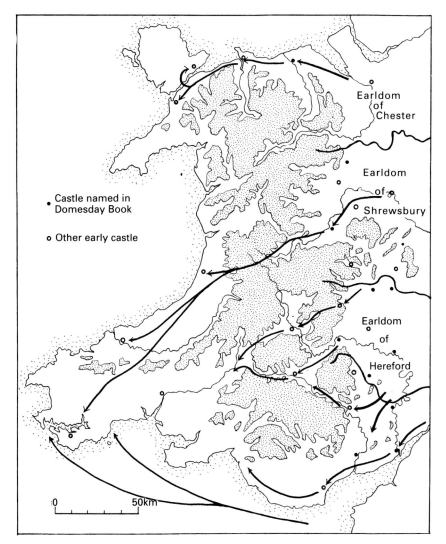

Castle named in
Domesday Book

Other early castle

Earldom
of
Chester

Earldom
of
Shrewsbury

Earldom
of
Hereford

0   50km

2.4 The Norman penetration of Wales by about 1100 from the Marcher earldoms of Chester,
Shrewsbury and Hereford. The stippled areas represent land above 250 metres.

descendants continued for most of the Middle Ages to serve as sheriffs.
Worcestershire and Gloucestershire thus slipped from the control of Marcher lords.
This was inevitable; the earl had 'advanced the frontier so far westwards that
[Gloucestershire's] marcher nature could be forgotten in a very short time'.[59]

The Marcher earldoms held little land in demesne. Most, in Shropshire and
Herefordshire was subinfeudated and held by tenants who, with the extinction of the
earldoms, became tenants-in-chief of the crown.[60] Typical of such families were the
Corbets, the Pantulfs, the Mortimers and the de Lacys. The first Corbet after the
Conquest was a tenant of Roger de Montgomery.[61] The centre of his power lay west

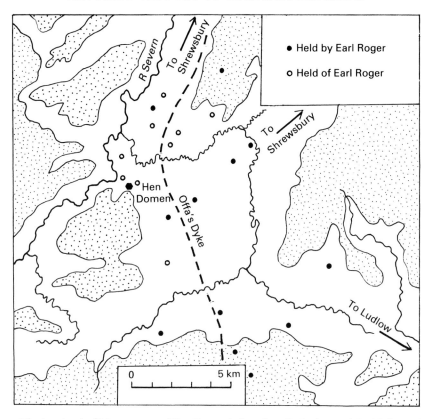

2.5 The 'castlery' of Montgomery (Hen Domen), based on P. Barker and R. Higham, *Hen Domen Montgomery*, RAI, 1982, pp. 8–16. The settlements shown probably contributed in some way to maintenance and defence.

of Shrewsbury, close against the Border. Here the Corbets appear first to have established themselves at a ringwork, now known as Hawcock's Mount, and then to have built Caus Castle, a mile to the west.[62] The latter is one of the largest and also one of the last motte castles to have been raised in this country. The Corbets themselves continued to play an important role in the politics and the warfare of the Welsh Border until the extinction of their line in the fifteenth century.[63] It was lords such as these who held compact blocks of land in each of which was their fortified *caput*. A list of these marcher lordships was compiled in about 1520, though by this time most had passed by inheritance to a small number of aristocratic English families.

There never was any restriction on castle-building within the March. Indeed it was expected of the Marcher lords, and the king even contributed on occasion to the cost of putting their castles in order. The ownership and occupation of quite minor castles was a constant preoccupation of the central government. Of the forty-eight castles named or inferred in Domesday Book, fourteen lay within the March and the density of earthwork castles, mottes or ringworks is far greater than in any other part

38

of Britain. Their total is as difficult to estimate as their date, but in the three Marcher counties cannot have been less than 150. At five of the Domesday castles in the Marches there is evidence of a castlery – *castellaria*, to provision and defend the castle. William de Scohies, for example, held eight carucates of land '*in castellaria de Carlius*' (Caerleon);[64] five carucates were dependent on the castle of Ewyas Harold.[65] But the most instructive case is Montgomery. Domesday records that *ipse comes* [Roger of Montgomery] *construxit castrum Muntgumeri vocatum*.[66] The castle was, of course, the motte-and-bailey now known as Hen Domen. It lay to the west of Offa's Dyke, the traditional boundary with Wales, and beside a ford across the Severn. Routes converged on the ford, beside which the Romans had established their fort at Forden Gaer. The site might seem in retrospect to have been an obvious one for the building of a castle to guard the river crossing and the routes which ran eastward to Shrewsbury and the English plain. But what gives Hen Domen particular importance in the present context is the way in which Domesday lists the manors – no less than twenty-two – which were dependent on the castle and formed its castlery. Most were held by Earl Roger himself; the rest by Roger Corbet or by a certain Eilward. Their precise obligations to the castle are not specified, but must be taken to have included the supply of men and provisions.

The Scottish Borders

The problem in northern England was different from that on the Welsh Border. The North was a region of transition. There was no acknowledged boundary between England and Scotland. Instead a debatable land reached from Cumberland and Northumberland to Dumfries, Roxburgh and Berwick within which the people 'had more in common with each other than with their fellow countrymen'[67] in Scotland or England.

Anglo-Norman power and authority intruded only slowly into the wasteland which made up much of northern England.[68] The Conqueror himself never exercised effective control much beyond York, even though in 1072 he led a raid into Scotland and established a castle at Durham.[69] Towards the end of his reign Odo of Bayeux built the New Castle on the Tyne, and shortly afterwards we first hear of a castle on the rock of Bamburgh, former centre of Northumbrian power. The Domesday surveyors, it might be added, ceased their labours in northern Lancashire and Yorkshire.

The Normans had an even freer hand in northern England than in the March of Wales. Large areas had been devastated in the course of both Scottish incursions and the 'harrying of the North' by King William. Domesday itself is evidence of the 'wasting', which was followed by a not inconsiderable movement of the population.[70] Peasants filtered down from the hills to the lowlands, where armies passed and much of the devastation had occurred. In some measure this movement was prompted by the need for labour in castle-building, but 'peasants who came to build remained to plough'.[71] It ceased to be possible in northern England to allocate to the Norman settlers the lands of specific Anglo-Saxon thegns. The previous ownership of land was imperfectly known, and for social as much as military reasons the Conqueror found it necessary to reward his followers with compact blocks of land.

English writers have often contrasted the land beyond the Trent with that to the south, and this perception goes back at least to William of Malmesbury.[72] The English did not so much rule Northumbria 'as make periodic forays into a land possession of which was disputed with the Scots down to the reign of Henry II'.[73] And English kings as late as John were content to leave the northern barons a degree of freedom and authority that would have seemed unusual even in the March of Wales. The North was dominated by compact and powerful baronies, each centred in a castle and providing men for its defence. Most 'possessed an obvious physical unity and identity as river valleys, distinct sections of river valleys or areas naturally cut off by mountain and sea'.[74] The traditional division of the land in the North was the 'shire', as was the hundred in the south and the 'commote' in Wales (see p. 156). The northern shire was a unit of land into which the lordship as a general rule was fitted, just as it was into the Welsh commote.[75] 'To travel south from the Border', wrote Holt,[76] 'was to journey from the simple to the complex', and this contrast is reflected in both the structure and the role of the castle. It remained significant, socially and politically, in the North long after it had become superfluous in the South. North of the Trent baronies were more compact and concentrated; Tickhill, Conisborough, the Peak and Pontefract all show this trend, which culminated in the lordships of Richmond and Holderness.[77]

Holderness is the lowland which lies to the north-east of the Humber.[78] It was important in view of Danish raids on the plain of York, and the whole region, with the exception of the lands of the church, was entrusted to Drogo de Bevrère, whose castle still rears its gigantic motte beside the sea at Skipsea.[79] From Drogo Holderness passed to the earls of Albemarle (Aumâle, Alba Marla), who held it until the thirteenth century, when all risk of Danish raids had vanished and the castle could be abandoned,[80] and the unfortified manor of Burstwick became the *caput* of the honour.[81] Drogo was owed the service of ten knights, whom he established on lands close to Skipsea. The small motte at Aldborough was probably put up by one of them.

If the honour of Skipsea had been designed to resist Danish incursions, that of Richmond was clearly intended to oppose the Scots. Of its purpose there can be no question. *Comes Alanus* [Count Alan of Brittany] *habet in sua castellata 199 maneria*, and almost two hundred manors spanned a wide area,[82] yielded a substantial income and represented a very considerable military and political power. The castle of Richmond, high above the river Swale had been built before the death of the Conqueror.[83] It exercised control over a distinct area, its *castelaria*, reaching from the Ure to the Tees. Its name Richmond*shire*, suggests that it was a traditional northern territorial unit (see p. 95), and within its limits the earls of Richmond administered their lands as a liberty.[84] For a time there was even a separate sheriff of

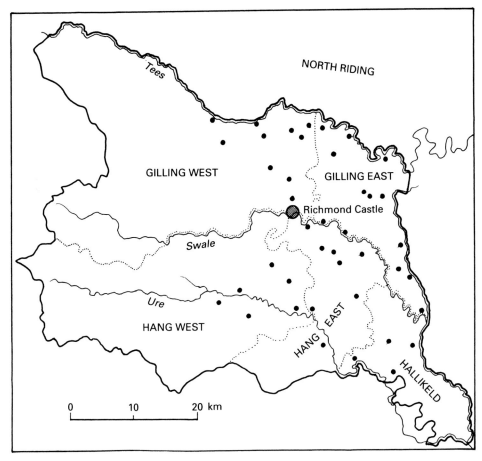

2.6 The Honour of Richmond. It was territorially compact, and formed the unit known as Richmondshire; it subsequently became the western part of the North Riding of Yorkshire. For administrative purposes it was divided into five bailiwicks, all dependent on Richmond Castle.

Richmondshire. The honour of Richmond was organised for war. No less than 174 knights owed service to the castle, each for two months in the year, and were so grouped that at least twenty-six were always on duty.[85] A further thirteen owed castle-guard in respect of lands outside Richmondshire and as far away as East Anglia, but they commuted their obligation for a money payment.[86]

Beyond Richmondshire lay the bishopric of Durham. The king had passed through its territory in the course of his expedition into Scotland in 1072, and on his return he founded a castle at Durham. The castle lay to the north of the cathedral; much of the surrounding land belonged to the patrimony of St Cuthbert, and it might have been impolitic to establish a lay baron in this important stronghold. It was thus entrusted to the bishop, and, with short interruptions, remained in episcopal occupation until the nineteenth century.[87] Durham was never surveyed for Domesday, but the gap was in some measure filled by Bolden Book, a record of the episcopal estates, nearly a century later.[88] There was no question here of the king creating a baronial honour and conferring it on one of his supporters. The complex of estates was already in the bishops' possession, and covered much of the county. The only lands which escaped their grasp were the Balliol possessions in Teesdale and those of Bruce in the south-east of the county. The bishopric of Durham came to be one of the most privileged 'liberties' in England, but this was not of King William's making.[89] Its exceptional jurisdiction came later, and was predominantly administrative and judicial, the bishop exercising those rights and privileges which in England normally belonged to the sheriff. These rights, furthermore, were not exercised throughout the county and see. The lands of lay barons remained directly dependent on the king. The patrimony of St Cuthbert did, however, include one distant outlier beside the Tweed in northern Northumberland. Here Ranulf Flambard, bishop from 1099 to 1128, built the castle of Norham on the Tweed and looking into Scotland. It was rebuilt by Bishop du Puiset at the king's command. Henry II claimed a superior jurisdiction, and took possession of the castle on the slightest pretext.[90] Nevertheless, the rise of the bishops of Durham had less to do with defence against the Scots than with the raw assertion of feudal power.[91]

The earldom of Northumberland was heir to the Anglo-Saxon kingdom of Bernicia. At the time of the Conquest its extent was ill defined and it was a prey to Scottish raids. It was granted to Robert Mowbray, presumably after the Conqueror's expedition into Scotland in 1072, and forfeited in 1095, when its focal castle, Bamburgh, was besieged and taken by Rufus (see p. 39). Northumberland remained in royal hands, despite the persistent claims and forays of the king of the Scots, until 1139, when Stephen granted it to Henry of Huntingdon, son of the Scottish king. The Scottish prince became earl, but held his earldom of the English king. The latter also held on to the castles of Bamburgh and Newcastle-upon-Tyne, and the Bishop of Durham, of course, continued to defend his distant outpost of England upon the banks of the Tweed.[92] In 1157 Henry II induced the Scottish king to surrender the earldom, but allowed him to keep the lordship of Tynedale, with its castle of Wark-upon-Tyne. In the meanwhile the earldom had been parcelled into baronies, larger than those found on the Welsh Border, but with fewer castles (Figure 2.7).[93] The absence of defensive centres offers a partial explanation for the ease with which the Scots were able to make incursions deep into England.[94]

The wastelands of the Pennine hills separated the baronial honours of Yorkshire and the North-east from the lowlands on the west coast. The latter were less extensive and their historic links had been with Galloway and south-west Scotland rather than with the more populous Tweed valley and Scottish Lowlands. Norman penetration into Lancashire and Cumbria came later than into Yorkshire and Durham. The region was remote, and Scottish pressure was felt less strongly.

The earldom of Chester, with its focus in Chester Castle, formed as much a frontier against the North-west as against Wales. Indeed, the area lying to the north of Cheshire, known as *inter Mersam et Ripam*, was merely an appendage of Cheshire, as northern Lancashire was of Yorkshire. The territory as far north as the

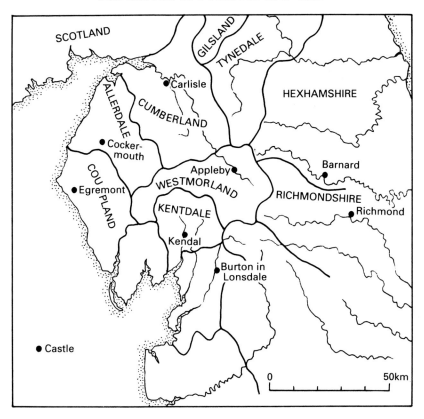

2.7 Lordships and castles in the north-west of England; after G. W. S. Barrow, 'The Pattern of Lordship and Feudal Settlement in Cumbria', *Jl Med Hist*, 1 (1975), 117–38.

Ribble was placed under Roger of Poitou, son of that redoubtable Marcher lord, Roger of Montgomery.[95] Roger of Poitou appears to have established a number of small baronies within the plain of southern Lancashire. He possessed a castle at Penwortham, the degraded motte of which survives above the steep south bank of the Ribble,[96] and another at Clitheroe, whose *castellata*, or castlery was recorded in Domesday.[97]

Both Penwortham and Clitheroe lay on the northern frontier of Roger's territory. At a later date a castle was established beyond it at Lancaster, but even under Roger the Normans were probing northwards between the Bowland hills and the sea, and a number of motte castles was built in the Lune valley and Furness. One of them became the considerable fortress of Burton-in-Lonsdale.[98]

The Normans merely nibbled at the flanks of the northern Pennines and Lake District hills,[99] until, in 1091, Rufus led an expedition as far as the Solway, built a castle at Carlisle, and entrusted it to Ranulf de Briquessart (le Meschin).[100] Within a few years northern Lancashire was divided into compact baronies, most of them focussing on a castle. A ring of baronies and castles surrounded the Lake District hills: Kendal, Appleby, Cockermouth, Coupland, Furness.[101] There is, however, no evidence that any of these castles was built before the twelfth century, though the Coupland castle at Egremont and both Brough and Appleby were built soon after, and the foundation of Carlisle.[102] The Norman colonisation of the hills to the east of Carlisle and the formation of the baronies of Gilsland and Langley did not take place until late in the twelfth century.[103]

The castle in rebellion and war

However much one may emphasise the domestic and administrative roles of the castle, its primary purpose was military: to give protection to its lord and his territory. Lordship consisted in the physical control of land, and for this the castle, garrisoned with mounted soldiers, was a prerequisite. The appearance of a hostile army was followed by retreat into the castle and re-emergence when the danger had passed. There were skirmishes and ambushes, but battles were rare. The forces engaged were small, and warfare consisted largely in destroying whatever resources might be useful to the other side; in protecting oneself in one's own castle, and in attacking the enemy in his. Both king and barons needed to call upon a body of armed men for their own protection and to oppose the forces of their rivals. To some extent this was done by paid retainers, known as household knights, but no less important a role was played in the early period of feudalism by the institution of knight-service. The Conqueror imposed on the barons whom he had endowed with land the obligation to serve him with a specified number of knights. It is not relevant to examine when and how these assessments were made. That Duke William brought with him from Normandy the institution of knight-service is now fairly clear; it is no less evident that in Normandy itself it was still fluid, a matter for negotiation between the duke and individual barons.[104] Not until 1166 do we find a clear statement of feudal obligations in England, and by this time knights' fees had begun to fragment and to be commuted for a money payment.[105]

The baron on whom had been imposed the obligation to serve with ten or twenty knights as a general rule passed the duty to his tenants, who served with horse and sword for the required period in return for the land they held. How they organised the *servitium debitum* was, by and large, the baron's business. Often enough they enfeoffed more knights than they needed, and the king was in due course to show great interest in the size of this surplus fighting force.

In the present context, however, there are two questions: how did the obligation to provide knights for the royal host relate to the duty to serve in the defence of castles, and, secondly, in what castles is there evidence for the performance of castle-guard? It later came to be assumed that service in the host and in the lord's castle were mutually exclusive. Castle-guard was an alternative to knight-service.[106] But it is doubtful whether this was initially the case. A pre-Conquest charter between Mont-St Michel in Normandy and one of its tenants appears – for the text is far from clear – to have given the latter the alternatives of serving in the castle with six

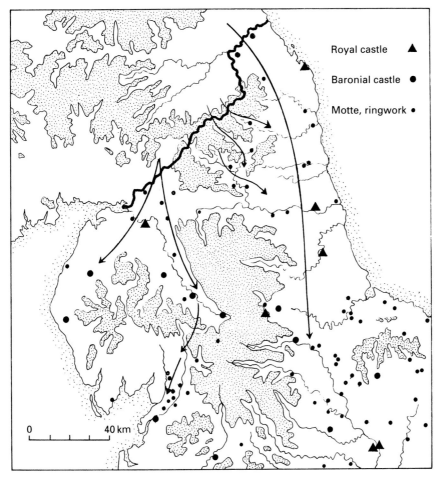

2.8 Castle-building in northern England during the first century of English feudalism. Mottes and ringworks are presumed to have been of this date. The arrows show Scottish invasion routes.

horsemen or in the field with two,[107] castle-guard being regarded apparently as less onerous than service with the host. In reality, as the history of warfare in England showed, there could be little difference between castle-guard and field-service, since garrisons were used to scour the countryside and field armies regularly retreated to castles.

Nevertheless, cases arose of quotas differing according to the nature of the service due. Cerne Abbey, Dorset, appears to have owed the king either two knights for service with the host or ten on guard in his castle of Corfe.[108] On the other hand, Walter Waleran held twelve fees but, over and above this obligation, had to provide five *ad custodiam castelli Sarrisbiriae* (Sarum)[109] and Gatelay (Norfolk) was held for one fifth of a knight's fee *et insuper duos solidos ad wardam castri Dovorie*.[110] Again the honour of Bywell in Northumberland, where there does not appear to have been an early castle, owed the service of five knights or alternatively thirty for the guard of the New Castle on the Tyne. Other such discrepancies are apparent in the obligations of Abingdon Abbey to guard Windsor Castle and in those owed to Dover Castle.[111] The bishopric of Ely was saddled with the obligation to provide forty knights, but it would appear that this included a number to guard Norwich Castle.[112] Henry I excused the latter obligation,[113] and Stephen similarly released the abbey of Bury St. Edmunds from its duty to furnish guards at Norwich.[114] The Bishop of Lincoln owed sixty knights, presumably for field service, but Stephen allowed some of them to be used by the bishop as garrison in his own castle of Newark.[115]

Much of the evidence for castle-guard relates to royal castles, for which there seems in some instances to have been elaborate provision. Specific baronies and lands were obligated to provide guards at Cambridge, Northampton, Rockingham and Sarum, as well as in castles, such as Dover and Norwich, thought important in national defence. Castle-guard duties were subsequently established at Newcastle-upon-Tyne and Bamburgh. The Danish threat to the east coast diminished, and guard duty was commuted for a payment. But in frontier areas the institution was retained. Here the need to keep castles on something approximating a war footing continued through the thirteenth century. The king called upon the barons of the Border counties for little service outside their own districts. William FitzAlan, for example, might not be called upon for ward service except at the castle of 'Blancmuster' (Oswestry) and, though he owed the king the service of ten knights, not more than five might be called upon to serve outside Shropshire.[116] The case of Chester Castle is even clearer. Here castle-guard was performed by the earl's knights from the rest of England, those from the palatinate serving in the field, and in the castle only in emergency.[117] In pre-Conquest Normandy, however, service in the field and as castle-guard seem to have been interchangeable. The Abbot of Mont St Michel owed six knights at Avranches and Coutances and one at Bayeux *quem faciunt vavassores nisi fuerint in exercitum*.[118] In other words, duty in the host took precedence over that of guard duty.

It seems clear that there was, at least in the early days, no general rule, castle-guard being sometimes in addition to, sometimes an alternative to service in the field. It was a question of what local circumstances required. In this, as in so many aspects of feudal custom, the trend was from the complex to the simple, from local custom to general rule. When in the Great Charter of 1215 the barons demanded that ward should not be demanded in addition to service in the host, they were only attempting to generalise a practice which had been most favourable to themselves.[119]

It would seem reasonable to assume that ward was provided from fees in the vicinity of a castle, if it were not apparent that this was not always the case. Fees owing guard to Richmond Castle were found in East Anglia, and Dover drew its knights from as far afield as Suffolk and the Midlands. This must surely derive from the imperfect knowledge of the feudal geography of England under the Norman kings. In general, however, the obligation rested on fees nearby. The inconvenience of relying on knights from distant manors was such that their obligations were commuted at an early date. The period of service owed each year varied from a week to half a year. Service of forty days was most common and seems to have been taken as the norm. Not infrequently it was required only in time of danger and was ill organised and haphazard, subject to change according to local circumstances.

If it is difficult to trace the development of castle-guard in royal castles, it becomes almost impossible in baronial. Those barons who had enfeoffed more knights than they were obligated to provide for the king's service clearly had a small force which could be used in their own castles.[120] But the evidence for this is slight. Castle-guard had once been owed to de Todeni's castle of Belvoir, but was commuted for a money payment.[121] Both Richmond and Chester were baronial castles, and here castle-guard was organised with some care and performed until a relatively late date (see pp. 48-9). But most of the evidence of 'ward' in non-royal castles comes from the frontier regions of the West and North. There is no question but that the tenants of the Marcher lords called for military service from some of their tenants, and that this service was an obligation on their tenancies. Bishop Foliot of Hereford (1148-63), for example, granted a tenement in North Ledbury in return for forty days' service at Bishop's Castle.[122] Puddletown (Dorset) was held of Christchurch Castle by a similar service,[123] and guard was owed at the Bishop of London's castle of Stortford by land at Layer Marney (Essex).[124] Other cases might be cited from the Welsh Border, but the practice of performing guard duty at baronial castles seems generally to have disappeared early. It seems, more often than not, to have been a sergeanty attached to certain tenements. It was of small value and was used to support a man-at-arms, the conditions of whose tenure could be varied at will.

The organisation of ward at Richmond Castle is known through a late inquest. The earls had an abundant reserve of knights, 186 of whom were divided into six groups, each serving for two months, with larger groups on duty in summer. A not dissimilar arrangement existed at Hastings Castle, where sixty knights were divided into four wards, each serving for three separate months.[125] At Pevensey also there seems to have been a similar organisation of the 'wards' provided from its Rape.[126] Norwich Castle was at first guarded by more than 150 knights drawn from a half-dozen baronies. Here, however, part of the ecclesiastical contribution was remitted (see p. 46) or commuted.[127] The guard of Dover Castle was organised in an even more complex fashion, a mark perhaps of the importance with which it was regarded.[128] The guard seems at first to have been entrusted to local barons, one of whom served as constable.[129] But before 1166 it had devolved upon nine separate baronies, one of which, the 'Constable's Honour', was located as far away as Haughley in Suffolk.[130] Some of the towers of Dover Castle perpetuate the names of these honours, and the obligation to garrison this key to England was felt throughout the centre and south-east of the land.[131] In 1216 Hubert de Burgh reformed the system in a way that was significant for the future: '. . . considering that it was not safe for the castle at different months to have new guards . . . every knight due for ward of one month should pay 10s., and . . . henceforth certain men chosen

2 Richmond Castle, viewed from the north. The drawing is in a fifteenth-century register of the honour. Above the drawing is a list of fees of the new enfeoffment; below is a list of eight of those who owed castle-guard, together with the places within the castle where they served (see Fig 2.9).

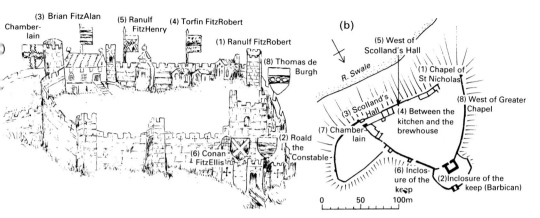

2.9 The stations of the eight knights listed in the manuscript have been located in (a) by the name of the knight, and in (b) by location. Based on *Early Yorkshire Charters*, vol. *V*, *The Honour of Richmond*, ed. C. T. Clay, 1936.

and sworn, both knights and foot soldiers, should be hired to guard the castle'.[132] Castle-guard came to be commuted in much of England; only in the border regions did knights continue to serve in person.

What did a knight do while serving his ward? Where did he sleep? Whose was the responsibility for feeding him, and did he in any way help to maintain the castle in serviceable condition? There are no clear answers. Painter is of the opinion that the knight was provisioned while on duty from his home manor, but this would have been impracticable for knights living far from the castle in which they served.[133] At Westminster twenty-five houses were allocated to the abbot's household knights, and at Ely they lived in the *aula ecclesiae* and were fed at the abbot's table, but this situation was shortlived.[134] More to the point is a clause in the *Descriptio Militum* of Peterborough Abbey: Hugo Olifard held land by service *in exercitu et in ward . . . cum corredio abbatis*.[135] In other words, he was fed by the monastery while doing the latter's ward at Rockingham Castle.

The accommodation of garrison knights is no less obscure. In Northumberland, several lords who owed the guard to Bamburgh Castle were obligated to keep *unam domum in eodem castro tempore guerre*,[136] and within Alnwick Castle and Newcastle tenements were allocated to specific baronies.[137] At Richmond Castle also specific quarters appear to have been allocated to particular wards, and the naming of the towers of Dover Castle probably records a similar practice.[138] Lastly, the Survey of Crown Lands of 1649–50 recorded of Launceston Castle, which was owed the service of seventy-two knights, 'every fee shall keep his garrett'.[139]

Castle-guard was not the only obligation owed to a castle. The castle needed to be supplied as well as guarded, and there were various menial jobs to be performed within it. Some of these were imposed as serjeanties on particular parcels of land or on particular families. Relatively few such obligations were recorded, possibly because they became customary and were enforced through the manor court. Even

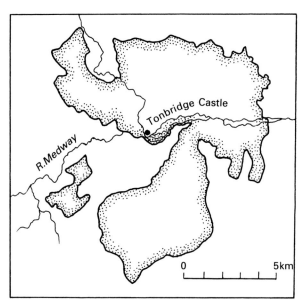

2.10 The 'Lowy' or Castlery of Tonbridge, Kent. After W. Y. Drumbeck, *Arch Cant*, 72, 138–47.

castle-guard might be detached from military fees and become a kind of serjeanty, a 'decadent military tenure'.[140] Such a service was owed to Porchester Castle by some of the inhabitants of neighbouring villages.[141] Many such obligations were recorded in the *Red Book of the Exchequer* and the *Book of Fees*. Some such obligations were more specific; they consisted of serving as porter, carpenter, smith or cook. The tenures which supported such serjeanties must have been in the close vicinity of the castle. The obligations must have been far more numerous than surviving documentation might suggest, but have lapsed with the passage of time or have been converted to a money rent.

This raises the question whether a discrete area around a castle was in any way separated off in order to serve its needs. The idea was not unfamiliar to the Normans, and Domesday Book mentions *castellaria* in the Welsh Border as well as at Richmond in Yorkshire. The Sussex Rapes can be seen as castleries, and Dudley (Staffordshire), Pontefract (Yorkshire) and possibly Tutbury (Staffordshire) were also recorded as the focal points of such areas. The term is, however, deceptive; it was not unusual to use *castellaria* for a baronial honour.

Castleries in the strict sense are largely absent from lowland England. The reason probably is that barons rarely held a block of contiguous manors. The Sussex Rapes form the most conspicuous exception. There was, however, one other example, and it lay significantly in the militarily exposed county of Kent. Here the 'Lowy' or *leuga* was the small but compact group of lands held by Richard FitzGilbert, around his castle of Tonbridge. Its boundaries were fairly definite,[142] and, though not referred to in Domesday Book, it was termed a 'castlery' in the *Domesday Monachorum*.[143]

One must assume that its primary purpose was the defence of Tonbridge Castle, though the specific obligations of its inhabitants are not known.[144]

The first century of feudalism was filled with revolts and sieges. The Conqueror was faced with rebellion within its first year, when Eustace of Boulogne attacked Dover Castle, was beaten off and fled the country. Eight years later, the rising of Ralph of Hereford ended with the siege and capture of Norwich Castle, and in 1076 there was an unsuccessful attack on Durham Castle. Rufus faced greater opposition than his father, chiefly because many of his barons also held lands in Normandy, now ruled by his brother, Robert Curthose, and claimed that they could not serve two masters. They aimed to reunite the two territories under the Norman duke. Odo, Bishop of Bayeux, held Rochester Castle against the king, and was joined by Robert of Mortain and other magnates. Rufus took Tonbridge and Rochester castles and Odo fled to join his brother Mortain in Pevensey Castle, which was starved into surrender. The castles of other rebels, Arundel, Norwich, and Bristol, surrendered, and the revolt was over. Not so the grievances of the barons. A fresh revolt in 1095 centred in the North. Rufus took the Mowbray castle of Tynemouth and besieged and took Bamburgh.[145]

The death of Rufus (1099) raised again the question of succession. Robert Curthose still had his supporters, and might reasonably have expected to inherit the English crown. In the event Rufus' younger brother Henry seized the Treasury at Winchester, the sinews of kingship, and had himself crowned three days after his brother's death. Again Curthose's English supporters prepared to resist in the only way they knew, by preparing their castles for defence. Robert of Bellême, heir to the Montgomery lands, prepared his castles: Arundel, Bridgnorth, Shrewsbury, Tickhill[146] (see pp. 27–8). He is also said to have begun another castle at 'Caroclove' (Carreghova).[147] The king first besieged Arundel, and 'having built forts against it, retired. He then ordered Robert Bishop of Lincoln . . to lay siege to Tickhill, while he sat down before Bridgnorth, and began to construct machines and erect a strong fort before it'.[148] Bellême surrendered; the revolt was over.

Revolts consisted of little more than sieges of baronial castles, and only a handful of them was ever involved. Small, earthwork castles were bypassed in the fighting, and an increasing number of the latter were transformed into manor houses, in which a veneer of castellation may have flattered the pride of their lords, but added little to their security.

Nevertheless, one is struck by the ability of earthwork castles with their wooden defences to resist a powerful and sustained attack. The records do not tell us how often a bailey was lost and the garrison took refuge on the motte.[149] At Tonbridge, Tickhill and Shrewsbury the mottes were large. Their summits could have provided space for a sizeable garrison, and their steep slopes might have been almost unscalable in the face of archers stationed on the summit. Castles seem to have been starved into surrender more often than they were taken by storm.

Lastly, one must not exaggerate the size of the forces deployed on both sides. They were small when compared with the armies of the later Middle Ages. It was almost impossible to invest a castle and cut it off from the surrounding countryside. There was much coming and going between the besieged and their supporters outside, and the postern gate, the small and unobtrusive opening through the outer walls, was, as a general rule, well used.[150]

The most common practice was for the besiegers to build some kind of protection for themselves within sight of the castle; to prevent aid from being brought, and then to wait for shortages and dissensions to sap resistance.[151] When Rufus besieged Bamburgh Castle, 'he build a fort before Beban-byrig, calling it "Malvoisin", and placed a garrison in it'. The cat-and-mouse game continued until the garrison surrendered. Henry I pursued a similar tactic at Bridgnorth, where a motte and weakly protected bailey, known as Pampudding Hill, survives from his siege castle. At Corfe also, an earthwork – the Rings – survives from Stephen's siege works of 1139.[152]

The Anarchy

The reign of Stephen offers the only instance of prolonged warfare in this country, and it was, by and large, a war of sieges. Stephen was a vacillating and indecisive ruler: 'a mild man, and soft, and good, and no justice executed', was the judgment of the English chronicler. The consequence is well known: 'every rich man built his castle', and held it against him.[153]

In the first year of his reign Stephen had to face sporadic revolts. Hugh Bigod seized Norwich Castle, and Baldwin de Redvers, Rougemont Castle in Exeter. Both were taken by Stephen, but Exeter only after a long siege, in the course of which he 'constructed machines for the assault and expended much treasure', as well as building a siege castle.[154] It was a ringwork, clearly recognisable early in the nineteenth century, but now obliterated.[155] Bampton Castle, in north Devon, was provisioned and held against the king, who was forced to dig in 'round the castle, post archers to act as pickets by night [and] detail others to lie in wait during the daytime'.[156] The following years were marked by local, uncoordinated risings in which castle after castle was attacked and defended. They included large and powerful castles, like Wallingford and Corfe, and castles of only local significance, like Harptree, Cirencester and South Cerney.

A picture emerges of frenetic activity as the king dashed from castle to castle, incapable of pursuing any objective consistently. Some order was introduced in 1139 by the return of Matilda, daughter of Henry I and claimant to the throne. Broadly speaking, Matilda's support came from the West Country; Stephen's strength lay in London and the South-east, but there was no clearcut boundary.[157] Each area contained castles loyal to the other side; Wallingford in the South-east remained loyal to Matilda[158] and Barnstaple in the West was for Stephen. But everywhere local feuds and enmities were subsumed within the general conflict. Much of the fighting, however, was in a belt of territory which reached from the West Country, through Oxfordshire to Bedfordshire, Cambridgeshire and Essex.

This area must have suffered severely, and it is here that the greatest density of small mottes and protective ringworks is found, as if the local population were striving to protect itself from the depredations of war. In this region, also, are several motte castles, which appear to have been left unfinished, as if their construction had been interrupted or the need for them had passed.[159]

The issues in the wars of Stephen's reign were clouded by his relations with the church. No monarch could have tolerated the dynastic ambitions of the family of Bishop Roger of Salisbury, Henry's Justiciar.[160] He took possession of Sarum Castle, within which his cathedral lay, and 'wishing to seem magnificent in [his] building, he erected . . . several [castles] . . . at Sherborne, Devizes [and] at Malmesbury . . . in the churchyard, hardly a stone's throw from the abbey'.[161] His 'nephew', Alexander, bishop of Lincoln, built Newark Castle[162] 'for the protection, as he said, and glorification of his diocese',[163] and at about the same time fortified his manors of Sleaford[164] and Banbury.[165]

Other bishops also felt this urge to build castles. Henry of Blois, bishop of Winchester and brother of the king, erected no less than six. Most important was Wolvesey, close to his cathedral, which he transformed from a hall-house into a lightly fortified castle with a keep.[166] At Taunton he added a keep to his manor house,[167] and at Farnham he built the curious motte castle which has already been described (pp. 13–14). At Downton (Wiltshire) and Merdon (Hampshire) he established earthwork castles and at Bishop's Waltham a fortified home.[168] The scale of building by the three bishops would have been difficult to parallel, even among the lay magnates, few of whom had resources equal to those of the more richly endowed bishops. In the event, Devizes[169] and Sherborne castles passed into royal possession, but the bishops of Lincoln retained their three considerable fortresses, and the Bishop of Winchester, Wolvesey, Farnham and Taunton.

The aftermath of the wars of Stephen's reign saw the destruction of many castles (pp. 30–1). They were essential in the warfare of the age; they were both the symbol and the reality of power, and Henry II, in reducing their number and exerting a control over those that remained, showed how well he had learned the lessons of the Anarchy (see pp. 75–6).

CHAPTER 3

A pattern of castles

fortissimas munitiones cum nimio sudore pagensium condiderunt

Ordericus Vitalis, VIII, iii

We cannot know what debates there may have been before the decision was taken to build a castle. In some instances little discussion may have been necessary. Both the need for the castle and its site were self-evident, and the element of choice was virtually eliminated. Such was the case at Pevensey, Hastings and Dover. But thereafter the establishment of a castle must have been a matter for serious deliberation. Reasons have been advanced in retrospect for the location of every significant castle in this country. They are alleged to have been put up to guard a river crossing or control a road, to protect the country from invasion or to overawe its unruly inhabitants. Castles have been seen as parts of an integrated scheme, planned and controlled from somewhere close to the king. One of the first to see such a scheme in the spatial pattern of castles was Alfred Harvey, whose book appeared even before the work of Ella Armitage; '[C]astles were not isolated fortresses', he wrote, 'but were arranged on a definite scientific plan'.[1] But the most extreme position has been taken by Beeler. He sweeps aside the cautious and scholarly statements of others, and ascribes to the Conqueror a topographical knowledge which few of us possess.[2] Coventry was elevated to the status of a 'communications center' comparable with London, and, like the latter, was surrounded by a protective screen of castles. The dates of foundation of all castles built before the end of the twelfth century were conflated, so that they appear contemporary, and, by implication, are ascribed to the early years of the Conquest. The rationalisation by which the siting of the humblest ringwork is explained verges on the ludicrous.

We repeatedly read that a castle was built to guard a river crossing, control a route, or block a passage through the hills. The castle in itself could do none of these things. It could provide a passive defence for its garrison; but it could control only such areas as it could command with its weaponry or scour with its horse- or foot-soldiers. It could offer a refuge for a field force which found itself threatened by superior numbers, but it could, as a general rule, be bypassed with little difficulty. It has, for example, been claimed[3] that the earthwork castles, which border the Chiltern Hills, were the product of Duke William's encircling march in 1066, and were intended to control gaps through the hills and provide a protective screen for

London. The Chiltern gaps, as any schoolboy knows, facilitated railway construction, but one cannot really suppose that William's men would have been deterred by the gentle slopes of these very modest hills.

In 1216 Prince Louis of France landed on the coast of Kent with a considerable force and invaded England as far as Lincoln and Winchester without ever having taken either Dover or Windsor. The castles built by the Anglo-Normans where the Welsh valleys opened towards the English plain were totally ineffective in themselves in checking raiders, who merely took routes over the intervening high ground.[4] Only when the latter returned by way of the valleys laden with booty and driving looted farm animals was it possible for a castle garrison to intercept them.

Professor Brown has claimed that 'the basic geographical knowledge was not available for such strategic planning from the centre even had the basic political and economic structure of the kingdom made it conceivable',[5] which it did not. 'Castle-building was a deliberate policy', wrote Barlow,[6] 'but it should not be thought that it was controlled by a strategic master-plan', and Painter wrote,[7] even earlier, that 'the Conqueror and his sons could not have had sufficient geographical knowledge to formulate a national scheme of castle-building, and there was no need for such a plan'. With these views this writer heartily concurs. It might be added that none of the kings, before the accession of Henry II, could possibly have exercised so complete a control over their tenants and subtenants that they could have dictated to the latter where to locate their castles, and it is very doubtful, except in a few instances such as the Sussex Rapes, that they made any attempt to do so.

Yet a cluster of castles, provided they shared some common control, represented a very considerable concentration of political power, as was shown in the partition of the East Midlands (pp. 8–9) and the Bigod control of East Anglia. It was to counter the latter that Henry II built his castle of Orford.[8] The political situation was always fluid, as honours were formed and reformed at the mercy of inheritance, marriage and escheat. If it could be shown that undertenants at some time maintained castles on their lands at the demand of their lords, there is no reason to suppose that the same relationship would obtain a generation later. One has only to consider the ways in which knights' fees were fragmented to see what could happen to any tenure.

Only along the borders with Wales and Scotland can a case be made for any kind of overall defensive scheme, because only here was there any kind of a unified control over a considerable area. It appears from the map that a screen of castles had been built west of Shrewsbury, to protect the English plain from Welsh attack. They 'form a chain of strong points linking the major castles of Roger de Montgomery at Shrewsbury and Montgomery' (Hen Domen), wrote Lily Chitty,[9] adding that they were 'part of a recognised system of defence of the Welsh Border surviving into the thirteenth century'. It is true that in 1225 Henry III called upon all who held mottes (*motas*) in the Vale of Montgomery to strengthen them. But to impose a common requirement on all earthwork castles in a restricted area is very different from saying that they all conformed in their location to a common plan.

The fact is that if one looks at the map of castles which are *likely* to date from the

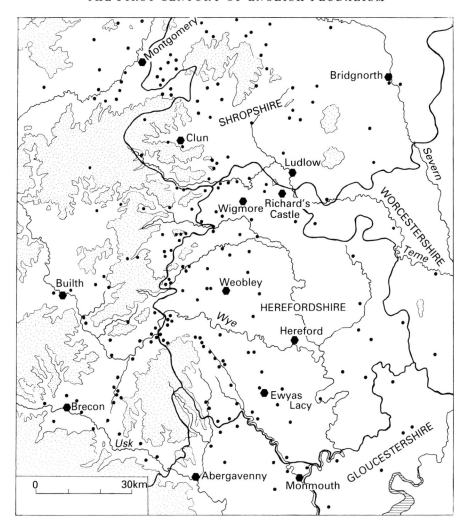

3.1 The middle and southern March of Wales. The larger symbols indicate major baronial castles; the smaller, motte castles or ringworks. Land above 250 metres is stippled. County boundaries are shown by a heavy line.

first century of English feudalism, one can read into it almost any pattern that one wishes. All such specious ideas are likely to be invalidated by the impossibility of demonstrating the contemporaneity of earthworks that have no documented history. It is more realistic to assume that each castle was built by the king, by one of his barons or by an undertenant according to local considerations. They needed a body of labour, access to water, food, timber and building materials. They took what advantage they could from the terrain. Above all, they had to build on land which they controlled. There are instances (see pp. 68–9) of the exchange of land to secure a particularly suitable site, but these are few. The most important factor in the analysis of the pattern of castles is not access to roads or proximity to river crossings – these were irrelevant – but the density of the population, which provided the prerequisite for castle building and castle living.

The spatial pattern of castles, wrote William Walters,[10] 'was remarkably even. They were noticeably absent only in areas like the Weald and the Pennines, where medieval population is known to have been scanty. Castles occur in significantly greater densities only along the Welsh Marches where life was more insecure, castle-building restrictions were less rigorous, and the feudal units more compact and better able to support castle construction. If castles were frequently found along roads and rivers it is only because most of the medieval population was found near them.'

The royal pattern of castle-building

King William, we are told, built – or ordered to be built – some thirty-six castles.[11] To these Rufus added Carlisle. Henry I was not a great builder, but he acquired, by confiscation or escheat, a number of baronial castles. Stephen's castle-building was largely dictated by the exigencies of war, and most of the castles which he erected were ephemeral. In 1154 Henry II had possession of forty-nine castles.[12]

If an overall strategic plan ever existed for the location of castles within England, it would surely be apparent in those which the king himself built. The sequence of events was, first, native resistance or revolt, and a successful military campaign, followed by the building of a castle to secure the conquest. Exeter, York, the Fenland and Midlands all conformed to this pattern. William would certainly have had from the start the intention to build castles. He did not, and could not, know in advance where he would establish them. This was dependent on the nature of the resistance and his success in suppressing it.

Yet there was some sort of pattern. Of thirty-seven royal castles (including Carlisle) established before 1100, no less than twenty were built within or against the defences of a town. In a country as feebly urbanised as eleventh-century England this is a remarkably high proportion. Twelve were in towns of Roman origin, whose defences had survived. Eight were within Anglo-Saxon burhs. All were populous, and, on the evidence of Domesday, large numbers of houses – up to 166 at Lincoln[13] – were destroyed to make way for them. The fact that King William was prepared to destroy, in the aggregate, at least 500 houses – there are no data for either London or Winchester – is proof that he thought it important to secure a site within each town.

There was a rudimentary road net, deriving in part from that left by the Romans. William used it, as, for example, when, on his return from York, he followed the Ermine Street and Via Devana, founding castles at Lincoln, Huntingdon and Cambridge along his way. If one looks for route centres of significance they were, apart from London, the Roman cities of Canterbury, Winchester, Leicester and Lincoln, where indeed castles were built, and Silchester and Cirencester, where they were not. Of some sixty points on the Ordnance Survey map of Dark Age Britain, where four or more roads converge, Norman castles were established at only fourteen. If the Norman kings set out to control a road net their failure was abysmal.

If, on the other hand, they aimed to dominate and control urban population and to command those centres from which the shires could be administered, their level of success was far greater. Figure 2.1 gives an indication of the size of the *larger* towns as recorded in Domesday.[14] The Domesday record is difficult to interpret; urban population fluctuated during the early years of the Conquest, and the map can be only the roughest of approximations. It is nevertheless apparent that more than half the castles which the king built and continued to control were to be found in the thirty largest towns. Their chief function must at first have been to overawe the citizens, but most eventually became centres for public administration. William cannot have known how important and wide ranging this administration was to become under his successors, but even within his own lifetime a link had developed between the sheriff and the castle which had been established in the county seat. When the Conqueror had chosen the site of Cambridge Castle, he left Picot, the sheriff, to complete its construction. That Picot continued to be associated with the castle is evident from the fact that a few years later he founded an Augustinian priory below its motte.[15] At Worcester, Urse d'Abitot was not only entrusted with the office of constable of the king's castle and the shrievalty of the county, but actually succeeded in making both offices hereditary in his own family.

The early Norman kings tended to play down the role of the earls, who had been the principal Anglo-Saxon officials in the counties. The office was, however, retained for a time on the Welsh border and in the North (see pp. 35–6), and here the royal castle – at Chester, Shrewsbury and Hereford – became the earl's principal seat. At Leicester, Northampton and Warwick, the castles, though unquestionably founded with royal approval, passed into baronial hands. They nevertheless remained the *capita* of their county earldoms, and Northampton, restored to the crown, became the seat of the sheriff's administration (see Chapter 4).

If the king visualised his urban castles as instruments of civil administration, he would have required a fairly even distribution throughout the land. That, in effect, is what he achieved, with a royal castle at the heart of almost every county. That there were gaps – Somerset and Derbyshire, for example – is self-evident. But one must regard his system as experimental, and not look for completeness and consistency in it.

The list of royal castles included some which could by no definition be considered urban. They included Dover, Corfe, Pevensey, Windsor and Rockingham. Some, including Corfe, were probably designed for coastal defence. For others, like Ely, Wisbech and 'Alrehede', the reason was shortlived, and they were either abandoned or allowed to pass into other hands at an early date. Rockingham Castle, on the other hand, remained important throughout the Middle Ages and considerable sums were spent on garrisoning and maintaining it. It nevertheless presents something of an enigma. It lies perched on a limestone cliff overlooking the Welland valley, in one of the least populous and most densely wooded parts of the East Midlands. Yet it was developed into a powerful fortress, and care was taken to secure the performance of castle-guard. One can only suppose that here, in this somewhat empty country, a royal presence was thought desirable.

One has not to look far for the rationale for William's third great rural castle, Windsor. It lies upon an abrupt inlier of the chalk above the south bank of the Thames. The king must have passed by it in the course of his march to Wallingford, and it is clear from Domesday that he was at pains to acquire half a hide from the manor of Clewer for the construction of the castle.[16] A royal residence outside but within a day's journey of London was eminently desirable, and the site of Windsor, it might almost be said, chose itself.

The pattern of baronial castles

Almost without exception the greater barons built castles, and, in general, they had considerable freedom to choose their sites. Except on the Welsh and Scottish Borders, lands were fragmented. The lords held clusters of manors, as Odo of Bayeux did in Kent and the Midlands (Figure 2.3); de Lacy in Yorkshire, Lancashire and the Welsh Border (Figure 3.5), and FitzGilbert in west Kent and East Anglia (Figure 3.3). Domesday gives the extent of baronial lands, in hides, together with their annual value, thus permitting a kind of feudal geography to be established. And this, in turn, offers some measure of the ability of lords to build and maintain a castle. According to le Patourel's estimates,[17] about three-quarters of the land passed into feudal occupation, and the rest continued to be held by the king.[18] About half the total land was in the hands of the *lay* baronage, and was used to support themselves, build their castles and discharge their obligations to the king. Some, in general the better endowed, built more than one castle; others, chiefly amongst the poorer, built nothing that can be positively identified as a castle.

There must have been about 170 baronies in England at the time of Domesday, each a complex of lands, rights and privileges which the baron held in return for services. Their value varied greatly. A great deal more than a half had gross incomes, as measured by the value of their lands, of less than £100 a year. W. J. Corbett divided them into five classes, according to their computed revenue:[19]

Table 3.1

Class	Value per year (£)	Number	Aggregate value (£)
A	over 750	8	9,000
B	400–750	10	5,000
C	200–400	24	7,000
D	100–200	36	
E	under 100	90–100	

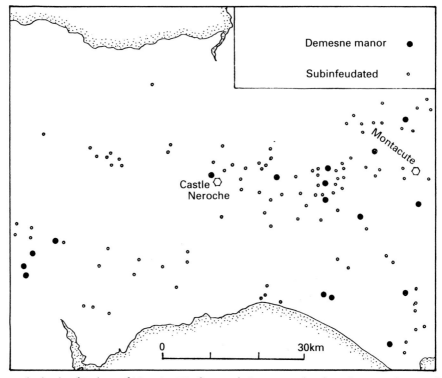

3.2 The lands of Robert of Mortain. His first castle is presumed to have been Castle Neroche, which was abandoned in favour of Montacute.

Classes A to C would have had the means to build a castle, and probably also those in class D, but possibly not those of class E. This table sets a kind of limit to the number of castles that could have been built by the tenants-in-chief of the crown. To this total, however, must be added those which might have been built by the under-tenants of the greater barons. The case is discussed below of the three motte-and-bailey castles which lay on manors which had been subinfeudated by the lord of Okehampton, presumably in return for some form of military service. Such instances could be multiplied. The problem is to relate an undocumented earthwork to a family that could have built it. This linkage can in many instances be made. Indeed the close proximity of a number of motte castles to a parish church is strongly suggestive of a manorial complex. There are, however, many exceptions.

Castle Neroche, built on the scarp of the Blackdown Hills in south Somerset, close to no inhabited place, may serve to illustrate the problem. The castle, a motte of massive proportions, was almost certainly built by Robert of Mortain, whose lands clustered in this region, though there is no documentary proof. After the defeat and exile of his son, William, in 1106, the lands reverted to the crown, and the castle was abandoned, except for a short period during the Anarchy.[20]

The castles of most of the greater barons, however, are documented and were, in most instances, continuously occupied. An examination of the sites of these castles in relation to the complex of lands which made up their baronies shows that local and tenurial factors predominated in the choice of site. Smallest of the class A baronies was that of Richard FitzGilbert, ancestor of the de Clare family.[21] It consisted of two clusters, one in West Kent, the other in Suffolk and Essex. These had been put together from the possessions of a number of Anglo-Saxon thegns. A castle was built near the centre of each cluster, Tonbridge in Kent and Clare in Suffolk. Both were motte-and-bailey castles of great size, such as only a baron of wealth and standing could have raised (Figure 3.3). We may presume that FitzGilbert first received the Kentish lands and built Tonbridge Castle, and was later given the lands north of the Thames, where Clare Castle was built.

The case of Odo of Bayeux is even more instructive. He was half-brother to the king, and served as Justiciar during William's absence in Normandy. At least six clusters of lands are credited to him in Domesday Book, ranging from the richest and most extensive in Kent, Surrey and along the lower Thames, to scattered possessions close to the Humber (Figure 2.3). Odo may well have received his more southerly lands within months of the Conquest, but the more northerly could not possibly have been granted to him before the next decade.[22] Manors remote from the centre of an honour were commonly committed to sub-tenants, but some, usually the larger and more conveniently placed, were held in demesne for the direct support of the baronial household. It was on a demesne manor that the castle was built. In barony after barony we find, centrally placed amid the cluster of rights and privileges, the lord's *caput*. If he held more than one cluster we might expect him to have a corresponding number of *capita*, though not all would necessarily have been castles.

Odo of Bayeux's career in England was short.[23] In 1088 he joined a conspiracy against Rufus, which ended with the siege and capture of his castle of Rochester and his retirement to his see in Normandy. His lands reverted to the crown and were later granted in smaller parcels to other and less distinguished tenants. In a period of some twenty years Odo had established two, perhaps three, central places from which to control his lands. The first was Rochester Castle in Kent, a royal castle established soon after the Conquest and entrusted to Odo.[24] The first castle was almost certainly the motte, known today as Boley Hill, to the south of the present castle. The latter was begun as a masonry castle under Rufus who commissioned Gundulf, bishop of Rochester and a builder of some eminence, to construct the enceinte.

Odo's second castle was at Deddington, in north Oxfordshire, centrally placed within his loose cluster of manors.[25] The castle which he built here is instructive, since excavation has demonstrated a late Anglo-Saxon occupation of the site, which may have been the centre of a pre-Conquest estate. Odo may also have had some kind of centre at Castle Rising, in Norfolk, which formed part of his manor of Snettisham. After his fall his Norfolk lands were granted to William d'Albini, whose son is credited with building the castle. Within the monstrous earthworks of the inner bailey, however, are the remains of a small church, abandoned when the castle was built. It is of late eleventh-century date and *may* perhaps be ascribed to Odo

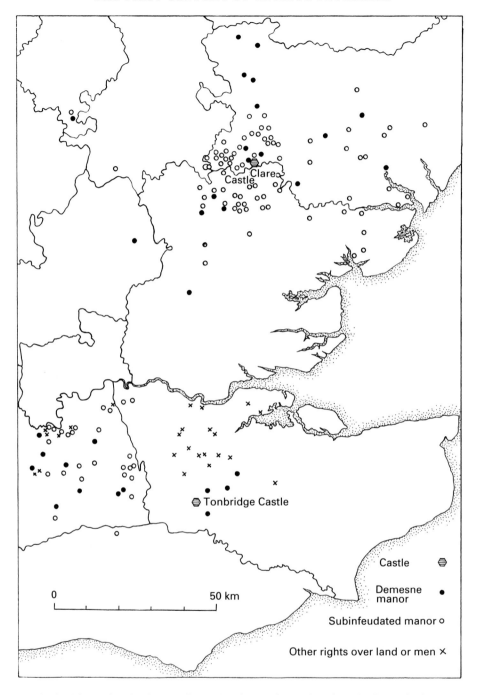

Castle ⬡

Demesne
manor ●

Subinfeudated manor ○

Other rights over land or men ✕

3.3 The lordships of Richard FitzGilbert (de Clare). The castles of Tonbridge and Clare were central to each cluster of holdings.

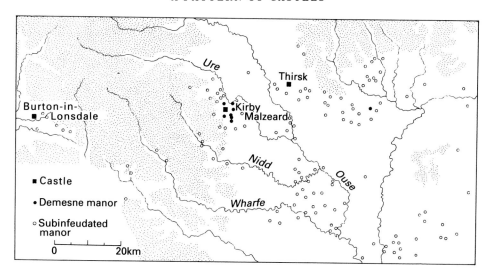

3.4 The Mowbray lands and castles in northern Yorkshire. Based on D. E. Greenway, *Charters of the Honour of Mowbray*, London, 1972.

himself. There is also evidence for pre-Conquest occupation of the site, thus raising the possibility that here, too, Odo had succeeded to a late Saxon estate.

The honour of Mowbray lay mainly in northern Yorkshire (Figure 3.4), in the Dales and on the edge of the Moors, with a small outlier in the Lune valley to the west. Most of their estates formed clusters around the castles of Thirsk and Kirby Malzeard, with that of Burton-in-Lonsdale serving as focus for the more westerly lands.[26]

The de Lacy lands lay mainly in two groups, in western Yorkshire and the Welsh Border respectively (Figure 3.5).[27] Robert de Lacy received his Yorkshire lands from the Conqueror and, before his death in 1091, had founded Pontefract Castle, one of the strongest and most important in northern Britain. Though not centrally placed within the scatter of de Lacy lands, it lay in the richest and most populous part of them. Although Pontefract was always the *caput*, there was also a castle on demesne land at Barwick-in-Elmet, to the north, and another at Almondbury, high up in the Pennines, within an Iron Age hillfort.

The Marcher barony of Weobley lay mainly to the north of Hereford (Figure 3.5), and was a more compact unit than that of Pontefract. It was held at the time of Domesday by Roger de Lacy.[28] Its *caput*, Weobley Castle, lies towards the west, as if protecting it from Welsh attack. There is no documentary evidence for Weobley Castle before 1138, but it is probable that the large ringwork and bailey, whose slight remains lie on the southern margin of the town, was established well before this date.[29] The de Lacys appear to have held only one other castle, that of Ewyas Lacy, or Longtown on the southern margin of their sphere. But there are motte-and-bailey castles on some of the manors held *of* de Lacy by undertenants, notably Eardisley, Almeley, Lyonshall, Mansell Lacy, Bacton and Munsley.

63

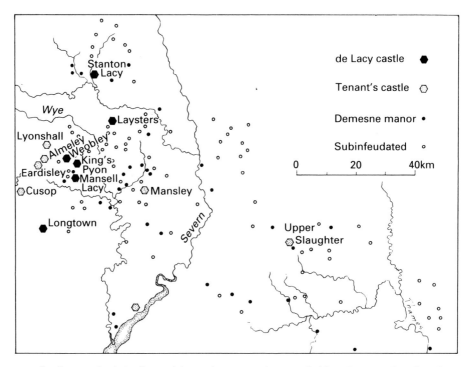

3.5 The de Lacy lands in the Welsh Border. Six castles were held in demesne, but the others were held by tenants of the honour. After W. E. Wightman, *The Lacy Family in England and Normandy, 1066–1194*, Oxford, 1966.

The honour of Okehampton, lastly, spanned much of Devon (Figure 3.6). It was held at the time of Domesday by Baldwin de Meules, who also served as sheriff and constable of the royal castle of Exeter.[30] He kept a dozen manors in his own hands and subinfeudated the rest, some 160. As the honour was later held for ninety-two knights' fees, one may presume that some of these manors provided the service owed.[31] The castle of Okehampton lay on the northern edge of Dartmoor. Its motte must be presumed to date from the earliest years of the Conquest, since Baldwin's possession of the lands probably dates from the suppression of the western rebellion in 1068.[32] A feature of the Okehampton honour is that, in a county not notable for the number of its earthwork castles, no less than three lay on manors which Baldwin had subinfeudated.[33]

Castle Neroche (p. 60) was almost certainly constructed by Robert of Mortain. Why then was it abandoned? Davison has argued persuasively that it was excentric to the main holdings of the count, and was probably built in the aftermath of the 1068 rising in the West (Figure 3.2). By the time of Domesday the count's *caput* was at Montacute, built on land acquired from the Prior of Athelney.[34]

It should be apparent from these instances that when a baron chose a site for his 'central-place' he was motivated primarily by his own convenience and security.

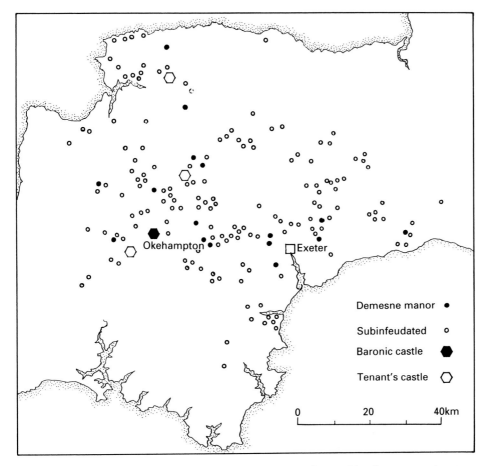

3.6 The lands of Baldwin de Meules, lord of Okehampton and constable of Exeter Castle. Motte castles are to be found on manors of three of his tenants.

Above all, he wanted access to the lands from which he derived his income and support.

Not all honours had been created by the time of Domesday. That of Pontefract 'did not begin to be formed until the 1080's',[35] and the creation of the northern honours belongs to the reign of Henry I rather than of the first two Williams. The honour of Ongar, in Essex, was not put together until late in the twelfth century, at a time when many in southern England had begun to disintegrate and fragment.[36] The removal of William of Mortain, Odo of Bayeux and Robert of Bellême without any designated successor meant that their undertenants were raised to direct dependence on the crown. Many would have joined Corbett's class E barons, with gross incomes of less than £100. The number of tenants-in-chief grew; very many lost their noble status, and in time a gulf emerged between those barons who were to receive a summons to parliament and the rest who eventually came to constitute the gentry class.

Other honours escheated to the crown, became extinct or were partitioned between heiresses.[37] The number of those which were extinguished by the lack of a male heir is evidence of the hazards faced by the nobility as well as by their inferiors. Neufmarché, Clare, Bohun, Braose, Corbet, d'Albigny are merely some of the more distinguished lines which ended in this way.[38]

A barony was 'a mass of varied rights over lands and men'.[39] As the number of possible baronies grew, so the poorer amongst them dropped out of reckoning, unable to support the obligations which this status entailed. A baron owed fealty and service in war and peace. He had financial and public duties, which he discharged from his *caput* or administrative centre. Indeed Bracton regarded the possession of a *caput* − an address to which writs might be sent − as the distinguishing mark of a barony[40] marking it off from lesser tenancies. Sanders listed 132 baronies whose existence before 1327 can be documented, together with a further seventy-two putative baronies.[41] A large number of the latter appear to this writer to have been indubitable baronies.

All baronies had a *caput*, but how many of them had at their centres structures which could be regarded as castles?[42] The honour normally was known by the name of its central-place. There were exceptions; the honour of Huntingdon had its seat at Fotheringhay, and that of Walbrook sometimes held its honour court at Arkesden in Essex.[43] But exceptions were few. We can, then, look at the central-places of honours for traces of the structure which must have stood there.

In only about 35 per cent of the honours was there a castle at their central-place. At others there was at most a manor house. The map, Figure 3.7, shows the location of known baronial *capita* and whether they consisted of castles or of lesser structures. Even allowing for the fact that some baronies possessed more than one, we cannot assume that the number of baronial castles ever greatly exceeded a hundred. To these should be added those built by the archbishops and bishops, but these would not have exceeded twenty.

The total of royal, baronial and episcopal castles at the accession of Henry II thus falls far short of the number of those whose physical remains can be attributed to the first century of English feudalism. Who then were the builders? A handful have with some degree of assurance been attributed to the undertenants of de Lacy, de Montgomery and de Meules. A more careful study of manorial history may lead to the ascription of a large number of such earthwork castles to the tenants of great lords. There is no other explanation of their proliferation in areas like the Welsh Border.

Another line of argument is to calculate the number of knights, since it is in the knightly class that one must look for the builders of many of the lesser motte castles. J. H. Round calculated that the total military obligation of the lay and ecclesiastical baronage at the time when the *cartae baronum*, the statements of feudal obligation, were drawn up was about 4,300 knights.[44] The total number of knights' fees, including those created over and above the *servicium debitum*, has been put at over 6,000 by Denholm-Young.[45] But there need never have been this number of knights,

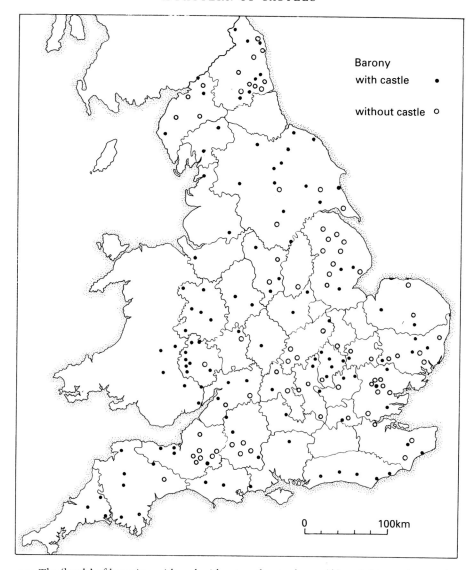

Barony

with castle •

without castle ○

0   100km

3.7 The 'heads' of baronies, with and without castles, in the twelfth and thirteenth centuries. The list of baronies is taken from I. J. Sanders, *English Baronies*, Oxford, 1960.

since service was commuted at an early date. Furthermore, many who held fees would have been impotent to serve, and the number of knights was in all probability a great deal less than that of knights' fees. Military obligations were most often fulfilled by mercenaries who are unlikely to have held any land. The mounted knights of Edward I at the time of the Welsh wars 'never consisted of more than 1000 to 2000 lances',[46] and the royal army could have been no larger a century earlier.

How then does this relate to the number of castles? Only an estimate can possibly be made of the number of the latter, and some of the totals proposed have been wildly extravagant. Rowley claimed over 150 motte-and-bailey castles in Shropshire,[47] while Barlow has claimed 'some 5 or 6 thousand castles . . . in England'[48] during the early years of the Conquest. Robert de Torigny's exaggerated total of castles destroyed by Henry II has already been cited (p. 30). If one includes those sites which were abandoned soon after the castle had been constructed in favour of another nearby and also those short-lived structures raised in the course of a siege, it is very difficult to find more than 900 which on documentary or archaeological grounds could be attributed to the period before 1154. And many of these are so degraded and uncertain that one can have no confidence in their identification.

The number of castles was very much smaller than that of barons and knights. Many of the lesser barons did not build castles; some undertenants did so. But their resources would have been limited. Whether they used them to build a castle or endow a church or in some other way is likely to have been determined by personal factors which must remain inscrutable.

The castle site

If the location of a castle in relation to others was, by and large, a matter of chance, the choice of its site was more likely to have been given serious consideration. The idea that a castle was sited primarily in order to give it the greatest possible security from attack dies hard. The castle perched upon a hilltop or above unscalable cliffs was rare in England and by no means common in Wales. Of course, it had to be as secure as local conditions permitted, but other considerations were fully as significant. A castle needed a source of water; it had to be accessible; it was part of a local community, as much a farm as a fortress, and ready access to the fields was important. Lastly, if a castle was to have any strategic value, ease of egress from it for a troop of cavalry was as important as its defensive capabilities.

A baron might have several manors within which he could site his castle, but he had to establish it on land which he already possessed. Not even during the Anarchy is there evidence of the outright seizure of land for the purpose of erecting a castle. The king might take liberties, but a baron rarely built on land which was not initially his. Lewes Castle was founded on a site which had been acquired by exchange, though the Domesday references are oblique and the transaction is obscure. More significant, Robert of Mortain acquired the hill of Montacute at the not inconsiderable price of the manor of Purse Caundle (see p. 64). At Berkeley a tract of land in Ness was allocated specifically for a castle,[49] and the Conqueror acquired the steep hill of Corfe from Shaftesbury abbey for a similar purpose.[50] There are other instances, including Windsor[51] and Warwick,[52] of the acquisition of land because it offered a favourable site for a castle.

It is no less clear that the site of a castle was sometimes changed, probably because the initial site offered little scope for development. At both Canterbury and Rochester the earliest castle, a motte, was replaced by a masonry keep on an adjacent site. The d'Albini castle in Norfolk was moved from Old to New Buckenham. Morpeth Castle, destroyed by King John in 1216, was replaced by another of more contemporary design only 100 metres away.[53] At Rhuddlan the motte castle of Robert of Rhuddlan, built by 1075, was replaced two centuries later and 300 m to the north by Edward I's concentric castle.[54]

At Montgomery the motte-and-bailey of Hen Domen, built by Roger of Montgomery before 1086, was replaced by the masonry castle of Montgomery in the 1220s, but continued to be used until late in the century.[55] At Aberystwyth there appear to have been two castles near the mouth of the Ystwyth, before Edward I built the masonry castle whose ruins today lie above the cliffs. The first was a motte castle lying south of the Ystwyth; the second, a castle built on a courtyard plan near the Rheidol river.[56] Middleham (Yorkshire), a masonry castle with a square keep, replaced a motte castle, which still remains half a km to the south,[57] and at Pickering a ringwork, which may have been a siege castle,[58] lies on a hill 600 metres away.

There are other instances, most of them probable if not proven, of the shift of a castle over a relatively short distance. The case of the Castell Madoc ringwork may serve as an example.[59] A ringwork, shown to have been occupied for only a short time, lies some 400 metres from a motte, which is presumed to have replaced it. It is suggestive that both earthworks lay within the grounds of a later manor house.

It should not, however, be assumed that when the remains of two castles occur in close proximity to one another, one of them replaced the other. There are instances of a kind of pre-emptive castle-building. Ascott-Doilly had a castle at each end of the village, which was itself divided between the d'Oilly manor to the east, and that of the earl of Gloucester in the west.[60] The building of the one castle probably prompted the construction of the other. Other such paired castles are met with in the Welsh Border. In the Kennet valley, west of Newbury, are no less than three mottes within 900 metres of one another, their relationship to one another being quite unknown.[61]

Within the broad constraints already outlined, the builder had a certain latitude in choosing a site. One cannot analyse his motives. One can only examine the sites used and indicate the statistical probability that one kind of site would have been preferred to another. Ease of defence was a significant factor, but possibly not one of overwhelming importance. Doubtless Corfe and Montacute were acquired because their height and steep slopes lent themselves to defence. Rockingham, Belvoir, Ludlow, Richard's Castle and many others were so located that nature gave them an adequate protection at least on one side. But the vast majority of English and Welsh castles were established on lowland or valley sites, even though they might take what advantage they could from the terrain. The reasons are clear. Most of the population and much of the cultivable land were to be found in the valleys, where the yielding soil of river terrace and flood plain facilitated the construction of earthworks. A statistical study of the sites of early castles suggests that a lowland or valley site was a matter of deliberate choice. The fact that a castle was overlooked by higher ground made little difference. The range of a crossbow bolt was little more than 300 metres,[62] and siege engines could not cast a missile more than half as far. The damp valley soil gave some protection against tunnelling, and, at a later date, facilitated the creation of moated defences.

The spatial pattern

Several hundreds of castles can be ascribed on archaeological or documentary evidence to the years before 1154. Their pattern is neither random nor regular. It shows very heavy concentrations in some areas and a relative sparsity in others. Such a map has certain shortcomings. It equates a castle of the strength and importance of the Tower of London with the humblest ringwork. One might expect the exposed coastal region of southern and south-eastern England to have been very well protected. Indeed it was, but by a relatively small number of strong castles. There were also comparatively few in the south-western peninsula, over the chalklands of southern England, the Fenland and the Weald, all areas of sparse population. On the other hand, the south-west Midlands and the Welsh Border show an extraordinary density of castle sites in regions which were by no means densely peopled.[63]

Clearly there is a factor other than the density of the population in the frequency of castles, and that can only have been insecurity. Major invasion was guarded against by great castles. But along the Welsh Border the danger arose, not from largescale invasion, but from the infiltration of small bands, which could creep, unseen and unheard, through the hills. It was not conquest but loot which they sought, and powerful, masonry castles offered little protection against them. Under such conditions each lordship, each manor and each village was thrown back upon its local resources. It needed to protect itself against the sudden and shortlived foray. No elaborate defences were called for. A motte, with a bailey to protect the farm stock, was generally enough, and that, indeed, is all we find. Along the valleys of the Usk, Wye, Severn, Dee and their mountain tributaries, where they begin to open towards the English plain, mottes and ringworks succeed one another like beads on a string. There was no overall plan of defence. Each castle could have been circumvented too easily for that, and the petty lords who built and occupied them could have possessed no armed force that could scour the surrounding countryside. They served only for local protection against an enemy who came by stealth and at night to forage and to loot. Similar conditions were to produce a similar reaction in the northern Borders at the end of the Middle Ages, when raids by moss troopers led to the building of tower-houses, bastles and barmkins to protect the local population and their stock (pp. 291–3).

The clustering of earthwork castles in the south Midlands must be ascribed to a similar condition of insecurity which arose during the Anarchy of Stephen's reign.

They provided at most some degree of protection against pillaging by both sides, without in any way influencing the course of the war. And when the wars ended their inhabitants abandoned their earthwork defences and withdrew to more commodious homes.

PART II

The thirteenth century

CHAPTER 4

The royal castle and public administration

The castle was at its greatest use in peace. It was an instrument of local power planted
to enforce authority and government.   S. Cruden

When, in 1154, Henry of Anjou succeeded to the throne he found himself in
possession of some fifty castles,[1] about half of which had been built by the first two
Norman kings. Most had been continuously in royal hands; some had been
temporarily aliénated, but were recovered; some, like Devizes and Sherborne, had
been acquired by Stephen and were passed on to his successor and the rest were
acquired by Henry from his barons.

In this Henry of Anjou displayed the ruthlessness that characterised his reign.
His policy, consistently pursued, was to render his baronage innocuous by
controlling their castles, and where this proved to be impracticable, to overawe them
with castles of his own. At the beginning of his reign, Brown claims,[2] baronial castles
outnumbered royal by five to one. By the end of his reign the two groups had been
brought more nearly into harmony, with baronial castles numbering less than twice
the royal. Some castles were acquired with little effort. Wallingford came to Henry
when its defender, Brian FitzCount, entered a monastery. The castles of Ranulf de
Gernons, earl of Chester, which included such vital fortresses as Nottingham and
Tickhill, were seized on the earl's death. Henry occupied Northampton Castle
during the minority of its heir, Simon de Senlis, and withheld the Shropshire castles
of Ellesmere, Overton and Whittington from the heir to the barony of Peverel of
Dover. Scarborough was taken from William d'Albemarle; Bridgnorth from Hugh
Mortimer; Hereford and St Briavels from Roger, earl of Hereford, and, lastly, a
formidable group of castles, including Norwich, Pevensey, Lewes, Reigate and
Castle Acre, from Stephen's son whom he had displaced as heir to the throne. After
he had been on the throne a year or two Henry felt strong enough to move against
the Bigod and Mandeville castles in East Anglia, taking some into his own hands and
demolishing others.

A number of the castles which thus passed into the hands of the king seemed to be
of little permanent value to him. They were militarily weak or were located where
there was little need for them. Furthermore, the cost of maintaining a castle was
high, especially when masonry was rapidly replacing the timber palisades of earlier
times. Many castles were thus restored to the families of their previous owners or
were granted to men on whose loyalty the king could rely. Throughout his reign it

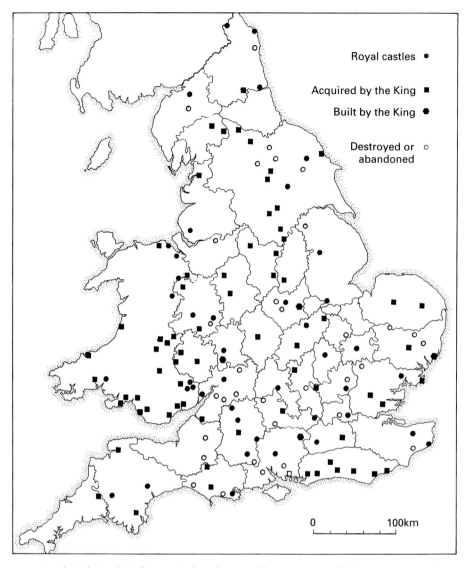

4.1 Castles inherited, built, acquired or destroyed by Henry II and his sons. It cannot be assumed that all the castles which he destroyed are shown here.

was implicitly understood that all castles were his to command, and that he could take into his own hands whatever seemed desirable in the public interest. Diceto and Torigny were certainly incorrect when they claimed that Henry had put royal officers into *all* castles, but few would have questioned his right to do so.

The royal acquisition of baronial castles was matched by a building programme as ambitious in its way as that of the first William. Data on royal expenditure comes from the Pipe Rolls, which record the annual accounting between the central exchequer and the sheriffs of the individual counties.[3] The Pipe Rolls constitute a

Table 4.1. *Expenditure on royal castles, 1154–1216*[4]

Dover	8,248.. 2..5½
Tower of London	4,019.. 1..4
Scarborough	2,973..18..7
Nottingham	2,269.. 6..7
Windsor	1,830..19..1½
Winchester	1,685.. 3..4
Orford	1,471.. 0..8
Corfe	1,405.. 6..10
Newcastle-upon-Tyne	1,315.. 8..8
Knaresborough	1,294..18..4½
Kenilworth	1,115.. 3..11½

continuous record from 1155 to 1216 and can be supplemented from other sources such as the *Misae* Rolls and, in the next century, the *Liberate* Rolls. The figures must, however, be regarded as underestimates of the total cost of building and maintenance. Keeping a castle in defensible condition involved a very considerable outlay, and the king must constantly have been torn between his desire to maintain a castle for reasons of security and his inability to afford its cost.

Nevertheless, a small number of strategically placed castles received what was for the time an immense investment. Part of the royal expenditure was in small amounts for repairs and minor extensions to relatively unimportant castles, but very large sums were spent on some dozen castles, which were, indeed, the 'keys of the kingdom'. By far the most extravagant outlay was on Dover Castle, where works included the building of the great keep, which has not ceased to dominate the site.

The 'Tower' of London had already been completed, and the heavy expenditure on it seems to have been largely on cutting a tidal moat and building a curtain wall on the north and west.[5] At Scarborough the tower-keep was put up at this time and, in all probability, much of the curtain wall.[6] At Orford and Odiham the expenditure was on building the round or polygonal tower-keeps, of which Orford survives intact.[7] In these instances we can see what the king got for his money and can thus formulate a very rough estimate of the monetary cost of castle building (see p. 149). Elsewhere expenditure was in the main on repairing and strengthening existing structures, and on replacing timber palisades and wooden towers with masonry.

Royal castle-building was far from evenly spread through the sixty years spanned by the reigns of Henry II and his two sons. The graph (Figure 4.2) shows, broadly speaking, three peaks in expenditure, in addition to the exceptional outlay in 1189–90, the first year of Richard I. Periods of high spending coincided with those of acute political tensions. The first began in 1160 with the build-up of discontent with the king's centralising and autocratic ways, and culminated in the rebellion in 1172–3[8] of Hugh Bigod and other leading barons. The heaviest expenditure was at first on Orford Castle, built to contain the activities of the Bigods, who had regained their

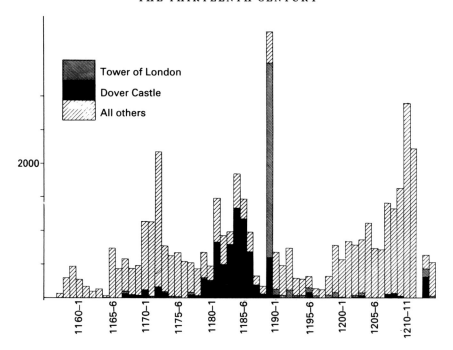

4.2 Expenditure by year of Henry II, Richard I and John on castles, based on the Pipe Rolls. There is no extant Pipe Roll over the period 1154–1216. The largest separate expenditures are on Dover and the Tower of London; these are distinguished by shading. Based on R. A. Brown, 'Royal Castle-Building in England, 1154–1216', *EHR*, (1955), 353–98.

castles of Bungay and Framlingham. Nottingham, Windsor, Winchester and Corfe castles were strengthened and at Newcastle-upon-Tyne the tower-keep was built. In addition, at the height of the troubles, a number of minor castles was garrisoned, munitioned and put into a state of readiness.

The suppression of the rebellion was followed by a lull in spending. Lesser fortresses appear to have been abandoned, some of them never again to come within the scope of public policy. On the other hand, the course of events in the rest of the Angevin empire was giving cause for concern. The French kings, Louis VII (1137–80), and his son and successor, Philip Augustus (1180–1223), were pursuing a policy of bringing the several duchies and counties of France under direct royal control. Flanders and Artois, across the Channel from Kent, were coming increasingly under the influence of the French king. Flemings had seized Dover in 1067, and in 1172 a Flemish army had penetrated East Anglia until it was routed at Bury. Against this background the king began to strengthen Dover Castle, which thus continued to absorb a large part of Henry's military expenditure until the end of his reign. At the same time there were more modest outlays at Hastings, Chilham, Canterbury and Southampton, and, though not recorded in the Pipe Rolls, at Porchester.[9]

Under Richard I (1189–99), outlay was relatively small, except at the beginning

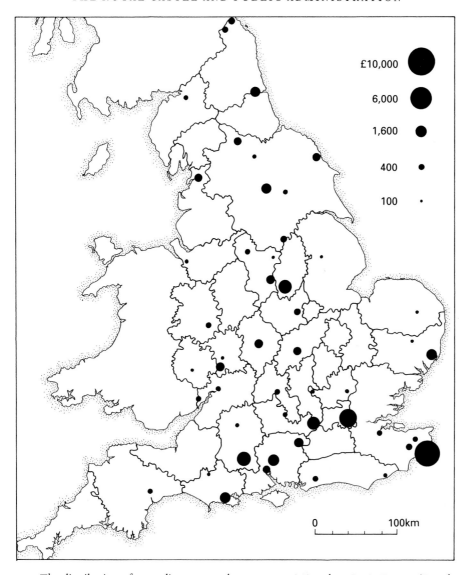

4.3 The distribution of expenditure on castles, 1154–1216. Based on R. A. Brown, 'Royal
Castle-Building in England, 1154–1216', *EHR* (1955), 353–98.

of his reign, when William Longchamp, Richard's chancellor during his absence on
crusade, invested a very large sum in the Tower of London. On the other hand,
Richard devoted immense resources to the defence of Normandy, and in 1197 began
the building of Château Gaillard above the Seine guarding the approach to his duchy
from the Ile de France. Over a period of two years no less than about £45,750
Angevin (about £11,500 sterling) was spent, greatly in excess of total expenditure
on Dover Castle.[10] This fact alone would account for the relatively small
expenditure within England. With the accession of John in 1199 the amount spent

on royal castles increased, and was greatly inflated during the middle years of his reign by the building of Odiham Castle and towards its end by the further strengthening of Scarborough.

Scarborough commanded the north-east coast and was significant in the defence of northern England. Odiham is more difficult to explain on military or strategic grounds. There had long been a royal palace nearby, where Henry I had spent the Christmas of 1116.[11] John evidently set some store by the site, and was at pains to acquire it from a tenant.[12] Its principal feature was an octagonal tower much slighter than that of Orford, and costing significantly less.[13] Odiham might seem a strange location for such an investment, with Windsor twenty miles to the north-east, and Winchester and Guildford even nearer. According to a contemporary, John built Odiham for his pleasure – *por lui deporter*.[14] It was, in fact, more a costly hunting lodge, like Ludgershall, and a staging point on the road to Winchester, than a significant fortress. Nevertheless, it was held for more than a week against the French in 1216 by only three knights and ten sergeants.[15]

Much of John's expenditure at Corfe went on the *domus regis*, the royal apartments within the inner bailey.[16] Elsewhere, too, there were instances of conspicuous consumption: at Arundel, Marlborough, Nottingham, Winchester, all with the purpose of converting a castle into a palace. But the military aspects of his castles were not wholly neglected. Money was laid out on northern castles which can have held little attraction for him: Knaresborough, Lancaster, Scarborough, Tickhill and even the Bishop of Durham's fortress, temporarily in crown hands, at Norham.

Castles in the Welsh March and Scottish Border were neglected. Small sums were spent on Hereford, Bridgnorth and Chester, though the last was, by and large, maintained out of the revenues of the palatinate. Fortresses on the Scottish Border were no more prominent in the royal accounts. The danger from Scotland might have been expected to give added importance to royal castles. In fact expenditure on Bamburgh and Carlisle appears to have been negligible and that on Newcastle and Wark far from significant.

There was, indeed, little need for the king to spend lavishly on the defences of his kingdom in the north and west. In the latter the 'palatine' earldoms of the Conqueror (see pp. 35–8) had broken up into compact baronies, far better adapted for defence than the scattered fiefs of England.[17] The so-called *Magna Carta* of Cheshire, for example, confirmed that no military service might be demanded from the palatinate beyond its eastern boundary.[18] Its knights were obliged to fight only against the Welsh, and, furthermore, if knights from England did service within the castle of Chester the local knights were relieved of duties except in the event of imminent Welsh attack. Though nowhere stated explicitly, it seems, nevertheless, that in Shropshire and Herefordshire also the local knights did service only within the March. The concern of the Norman and Angevin kings was 'to contain the Welsh threat',[19] and this the Marchers, with their castles and small, compact baronies, were well qualified to do. They claimed an almost absolute control within their lordships, and in this the king was generally happy to acquiesce. In 1199 William de Braose, lord of Bredwardine in Herefordshire, claimed that 'neither, the king nor the justiciar nor the sheriff ought to interfere in his liberty'.[20] Similar rights to do what they liked, as long as their activities were directed against the Welsh, were claimed by the FitzAlans of Clun and Oswestry, and, indeed, by most other lords. They were, in the words of J. G. Edwards, 'outside the sphere of the king's courts of common law; they had the right to build castles without royal licence; and they had the right of levying war'.[21] The English kings may occasionally have resented this liberty, but they were powerless to oppose it. On occasion they even encouraged it, as when Henry III helped Corbet with 50 marks in strengthening his castle of Caus.[22]

The border with Scotland differed from the March only in its greater distance from the focus of power in England.[23] One finds the same intense pattern of landholding; the same preoccupation with defence against the Scots – a euphemism for raids into Scotland – and the same contempt for the distant authority of the king. There was, however, one important difference. The North was less developed, socially, administratively and politically. English kings rarely went beyond the Humber or even the Trent and when they did so it was only with an effective military force. 'They did not so much rule "Northumbria"', wrote Miller,[24] 'as make periodic forays into a land possession of which was disputed with the Scots down to the reign of Henry II'. The English system of shire administration was only slowly extended beyond Cheshire and Yorkshire, and 'many aspects of normal hundredal administration were in baronial hands',[25] and so continued throughout the Middle Ages. Henry VIII's Council of the North was a recognition of this continuing spirit of independence well into the sixteenth century.

Henry III

When Henry III succeeded to the throne in October 1216, the country was being invaded by Prince Louis of France and a significant part of the baronage was in revolt against him.[26] The French forces advanced north to Lincoln and west to Marlborough and Winchester. Castles were besieged and taken (see pp. 116–17) but it was a desultory war. The death of John had deprived the French of the chief reason for their invasion, and, despite their possession of the most modern 'engines', they failed to take Dover or Windsor, and were defeated amid the streets in the so-called battle of 'Lincoln Fair'.[27] They then withdrew and the disaffected barons returned to their royal allegiance.

The effect of the war was to demonstrate that castles were still of great military value and could be held against the newest weapons of war if well built of masonry. Gone were the days when earthwork and palisade gave real protection. Masonry walls, with crenellation, fighting platform and projecting towers to deliver flanking fire, were becoming necessary. Defence could no longer be left to a local levée; instead, the trained mercenary was increasingly important. And castles, and the soldiers to defend them, became more and more expensive. These changes were reflected in the management of those castles which remained in royal hands.

It is not easy to formulate an estimate of royal expenditure on castles during the reign of Henry III. Previously most of the outlay had been channelled through the sheriffs and recorded in the Pipe Rolls. Now such expenditure might be recorded elsewhere. The sheriffs continued to account for part of the outlay on castles, and the practice developed early in the reign of allowing them a discretionary power to spend up to 100s a year on building and renovation at each castle in their charge. The Pipe Rolls record with an almost monotonous regularity the expenditure of this sum *in emendatione domorum castri de . . ..* The crown, however, also devised other ways of paying for work done on castles. Increasingly payments were authorised directly by the exchequer. The Liberate Rolls for Henry III's reign record an infinity of payments for building and services within the royal castles. Materials, especially timber from the royal forests, were supplied without recorded payment except for transport. The administrators of episcopal lands during a vacancy in the see were called upon to make payments, or the rent of a manor or the farm of a borough might be diverted to the repair or extension of a castle.[28]

Colvin has estimated that castle expenditure during the whole reign amounted to about £85,000, an average annual outlay of over £1,500.[29] A study of the Liberate Rolls suggests that this might be a minimum figure, and that the total would have amounted to more than a tenth of crown income.[30] It was inevitable that the king and his advisers should attempt to reduce this expenditure. This they could do in only two ways. The first was by neglecting castles of little military importance. Many were urban, located in shire towns and administered by the sheriff. They were commonly kept in order only to the extent necessary for him to carry out his duties. The second method was by giving them up. Some were destroyed, like Mountsorrel. Others were granted, together with whatever lands went with them, as *apanages* to the king's relatives and friends. Many of these, however, like the grants to Richard of Cornwall, Thomas of Lancaster, or Prince Edward himself, ultimately returned by inheritance or escheat to royal control. Nevertheless, the number of castles in the king's hands was reduced from fifty-eight at the beginning of his reign to forty-seven at his death.[31]

Expenditure on castles was more narrowly focussed than it had been under Henry's predecessors. A small number of castles received each a heavy investment, and only three new castles were begun – Montgomery, Deganwy and Dyserth. Beeston Castle in Cheshire was begun in 1225, but came into the king's hands only when it was nearing completion. Little was spent on it, and it might never have been built if Ranulf, earl of Chester, had died a few years earlier. The largest outlay was on Dover Castle,[32] where some £7,500 were spent during the reign. Work included the repair of damage inflicted during the siege of 1216–17; extending the curtain to the cliff edge and building a new gatehouse, to replace the older northern entrance, which had proved the weakest point during the siege.[33] Large sums were also spent on York Castle, where the existing quatrefoil keep was built on the motte;[34] at Nottingham, where the outer bailey was walled in masonry, and at Bristol, Gloucester and Rochester. These may be deemed military expenditures, in so far as the maintenance of these castles was thought necessary for the defence of the realm. But the amounts spent on Windsor, Winchester and the Tower of London were even greater. Gatehouses, towers and curtain walls were built or extended, but far larger sums were spent on their internal conveniences. They became palaces without ceasing to be fortresses. The Liberate Rolls show, in addition to large sums allocated 'for works' – ad opera – more specific amounts for beautifying the royal apartments, building a new kitchen, or constructing pentices to link various buildings within the castles.

At the Tower of London, in 1240, order was given for the 'queen's chamber to be wainscoted . . . and to be painted with roses . . . a wall to be made in the manner of panelling between the said chamber and the wardrobe of the chamber [and] to be tiled outside'.[35] The king's chamber was to be painted with the royal arms. There was greater attention to the niceties of life than before. A turret was ordered to be built in the corner of the king's chamber, 'so that the drain . . . shall descend to the Thames'.[36] At Windsor separate suites were built for the king, his queen and the young Lord Edward. At Winchester the number of private chapels began to proliferate and the king's chamber was fitted with windows that could be opened and closed, and painted with scenes from the Old and New Testaments.[37] At Devizes, Marlborough and Ludgershall, also, considerable sums were spent on enlarging the halls, extending the kitchen, building a saucery and decorating the royal apartments. It is impossible to assess the relative expenditures on military works and on conspicuous consumption. It is clear, however, that the cost of creating gracious homes for the monarch and his dependants was beginning to absorb an increasing part of total expenditure.

Henry III is known for his discriminating taste, and for the elaborate decoration of his buildings. He had his favourite motifs. The legend of Dives and Lazarus was represented in the great hall of Ludgershall full in the king's view, and was repeated in that of Northampton Castle, and 'opposite the king's seat' in Guildford Castle.[38] There was an elaborate scheme of decoration at Winchester, Windsor and Nottingham castles. The legend of King Arthur was used in the decoration of Dover Castle, and the round table at Winchester shows how popular it was.[39] One cannot be sure how widespread was this internal decoration. That the walls were plastered seems probable but the refinements found at Winchester were probably rare.

The lavish expenditure on a small number of English castles illustrates another aspect of their role. The Angevin kings were peripatetic; they were constantly in motion. Theirs was 'a government of the roads and of the roadsides . . . England had no capital but the king's highway'.[40] In the year 1205 King John is said to have spent only twenty-four days in London or Westminster. The Angevin kings had castles and manor houses scattered up and down the country, some of them, like

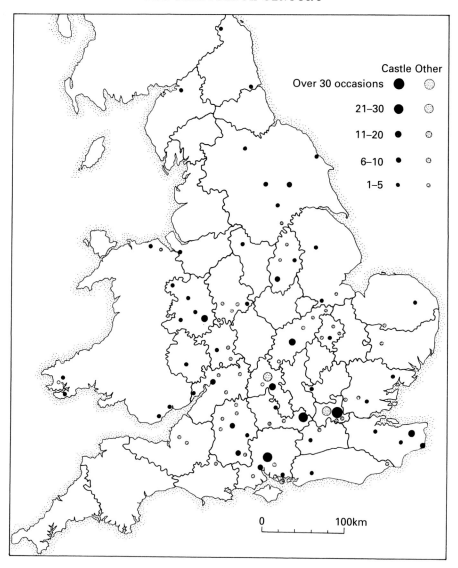

4.4 The itinerary of Henry II, showing the number of nights spent at each site. Some 50 per cent of the nights was spent in castles. Based on R. W. Eyton, *Court, Household and Itinerary of King Henry II*, Dorchester, 1878.

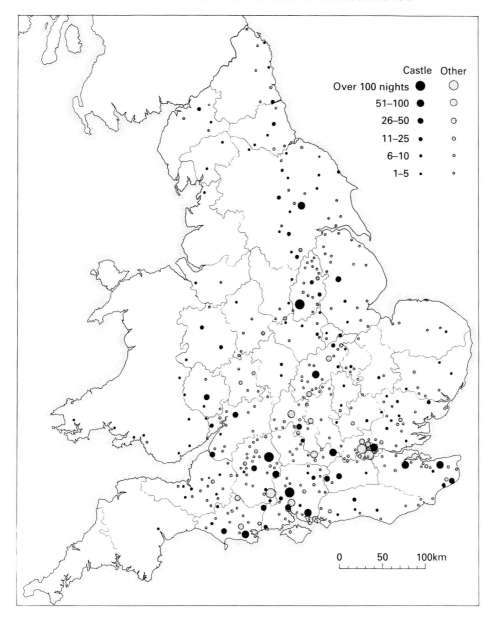

Castle Other

	Castle	Other
Over 100 nights	●	◯
51–100	●	○
26–50	●	○
11–25	●	○
6–10	·	○
1–5	·	○

0   50   100km

4.5 The itinerary of King John, the most peripatetic of English kings. Based on T. Duffus Hardy, Introduction to *Rot Lit Pat*.

Clarendon, Clipstone and Havering, in forest areas where they were accustomed to hunt. But they also resided at their own castles, and, when nothing else offered, exercised their right to demand hospitality of a monastic house. The itineraries of Henry I[41] and II[42] are known only in broad outline. More detail is available for Richard I, though much of his reign was spent outside England[43] but not until the reign of John can the monarch's movement be traced from day to day.[44] Figure 4.5 shows the breadth of his travels and the relatively considerable time spent in some favoured castles and palaces.

Things began to change under his son and successor, Henry III. To begin with, his minority lasted until 1227, and thereafter he preferred to spend his time in the relative luxury of Winchester Castle or the Palace of Westminster to travelling the country in discomfort and using whatever accommodation his servants could contrive.

In addition to providing a home for the king in the course of his travels the royal castles were extensively used for the accommodation, temporary or otherwise, of his relatives, dependants and friends. Indeed, some of them became virtually grace-and-favour homes. A common practice was to instruct the sheriff that certain persons were to dwell in the castle and that he should make provision for their accommodation.[45] In 1230 Henry III's sister and her family were admitted to Marlborough Castle, and in addition to fixing them up with suitable accommodation, the sheriff provided sufficient firewood.[46] Sometimes all that we learn is that a 'lodger' is to have wood *ad focum suum*.[47] Ela, countess of Salisbury, who had been billeted on Sarum Castle, was to have five *dolia* (casks) of wine, to be brought from Bristol.[48] Deserving widows were frequently given such accommodation; Joan de Valence at Winchester in 1266;[49] and Eleanor de Courtney at Sherborne in 1294.[50] Amice, countess of Devon, was given shelter in Winchester Castle, together with her household, 'in the queen's great chamber adjoining the chapel towards the hall and in the adjoining houses, provided that the castle be not less safely kept by reason of this'[51] – a euphemism, no doubt, for as long as they don't get in the way.

Towards the end of the century the long-suffering sheriff began to be burdened with another category of guest. In 1295 the constable of Richmond Castle was ordered to provide the wife of Miles de Stapelton with 'some suitable houses wherein she may dwell with her household ... as Miles is shortly going to Gascony.'[52] The same happened at Rockingham[53] and Skipton.[54] It was but a short step from treating the castle as a safe home for unprotected families to housing therein a whole nursery of young children. The children of Joan de Clare were assigned houses in Bristol Castle, 'except in the tower',[55] and similar use was made of Windsor Castle.

Hostages taken in the Welsh and Scottish wars, and, later, the French wars were another category of guest frequently found in some royal castles.[56] Among the castles favoured for their safe keeping were Corfe and Rockingham, for reasons that are readily apparent. Occasionally, hostages were kept close to the scene of fighting,[57] but usually they were moved deep within England. The constable was obligated to prevent their escape and was heavily fined if they did so. But in other respects they may have presented less of a problem than the presence of a well-endowed dowager or the teeming family of an impecunious knight. As a general rule, an allowance was made for their keep, commonly from 4d to 1s a day, according to their rank.[58] The more exalted amongst them were allowed a retainer or servant, and the most exalted ever to be held in an English castle – King John of France after Poitiers, 1356 – was held at Hertford and Somerton castles at a very considerable cost to the exchequer.

The constable and his staff

A royal castle was in the charge of a constable appointed by royal writ. In a few instances the office had become hereditary, as at Worcester. There are elsewhere instances of members of the same family holding the office for two or three generations, but normally the constable held it for only a few years, at the end of which he was replaced. The list of constables of Bristol Castle[59] shows that during the thirteenth century the average tenure of the office was little more than two years. In almost half the royal castles the constable was also sheriff. On appointment he was entrusted with 'castle and county', and held both until replaced. There were, however, occasions when the sheriff was denied possession of 'his' castle. Few sheriffs held office for more than three or four years, but, like constables, were sometimes reappointed at a later date.[60]

There were varied and devious ways of paying the constable for his services, which included holding the castle, keeping it in good condition, guarding prisoners, entertaining guests and managing its fields, mills and other assets. In many instances, of which Windsor is only the most familiar, the castle had attached to it a park or forest which provided hunting as well as timber for construction and firing. In many instances there were craftsmen, and the constable had usually to provide them with suitable 'houses' and materials, and often enough to transport the products of their work. The castle had a store of food and weapons, which deteriorated with keeping. Wine went sour, grain developed mildew, and at intervals the constable would be instructed to inspect the *warnistura* in his charge and to dispose of whatever was not good enough for king or constable for whatever it would fetch in the market, and to purchase fresh. Weapons became corroded and bowstrings slack. All had to be inspected and, when necessary, refurbished. There were staff and servants to hire and, in times of stress, a small garrison to be recruited. The king sometimes imposed a 'janitor', a gaoler or a watchman from among the retainers around his court on the constable. But whether such appointments were to be considered rewards for service or a means of getting rid of the elderly or incompetent is not always clear.

The constable's salary varied with his obligations and the status of his castle. In 1287 the Close Rolls recorded the payments to the constables of twenty-three royal castles. Rearranged in rank-order these were:

Table 4.2.[61] *Fees paid to*
constables, 1287

	£
Tower of London	50
Chester	40
Bristol	30
Windsor	30
Bamburgh	20
Corfe	20
Norwich	20
Nottingham	20
Oxford	20
Rhuddlan	20
Rochester	20
St Briavels	20
Winchester	20
Carlisle	15
Northampton	15
Bridgnorth	10
Canterbury	10
Odiham	10
Rockingham	10
Sherborne	10
Shrewsbury	10
York	10
Cambridge	5

The Justiciar of Chester combined the guardianship of Chester and Rhuddlan castles, and seems also to have had charge of Beeston.[62] Twenty pounds for keeping the comparatively unimportant castle of St Briavels in the Forest of Dean was due to the fact that the office carried with it the far more onerous duty of managing the Forest (see pp. 109–10). In five instances – Sarum, Sherborne, Shrewsbury, Oxford and Winchester – the constable was also sheriff and his fee was for the fulfilment of both offices.

These figures may not represent the true rewards of office. There were perquisites – income from castle mill and meadow, which was not always accounted for; profits from keeping hostages and other prisoners; fuel from the park and periodic gifts of wine and a robe.[63] On the other hand, these advantages were offset by other problems. The king was always a bad paymaster. The constable, acting on instructions, commissioned work on the fabric of the castle, but was all too often left paying the bill. Of course, he was promised payment, but there are records of accumulated royal debts to the constable spanning several years.[64]

Even when the constable received his fee promptly, he had often to collect it from several sources. Sometimes he received a fixed amount per day or per year, from which he had to pay the wages of officials and servants. A constable of Carlisle received 4s a day – on the face of it a good income – but had to support two grooms, or servants.[65] The income from castle-wards, London merchants, the Cinque Ports and other sources was earmarked for the support of the constable of Dover Castle, but out of the princely salary of £300 he was obliged to support chaplains, servants, watchmen, craftsmen and grooms.[66] In 1332–3 a constable was placed in Wigmore Castle during the minority of Roger Mortimer at 6d a day, and another in 'Kentles' (Cefnllys) Castle at only 4d. This very low rate was justified only by the temporary nature of the appointment.

Another device, especially if the castle included a profitable manor or castle-guard rents, was to let the office of constable at farm. Thus John de Warren held Bamburgh Castle for nine years, paying in all £990 to the exchequer, as well as £570 on munitions, repairs and the keep of prisoners.[67] In return, he was expected to cover his outlay from the income of the castle and to make a profit for himself. In this instance he failed to do so, and claimed reimbursement. Hugh Bigod paid £40 a year for the privilege of keeping Pickering Castle.[68] Robert de Maris gave only 16 marks (£10..13..4) for the evidently less profitable castle of Porchester,[69] and the farm of the relatively remote and unimportant castle of Sauvey in Leicestershire was worth only 5 marks (£3..6..8) to the Exchequer.[70] Robert de Tatteshall held Bolsover Castle together with the farm of the town at £30.[71] Occasionally there was no monetary transaction between the constable and the Exchequer. Henry, son of Richard, held Rockingham Castle 'on condition that he be not held to answer for the issues, provided . . . he maintain the castle and houses and finds the stipend of a chaplain for the king's chapel'.[72] At Sherborne the king lent the *corpus* of the castle to Nicholas de Molis 'to put his wife and household in' while he was at the wars.[73]

Such a system was clearly open to abuse, and there are numerous cases where the survey, conducted when the constable vacated his office, showed a grave neglect of the fabric. In such cases it was usual to call upon the former constable for repayment. Continually we find the king striving to keep his castle garrisoned, provisioned and in good repair with an expenditure totally inadequate for the task.

It was doubtless the need to economise that led to the practice of allowing a constable to manage two or even more castles. Bolsover was almost always held along with Peak (Peveril); Pickering with Scarborough; Shrewsbury with Bridgnorth; and Hastings with Guildford. The constable of Windsor often had responsibility for Odiham, and sometimes also for Berkhamsted. The Justiciar of Chester held Rhuddlan and occasionally Beeston, and the 'Three Castles' of Monmouthshire – Grosmont, Llantilio or 'White' Castle, and Skenfrith – always shared a common keeper. Who then were these men who held the king's castles? They did *not* include the greater barons, whom the king would not readily trust. Nevertheless, lists of constables show many familiar names. They were the petty tenants-in-chief of the crown and junior members of baronial families. But they included many of humble origin, men who had risen in the king's service and owed everything to him.[74] Some were moved from castle to castle to bring order to their troubled administration.[75] They constituted the upper ranks of an effective civil service. Some were mercenary soldiers, many of them recruited under John, but continuing under his successor to rule some royal castles.[76]

The constable sometimes had a deputy, who rarely emerges from the shadows into the light of the public records. If the constable was also sheriff, he was frequently absent from his castle, and left an assistant in control. There was usually a deputy in castles of national importance like Dover. But in lesser castles there was none, nor was there business to employ one.

The staff of a castle varied with the political situation. Any threat of insurrection or invasion, and letters were sent to sheriffs and constables, ordering that the castles be stoutly manned and diligently held. The question of the size of garrisons and the provision of armament is deferred to the next chapter. There was, however, a small permanent staff. As a general rule, one found a gatekeeper, janitor or porter; a watchman and a chaplain, sometimes two or even more of each. At Windsor the staff consisted of a watchman and a porter who each received 2d a day, and a gardener at 2½d. There was a maker of crossbows (*atilliatorus*) who earned 5d, a 'viewer of works', various building craftsmen and eight chaplains, who each earned 50s a year, less than 2d a day.[77] On the military side there were four sergeants at 9d a day, rather more than was commonly paid. At Pontefract in 1241 sergeants came a little more cheaply, at 4d a day.[78] At Rhuddlan at about the same time they were getting 7½d a day, porters 2½d but watchmen only 2d. The more skilled craftsmen − master-masons, crossbow artificers and the builders of siege engines − commanded much higher wages, up to 12d a day in some cases − far more than some constables were getting. A feature of this wage structure was the very wide range in rates of remuneration. The lowest rate of pay was that for priests and chaplains, less than the wage of unskilled watchmen. They were, of course, a very numerous class and were, without doubt, housed and fed within the castle, so that their *real* wage would have been higher. The more responsible members of the castle's staff were distinguished, not by the level of their wage, but by the methods of payment, a distinction not unknown today. Constables, chaplains and a very few highly skilled officers were paid by the year, whereas humbler members of the staff had their wage reckoned by the day. It is evident from the odd sums paid out that many of the latter served for only short periods.

The permanent staff at Windsor, Marlborough or any other castle regularly visited by the king was small, but was augmented when the king arrived with his train of retainers and servants. The Tower of London, by contrast, housed an immense and wide-ranging body of craftsmen, clerks and officials. The castle contained part of the wardrobe; it was an arsenal, where weapons were made and stored. Records were kept here, and here was the country's most important mint, where metal was assayed, dies cut and coins struck.

Wardship and escheat

All tenants-in-chief held their castles of the crown and were obliged to use them in its service. If for any reasons this obligation could not be discharged, as, for example, when the estate passed to a minor, the king had the right to take possession of castle and lands. The officer of the crown charged with watching such matters was the escheator.[79] The office first appeared late in the twelfth century. Its duties had previously been executed by the justices, and for a period after this date were sometimes carried out by the sheriffs. But in the course of the thirteenth century a system emerged whereby one escheator looked after the king's interests in central and southern England and another beyond the Trent.

The death of a tenant-in-chief was followed by an inquiry – *inquisitio post mortem* – into his lands and obligations, and into the competence of his heir to assume them. If the latter was a minor, he or she became a ward of the crown; revenues were collected by the escheator and paid into the Exchequer, and if there was a castle of any significance, it received a royal constable or was placed under the authority of the sheriff.

Archbishops, bishops and abbots, no less than laymen, were barons and had obligations to the crown. They owed military service, and the king could call on them for aid and advice. A period, more or less long, always intervened between the death or, more rarely, the translation of a bishop and the enthronement of his successor. The king could claim that obligations to the crown were not being discharged during this period, and his servants took the lands and privileges of the see into his own hands.

This regalian right was first exercised, *sede vacante*, by Rufus, and reached its final form under John.[80] In this way episcopal castles as well as manor-houses came into the king's possession. Some were of military importance like the castles of the bishops of Durham, Lincoln and Winchester.

A further aspect of regalian right was that the income of the see accrued to the crown as long as the vacancy lasted. The sums involved were considerable. The issues of the York diocese in 1279 largely paid for building Rhuddlan Castle, and those of Winchester built Flint and Harlech.[81] 'This allocation of the profits of vacancies to a large constructive project was perhaps the most purposeful and discriminating use of casual revenue that had been achieved'[82] up to this time.

The king, lastly, claimed, and on rare occasions exercised, the right to take a baronial castle into his own hands merely because this was in the national interest (see pp. 141–3). This was likely to happen only in time of grave emergency. The king, for example, prolonged his occupation of Norham Castle, and took possession of the de Brus castle of Wark-on-Tweed and garrisoned and held it for a considerable period of Border unrest.

The sheriff and his castle

When the Normans came to England they found a system of counties and in each a military leader or earl (*comes*) and his deputy, the *vicecomes*, shire-reeve or sheriff. The earls soon ceased to be significant in local administration, and their title became largely honorific,[83] leaving the sheriff as head of the shire. Before the end of his reign the Conqueror had replaced the Anglo-Saxon sheriffs by his own nominees.[84] The latter were drawn from the ranks of the lesser nobility, men with the wealth to support their office, but not rich enough to act with any degree of independence. For the sheriff was the arm of the king within the shire, his local agent, watching his interests and doing his bidding.[85] The baronial sheriff of the first century of the Conquest was gradually transformed into the ministerial sheriff of the thirteenth century, and as such he played a vital role in governing the county and enforcing the rule of law.[86]

The duties and obligations of the sheriff were gradually defined during the thirteenth century, which became 'the sheriff's golden age'. He collected the king's revenue and accounted for it at the Exchequer; he managed the king's estates and disbursed whatever was necessary to maintain them. In theory, he led the armed forces, the *levée en masse* of the shire, though in fact such a body had virtually ceased to exist. He represented the king as fountain of justice. He arrested and imprisoned wrongdoers, empanelled juries, and presided over the courts of the shire and its hundreds in both civil and criminal matters. The sheriff received a continuous flow of writs from the central government, to which he was called upon to return a reply.[87] Complaint had been made to the king that navigation on a river had been obstructed; that the towpath had been washed away; that a bridge was ruinous. All were passed to the sheriff, coupled with the injunction that he look into the matter and report.

There were, apart from the 'palatinates' of Chester and Durham, twenty-seven shrievalties in England. Except in Glamorgan and Pembroke, there was no system of counties and sheriffs in Wales before the Edwardian conquest.[88] Almost from the first some counties were grouped in pairs and placed under a single sheriff. Templeman has suggested that this was due 'to the difficulty of securing sufficient men who were both competent and reliable'.[89] This may have been the case, but it is suggested below that there was another and equally powerful reason.

The Conqueror found in some twenty-five of the counties a central-place which had been created by the Romans or Anglo-Saxons. In most instances the central-place was a town of some size and importance. In these, and indeed in most other urban central-places, he established a castle, which then or at some future date passed into the charge of the sheriff. But there were exceptions. Some counties lacked an urban central-place; Cornwall and Somerset had no such focus. There was no obvious capital in Suffolk or Derbyshire or, at this time, in Berkshire where Wallingford, the obvious candidate, was not retained in royal hands.[90] The unity of Sussex was broken by the semi-autonomous Rapes. Bedfordshire, Buckinghamshire and Huntingdonshire and, in the Midlands, Leicestershire and Warwickshire, however, each had unequivocal central-places – the towns which give their names to the counties – and in each a castle was built soon after the Conquest by the king or his barons. But the king failed to retain control of the castle for reasons which are unclear. It is too simple to accuse the early Norman kings of lack of consistency. They did not, and could not, anticipate the expanding role of the sheriff and his need

Table 4.3. *Counties and administrative castles*

Shrievalties	Castle
Bedfordshire–Buckinghamshire	—
Cambridgeshire–Huntingdonshire	Cambridge
Cornwall	Launceston
Cumberland	Carlisle
Devon	Exeter
Essex–Hertfordshire	Colchester
Gloucestershire	Gloucester
Hampshire	Winchester
Herefordshire	Hereford
Kent	Canterbury
Lancashire	Lancaster
Lincolnshire	Lincoln
London–Middlesex	—
Norfolk–Suffolk	Norwich
Northamptonshire	Northampton
Nottinghamshire–Derbyshire	Nottingham
Northumberland	Newcastle
Oxfordshire–Berkshire	Oxford
Rutland	—
Shropshire–Staffordshire	Shrewsbury
Somerset–Dorset	[Sherborne]
Surrey–Sussex	Guildford
Warwickshire–Leicestershire	—
Westmorland	—
Wiltshire	Sarum
Worcestershire	Worcester
Yorkshire	York

to control the castle of his shire. At some early date in the Conquest it seemed convenient to throw a county, such as Somerset or Suffolk, which lacked an obvious central-place, in with another which had one.

Even so, some sheriffs were left without a focal castle. The castles of both Warwick and Leicester came into baronial possession and remained so. Leicester Castle passed ultimately to the duchy of Lancaster, and reverted to the crown only with the accession of Henry IV. Similarly, the castles of Bedford[91] and Buckingham[92] appear to have been baronial from the start. The castle of Huntingdon was, like that at Cambridge, established by the Conqueror, but became the shortlived *caput* of the barony of Huntingdon.[93] One might have expected the castle of Dorchester to have become the administrative centre for the counties of Dorset and Somerset.[94] In fact, almost nothing is known of the castle, and documentary references suggest that it was more a manor house than a castle. Corfe Castle was established by William I, and remained in royal hands until early in the

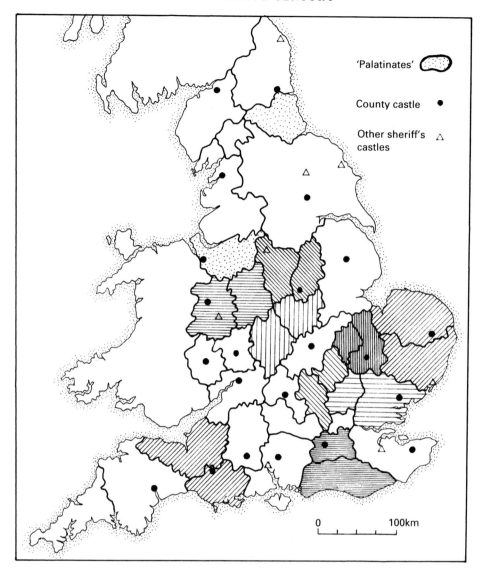

4.6 The historic counties and their shrieval castles. Where two adjoining counties were held by the same sheriff they are shown by the same shading.

fifteenth century.[95] The records show that the sheriff of Somerset–Dorset had general supervision over it, and that he used it occasionally in his shrieval duties. But it was Sherborne, seized by King Stephen from the Bishop of Sarum that appears during the thirteenth century to have focussed the sheriff's activities more than any other site.

In 1070 the Conqueror built a castle at Stafford, now represented by a large motte 2.2 km south-west of the town.[96] Why William departed from his usual practice of building an *urban* castle we do not know. In any event, the castle had been destroyed before the compilation of Domesday Book and a baronial castle was built later.[97] And so the county of Stafford shared its sheriff with neighbouring Shropshire, and was administered from Shrewsbury Castle.

The system of shires was introduced into northern England by the Norman kings. In Northumberland the first sheriff was appointed in 1076, and administered the county from Bamburgh, once the seat of the kings of Bernicia.[98] Bamburgh Castle remained for many years an appendage of the shrievalty, and even when the New Castle-upon-Tyne became the sheriff's chief charge, Bamburgh was often specifically named as in his custody. The county of Cumberland was created as a dependency of Carlisle Castle, which Rufus had founded in 1092. Both Cumberland and Northumberland were ceded by Stephen to Henry, son of the king of the Scots, and when they were recovered by Henry II in 1157, sheriffs were appointed on the English model and ran their counties from, respectively, Carlisle and Newcastle-upon-Tyne.

Durham had been part of the former earldom of Northumbria, but much of its territory had been acquired by the see of St Cuthbert. In this 'vast, sparsely populated and remote area ... jurisdiction was less a privilege than a frequently fatal duty'. The Bishop of Durham successfully resisted the attempts of the sheriff of Northumberland to extend his authority south of the Tyne. This he could do since he held 'the essential requirement of government and survival, Durham Castle, the only secure refuge between Tyne and Tees. Away from it neither earl nor bishop could stay alive'.[99] In fact the immunity which the bishop claimed extended also to those parts of Northumberland which belonged to the see of Durham. Norham Castle was outside the control of the county's sheriff.[100] Only during a vacancy in the see, when the king took possession of the bishop's lands, did the sheriff enter what could well have been his most important fortress.

The county of Westmorland was a latecomer among English counties. It was mountainous and consisted essentially of the baronies of Appleby and Kendal. The sparse population and restricted resources, combined with the tight control exercised by those who held the two lordships, made this the least onerous of English counties to administer.[101] There was a sheriff at least as early as 1129, but he appears to have had no castle and his rights and duties were slight.[102]

Lastly, the county of Lancashire evolved slowly, filling the gap between Cheshire, on which it was at first dependent, and Cumbria. Though not a palatinate like Chester, Lancashire nevertheless appears to have enjoyed a measure of independence not found in most English counties,[103] and in 1267 was erected into an earldom which was granted to Edmund, youngest son of Henry III. It had a sheriff from 1164, who accounted at the Exchequer like any other.[104] He appears to have operated from Lancaster Castle, but his scanty correspondence with the central government suggests an uncommon degree of independence.[105]

The thirteenth-century sheriff was the king's man, appointed by him and liable to dismissal without notice or excuse. This was the royal view of his office. In reality, sheriffs sometimes proved more obdurate, and to remove them from office and get them out of royal castles was occasionally a task of some difficulty. The Conqueror could not be too discriminating in his choice of men to fill the office; he had too few from whom to choose. And he lacked the means to control them closely once they were in office. Not unnaturally some tried to make their office hereditary, and a few were successful. The most conspicuous cases were in the counties of Devon, Gloucester and Worcester.[106] Although the shrievalties of Devon and Gloucestershire, with their respective castles, were ultimately regained by the crown, that of Worcester remained with the Beauchamps, heirs of Urse d'Abitot. The sheriff of Worcestershire and constable of its castle was effectively beyond the control of the king. This is reflected in the curious history of Worcester Castle itself. It lay just south of the cathedral and, according to William of Malmesbury, spread over a large part of the monks' cemetery.[107] Royal though it was, the king had little authority over it, and it was occupied most of the time by the hereditary sheriff. In 1215 John, as a gesture of reconciliation, returned to the cathedral-priory the land which had been filched from it nearly a century and a half before. The castle, thus emasculated, ceased to have any military value. Its walls became a quarry, the motte, grazing land, and of its former buildings only the sheriff's gaol remained.[108]

The county of Middlesex and its principal city, London, constitute an exception to all that has been said of the functions of the sheriff and his castle. London's castle, the Tower, had been begun early in William's reign. At the end of the eleventh century there appears to have been a sheriff of Middlesex, the son of Ansgar the Staller, who was also constable of the Tower.[109] Amongst his successors in both offices was Geoffrey de Mandeville. But thereafter the sheriffdom of Middlesex developed in a different direction from that taken in other counties. He became more a representative of the citizens than of the king, and the constable within the Tower was the chief royal officer. Indeed, the first act of the sheriffs of the city of London was to pay their respects to the constable.[110]

The functions of royal castles

Royal castles which became the centres of shrieval administration must be distinguished from the rest, which served for the protection of the realm or the residence of the king. The former were few in number – only about twenty. They ceased, with a few exceptions, to have any military significance, and, in extreme cases, were allowed to fall into decay except for the buildings essential for the sheriff's administration.

The sheriff's jurisdiction was not, as a general rule, restricted to castles under his direct control. He had some limited authority and responsibility, which differed from one shire to another, over the other royal castles. He supervised building operations, made repairs and accounted at the Exchequer for their income and expenditure. But he was not their constable. Nor was the sheriff in continuous possession even of his own castle. He held both castle and county at the will of the king, and was always liable to be ousted in favour of a royal servant or favourite.

4.7 A sheriff's seal commonly showed his own arms superimposed on a castle, symbol of his office: (left) the seal of John Giffard, sheriff of Hampshire, 1432–3, (right) the seal of William Harcourt, sheriff of Oxfordshire and Berkshire, 1491–2.

When Robert Echyngham was made sheriff of Surrey and Sussex in 1390, his writ added 'by virtue of which he has custody of the castle [of Guildford]'.[111] This was, indeed, the usual case, but at Nottingham in 1255–6 Ralph, son of Nicholas, was given the *corpus* of the castle and the sheriff was left to run the county from whatever place he could.[112] Gloucester Castle was not infrequently separated from the shire, but always in the end it 'rejoined the body of the county'. Clearly the separation of castle and county was considered unusual as well as inconvenient. The sheriff had to have an office and his status required that this be a castle. The seal of the sheriff almost always showed a castle gate. Nevertheless, there are instances of a sheriff acquiring a building outside the limits of the castle from which to carry on at least part of his activities. At Norwich there was a shirehouse in the city which belonged to 'the fee of Norwich castle' and for which exemption was claimed from the jurisdiction of the city authorities.[113] At Nottingham, which must have been a particularly congested castle, the sheriff had a gaol in the city[114] and at Winchester, the constable took over premises in the town.[115]

The sheriff of Norfolk and Suffolk, denied access to *his* castle, was on one occasion placated by being allowed to keep the castle-guard rents which accrued.[116] At Oxford compensation was paid to a former constable because for three and a half years he 'had neither dwelt in the castle, nor had the profitable custody of prisoners', and at Oakham, where the sheriff of Rutland did not have possession of the castle, he was allowed a small space to keep his prisoners and 'the writs, memoranda and other things'.[117]

The sheriff's duties can be subsumed under four heads. His foremost obligation within his county was to enforce the law in the name of the king. Secondly, he was responsible for the collection of taxes and their transmission to the Exchequer. He received royal rents and farms and made disbursements for the repair of crown buildings and the support of royal chapels and charities. The smooth running of the shire, thirdly, was his responsibility and, lastly, he had a residual military function as commander of the local *levée*. In time many of these functions passed to other bodies, like the itinerant justices or the justices of the peace.

In the thirteenth century each of the sheriff's tasks involved paperwork. There was a continuous flow of writs from the king's council. Each had to be 'returned', and if the sheriff was slow in doing so the order would be repeated in more peremptory terms. There were felons to be arrested and brought before the courts. Juries had to be empanelled and gaols and courtrooms kept in order. There were Hundred courts to be visited — the sheriff's turn — and endless complaints to be answered. So the castle had to embrace not only offices where the county administration could be carried on, but also court and gaol, and if these were not well maintained, the justices complained and the prisoners escaped. At Hereford in 1249 the sheriff was called upon to repair the great hall of the castle, where courts were held, as well as the exchequer building, grange, gaol and the county hall — *domus comitatus*.[118]

The sheriff's court was a court of record. Its proceedings were written down and served as evidence or precedent in future cases.[119] The storage of court records was thus of great importance. They had to be available for consultation and were transmitted with care by one sheriff to his successor. The chronicle of Barnwell Priory records that the prior often needed to consult a table of the tax liabilities of his house which was kept in Cambridge Castle, and sent a monk to make a copy.[120] A similar case arose at Oxford, where a court ordered the constable of the castle to produce his records. Sometimes records were destroyed; more frequently they were transported from one castle to another for safety or for consultation.[121] In 1264 Matthias Bezil, constable of Gloucester, complained that charters had been taken from his castle during the Barons' War.[122] At Corfe Castle, the records were kept *in capella nostri castri*.[123] In royal castles there was an archive, the clerks in charge doubtless hoping that they would not be called upon to clean them up and produce them for the justices.[124]

But it was the Tower which in the end became the chief depository for records.[125] Provincial collections accumulated in castles like Tonbridge, Tutbury and Pontefract, but eventually most made their way to London where they were stored in ever-worsening physical conditions. In 1312, in the course of the reorganisation of the records instituted by Walter Stapleton, the chapel in the White Tower was fitted up with 'presses' for the storage of rolls and other documents.

The shire court was not the only one to meet in the sheriff's castle. It was of declining importance, as its business passed to the king's justices and the king's courts.[126] From the time of Henry II royal justices visited the counties and from early in the thirteenth century they carried with them commissions of gaol delivery. The courts usually met in the great hall of the castle, which alone could acccommodate the throng of jurymen, mainpernors and petty officials.[127] At Norwich, on one occasion, the court, which met in the 'Shire House', was obliged by the throng of people to adjourn to the castle.[128] At York Castle a hall was assigned especially for the courts, together with 'other buildings necessary and convenient for the sheriff's business',[129] and at Nottingham houses in the outer bailey were used by the justices in eyre.

The sheriff or his bailiffs arrested suspected felons and held them until the arrival of the justices. Suitable gaols were rare, but the sheriff had authority to use any private castle. In 1274, there was an assault at Tempsford (Bedfordshire).[130] The suspected felon was caught and taken to Eaton Socon Castle, which lay nearby. The castle must by this date have been almost derelict, and he was held only until he could be taken to the greater security of Bedford gaol, where he awaited the next gaol delivery.[131] On the other hand, a felon arrested in Surrey was taken to Reigate Castle, where the constable refused to admit him. He had then to be taken to Guildford Castle, 20 km away.[132]

The Assize of Clarendon of 1166 required the sheriff to have his own gaol in a royal castle or borough. Without exception the shrieval castles became the county gaols.[133] More than one gaol was eventually found necessary in most counties,[134] but always the castle was the strongest and most important.[135] The constable, whether or not he was also sheriff, was responsible for the safe-keeping of prisoners and it was he who was fined if any escaped.[136] The sheriff's gaol was often insecure and desperately overcrowded. In Shropshire it was objected that only the gaol in Shrewsbury Castle was available for the sheriff to use and that it was so ruinous that prisoners were continually escaping. In 1275 the sheriff of Northumberland was obliged to petition for a gaol delivery because he could hold no more prisoners.[137]

If security was often neglected, we can be sure that the comfort and well-being of prisoners was ignored. The constable expected to make a profit from his custody of prisoners. The case of the Oxford constable who received compensation for the loss of this source of income has already been mentioned. A prisoner in the 'tower' (keep) of Norwich Castle complained that he was 'exposed to the elements'.[138] There are numerous cases of maltreatment and even of starvation. Another prisoner in Norwich Castle reported that the constable had forced him to make an 'appeal' (false accusation) through 'tortures, beatings and starvation', and that he had been kept 'in the lowest room of the gaol.'[139] The catalogue of the deaths through starvation of prisoners in Northampton Castle provides the worst instance of maltreatment.[140] Of eight prisoners who died in the castle while awaiting trial, six succumbed to 'hunger, cold and privation'.

Most of those who were thus mistreated were suspected felons awaiting trial. The courts very rarely imposed what would today be called custodial sentences. With a mandatory death sentence for offences of the most trivial order, we find that prisoners were found 'not guilty' or were hanged. The severity of the law was at least tempered by the frequency with which a 'not guilty' verdict was given.

Long-term prisoners were, as a general rule, political. They were hostages or prisoners for whom a ransom could be demanded. Such persons were kept in greater security and comfort than ordinary felons. A daily allowance was made for their support, and, if their rank warranted it, they were allowed a servant to attend to their needs.[141] The low relief carvings on a wall on the second floor of the keep of Carlisle Castle are almost certainly the work of Scottish hostages in the late fifteenth century. They display a level of sophistication not likely to be found amongst common prisoners.[142] The constable did not always welcome such high-born prisoners, and at Bridgnorth he refused to receive them until provision had been made for their clothing and entertainment.[143]

The actual care of prisoners devolved upon the gaoler. The location of the gaol varied greatly. The Assize of Clarendon provided for timber to build what may have been a free-standing structure.[144] With the decline in the castle's military significance, a gatehouse, tower or even the keep was used for prisoners. In fact, there was commonly more than one gaol, and a prisoner's social status determined the one in which he would be incarcerated. In 1283 a mixed group of prisoners was held in Carisbrooke Castle, 'some, like the monks in the more comfortable prison; some, like the lay brethren, in the gaol, and . . . the laymen according to the status of their persons', and on their release, the gaoler demanded 4d from each.[145] At York Castle, there was a gaol for women prisoners.[146] There was a subterranean cell for more dangerous prisoners at Canterbury, Leicester, Norwich and Wallingford.[147] Though such cells often had a grating in their roof to admit light and air, they seem generally to have been entered by a door.

During the later Middle Ages the common gaol seems increasingly to have been located in the gatehouse, and the porter to have served as gaoler. At Skipton in Yorkshire a tenement in the town was held by the serjeanty of 'keeping the gate of Skipton castle [and] finding irons for all the prisoners and guarding them'.[148] The gatehouse of Cambridge Castle survived into the nineteenth century because it served as the county gaol,[149] and at Bridgnorth, Lancaster and Newcastle-upon-Tyne the gatehouse was long used as a prison.

In addition to being the chief judicial officer the sheriff was also the king's local financial agent. It was in the castle that the sheriff's clerks conducted their audits. Money which accrued from rents and fines, from the sale of timber and other assets, and from the goods of convicted felons all passed through their hands. Out of thirty designated places for the collection of the scutage of 1235, nineteen were royal castles.[150]

The sheriff had also to assess the mental condition of testators and establish the pregnancy of women whose husbands had died while holding land of the crown. Posthumous births were supervised by the sheriff, and the women had to 'remain in the castle until the question of her offspring can be settled'.[151]

How the sheriff's clerks handled this volume of work we have no means of knowing. Jenkinson has postulated 'a permanent, efficient and fairly numerous clerical staff at the sheriff's office, the standard of whose work did not fall below that of the central government'.[152] At most castles there would have been a strong room in which to keep the king's treasure. The castle treasury must have resembled the Pyx Chamber in Westminster Abbey.[153] The national treasure, *thesaurus Angliae*, was located mainly in London, distributed between the Tower, the Temple and

Westminster,[154] but the king and his *curia* were in constant motion. They needed access to their treasure, and sums had to be despatched to all parts of the kingdom. King John adopted the practice of dispersing his treasure in a number of castles. John favoured Marlborough in the south of England and Nottingham in the north, but he also used Bristol, Devizes and others. Towards the end of his reign, as danger mounted, he came to prefer the fortress of Corfe. Constables continued to receive direction to send specified sums, usually expressed in marks, to the king or to an army in the field. It was transported by cart, packed in leather bags. It took fifteen 'long-carts' to move 50,000 marks from Bristol to Corfe in 1213.[155]

The treasure was held as minted coin. The principal mint was in the Tower. Here, 'between the ramparts . . . and the Inner or Ballium wall was a narrow street called Mint Street'.[156] Here were the 'houses' in which the moneyers and assayers lived and carried on their work. Theirs was a complex and highly organised craft.[157] At its head was the warden, and under him were the 'master-worker', assayer, clerk and engraver, each with a small staff. Outside the limits of the mint the royal exchanger acquired metal for minting.

The private right to mint coins had been retained by the two archbishops and by the Bishop of Durham, but little use was made of it.[158] The Bishop of Lincoln claimed in the *Quo Warranto* proceedings to have *cuneum* [mint] *in castro suo de Newark ad monetam faciendam*.[159] A short-lived mint was set up in York Castle to remedy a scarcity of coin in the North.

Castles were the crown's only effective depositories for an endless range of goods including food and drink, and a vast range of weapons and armour. The breadgrains, meat and fodder were available at most places where the royal party halted and the constable or steward was usually warned in advance to have sufficient on hand. But not all castles could produce venison from their own resources, and those constables who also had charge of parks were instructed to deliver deer and game for the king's table. But the commodity most commonly moved around the country was wine. England's vintage may have satisfied the requirements of the church, but was not up to the standard demanded by the royal table. Wine was imported in vast quantities from Gascony and the Rhineland. It was held in castles near the ports of entry: London, Southampton, Winchester, Bristol and from here was distributed. What this did to the quality of the wine may be surmised from the frequency with which stocks were tasted, found to be sour, and sold to those with less discriminating palates.

CHAPTER 5

The castle in peace and war

Idem rex . . . ad Orientalem egrediens Eliensi episcopo cancellario suo vices suas in administratione regni commiserat cum ejusdem regni ossibus, id est munitionibus regiis.
William of Newburgh, I, 331

When Henry II came to the throne most castles were still of earthwork and timber. Their principal defence lay in their rampart and motte, crowned with palisade and wooden tower. In very few of them was masonry significant, and not more than a dozen stone keeps had been built. There were stone curtain walls at only a few castles, like Rochester and Eynsford, and gate-towers at Exeter, Newark, Ludlow and Richmond.[1] There were a few stone buildings, like Scolland's Hall at Richmond, within the bailey. But elsewhere timber was the chief building material.

The advantages of such construction were obvious. It was quick, cheap and called for few skilled craftsmen, and the resulting castle, if well sited and carefully put together, could be remarkably strong. But it was not durable. Timbers rotted and towers collapsed, and those who could afford it were beginning to look for a more permanent, more defensible and, above all, more comfortable home.

The century and a half following the accession of Henry II saw important changes in both the form and the role of the English castle. In the first place, masonry replaced timber on a considerable scale. The motte and then the freestanding keep were gradually abandoned. Instead, the court with angle towers became the norm. Curtain walls became thicker. Crenellations and over-sailing brattices were added. Gatehouses became stronger and more elaborate in their construction. The entrance tunnel was fitted with a portcullis, and its surrounding ditch was crossed only by a 'turning' or drawbridge.

The new type of castle represented a very large investment. No longer did it lie within the resources of any petty lord of a few manors, and the masonry castle was the mark of a baron of wealth and standing. In consequence, the number of active castles declined during the period. By the end of the thirteenth century the right to have a castle and the ability to pay for its construction, modernisation or extension had become the prerogative of the few.

This narrowing of the range of those able to build and maintain a castle was paralleled by the growing practice of applying to the king for a licence to crenellate whenever such a construction was contemplated. This practice was not new. Even Geoffrey de Mandeville, during Stephen's reign, had sought charters from both

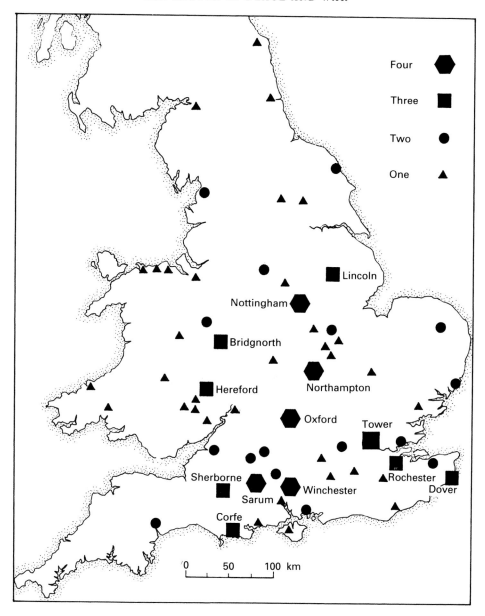

5.1 On several occasions (1223, 1258, 1260 and 1297) the king sent missives ordering constables to see that their castles were securely held. The map shows the number of times individual constables received an injunction to see that the king's castles were securely held, in the thirteenth century.

Matilda and Stephen authorising him to build a castle (see p. 30). Henry II, who would have been very chary of making such grants, none the less authorised the building of Berkeley Castle.[2] During the thirteenth century the number of requests for permission to crenellate began to increase. In some instances the grant of a licence was followed by the building of a substantial castle, as at Brougham or Hadleigh. In others no recognisable building ever resulted, and the licence would appear never to have been acted upon.[3] In many the fortifications erected were of little military significance. They include, if we look only at those built before 1300, Acton Burnell and Stokesay in Shropshire, Somerton in Lincolnshire and Weoley in Warwickshire,[4] all castles of pretence rather than fortresses. On the other hand, we find a few castles of not inconsiderable military significance built without any authorisation that has been discovered, among them Dunstanburgh (Northumberland), and Compton and Powderham (Devon). Others were strengthened or enlarged during the century, sometimes with, sometimes without licence. Nafferton Castle, west of Newcastle, was build without licence by Philip de Ulecotes. His near neighbour, Richard d'Umfraville, complained that this was to the detriment of his own castle of Prudhoe, only 4 km away,[5] and in 1221 the sheriff was authorised to destroy Nafferton Castle, and to use its timber at Bamburgh and Newcastle.[6] There was probably an element of local jealousy in this incident.[7]

Beverston Castle in Gloucestershire offers an analogous case. The castle was built before 1225 by Maurice de Berkeley, who was pardoned by Henry III for not having obtained permission, on payment, doubtless, of a fine.[8] Both Nafferton and Beverston were castles of some significance, which the king probably felt that he could not ignore. But why did so many builders of what were only strong manor houses seek and obtain a royal licence to build? It could hardly have been to protect themselves from an overzealous sheriff or jealous neighbour. The reason lay more probably in the self-conscious pride of the gentry and lesser nobility, who could at least say 'we *could* have built a castle if we had wished'. The list of licences to crenellate is an uncertain guide to castle-building in the thirteenth century. It demonstrates little more than the pretensions of the lesser nobility. The greater barons already had castles enough, and probably, if they had wished to add to their number, would not have bothered to seek a royal licence.

Despite many castles built *ab initio* during the thirteenth century, their total number was declining. It is impossible to be precise; many slipped out of the records unnoticed. Manorial extents increasingly fail to mention that at the centre of the manor lay an earthwork castle, or merely state that there is an old castle of no value.[9] The castle site could not readily be obliterated, but it had become irrelevant. In the county of Dorset, the considerable earthwork castle of Powerstock escheated to the crown and was, along with its lands, granted by Henry III to Sir Ralph Gorges, who lived elsewhere.[10] The castle was abandoned and left to decay. A similar fate awaited Marshwood Castle (Dorset), *caput* of the barony of Marshwood.[11] The barony was forfeited in 1264, and henceforward there was no use for the castle. There were many such instances. Usually they arose from the forfeiture or escheat of a barony or from the marriage of an heiress into another family which had no need for it.[12]

At the head of any scale of castles must be those strongholds, both royal, like Dover and Scarborough, and baronial, such as Pontefract, Ludlow and Warwick, which were extensively rebuilt and modernised. Their number was relatively small, and they continued to play a role in political affairs.

Secondly, there were new castles built on virgin sites, with or without an enabling licence from the king. Among these were Beverston, Codnor and Somerton. They were courtyard castles, subrectangular, with strong corner towers and a well-protected gate. Some had a second and more lightly protected bailey to one side, which commonly resembled a farmyard more than a fortified enclosure (see Chapter 10).

On a lower plane were defended homes, capable of resisting an armed band for a short while but quite unable to withstand a siege. Such was the castle of Eaton Bray, surveyed in an inquest *post mortem* of 1274, held on the death of George de Cantilupe:[13]

... a manor, enclosed with moats and walls, and two drawbridges, and gate [houses?] ... roofed with shingles. Within the chief court is a hall with two chambers at its ends; where of one with chimney, roofed with shingles; the other ... pantry and buttery, roofed with tile. A large chamber ... an outer chamber with a chimney ... well roofed with lead, with a passage between the hall and chamber, roofed with tile. He has a chamber with [wa]rdrobe roofed with shingles. A certain small building as a larder in place of a kitchen because there is none. A bridge [across the moat] towards the park, weak, with drawbridge and gate ... [un]roofed and shaky. A new chapel without glazing. A good granary ... In the second court a stable good for sixty horses ... an adequate barn, thatched; a cowhouse also thatched; a stable for cart and draught beasts, thatched. A poor building for a bakery, and two little buildings for [calves?] and swine, thatched.

This description makes Eaton Bray Castle seem more like a farm than a castle; certainly its military pretensions were minimal. Yet the Dunstable chronicler could say that it had been built *in grave periculum Dunstapliae et viciniae*.[14] Perhaps a lightly fortified home seemed more formidable in the twelfth century than in retrospect it does to us.

A more familiar castle of this type and period is Stokesay Castle in Shropshire. Its builder was a prosperous wool merchant, Laurence of Ludlow, though the lower part of the north tower had been built by the de Says, from whom he had bought the site. Laurence clearly intended Stokesay to be both pretentious and comfortable. He completed the north tower and built the more southerly, and between them laid out a hall-house with a princely solar block.[15] The site was surrounded by an insubstantial wall and a moat, and must have had some form of gatehouse. The present timber-framed gatehouse is of the seventeenth century.

Many, perhaps most of those for which licences were granted must have approximated to Eaton Bray and Stokesay. They were what one might have expected of an aspiring middle class who had more money than many of the lesser barons and were beginning to marry into the ranks of the noble families.

Lastly there were what one might call protected homes. They included moated sites, sometimes entered by way of a flimsy drawbridge.[16] There were hundreds of such sites in lowland England, especially on the claylands of the Midlands and East Anglia, where the moat could be filled without difficulty. The sites differed from ringworks in the absence of any form of rampart, though the moat may well have been supplemented by a wooden palisade. Within the moat there was, as a general rule, a simple manor house. Moated sites are difficult to date. They include 'the near-castle and the unpretentious house of the proto-yeoman, the rectory, the park-lodge and the monastic grange'.[17] Some unfinished castles of the Anarchy bear a close resemblance to moated sites. At Aughton (Yorkshire) the moated enclosure 'seems to cut into the bailey [of a motte castle] and to replace it in large part'.[18] In other cases the moated manor house adjoins a motte-and-bailey castle, and appears to have been constructed to replace it. In Warwickshire, where moated sites are particularly numerous, they appear to characterise the colonisation of forested claylands at a time when the motte was already obsolete.[19]

The spectrum described here is a broad one. Structures which a century earlier could be regarded as castles were much less diverse. Most were mottes or ringworks, with or without an attached bailey. The humble lord of a few manors built a castle broadly similar in *form* to that put up by a Richard FitzGilbert or a Robert of Mortain. A consequence was that all, whatever the rank or wealth of their creators, could play a role in the rebellions of the early Norman kings or in the wars of Stephen. The annals record attacks on earthworks which must, to judge from their surviving evidences, have been very low in the scale of castles. Given the level reached by the art of war at this time, the smallest motte-and-bailey was a defensible unit.

As we move into the thirteenth century, important castles became more formidable, as masonry walls replaced palisades, and gatehouses became ever more complex in design. The rest, with few exceptions, were abandoned, replaced by homesteads with little or no military pretension or political significance. It was of no concern to the king who owned them. On the other hand, a group of castles emerges in which the king and his servants took a deep interest. They were large, strong and increasingly they were built of masonry. Each could hold a large garrison and a store of food and weaponry. They were, indeed, 'the bones of the kingdom'.

Siegecraft and defence

The strengthening of the defences was paralleled by improvements in the art of war and, in particular, in the methods of siegecraft. In the wars of Stephen castles were attacked and defended, usually by small bodies of men equipped with sword and short bow, such as are portrayed in the Bayeaux Tapestry. Modes of attack were limited to direct assault, in which the balance of advantage lay with the defenders. A

5.2 The shutters (*fenestrae volantes*) which gave some protection to those who manned the battlements. These survive in the crenellated wall of St Mary's Abbey, York.

wooden castle was susceptible to fire, as is seen in the Bayeux Tapestry's portrayal of the siege of Dinan. But in many early sieges the chief weapon was starvation. The construction of siege-castles, itself a laborious process, was a means of watching a castle and of preventing it from receiving supplies.

After the accession of Henry II castle warfare began slowly to take on a different character. On the one hand, defence was assisted by developments in the plan and construction of castles; on the other, the weaponry of attack was greatly improved. In the castle itself walls became thicker; corner and mural towers were built to give enfilading fire. Loops were located in the walls with increasing regard both to the field of fire which they could control and to the convenience of the archer.[20] The walls were crowned with battlements which gave protection to the defenders, and the gaps between the merlons were often guarded by hinged flaps, such as still remain in the wall around St Mary's Abbey, York.[21] Further, wooden brattices or machicolations were sometimes built in front of the crenellations. The entrance, always the most vulnerable point in the circuit of walls, was protected by a gatehouse, which, when fully developed, consisted usually of an entrance tunnel set back between drum-towers and further protected by drawbridge, portcullis and stout oaken gates.

The defence was assisted from the later years of the twelfth century by the introduction of the crossbow. The traditional English bow was the short-bow, with a range of no more than 200 metres.[22] The medieval crossbow derived from the classical *balista*. It was a more accurate weapon, with a longer range, and the quarrel which it fired was in all respects more deadly than the simple arrow. It had been condemned by the Papacy in 1139, but never ceased to be used. It was adopted in England in the later years of the twelfth century.[23] Richard I favoured it, and from the time of John small bands of *balistarii*, or crossbowmen, were stationed in the more important castles. They clearly ranked high among the mercenaries of the king. Their wage was from 4 to 6 pence a day, greatly in excess of that of ordinary serving soldiers. They were mentioned in writs sent to constables, and a half-dozen made a useful garrison. Sixty crossbowmen were sent to Dover Castle in 1242,[24] and small companies were despatched from castle to castle as need arose.

The records distinguish between 'one-foot' and 'two-foot' crossbows, according to whether or not both feet were used to hold the bow when drawing back the cord. Sometimes the bowman drew the cord by means of a loop attached to his belt.[25] In 1270 six such belts, at the cost of 7s, were sent from Windsor to the king's forces besieging Kenilworth.[26] Yet another type of crossbow had a winch for drawing it — *balasterii ad turnum*.

The sheriff of Hampshire was ordered to buy ten 'good crossbows',[27] but as a general rule they were manufactured for the king's use at the Tower of London, or by travelling *attiliatores*. In 1258 Henry Teutonicus was *factor balistarum regis apud Turrim*.[28] In 1260 Thomas de Sancto Sepulcro was attiliator at the Tower[29] and in 1272 received timber for bows from the forester of Hadleigh Forest.[30] A large store of crossbows was kept at both Windsor[31] and the Tower, and from here they were despatched all over the country.[32]

Large numbers were also given to individual barons. The Lord Edward had, for the defence of Odiham Castle, 'five crossbows of horn (*de cornu*) *cum eorum atillio*, of which two were *ad duos pedes* and three *ad unum pedem*, together with three buckets (*bokettos*) of quarrels of different sizes'.[33]

Bows deteriorated readily, and 'engineers' were sent from castle to castle to repair them. The sheriff of Northumberland was directed to send Master Gerard the engineer to Bamburgh and Newcastle castles to repair the bows,[34] and when he had finished his tools were to be returned to Nottingham Castle, which appears to have been the chief store of weaponry in the North.[35] At the Tower Philip le Convers received $4\frac{1}{2}$d a day for repairing crossbows,[36] and in 1242 all the crossbows in the Tower and at Dover Castle were ordered to be tested, so that the king might know whether he could rely on them.[37]

The number of crossbows in use during the thirteenth century may not have been great, but their consumption of quarrels or bolts was immense. The latter were fairly short, tipped with iron and feathered. They came in at least two sizes, for the one-foot and the larger two-foot bow. They were made of a hardwood, and represented an immense consumption of timber. Whereas crossbows were made at castles like the Tower, their quarrels were produced largely, if not exclusively, in forested areas where the materials were at hand. Most important of these was the Forest of Dean, a royal forest which also held easily worked deposits of iron ore. The manufacture of quarrels was concentrated in the castle of St Briavels, on the western edge of the forest.[38] John Malemort, the chief quarrel-maker, was said in 1256 to be producing 25,000 quarrels a year.[39] Malemort himself was expected to make 100 quarrels a day, for which he was paid $7\frac{1}{2}$d, with a further 3d for feathering them – a not inconsiderable wage for a craftsman, somewhat more, in fact, than the king's crossbow maker was receiving in the Tower.[40] He was supplied with wood, iron, charcoal, lard, bran, a grindstone and barrels in which to pack his product.[41] The only other manufactory for which there is evidence was in the Tower itself. Here Henry le Fevre was the king's quarrel-maker, receiving $4\frac{1}{2}$d a day, together with the materials required.[42] Far fewer quarrels were distributed from the Tower than from St Briavels. It is difficult to determine the normal ratio of quarrels to crossbows. The constable of Winchester Castle was ordered to send eight crossbows to Portsmouth, evidently for shipment, together with 50,000 quarrels[43] but this may have been for a long military campaign. The allowance of three buckets for five crossbows, made to the Prince Edward seems more reasonable.[44]

Quarrels were shipped throughout the land, and were sent overseas. They were packed in barrels and carried in long-carts. Some castles held a large store to serve the needs of their local regions: Windsor, Corfe and Bristol castles in the South, and, probably, Nottingham and Chester in the North. But the largest store appears to have been in Hereford Castle, probably the chief supply centre for the Marches, as Chester was for North Wales.[45]

The crossbow gave the defence a considerable advantage during the thirteenth century. But its rate of fire was slow and the archer needed protection while drawing his bow. Loops facilitated sighting the bow, and the wide internal splay gave the bowman room to handle his weapon. The crossbow was a remarkably accurate weapon, capable of picking off defenders on the walls and even of shooting a quarrel through a loop and hitting the defender. Its accuracy and range led to the construction of wooden shutters and bretaches over the tops of castle walls.[46]

Attack was assisted by a variety of 'engines' which threw missiles, usually stones, into the castle. They made use of tension, as in a bow, of torsion and of counterpoise. Most had been used in classical times. All were used in the Middle Ages to beat down walls and crush buildings and also by defenders against all that approached their walls too closely. The nomenclature used for siege engines is far from clear, and one is often uncertain from the written record of their precise nature.[47] The term 'ballista' usually denoted a great crossbow operated by the tension of the bow; the springal relied on the tension of a bent beam of wood, and the mangonel on the torsion of tightly twisted rope.[48] Only one engine was the invention of the Middle Ages, the *trébuchet*. It relied on a counterpoise and was simpler in design and construction than most others. Prince Louis of France is credited with bringing it to England in 1216. The curious mounds which surround Berkhamsted Castle (Figure 5.4) may have been erected by the French during the siege of 1216 to support such machines.[49]

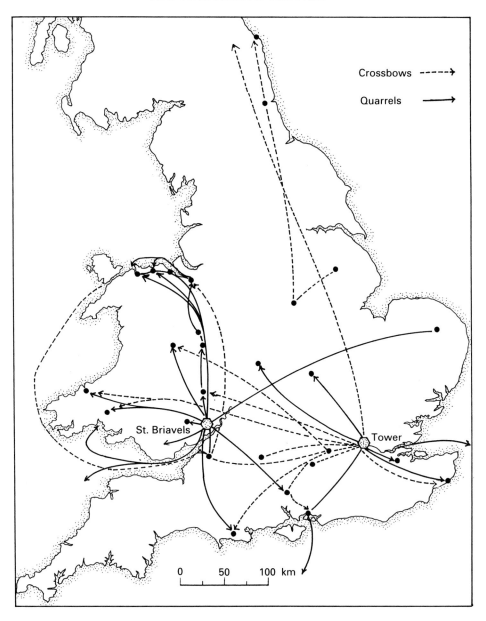

Crossbows ----->

Quarrels ----->

St. Briavels

Tower

0   50   100 km

5.3 The supply of crossbows and quarrels to royal castles. The Tower was the chief place of manufacture of crossbows, but quarrels came mainly from the Forest of Dean, with its administrative centre in St Briavels Castle.

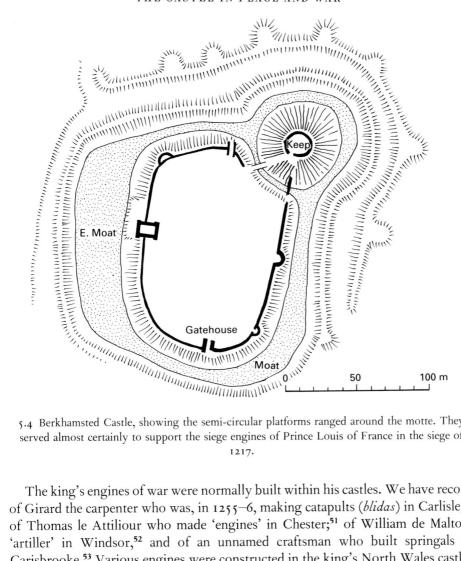

E. Moat

Keep

Gatehouse

Moat

0   50   100 m

5.4 Berkhamsted Castle, showing the semi-circular platforms ranged around the motte. They served almost certainly to support the siege engines of Prince Louis of France in the siege of 1217.

The king's engines of war were normally built within his castles. We have record of Girard the carpenter who was, in 1255–6, making catapults (*blidas*) in Carlisle;[50] of Thomas le Attiliour who made 'engines' in Chester;[51] of William de Malton, 'artiller' in Windsor,[52] and of an unnamed craftsman who built springals in Carisbrooke.[53] Various engines were constructed in the king's North Wales castles of Deganwy and Dyserth, where four 'switches' were built for catapults and mangonels.[54] At both Dover[55] and Hereford[56] buildings were erected for storing engines. In 1233 a *trébuchet* was built in the Forest of Dean by master Nicholas the carpenter,[57] the only instance found of their construction outside the limits of a castle though within the jurisdiction of St Briavels.

But the most important manufactory was without doubt the Tower. In 1312 four *ingenia* and six springals were under construction there.[58] In 1340 Robert de Bredon held the office of 'artiller' in the Tower at 6d a day;[59] thirteen years later John de Byker held the same[60] but at 12d a day, and his son succeeded him at the same wage.[61]

It was usual to drag these machines around the country as need arose. One of the engines at the Tower was taken to Sandwich for shipment to France, and brought back again because there 'were not ships enough for the passages of the king and the engine'.[62] After the siege of Kenilworth Castle (1266), the king's engines were dismantled for shipment.[63] They decayed readily. In 1278 the king's engineer in the Tower was allowed seven oak trees and five beeches for their repair.[64] A store of such engines was kept at Winchester and Porchester – evidently for shipment abroad[65] – as well as at Nottingham and the Tower.[66] Even a minor baronial castle like Chartley in Staffordshire was found, when taken into the king's hands in 1276, to have a store of hardware (*ferramenta ingeniorum*) for engines.[67] Master Girard, doubtless the same engineer who built catapults in Carlisle Castle, was in 1244 making engines for Dover – 'a catapult, a trébuchet and a ram'[68] – and in 1255 was sent to North Wales 'to view the king's works and engines in . . . Gannok [Deganwy] and Dissard' [Dyserth]. The fact that Girard not only built such machines at the Tower, but was sent about the country to inspect and repair them suggests that such craftsmen were few.[69]

The attackers had a range of options. They could pulverise both the external walls and buildings within by their artillery; they could pick away at the walls with a 'bore', or undermine them by tunnelling, and they could make a direct assault either with ladders or by building a mobile wooden tower which could be advanced to the walls. In the last resort a castle could be isolated and forced into surrender by starvation. All methods were used. Rochester Castle succumbed in 1215 to a mine driven under the south-east corner of the keep. Prince Louis of France in 1216 failed to take Dover and Windsor castles with his artillery, but reduced the weaker castle of Hertford in twenty-five days with his hail of *damnosi lapides* and Berkhamsted in twenty.[70]

Most of the siege engines were capable of throwing a stone of 300 lb. or more a distance of at least 150 metres. Stones of this weight have been excavated at Kenilworth Castle, where they were probably used in the siege of 1266. A store of them would have been kept, as at Alnwick in 1244,[71] but they could not have been carried around the country with the machines which threw them. Stones must have been acquired locally, and this would, for geological reasons, have been difficult in some areas.

Siege engines were heavy and clumsy. Kendall claimed[72] that the seven *trébuchets* used at Berkhamsted called for fifty-six long-carts for their transport. It seems more likely that siege engines were constructed at the site, as they were when the Welsh attacked the castles of Mold and Dyserth, and during the siege of Kenilworth Castle.[73] Wooden towers were sometimes pushed close to the walls, which were then assaulted by foot soldiers gathered on their upper level. The Justice of Chester was in 1244 ordered to have four 'good strong wooden towers' built in the forest of the Wirral[74] and to have two such towers made as close as possible to the Border 'to carry wherever the king may wish in Wales'.[75]

The cost of repairing walls and buildings after a siege gives us an idea of the damage that 'engines' could do. It was, for instance, almost half a century before that inflicted in the siege of Bedford Castle in 1224 was fully repaired. 'Engines' were, however, costly and difficult to move about the country. The expense of transporting and mounting 'the king's great engines' before Kenilworth Castle in 1266 was very considerable.[76] Nor were the problems of building them on the spot small. The transport of timber to make a siege tower cost 15s 9d, a sum equivalent to more than could be earned in ninety man-days.

Not surprisingly, the long, slow siege was preferred, and for this reason castles that were at risk were usually well stocked with food. Most provisions, however, had only a short 'shelf-life' and had to be frequently renewed. For the most part the attackers put their trust in having sufficient time for the slow process of starvation to compel the surrender of the castle. The besieged, however, always counted on the timely arrival of a relieving force. A set of rules was worked out and was normally adhered to. A siege became a kind of poker game governed by strict rules. In the siege of Dolforwyn 'the garrison gave eight hostages, the best after the constable, as a guarantee that they will surrender the castle on the Thursday after the close of Easter unless they are relieved by Llewelyn, and if they are relieved, the hostages are to be returned to them'.[77] The choice of a date by which the castle should be relieved or surrendered was crucial and represented the gamble in the negotiation. Whenever a castle was yielded the garrison was usually allowed to march away. Only when it was taken by assault do we find evidence of a wholesale slaughter. The case of the siege and capture of Bedford Castle, held against the king for Faulkes de Bréauté in 1224, was quite exceptional in that almost all the garrison was captured, and eighty of them, including a number of knights, were hanged. This made a great impression at the time, and no less than eight contemporary chroniclers left a record of it,[78] differing from one another only in detail, and Matthew Paris was moved to make a marginal sketch of the scene in his *Historia Anglorum* (Plate 3).[79]

Castles in medieval warfare

Warfare within England was, until the beginning of the Barons' War in 1264, virtually restricted to the siege and defence of castles. There were three such periods of warfare: the rebellion of dissident barons in 1172; the war between Longchamp and Prince John during the absence of Richard I; and, lastly, the wars which preceded the sealing of Magna Carta in 1215 and continued intermittently until the siege of Bedford Castle in 1224.

The rebellion of 1172 has already been discussed (pp. 77–8). The war of 1189–91 was similarly one of sieges. Richard I spent only a few months in England before he departed for the Third Crusade. During this period his generosity was 'liberal to the extent of folly' and in his choice of those who were to represent him during his absence he showed little judgment.[80] The North was left in the hands of Hugh de Puiset, and England south of the Trent in those of William Longchamp, Chancellor and bishop of Ely. Longchamp quickly took control. He boosted his power by a lavish expenditure on the Tower of London, which he strengthened by a ditch, new curtain walls and towers.[81] He took the royal castles of Windsor and Newcastle,

3 The siege of Bedford Castle, 1224, as represented in a marginal drawing of Matthew Paris.

previously held on behalf of the king by the Bishop of Durham, under his own control, and replaced the sheriff in York Castle by his own man. At this juncture Richard's younger brother, John, count of Mortain, returned to England and at once became the rallying point for all disaffected with the rule of Longchamp. Gerard de Camville, constable of Lincoln Castle and sheriff, threw his weight behind John, who also seized the royal castles of Nottingham and Tickhill.[82] At the same time Roger Mortimer of Wigmore declared for him. Longchamp managed to take Wigmore Castle, but opposition to him was growing and he reached an agreement with Prince John. At the heart of the accord was the control of castles.[83] Gerard de Camville retained Lincoln and John acquired Wallingford and Windsor, but gave up Nottingham and Tickhill, which were entrusted to men whose loyalty to King Richard was beyond suspicion. Furthermore, castles erected since the troubles had begun were to be demolished. The war ended with Longchamp holding out in the Tower until his escape to France. Its course showed conclusively that in the minds of contemporaries control of England consisted in the mastery of its more important castles.

The wars of the later years of John and of the minority of his son, Henry III, demonstrated this fact yet more clearly. As hostility mounted between the barons and the king, the former besieged Northampton Castle, but failed to take it, and moved on to Bedford Castle and London. They obtained a promise of siege engines from the king of France, while John hastily repaired his castles and placed large numbers of foreign mercenaries in them.[84] Hostilities were interrupted by a truce when the Great Charter was accepted and sealed by the king. It was a statement of feudal custom as this was conceived at the time, and in so far as castles were concerned it laid it down that no constable might force a knight who owed guard duty to commute his service if he wished to perform it in person, and if he should accompany the king on field service he was to be exempt from castle-ward.[85] Timber might not be seized for castle works, evidence of the extent to which construction was still in timber, and royal sheriffs and bailiffs might not seize horses and wagons for its transport.

The barons at once began to throw away their advantage by quarrels among themselves. They were a disparate group, with widely varying interests and ambitions. Some of the northern barons began to ready their castles for defence. They were acting, in the words of A. L. Poole, 'without right or provocation',[86] but with the personal and political causes of the war we are not concerned. The king was in Kent in September 1215, and on his return to London found the royal custodian of Rochester Castle displaced by the dissident barons.[87] The siege which followed lasted from 13 October to 30 November, almost fifty days. Every device was used to take the castle: engines battered its walls and crossbowmen shot at everything that moved on them.[88] The bailey was stormed, but still the large garrison, put at 95 to 140 knights with crossbowmen and serving soldiers, held out in the keep. Its passive strength defied attempts to batter it. A relieving force from London was turned back, and John resorted to the only means left to him. Picks were obtained from Canterbury, and a mine was driven under the southern corner of the keep. The roof of the mine was supported by timbers, which were then fired. For this the fat of forty bacon pigs — specifically 'those less good for eating'[89] was used. The tower collapsed, but the defenders continued to hold out in the north-western half of the keep, protected by the internal cross-wall, until they were eventually forced into surrender by starvation.

The siege and capture of Rochester Castle made a great impression on contemporaries. It was, in Brown's words, 'the greatest operation of its kind in England up to that time'.[90] 'Our age', wrote the Barnwell chronicler, 'has not known a siege so hard pressed nor so strongly resisted'.[91] Rochester Castle was, by common consent, one of the strongest in the country, and after its fall, the chronicler added, 'few cared to put their trust in castles'.[92]

After his success at Rochester John moved to the North where the focus of baronial resistance lay. The castles of Nottingham and York were taken and during his return he captured Colchester. At this juncture Prince Louis, heir to the French crown, landed on the coast of Kent in answer to the barons' repeated calls for help. Part of his force settled down to besiege Dover Castle, while the rest fanned out over south-eastern England, taking castle after castle, until only Dover, Windsor and Lincoln held out for the king (Figure 5.5). For his part, John, in a frenzy of activity, dashed from castle to castle, trying to stir up resistance to the invader, until, worn out by the rigours of the campaign, he died at Newark Castle on 18 October 1216.

The death of John made little difference to the war, which was far more than a simple dispute between king and barons. It subsumed the feuds among the barons themselves, hostility towards the regents of the young Henry III, and a certain element of anti-French feeling.[93] The war was pursued in a desultory manner, punctuated at intervals by sieges. Prince Louis took the chief castles of the South-east: Berkhamsted, Cambridge, Colchester, Hertford, Norwich, Orford and Winchester, as well as the baronial castles of Hedingham and Pleshey. 'It was a war not of battles but of sieges, carried on between rival castellans . . .'[94] London with the Tower was in his hands. Mountsorrel Castle in Leicestershire adhered to the barons, but Nicola de la Haie, widow of Gerard Camville and castellan of Lincoln in her own right, continued to resist the northward pressure of Louis' army, and it was at Lincoln that the turning point in the war was reached.

Louis' continued success depended on linking up with the dissident barons in the North, but in his path lay the royal strongholds of Nottingham and Lincoln. And so the French and their allies laid siege to Lincoln Castle. What followed is far from clear. The castle was held by the redoubtable Nicola de la Haie. It lay in the south-western quarter of the walled upper city. To the east was the cathedral and the episcopal precinct. The French established their engines in the 'Baile', between castle and the cathedral, leaving the external wall of both town and castle on the west relatively clear. The regent, William Marshall, approached Lincoln and timed his attack to coincide with an eruption of Nicola's forces from inside the castle. This much is clear, but the contemporary accounts embroider the event with conflicting detail, much of which must be apocryphal.[95] 'Nearly every one of these details, it has been said, is either unintelligible or incredible'.[96] What is certain, however, is that the battle spread through the streets of the city and that in these close quarters the French suffered disastrously. They never recovered. The siege of Dover was lifted, and they withdrew to France. The invasion was over, but hostilities, spawned by the bitter conflicts of the last two years, continued. The terms of peace included the restoration of lands which had been confiscated. But it was sometimes difficult to distinguish, in the acrimony which surrounded events, between genuine alienation and outright confiscation. The line between hereditary rights and possessions and those held only by temporary grant of the king had become blurred, and there were many who aimed to translate the one into the other. There were those who thought they could defy the advisers who surrounded the infant king by clinging to castles which were not theirs, and, lastly, there were the mercenary captains whom John

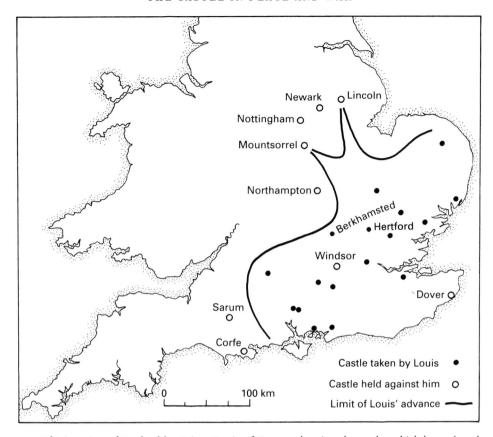

Newark
Nottingham ○
Mountsorrel ○
○ Lincoln
Northampton ○
Berkhamsted
● Hertford
Windsor
○
Dover ○
Sarum
○
Corfe
○

Castle taken by Louis ●

Castle held against him ○

Limit of Louis' advance ━━

5.5 The invasion of England by Prince Louis of France, showing the castles which he took and those which resisted him.

had brought in to support him against the barons and whom he had rewarded with high office. None was willing to abandon the rich pickings they had enjoyed. The pretensions of the barons hinged on their control of castles. In the words of Roger of Wendover 'they presumed to keep in their own hands castles and other lands contrary to the king's prohibition'.[97] They had come almost to regard the castles which they held as their own, and they did not expect to be ejected by those whom they had served.

Amongst these men were Robert de Gaugy who had occupied the Bishop of Lincoln's castles of Newark and Sleaford; Engelard de Cigogné, a French mercenary brought to England by John, held Windsor and Odiham, which he had defended against Prince Louis; Peter de Mauley, a Poitevin, held Corfe; and Faulkes de Bréauté, the Norman adventurer who came to typify these men, seized Plympton (Devon), Christchurch (Hampshire) and Carisbrooke (Isle of Wight) and clung to Bedford Castle. William de Forz, or Fortibus, was, in terms of his castles and lands, even more formidable and proved to be more turbulent than any.[98] His father was a Poitevin, but through his mother he had inherited the Albemarle lands. His holdings included the castles of Skipton, Cockermouth, Skipsea and Driffield. John ordered the constable to admit him to Scarborough,[99] and in 1215 he was entrusted with Rockingham Castle, as well as with the newly constructed Sauvey Castle. But it was the affair of Castle Bytham which brought him into conflict with the king and the law. The castle and manor of Bytham, within 30 km of both Rockingham and Sauvey, had been part of the honour of Holderness, but was alienated to the de Colevilles. William de Coleville adopted the cause of the barons, and his lands were occupied, with at least the tacit consent of the king, by William de Forz. The peace of 1217 required their return to their legitimate owner. The king's advisers agreed, but instead of handing over the castle, de Forz garrisoned it, ravaged the countryside, seized Fotheringhay Castle and attempted to take possession of Sleaford and Newark.[100] The escapades of William de Forz bore a certain resemblance to those of Geoffrey de Mandeville in the previous century, but on this occasion they brought upon him the hostility of much of the baronage and the denunciations of the church. A royal force was gathered at Northampton Castle to suppress the revolt. A siege train from Nottingham Castle went first to Fotheringhay, which was found abandoned, and then on to Bytham, which was assaulted and taken.[101]

Not all who held on to castles in defiance of the treaty and the courts were foreign adventurers. William Earl Marshall had been granted the custody of Marlborough Castle in 1217, and the castle was claimed by his son. The young Marshall proceeded to strengthen it, but made his peace with the king, and was given instead Fotheringhay Castle, fortified by the king of the Scots.[102] The honour of Huntingdon, of which Fotheringhay was the *caput*, was later restored to Alexander II of Scotland, but William Marshall held on to the castle for another year. In the North the castles of Tickhill, Mitford and Prudhoe were handed over to the king only after a long delay, and Newark after a siege. On the Welsh Border the king tried to get possession of Marshall's castle of Caerleon and to limit his control of castles in west Wales,[103] but in this he failed.

Royal control of castles was vital in restoring order. Under a weak government they threatened to become the centres of small areas in which the king's writ scarcely ran. The problem was two-fold. The first was the difficulty of drawing a distinction between baronial castles held in fee and those in which the baron was merely an agent or appointee of the crown. Memories could on occasion be short and records were either improperly kept or lost. The status of a castle was often obscure, and made more so by the obfuscations of its constable. The second difficulty lay in the undisputed right of the king to take over a private castle in an emergency, but the lack of any clear understanding of the conditions under which this might be legitimate set limits to the royal prerogative. Henry III's demand for Caerleon Castle was probably an attempt to see how far he could go[104] and when an attack by Llewelyn ap Iorworth threatened, Henry quickly withdrew. The king and his advisers had, in fact, an unclear idea of the status and attitudes of castellans. In

Walter of Coventry's words he 'travelled through the land to discover whether those who had been entrusted with castles by his father would be willing to give them up quietly'.[105] He just did not know.

The last of these castellans to cling to castles to which they had little or no right was Faulkes de Bréauté. He had been a loyal if somewhat unscrupulous servant of King John and of the young Henry III. He had been given Bedford Castle during the rebellion of William Beauchamp. But it is far from clear whether the latter, though holding the honour of Bedford, actually held the castle in fee. Whatever the situation may have been, Faulkes made Bedford Castle the focus of his activities, greatly strengthening and expanding it and destroying the church of St Paul in the process. When in 1224 the royal court moved to outlaw him for his continued offences against the peace of the realm and the authority of the courts, his brother, William de Bréauté, seized a justice who was holding an assize in Dunstable and took him presumably as a hostage to Bedford.[106] The king had no alternative but to move against the castle.

Bedford Castle was larger and stronger than Bytham, Newark or Sauvey, which the royalist forces had recently taken,[107] and its siege called for the resources of the whole kingdom. The king and archbishop were present, together with many of their barons and leading clergy. The Dunstable chronicler, who was near enough to know just what went on, described the erection of 'engines' around the castle, and two wooden towers, or *beffrois*, were advanced to dominate the wall around the bailey.[108] In its scale, though not in its consequences, the siege of Bedford Castle was comparable with that of Rochester. The countryside was scoured for labourers and materials. Stone was quarried and shaped to make missiles.[109] Miners were brought in from the Forest of Dean. The castle was taken by assault, first the barbican, then the main bailey, then the court on the summit of the motte, and, lastly, the tower within it (Plate 3), was mined and collapsed.[110]

The king ordered the castle to be destroyed in a writ of quite unaccustomed length and detail.[111] The bailey walls were to be flattened and the ditches filled and everything reduced to *plana terra*. The walls of the court upon the motte were to be lowered and their crenellations destroyed, and what remained was returned to William de Beauchamp, with leave to build there a *mansionem* if he so wished. The castle was demolished. The sheriff of Hertfordshire was called upon to supply carts and men with spades, picks and shovels and to remain in Bedford *donec mota sit prostrata et fossata sint palata*.[112] Stone from the castle was given to rebuild St Paul's church in compensation for that removed to make missiles.[113] Today the base only of the motte stands in a public park, its summit 49 m in diameter and rising $7\frac{1}{2}$ m above the level ground.

The next forty years were a period of peace, of relative prosperity, and of increasing maladministration. Henry III was a weak and impetuous ruler at a time when his barons were looking for a larger role in running the country. The latter succeeded in putting their nominees in control of royal castles and were thus in a commanding position. But the situation was quickly reversed, and Henry's failure to abide by the compromise reached with the barons – the Provisions of Oxford – led directly to war.[114]

The Barons' War consisted essentially of two short campaigns. In the first in 1264, the barons were triumphant at Lewes. During the following year dissension spread through their ranks and their cause crumbled. In the Evesham campaign of 1265 they were defeated and their leader, Simon de Montfort, killed. In neither campaign did castles play any role at all in England, though things were different in the March of Wales. The survivors of the rebel barons – the 'Disinherited' – were dispersed and hunted down by the Lord Edward. One might have expected them to hold out in castles, as had happened during the king's minority. They did not. There was some resistance by John de Vescy at Alnwick Castle; a group took possession of the Isle of Ely, and another tried to put Southwark, across the Thames from the city of London, into a state of defence. But the only castle to be effectively defended was Kenilworth, the chief seat of de Montfort's barony. It was a castle of quite exceptional strength because the small river beside which it lay had been dammed to form a large lake.[115] For this reason, a mine, such as had been effective at Rochester and Bedford and had only just failed at Dover Castle, would have been quite ineffective. The lake also kept siege engines at a distance and prevented the use of a wooden tower to scale the walls. The impasse was ended by the familiar medieval practice by which both parties agreed on a time limit – forty days in this case – at the end of which the garrison would surrender unless relieved. There was no chance of the younger Simon de Montfort bringing help, and the castle was duly surrendered in December, 1267, after a siege which had lasted a little over six months.

The long defence of Bedford and Kenilworth did something to restore a degree of confidence in the military role of the castle. In Wales its significance had never been in question. But only castles of great strength, built on commanding sites and immune to mining, held any value. The rest could offer no prolonged resistance to a well-equipped field force. It is not surprising, then, that a list of what may be termed 'key castles' began to emerge. It was a fluctuating list made up of those whose importance was wholly strategic, such as Dover and Scarborough; those which served as administrative centres, like Northampton and Sarum; a few, like St Briavels, which served for the manufacture and distribution of military equipment; and some, like Ludgershall and Odiham, which were little more than hunting lodges and staging points on the king's journeys. In 1223, when the king was anxious to secure the loyalty of those who kept his castles, he was at pains to put new and, presumably, trustworthy constables into no less than thirty-three of them.[116] The list does not exhaust those of national importance, since some were already in the hands of trusted supporters, and called for no change. Over half were entrusted, at least temporarily, to bishops.

The next wholesale change in the control of castles came in 1258, when the crisis between Henry and his barons was coming to a head. Those who held the royal castles were called upon to swear that they would 'keep [them] loyally and in good faith to the use of the king and his heirs, and that they will restore them to the king or his heirs and to no other, and this by his council and in no other way'.[117] Fourteen castles, most of them in Wales and the Borders, were entrusted to Prince Edward.[118] At the same time, John of Gloucester and Alexander, respectively the king's master mason and master carpenter, were instructed to visit castles 'on this side of the Trent and Humber, to view and amend the defects [and] to provide for the masonry and carpentry works'.[119]

As the political situation deteriorated, so changes were made in the table of constables. Eight of the most important castles received new guardians, and in the following year no less than twenty-five changes were made.[120] In most of them administration of the county went with the office of constable; at no time was the link between castle and county closer. Corfe was designated as the castle of Dorset, Sherborne of Somerset, and in Leicestershire and Warwickshire, where there had been no shrieval castle, Sauvey was elevated to become the sheriff's castle. Indeed, only three counties were not attached to their principal castles. At the same time the keepers of ten of the castles were ordered to lay in a store of foodstuffs, which were to be kept on behalf of the king, 'unless by reason of war they are consumed in [their] defence'.[121] Allowances were made for 'reasonable costs for munition'.[122] The Dictum of Kenilworth, the conditions of surrender of Montfort's supporters, called for the outright surrender to the king of three castles, Eardisley (Hereford), Bytham (Lincolnshire) and Chartley (Staffordshire), since it seemed 'dangerous that castles should be in the power of those who have acted badly against the king'.[123] It seems, in fact, that all three were in the end restored to their owners.

The Barons' War had begun with the capture by the king of Northampton Castle. It ended with the siege of Kenilworth. But, apart from these two events, castles played no significant role in the war. Yet the memory was always present of a time when warfare consisted of little more than attacking and defending castles. Both king and barons were always anxious to keep castles in the hands of their own supporters, and changes in political fortunes were always followed by changes in the ranks of constables. Amongst the castles which received the king's writ immediately after the battle of Lewes ordering them to preserve the peace was Benefield, a very minor castle lying between Rockingham and Oundle.[124] It could have had very little military value, yet its possession was deemed of political importance.

The war which ended with the siege of Kenilworth Castle, probably the longest in English history, marked a turning point in the role of the castle in English life. Castles retained their importance on the borders with Wales and Scotland, and great care was taken to maintain the defences along the south-eastern coasts. But within England the castle began to lose its military importance. It survived as a prestigious home. New castles continued to be built, with royal licence, but they became increasingly a facade, a 'martial front', behind which the baronage could live in comfort (see Chapter 10).

Garrison and supplies

It would be a mistake to assume that all castles had some kind of garrison, always at the ready. Except in a few castles in the borders or on the coast there were no knights and serving men on permanent guard. At most one would find a constable together with a porter and a watchman. If the constable happened to be sheriff, he would have a staff of clerics, bailiffs and messengers (see p. 90) but it is very doubtful whether these could have contributed materially to the security of the castle.

A well-sited and well-built castle needed few defenders unless a major assault was planned, and the cost of maintaining a garrison was high. The acceptable rate for a watchman was 2d a day, and that for a porter, clearly reckoned to be a more responsible position, was up to 4d.[125] There were, however, instances of much lower rates of payment. Peter le Porter was appointed to keep the gate of Winchester Castle at only 1½d,[126] but this was a reward 'for long service', and we must regard it as a sinecure in lieu of a pension. At Windsor a gatekeeper received 6d a day, but for this he also served as 'viewer of works'[127] (see pp. 184, 196). There are numerous instances of the use of a petty office within a castle to reward an elderly and ailing retainer, a practice which can have done nothing to increase the military security of the castle.

Where there was a garrison, it was paid considerably more. That at Rhuddlan in 1241 consisted of:[128]

10 knights at	2s a day
13 serjeant crossbowmen	12d a day
5 serjeants at	7½d a day
3 crossbowmen on foot	3½d a day
2 porters at	2½d a day
2 watchmen at	2d a day
2 carpenters at	9d a day

In all, the garrison, apart from the constable, cost 39s 3d a day. A garrison at Dyserth cost less, about 14s a day, because only two knights were present.[129] There might also have been an 'engineer' to maintain the stone-throwing machines, and sometimes also a craftsman who looked after armour and crossbows. Such men do not seem to have been part of a regular garrison, but to have travelled from castle to castle as their services were called for.

In the peaceful heart of England such garrisons were rare. At most there might be a small group of knights, a sort of sheriff's posse, sent there by the king to cover a temporary emergency. In 1232, for reasons which are unclear, Amaury de Sacy, 'with some other knights', was sent to Berkeley – not a royal castle – 'to keep the peace in those parts and the passes and passages',[130] and Thomas de Berkeley was called upon to receive them and, doubtless, to feed them at his own expense. It is just possible that they were intended to check any Welsh incursion from beyond the

Severn. Bramber Castle in Sussex may be taken to represent the peaceful and bucolic conditions that generally prevailed. William de Braose granted in dower to Lady Mary de Braose 'his barn within his castle of Bramber, so that she may enter it and store her corn therein'. Furthermore, she was permitted to reside in the castle during the winter half-year, and have there a keeper to look after her corn.[131] But William 'shall maintain his constable and porter with the ward of the gaol throughout the year'.

The Hundred Rolls contain some evidence for the cost of maintaining a castle. Jurors stated that Devizes Castle could be kept in time of peace for 25 marks a year, barely enough for a porter, watchman and a constable.[132] The cost of keeping the castle of Old Sarum was somewhat higher, 30 marks,[133] but there the constable also received £10 a year.[134] The castle of North Ledbury (Bishop's Castle) could be kept for £23..5..4 in time of peace, but in time of war the cost varied 'according to circumstances'.[135] Nicholas de Segrave, who was constable of Northampton Castle from 1308 until 1315, left a careful record of his income and expenditure. In the second year of his tenure of the office, his income from castle-guard rents, the keeping of prisoners and other local sources amounted to £26..4..0, and his outgoings to £24..5..4. This last sum was made up of £5 for repairs; £2..5..2 for maintaining an 'approver' (an informer waiting to give evidence), and the rest in wages.[136] The last was just sufficient to cover 12d a day for the constable and 2d each for a porter and watchman, costs which confirm what was said a few years earlier in the Hundred Rolls. Over the whole period of his constableship his expenditure was £222..16..0, his income during this period being £205..10..9½. We may perhaps assume that under normal conditions many castles could be very nearly self-supporting, except for major expenditure on construction and repairs.

It is evident that a garrison could be mobilised at short notice, but without food its ability to resist attack would have been gravely restricted. Most castles held a store. Some used the product of their own fields but others relied on local markets. Bridgnorth Castle was on one occasion provisioned from the market at Stottesden, seven miles away.[137] Windsor Castle was supplied from nearby manors.[138] The amount of food stored in any castle varied with the likelihood of a siege. The knowledge that it was well provisioned could itself be a safeguard against attack. But where attack was improbable stocks were run down. Constables reported, on taking over their castles, that they had no food in store[139] and at Dunstanburgh the constable, on one occasion, even disposed of stocks in order to pay his garrison. Food provided for Marlborough Castle cost 5 marks,[140] which would hardly support a garrison for long. The sheriff of Somerset and Dorset was ordered to expend only 100 marks on a store of foodstuffs, which was to be kept there unless 'it happen to be spent in the maintenance of the castle'.[141] This is an unusually large sum and it may be that this stock was intended to be a reserve for general use in those parts, and not specifically for consumption in the castle. The sheriff of Gloucestershire bought 100 quarters of wheat from the abbot of Gloucester for the use of the castle.[142] But this was during the Barons' War, when larger stores were maintained. Indeed, the king undertook in advance to cover the costs of laying in foodstuffs at certain of his castles.[143] A few years later purchases for Rougemont Castle, Exeter, amounted only to thirteen quarters of wheat and three of barley, together with small quantities of malt, beans and peas.[144] Supplies consisted mainly of cereals and oats for the horses, but sometimes malt was obtained for brewing. Meat was, in general, limited to sides of bacon, which had been salted or smoked. Occasionally saltfish was bought, and in a very few instances live animals were brought into the castle, presumably to be slaughtered as need arose. This method of securing a supply of meat would have necessitated a store of fodder, and must surely have been regarded as impracticable in most cases. Salt was usually kept together with wax for candles. Some castles (see p. 124) held a store of wine, but this was usually for the use of the king and his barons and did not form any significant part of emergency supplies. Occasionally we find the record of the purchase of more sophisticated foods, as for Edward I's coronation feast at Windsor in 1274[145] and at Odiham Castle in 1311 in anticipation of a visit by Edward II.[146]

In most castles there must have been a barn or granary. In 1270 the sheriff of Wiltshire was instructed to have 'a granary [built] in a fit place within the castle'.[147] Castles were no doubt infested with rats and mice, and the prevailing damp would have led to a rapid deterioration even of unmilled grain. This was recognised, and constables were instructed to sell 'the victuals which the king ordered to be purveyed . . . for the munition of the said castle and which cannot be retained further . . . on account of the deterioration of the same.'[148] In 1326 the constables of no less than ten castles including the Tower of London, were ordered to inspect their stores and to sell 'those not fit to keep'.[149] At Nottingham Castle where the sides of bacon were not keeping well, 400 were ordered to be sold and 100 were bestowed as a royal gift on the nunnery of Derby.[150]

Sheriffs and constables were sometimes guilty of excesses in provisioning their castles. The quantity of food required must have placed a strain on the local area. Magna Carta recognised the abuse, but failed to end it.[151] The Hundred Rolls report many such incidents. Robert of London, for example, was accused of forcibly taking thirty-two quarters of wheat for Windsor Castle and of paying only with a tally,[152] and ten head of cattle were seized for Lydford Castle.[153] During the troubled later years of Edward II abuses became so extreme that knights in Knaresborough Castle had to be 'reminded not to attempt anything contrary to the proclamation forbidding the taking of corn victuals or other goods against the will of their owners'.[154]

The provisioning of strategically important castles, on the south-east coast or on the Borders of Wales or Scotland, contrasts with the haphazard way in which stores were kept in castles in the interior of England. The memory of the great siege of 1216 meant that great attention was given to the provisioning of Dover Castle. In 1255 Bertram de Crioyl accounted for the purchase of:[155]

wheat	227 quarters
barley	425 quarters
oats	75 quarters
wine	125 tuns
wax	500 pounds

In 1268 purchases included seven lasts of herring and 200 cod.[156] In 1242, no less than 700 quarters of wheat and 500 of oats were demanded of the archbishop's estates in Kent.[157] In general it was the sheriff who was called upon to make these massive requisitions, and then to commandeer carts to carry them to the castle.

Other coastal castles, such as Pevensey,[158] Orford and Scarborough,[159] were usually well provisioned, and a varied store of wheat, malting barley, oats, beans, peas, bacon hogs, live cattle, salted conger and cod were acquired by the sheriff of Hampshire for Carisbrooke Castle, which, in its island location, must have been difficult to provision. The castles in the March of Wales were also well provided for. Food was accumulated at such points as Bristol and Chester *ad castra in Wallia munienda*.[160] The supply of Rhuddlan, Dyserth and Deganwy was particularly difficult because their local regions provided no surplus. In 1247 the sheriffs as far afield as Nottinghamshire and Leicestershire were called upon to purvey large quantities of wheat.[161] Amounts sent by sea from Chester to Deganwy were immense. In 1245 1,000 quarters of wheat, the same of oats, 100 flitches of bacon and 100 quarters of salt were sent.[162] This was further supplemented by supplies from Ireland. Two boats, each of twelve oars, plied between Chester and the North Wales castles,[163] but, if the weather was bad, supplies had to make the hazardous journey overland.

From Bristol, supplies were taken by sea to the king's castles in South Wales: Carmarthen, Cardigan, Llanbadarn (Aberystwyth), and from there were distributed to castles in the interior. Another base for the provisioning of castles deep within the hills was Hereford Castle.[164] The sheriff of Herefordshire was accustomed to send grain and salted meat, doubtless under heavy guard, to such outliers of English rule as Builth and Pain's Castle.[165]

Food and weapons were not the only stores customarily kept in an important castle. A stock of fuel was almost as necessary. Most foodstuffs had to be cooked and some form of heating was necessary during the greater part of the year. Wood and in some areas, perhaps, peat was used. Wood was not as abundant as is commonly supposed, and frequently the constable or the sheriff was strictly enjoined to use only fallen or dead timber. Important castles also held a stock not only of weapons, but also of the varied goods needed both for defence and for equipping a military expedition. In 1326, for example, 10,000 horseshoes and 160,000 nails were ordered for the Tower of London.[166] A list of items supplied from the Tower armoury gives some idea of the range of its stores and of the book-keeping involved.[167]

Building and maintenance

The history of most castles in England is one of gradual decay punctuated by short periods of frantic repair and rebuilding. The quality of construction was in general greatly inferior to that met with in churches. Building was more hurried, inferior materials were used, and a far greater employment was made of timber. The period from the mid-twelfth century to the end of the thirteenth was marked more by repair, renovation and extension than by new building. Records of this work are abundant if not always specific. Nevertheless, the Close and Liberate Rolls, together with Ministers' Accounts, provide enough data to establish a picture of the problems which faced those who kept the king's castles.

The replacement of wooden palisades by masonry walls was making progress throughout the period, but timber defences were still common in the mid-thirteenth century, and wooden 'bretaches' or 'hourdes' were often erected over the curtain walls. The 'wooden walls' presented serious problems. The palisade which surrounded the bailey of Colchester was *prostratum per tempestatum* and timber was supplied from Kingswood Forest for its repair.[168] A similar fate attended numerous other wooden defences.[169] At Dover Castle wooden buildings within the bailey were flattened by the wind.[170] At Pontefract an old wooden tower (*bretachia*) collapsed, destroying a bridge.[171] Nor were masonry walls immune. There is evidence for collapsing masonry at Kenilworth, Scarborough, Winchester, Windsor and elsewhere.[172] The sheriff of Nottinghamshire reported that the king's chamber in Nottingham Castle had collapsed through the instability of its foundations.[173]

The reasons for the insecurity even of masonry building are not far to seek. Walls were often built without sinking the foundations to bedrock. The materials of mottes and ramparts slipped and slumped, sometimes taking sections of wall with them. The motte of Shrewsbury Castle, for example, partially collapsed into the Severn. Then, too, the walls were, more often than not, of rubble masonry bonded with lime mortar of uncertain quality. The walls of ruined castles in the care of HBMC are in far better physical condition today than they would have been during the Middle Ages.

Much of the building within the bailey was of wood and the excavation of Hen Domen, a castle which continued to be used until late in the thirteenth century, has shown how closely packed and shortlived much of this construction was. At Windsor in 1236 timber was supplied for the repair of the king's wardrobe *que inclinata est in unam partem*.[174] One cannot even count the occasions when a surveyor reported, without specifying the cause, that a building would collapse unless it were repaired. The roof was often the most vulnerable part of a building. Roofs were mostly of truss construction, supporting the actual roofing material. The latter was commonly of wooden shingles or thatch. The fact that shingles were supplied in immense quantities is itself evidence of the speed at which they rotted and had to be replaced. The constable of Rockingham was allowed six oaks *ad scindulas . . . ad domos castri*.[175] In 1245 30,000 shingles were sent to Ludgershall to roof the king's hall and the queen's chamber, the bark and waste to be used as fuel. Such examples could be multiplied endlessly.[176]

Alternative roofing materials were thatch and tile.[177] Thatch appears to have been commonly used for the less important buildings. Clay tile and slate were rarer.[178] Lead beaten into thin sheets was the most secure material, and had the further advantage of being proof against fire. Its disadvantage was a tendency to develop thin cracks which admitted water. This accounts for the quantities of 'old' lead that were met with at castle sites, waiting to be remelted and hammered into fresh sheets. It was also heavy and called for stronger roof timbering than other materials.

Lead sheeting was also used for gutters (*gutterae*) to carry away rainwater from the roofs, for cisterns and for weighting the counterpoise of drawbridges and 'engines'.[179] In tower-keeps, where the pitched roof was hidden behind the walls of the keep itself, there was great difficulty in preventing the accumulation of water, and lead flashing was used, just as it would be in modern construction.

There was a large and continuous demand for timber for repair and rebuilding. Large timbers – *grossum maeremium* – were needed for pillars in the hall, joists (*gistae*) in the great tower; and planks (*plancias*) for the upper floors, roof trusses (*copulae*), ties (*laquei*), and wall-plates (*pannae*).[180] It was not the initial construction that placed great demands on forest resources, but the frequent repairs. For any major work it was often necessary to go far afield for suitable timbers. Materials from the Vale of Blackmore were used in Corfe Castle;[181] Winchester drew on the forests of Bere, Alice Holt, Merdon and the New Forest,[182] and Dover Castle received timbers by sea from the forests of Essex.[183] The choice of suitable timber was a serious matter. In 1235 the sheriff of Hampshire even excused himself from attendance at the Exchequer on the grounds that he was in Bere Forest *pro maeremio prosternendo ad operationes castri* (Winchester).[184] Nottingham Castle was supplied from Sherwood Forest, and Rockingham and Sauvey castles from the extensive forest of Rockingham, but a timber supply was less easy for most urban castles and for many in South and North Wales. For the latter it was even imported from Ireland. Extensive use was made of coastal shipping in the transport of timber; a consignment from Porchester (probably from Bere or Alice Holt) to Corfe Castle was lost *pro defectu navium*.[185]

Most building stone was taken from quarries close to the site where it was used.[186] This was made possible by the fact that walls and towers were generally of roughly coursed rubble. Some stone was supplied from the excavation of the castle ditch.[187] Superior stone was, however, needed for window tracery and door jambs and also for quoins, offsets and string courses. In few cases was this readily available. Sparing use was made of limestone from Northamptonshire and Lincolnshire in such East Anglian castles as Norwich and Castle Rising. Much of the masonry of Cambridge Castle was from the same source. The Tower of London was built wholly of stone brought from a distance, and in 1241 order was given to open a quarry on land of Warenne for the supply of stone.[188] This would in all probability have been Reigate stone, a Lower Cretaceous sandstone much used in southeast England. At the same time the monks of Merton Priory in Surrey were asked to allow stone to be taken from their land.

It was doubtless the poor quality of much of the masonry that led to the whitewashing or even rendering of the surface of many of the great tower keeps. That of Corfe Castle, for example, was ordered to be covered with a roughcast (*morterio perjactari*) 'where there were cracks', and to be whitened all over.[189] Several keeps are known to have had a coating of white lime. The keep of the Tower of London owes its familiar name of the White Tower to this fact.

The rubble masonry used in the construction of most castles was inordinately extravagant of mortar. The first task, whenever masonry construction was undertaken, was to build a kiln for burning lime. In 1242 the sheriff of Devon was ordered 'to make a kiln near Lundy for the work of fortifying a castle there; to dig stone there and take it to the works; if no stone there, then where it can best and most conveniently be got'.[190] At Windsor Castle the kiln itself cost £22 to build, but, then, it had to have a capacity of 1,000 quarters of lime.[191] This was probably the kiln referred to in the Close Rolls when permission was given to take stone for its construction from the castle ditch.[192]

The burning of lime called for both limestone and fuel. The former was highly localised, and was not available over the claylands which made up much of lowland England. No doubt the waste from scappling and carving freestone was used, but there must have been a not inconsiderable transport of limestone for this purpose. Limestone was also notably absent from the South-western peninsula and from parts of Wales, and lime had to be imported. The supply of fuel was at times no less difficult.[193] A kiln at the Tower of London used fuel from the forest of Havering in Essex, and that in Bristol Castle from Kingswood Forest.[194]

Construction on any castle site called for a range of other materials. Nails were used in their thousands, chiefly for affixing shingles to the roofing lathes. Iron was forged into hinges and door clasps, into bars for windows and the chains for portcullis and 'turning' bridge. And, since the more important castles served also as gaols, manacles were also needed. Lead was used, not only for roofing and guttering, but also for securing iron work into masonry. There were few sources of lead in Britain, and most of that which can be traced came from the southern Pennines. Its transport was difficult, usually down the Yorkshire rivers and around the coast. Coastal castles often held a store of lead, and directives were at intervals received to send so many fothers[195] to this castle or that.

Inventories were occasionally compiled of the gear in store or just left in the bailey of a castle. They included stone and timber; lead and lime; pieces of iron awaiting a smith to forge them into bars and hinges; lengths of chain; bales of hemp, and coils of rope.[196] One gets the impression that very little was ever thrown away. Even the stone and timber from a demolished building was useful. At Sauvey Castle the stone from a fallen stable was used for a chapel which the king had ordered to be built.[197] At the Tower of London the constable was instructed to recover from 'the tower recently fallen ... the timber and freestone and put them in a suitable place and cover them up [and use] to roof the two turrets . . . and [to] finish the building begun between the hall and kitchen and other repairs'.[198] In 1241 the king gave the Bishop of Hereford two *bretaschiae* which were in store at Montgomery Castle to strengthen his castle at North Ledbury (Bishop's Castle).[199] The sheriff was called upon to organise the transport of this bulky material.[200] At Oxford, where timber had been supplied to repair a fallen tower, the constable was ordered to keep the offcuts as fuel for the lime kiln.[201]

In reading the king's directives one is constantly impressed, on the one hand, by the extraordinary wastefulness of the technology and, on the other, by the extreme economy practised. Nothing was deliberately wasted; everything left over from one building operation was husbanded for the next. It seems scarcely possible, for example, that the sheriff who looked after Tintagel Castle in Cornwall should be instructed to remove the roof trusses from the great hall and to store them so that they would not suffer harm from the damp when the hall was not in use.

CHAPTER 6

The baronial castle

> Were I in my Castle of Bungaye
> Above the Water of Waveneye
> I would ne care for the King of Cockneye
> And all his meiny

A very fine line separates the baronial castle from the royal. The king took baronial castles into his own hands and entrusted his own castles to favoured barons and members of his own family. Some such castles returned to royal possession; others were permanently lost. His servants occupied the castles of minors and episcopal castles whenever the see was vacant. And when it seemed desirable he helped his barons by putting his own mercenaries in their castles and providing money for their repair.

Baronies and honours

Nevertheless, a certain number of castles were without question baronial in that they were the chief seats of important barons and centres of baronial administration.[1] Every honour had its *caput*, but the *caput* did not always give its name to the honour. Nor was the *caput* necessarily a castle. It could be a rural manor house or, as in the case of the twelfth century honour of Walbrook, merely a place within the city of London.[2] Many a small and impoverished honour never aspired to the dignity of a castle, while rich and widespread honours might have several. It all depended on the resources of the barony and how the baron saw himself amongst his peers.

Figure 3.7 shows the *capita* of what may be judged a fairly complete list of honours and putative honours in the twelfth and thirteenth centuries, with differing symbols for those which incorporated a castle as their administrative focus and those which did not.[3] It is difficult to say why some indubitable honours lacked that essentially feudal asset, a castle. A castle was, as a general rule, considered to be an indivisible component of an honour, because its military effectiveness would be diminished by partition. Notwithstanding, there are instances of the physical division of a castle between two parties. Whatever the reason, no less than a third of honours show no indication of ever having had a castle as the seat of their lord and meeting place of their honourial court. It is a measure of the peace that prevailed that the castle, the 'condition of lordship and its guarantee',[4] was lacking from so many.

But the nature of the barony and the role of the castle in the frontier regions was so different from the situation in the rest of England that a discussion of this is postponed to the next chapter.

In England baronies consisted, at least until the end of the thirteenth century, of a group of scattered manors. The high cost of transport 'made small isolated estates almost useless', and 'the only principle that seems to have been applied in almost every barony was to keep in demesne the more valuable estates while granting the smaller . . . as fiefs'.[5] The location of the honourial castle or seat had far more to do with access to the component rights and manors than to any strategic considerations. 'If a baron had fairly important properties in a region, he wanted an administrative seat there and a fortress to watch over his interests.'[6] Not all possessed the fortress, but the focus of an honour was established so as to minimise travel time to its members.

It is not difficult to map the component units of an honour at the time of Domesday. But there was no subsequent record of landholding. At most we have the lists of feudal obligations embodied in the *Red Book of the Exchequer*, and the later *Book of Fees*.

By the time they were put together, the feudal honours had begun to disintegrate. 'As time went on, the old baronies escheated and were regranted in parcels, became minutely divided among heiresses, or were alienated by their lords. When the hereditary Parliamentary baronage became well established [in the fourteenth century], few tenurial baronies remained intact or even in portions large enough to be of much significance.'[7] The feudal obligations of the original honour had all become so subdivided and attenuated, that by the end of the Middle Ages many of them were 'lost'. The number of tenants-in-chief of the crown increased as the extent of their lands diminished, until by the end of the thirteenth century their number greatly exceeded that of all the castles there ever were in this country.

When first established, an honour was measured in terms of knights' fees, the obligation to provide a stated number of knights for the king's service for a certain period in each year. The lord of an honour passed on the obligation to his tenants, but not infrequently enfeoffed more knights than he needed to discharge his obligations.

Among the honours for which both the location of fees and the names of tenants are recorded in the *Red Book* are those of Rayleigh, Haughley and Wormegay, which together span the whole of East Anglia.[8] The honours of Rayleigh and Wormegay (Figure 6.1) are largely clustered round their castles, but Haughley, which was in origin a perquisite of the Constable of Dover Castle, shows no such pattern.[9] The honour of Richard's Castle in the Welsh Border, surveyed in 1211–12, is similarly scattered. Its focal castle, a motte and bailey with masonry keep and curtain walls,[10] is somewhat excentric to its dependent fees, lying as it does on their exposed western margin.

We know little of the internal administration of these four honours. Each had a central-place, a castle, where stewards accounted to their lords. The organisation of

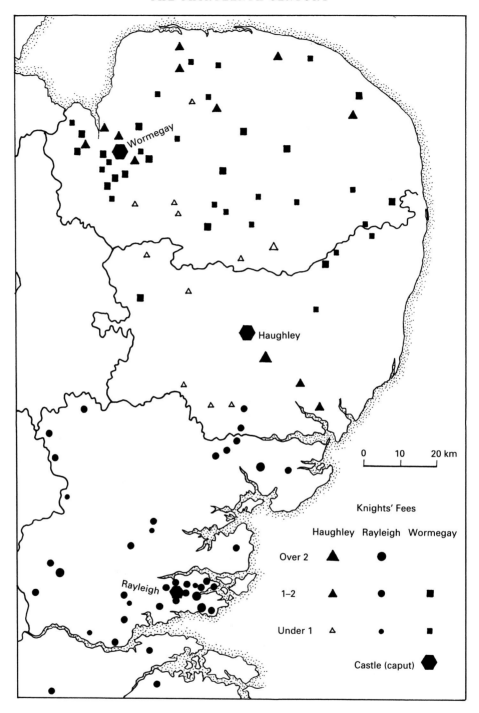

6.1 The lands and castles of the East Anglian honours of Rayleigh, Haughley and Wormegay. A strong motte castle lay at the centre of each honour. Based on *Red Book of the Exchequer*.

larger and more widespread honours was more complex. The barons 'with much inconsistency . . . were organising their own establishments on the very model of that [the king's] which they were opposing'.[11] They were arranging their estates in local groups, each with its bailiff who reported and accounted to the lordship, just as the sheriff did to the Exchequer. This baronial organisation was not present under the Norman kings. It developed slowly, like the shrieval administration, and was probably not fully developed until late in the thirteenth century.

The honour of Leicester was one of the larger baronies in thirteenth-century England. At its heart lay the estates granted by the Conqueror to Hugh de Grantemesnil, who probably built the earthwork castle within a corner of the Roman city of Leicester. From Ivo, his son, it passed to Robert de Beaumont who added the Grantemesnil lands to his own extensive holdings.[12] His grandson forfeited some of his possessions, including the castles of Mountsorrel and Groby, following the rebellion of 1172. Leicester Castle was itself ordered to be torn down, but if this was indeed done, the castle must have been rebuilt soon afterwards. The last of the Beaumont earls died in 1204, and his lands were divided between his two sisters. Amicia, the elder, married Simon de Montfort, who thus acquired the earldom and castle of Leicester as well as the East Midland estates of the honour (Figure 6.2).[13]

Leicester Castle was the focus of its administration. Here its court met and the audit of accounts of even the remotest estates was held. Here too the earl stayed on occasion and was even visited by the king himself. The castle had a regular staff. At its head was the steward (*senescallus*), the earl's chief administration officer.[14] He was also constable of the castle, and in his double role he mirrored the activities of a royal sheriff. His importance is reflected in his relatively high salary of £16 a year. He was likely to be a member of the knightly class, and had a *domus* within the castle. Under him was a receiver, the chief financial officer, who had a counting table with a chequerboard pattern on which his regional bailiffs rendered their accounts, just as the sheriffs did at the king's exchequer.

The only other official recorded in the Leicester accounts was the porter, whose duties were a great deal broader than the keeping of the castle gate. He kept the honourial gaol, served writs and collected rents. His basic wage was small – only 1d a day – but he also enjoyed fees and corrodies which may have amounted to a considerable sum. There would, in addition, have been a clerical staff which combined spiritual duties with the more mundane keeping of records and returning of writs.

For the convenience of management the estates were divided into eight bailiwicks, each of them a cluster of manors. Each was managed by a bailiff who had a central office within it. In no instance was this central-place a castle, though there were a number of earthwork castles, in all probability long abandoned, on manors of the honour.[15] In each manor was a reeve who accounted to his regional bailiff who, in turn, settled his accounts across the chequered table in Leicester Castle.

The de Lacy honour had its nucleus in the honours of Pontefract and Weobley

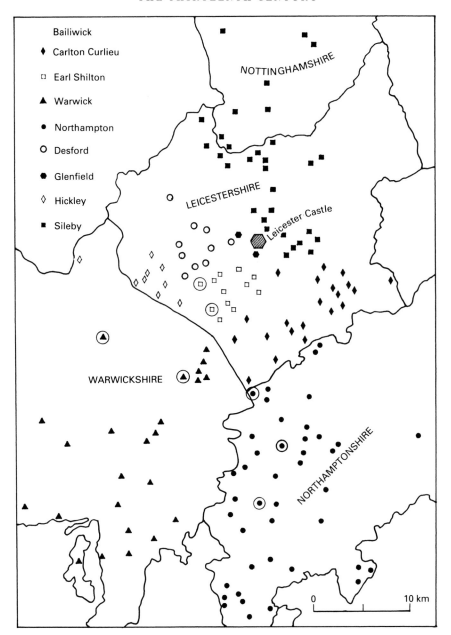

Bailiwick

♦ Carlton Curlieu

▫ Earl Shilton

▲ Warwick

● Northampton

○ Desford

◕ Glenfield

◇ Hickley

■ Sileby

NOTTINGHAMSHIRE

LEICESTERSHIRE

Leicester Castle

WARWICKSHIRE

NORTHAMPTONSHIRE

0   10 km

6.2 The organisation of the estates of the Earl of Leicester into eight bailiwicks, all of which were dependent on Leicester Castle. Dependent castles within the honour are shown each by a circle around the manor symbol. After L. Fox, 'The Administration of the Honor of Leicester in the Fourteenth Century', *Tr Leic AS*, 20 (1938–9), 289–374.

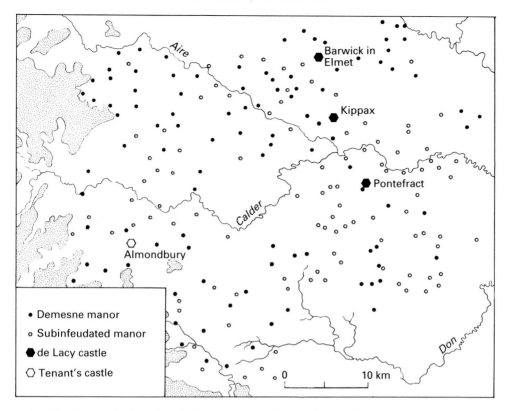

6.3 The de Lacy lands and castles in western Yorkshire in the twelfth century. Pontefract was the head of the honour, but the castles of Barwick-in-Elmet and Kippax were held in demesne. Almondbury was tenanted. Based on W. E. Wightman, *The Lacy Family in England and Normandy, 1066–1194*, Oxford, 1966.

(see pp. 63–4).[16] To these were added the county of Lancaster and the earldom of Lincoln, from which de Lacy derived his title. Two *compoti* allow the intricacies of honourial administration to be explored. It was less centralised than that of the Leicester honour, and rested upon 'a chain of receiverships, corresponding with the honours and lordships'[17] that had been acquired by the de Lacys. Each receivership was located in the castle of a subordinate honour: Clitheroe, Bolingbroke, Denbigh, Halton, Pontefract and the palace of Holborn in London, which served as accounting centre for the whole of de Lacy's estates.[18] They had, with the exception of Lincoln Inn in Holborn, been the heads of independent baronies before being absorbed into the vast holdings of de Lacy, 'each depending on its own incomes, bearing its costs of maintenance and making whatever expenditures were required of it'.[19] The accounts for the Cheshire and Lancashire manors include not only the rents, wardships and profits of courts and mills, but also the costs of repairing Halton and Clitheroe castles, of cutting their winter fuel and paying the officers of the honour. The constable of Clitheroe Castle, for example, received £7..10..0 a year, a sum which included the cost of buying a robe. His master, the steward in respect of this castle, received 10s for only nine months, while the porter, the only other official to appear, had £2..5..6 a year, or less than $1\frac{1}{2}$d a day.[20] Small amounts were spent on maintaining the 'houses' within the castle, on bringing in hay and winter fuel, and on keeping a lamp burning for the soul of Earl John.[21]

The costs of transport were recurring items in most accounts. The profits that arose from the de Lacys' estate management in northern England were carried to Pontefract, for Pontefract Castle was 'the strongest fortress and military base in all these parts, within the walls of which were a great chamber and a wardrobe . . . an armoury filled with artillery, while its treasury, dignified by the name of exchequer, was not only a counting-house but the main depository of records for the region'.[22] It was, indeed, in the words of a charter 'the key to Yorkshire'. If Pontefract Castle was the principal exchequer of receipt, Bolingbroke Castle in the south of Lincolnshire was the chief centre of consumption. It was the earl's main residence, if a person so constantly in motion could be said to have one. Its administration was more centralised than that of the northern honours, but its income was insufficient to support the immense expenditure of its lord.[23] When he was resident the earl's retinue might have risen to 200. Money was channelled from Pontefract to Bolingbroke and some was passed on to Lincoln Inn in London.

Henry de Lacy died in 1310. His sons had predeceased him and his lands and titles were divided between his two daughters. Of these the elder, Alice, married Thomas, second earl of Lancaster and son of Edmund 'Crouchback', the first earl and youngest son of Henry III. Edmund's honours and estates began to accumulate in 1265 when his father endowed him with the honour of Leicester, forfeited by Simon III de Montfort.[24] During the following years he received the de Ferrers honours of Tutbury and Duffield, each with an important castle. Kenilworth Castle was acquired after the great siege, followed by Chartley Castle (Staffordshire) and Liverpool Castle, which had formerly belonged to the earls of Chester. The Prince Edward, who had been granted castles and lands in Wales and the March passed the castles of Carmarthen and Cardigan, with their dependent counties, on to his younger brother.[25] Edmund held them for only a short time before surrendering them to the crown, receiving instead the 'Three Castles' together with Monmouth Castle. The summit of his power was reached in 1267 when he received from his father the castle of Newcastle-under-Lyme, the honour and castle of Pickering (Yorkshire) and, most important of all, the 'honour, county and castle of Lancaster'.

The earldom of Lancaster, as thus constituted, embraced property in no less than 632 places in England and Wales, including forty-nine demesne manors and fourteen castles.[26]

Leicester	Kenilworth
Duffield	[Carmarthen]
Tutbury	[Cardigan]
Lancaster	Monmouth

Liverpool	Grosmont	}	'The Three
Dunstanburgh	Skenfrith	}	Castles'
Chartley	Whitecastle	}	

Earl Edmund died in 1296, and most of his possessions passed to Thomas, the second earl, who had married Alice de Lacy, making him the richest baron in the land. He, none the less, continued to put acre to acre, at the same time making his administration more centralised. Kenilworth Castle became his treasury and exchequer of receipt, with a counting table for which three ells of green cloth had been bought.[27] In 1303 the receipts of the Kenilworth treasury amounted to the very considerable sum of £2,377. As a social centre Kenilworth had replaced Bolingbroke. The great causeway, known as the Tilt-yard, was the scene of tournaments which, with other excesses of the earls, required the supply of revenue from other exchequers of the earldom. There was continuous building and rebuilding at Kenilworth, culminating later in the century in the erection of John of Gaunt's Great Hall.

Thomas of Lancaster became a leader in the revolt against Edward II's system of governing by the 'household system', but he proved incapable of transforming the movement into a national opposition to corrupt and inefficient rule.[28] He was defeated at Boroughbridge, and executed within his own castle of Pontefract in 1322.[29] His titles lapsed and his lands reverted to the crown, most to be granted to his younger brother Henry, who became the third earl. Henry was succeeded by his son, Henry of Grosmont, the fourth earl, and first duke of Lancaster, who died in 1361 leaving only a daughter, Blanche, the most eligible heiress in Europe. Her marriage to John of Gaunt, the younger surviving son of Edward III, laid the foundations of the Lancastrian dynasty. Its possessions differed only in detail from those which had been held by Earl Thomas. They were even increased by the addition of the castles and lands of Hertford, Knaresborough, the Peak, Pevensey, and Liddell Strength on the Scottish Border. The county of Lancaster had been erected into a palatinate with somewhat restricted powers of self-government, and this privileged status was inherited by John of Gaunt.

John of Gaunt possessed more than thirty castles, several of which were in fact royal castles which had been alienated to him. These, with the honours and lands which went with them, represented 'a power which no other feudatory . . . could rival. He appointed a constable to each castle, maintained a store of weapons, and was assured of its military efficiency. The income from his lands was exceeded only by that of the king himself, and the organisation of his administration was modelled on the royal household'.[30] This concentration of raw power would have boded ill for the country had it not all in 1399 reverted to the crown with the accession of Henry Bolingbroke, John of Gaunt's son, as Henry IV. Henceforward the monarch has been duke of Lancaster, and the ducal lands and castles have been vested in the crown.

The vast Lancastrian estate consisted essentially of a number of disparate baronies. Other such honours at this time had been put together in much the same way. The nucleus of the earldom of Cornwall was the honour which centred in the castle of Launceston. Earls Richard and Edmund had in the course of the thirteenth century acquired – by purchase, be it noted – the Valletort honour of Trematon and the honour which the Cardinhams held at the castle of that name.[31] Even before their extinction the Cardinhams had begun to build Restormel Castle near their borough of Lostwithiel. Cardinham Castle, a ringwork on the margin of Bodmin Moor, was abandoned, and the earldom (after 1337 the duchy) retained the castles of Launceston, Trematon and Restormel, together with the remote, cliff-top castle of Tintagel.[32] The honourial organisation of the earldom had been abandoned by the time the earliest surviving survey, that of 1296–7, was made. Instead a new administrative centre was created, the so-called Duchy Palace, in Lostwithiel.[33] The discrete honours were subordinated to it, and all distinctions between them obliterated.[34]

The Cornish lands of the earldom were composite in origin, but at the time of the 1296–7 survey comprised a single bailiwick within the comtal lands. The remaining lands of the earl were subsumed under the bailiwicks of Knaresborough, Oakham, Wallingford and elsewhere.

Few honours of the thirteenth and fourteenth centuries have retained documentary sources comparable with those of Lancaster and Cornwall. The honour of Clare, with bases at Clare and Tonbridge in England, and at Cardiff, Caerphilly and elsewhere in the March, was, when the last male of the line was killed at Bannockburn (1314), moving towards a similar structure of logically conceived bailiwicks.[35] The estates of Isabella de Fortibus, heiress of both Albemarle and de Redvers, were organised on the basis of local exchequers of receipt, centring in castles, and a central treasury.[36] The honours of Bohun, Bigod and Warenne were all moving administratively in the same direction.[37]

These aggregations of estates were administered first as a group of semi-independent units, each with its receiver and accounting office, located as a general rule in the principal castle. But this system gradually underwent a process of rationalisation. The constituent units – by and large separate manors – were regrouped; new local exchequers were established, and a tighter control imposed from the centre. This process seems to have been actively pursued on the Lancaster estates in the earlier part of the fourteenth century, so that the structure of John of Gaunt's duchy differed fundamentally from the earldom of Edmund 'Crouchback'. Baronial officials were in this following the example set by the royal administration. Denholm-Young, writing of the lawless magnates of the Welsh March, was compelled to admit that their administration 'corresponded most nearly to that of which the royal household was the centre . . . the earl's writ [replaced] the king's writ, the earl's chancery the king's chancery, the earl's exchequer the king's exchequer . . . There was no difference in kind, but only one of degree, between the administrative problems which beset the barons and those of their kings: as the Crown developed its organs of government so did the barons'.[38]

The changing structure of baronial administration was reflected in the role of the castle. The latter was a costly luxury, and the barons were discovering, as the king had already done, that its maintenance could sometimes stretch their resources. The inquest held on the death of Earl Edmund of Lancaster found that 'the custody of the castle exceeds the value of this extent by 100s [a year] at least, besides [the cost of] works'.[39] In other words, its upkeep and custody had to be paid for in part from other sources. The important northern castle of Helmsley, the jurors reported on the death of William Roos, should be kept by a constable receiving 3d a day and a robe to the value of 20s and they said that 'the walls of the castle, the houses and buildings . . . cannot be maintained and repaired for less than 100s yearly if they were to be kept in sufficient state'.[40] In other words, even without porter and watchman, the castle demanded an outlay of almost £12 a year. The minor Yorkshire castle of Skelton required 10 marks a year for repairs.[41] Whittington Castle in Shropshire was 'worth nothing . . . because it needs £40 yearly for repairs',[42] while Ruthin Castle in Flintshire could be kept in repair only by the annual expenditure of £10.[43]

The cost of maintaining a castle and keeping a skeleton staff within it must be measured against baronial incomes. Apart from the Lord Edward and Richard of Cornwall, wrote Denholm-Young, 'not half a dozen of Henry [III's] subjects had more than £3000 to £4000 a year'.[44] At a later date Thomas of Lancaster may have had £8,000, but an average earldom was worth only £1,600 and a well-to-do baron had little more than £300. The poorer tenants-in-chief of the crown, as shown in the *Inquisitiones post mortem*, can have had little more than £50 to £100 a year. Clearly they could not, from their regular, landed income, afford the luxury of a castle which could consume a quarter or more of their gross revenue.

If a baron of the status of de Warenne or de Clare maintained a large castle with constable, porter, watchman and servants it must have cost him at least £50 a year. Earl de Warenne had four such castles; de Braose had ten or more;[45] de Clare more than half a dozen, including several in the March of Wales where current dangers required a permanent garrison.[46] Earl Edmund of Lancaster had fourteen castles, including Kenilworth, and six of these lay in Wales and the March. Garrisoning his castles and keeping them in good repair *could* have absorbed up to a quarter of the earl's gross income.

These castles stood at the summit of the baronial hierarchy. They were regularly maintained and not infrequently visited by their lords. They were masonry-built, were kept in a tolerable state of repair, and would have had a resident constable or steward and a skeleton staff or garrison. They would have contained accommodation, however constricted, for the large company which followed its lord from one castle and one manor to another, eating its way through the accumulated store of food.[47] In a great lordship there were several such castles, which served both as administrative centres and as meeting places for the honourial court and sometimes for those of hundred and manor. There would have been a store of weapons, inspected and repaired at rare intervals, as well as of food, kept more in anticipation of the lord's visit than to sustain a garrison during a siege.

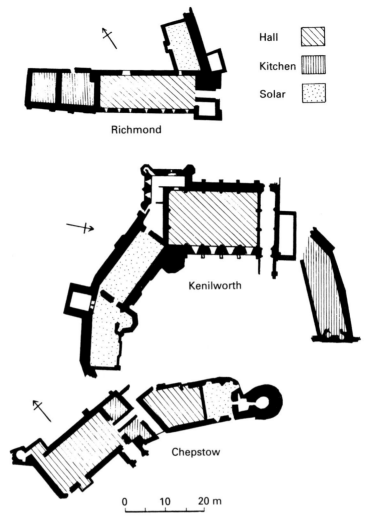

Hall	⧄
Kitchen	⦀
Solar	⋰

Richmond

Kenilworth

Chepstow

0   10   20 m

6.4 The hall-solar complex at three baronial castles.
The more easterly 'hall' at Chepstow is now seen as a kitchen.

The halls and chambers of a castle were adjusted to the needs of a great household, no less than storage space and stabling. In those regularly visited by Henry III separate chambers were set aside for king and queen, in addition to the accommodation of the constable.[48] These suites of rooms were, as a general rule, plastered and painted or wainscoted, and had usually an *en suite* garderobe. The purpose of this was to provide comfort and privacy and to segregate social classes from one another. In the course of the thirteenth century this practice spread to the more important baronial castles. At first two or more chamber blocks were associated with a common great hall, as, for example, at Ludlow Castle. The next step was to eliminate the common hall as the focus of the whole community and to build smaller halls each related to a particular set of chambers. At Corfe the original hall was retained in the keep, but additional sets of hall and chambers were built in the inner and middle baileys, and perhaps also in the outer.[49] Here they were fitted where practicable within existing structures. But when in the second half of the thirteenth century the lower bailey was begun at the Bigod castle of Chepstow, a hall of considerable magnificence was built along the northern and least exposed side, together with kitchen and private chambers. A further hall, possibly the constable's, was contrived in the gatehouse.[50] All this was in addition to the original spacious and elaborate hall in the Great Tower or keep. Similar developments took place at Pembroke, Middleham, Carisbrooke and elsewhere.

Caerphilly Castle was contemporary with the new development at Chepstow. Here a single great hall was built within the inner bailey, serving two separate solar blocks with further hall-suites in the gatehouses.[51] At Beaumaris and some castles built later this articulation of living space was carried to a logical conclusion (see pp. 273–4). Where we find two or more discrete halls and solar blocks it is not difficult to determine the rank of those who would have occupied them. At no time was social status reflected more clearly in building construction and embellishment.[52]

Royal control of Baronial castles

The policy of the English kings towards the building and maintenance of castles during the first century of feudalism has already been discussed (pp. 27–33). They claimed the right both to license the construction of private or baronial castles and to take them into their own hands if the political or military situation should make this expedient. The events of 1162–74 were a triumphant assertion of these rights, and there was never again a period when the subject enjoyed complete liberty to do what he wished with his own castle in defiance of the king. Though there were numerous rebellions during the next century and a half, and castles were on many occasions held against him, his right to occupy them was never seriously disputed. Yet this right was conditioned by feudal law and custom.

There were several occasions on which the king was permitted by feudal custom to take over and garrison a private castle. In the first place, it was recognised that if a tenant-in-chief of the crown was not able to fulfil his obligations, then the king could step in and see that they were properly discharged. The most obvious and frequent of such occasions arose when a tenant-in-chief died leaving only a minor to inherit. The minor became a ward of the king, who assumed the administration of his estate and the control of his castles.

A simple example of this is the death of William de Fortibus, earl of the Isle of Wight and the succession of a minor in 1242. The sheriff of Hampshire was ordered to occupy the earl's castles of Carisbrooke and Christchurch, and subsequently to hand them over to the Bishop of Winchester, in whose charge they remained until the heir came of age.[53] A year or two later, the king received the homage of William's heir, on attaining his majority, and the escheater was instructed to hand back to him his father's castles and lands.[54] The FitzAlan castles of Clun, Oswestry and Shrawardine in Shropshire, were similarly held by the Justiciar of Chester during the minority of John FitzAlan.[55] Tattershall Castle, in Lincolnshire, was farmed by the king to Henry de Percy and John de Neville for the very considerable sum of 350s a year.[56] The castle, a modest motte-and-bailey which preceded the fifteenth-century tower of Lord Treasurer Cromwell, can have had little military value; the attraction clearly lay in the revenue from the dependent lands.

The problem of inheritance by a minor was compounded if that minor should be female. The king then insisted on controlling her marriage for fear she might carry the castle with her into hostile or unfriendly hands. The heiress thus became a ward, to be married only to one who enjoyed the confidence of the king. The castles of Appleby and Brougham were thus in 1268 entrusted to Roger de Clifford to hold for the king and on behalf of Isabel, heiress of Robert de Vieux Pont.[57] In this case, the son of Roger married the heiress, thus initiating the long line of Cliffords of Westmorland. As a general rule, the castles were returned when the heiress married, and her husband did homage for them.

Analogous to the seizure of castles and lands during a minority was the possession of episcopal lands during the vacancy in a see (see p. 91). Some bishops held castles of not inconsiderable military importance on which the king not infrequently cast envious eyes. Such were the Bishop of Durham's castles of Norham and Durham,[58] which were apt to remain in royal hands for a longer period than the see remained vacant.[59] In 1249 the newly elected bishop, Nicholas Farnham, was given seisin of the two castles,[60] but was induced to commit Norham to Robert de Neville to hold against the Scots, and was mollified by the promise that it would be restored when the war was over.

The Bishop of Lincoln possessed no less than three castles: Banbury, Newark and Sleaford. Order was given to the sheriff to occupy them as soon as the death of a bishop was known, and this was invariably followed by the appointment of a trustworthy constable responsible to the king or his sheriff. The Bishop of Winchester had been able to salvage three of the castles held or built by Bishop Henry de Blois early in the twelfth century: Wolvesey (which occupied the south-east corner of the walled city of Winchester), Farnham and Taunton. All three were of considerable interest to the king. Farnham Castle lay too close to the capital for comfort, and in 1261 the king wrote to those who kept the temporalities of the see, ordering them to take steps to ensure that the castle *salvo et secure custodiatur* and that it be garrisoned and provisioned – at the expense, presumably, of the see of Winchester.[61] Similar attention was given to the bishop's castle of Taunton, which was handed over to a royal appointee who was to munition it 'with men and victuals more than usual', in view of the current disturbances.[62]

The residences of most bishops had little in them to attract the king other than the revenue they could yield, but the Bishop of Hereford possessed in western Shropshire the castle of North Ledbury, later known as Bishop's Castle. It lay amid the lands of de Lacy, Corbet and Mortimer, in an area, south of Montgomery, regularly ravaged by the Welsh. Its possession was of political no less than military significance and, whether in royal hands or episcopal, its maintenance in good condition was of great importance.[63] In 1241 the king gave to the bishop two *de melioribus bretaschis* which lay at Montgomery Castle, 12 km away, and ordered the sheriff to arrange for their transport.[64]

No castle was held absolutely by its lord; it was held of the king in return for services which might have been minimal and could even have lapsed with the passage of time. If a tenant-in-chief of the crown died without heirs, his possessions reverted to the king. This did not frequently happen, but during the thirteenth century no less than eight earldoms lapsed, together with two, those of Leicester and Derby, which were forfeited by rebellion.[65] Their titles, lands and castles were largely regranted by Henry III or by his son Edward I, mainly to members of their own family. It became the policy of Edward I to absorb these concentrations of power 'into the sphere of royal influence. He strove to acquire for the royal family as many of the earldoms as he could, and thus to turn to the service of the crown resources which for many previous generations had been employed in keeping the crown in check'.[66] The resulting concentrations of lands and castles in the hands of the earls of Cornwall[67] and Lancaster has already been mentioned. It meant that the crown came to control a large number of baronial castles, either directly or through members of the royal family, and in the course of time many others reverted to the crown.

The king's right to take over and use a private castle for the defence of the nation was not seriously disputed, but this right was ill-defined, and there were times when his assertion of it seemed arbitrary. In 1267 Henry III directed that Carisbrooke Castle, then in the possession of Isabella de Fortibus, be taken in hand 'owing to disturbance' and entrusted to John de Insula, 'keeper of the peace in the Isle'.[68] The king had reason on his side. Not only was Isabella de Fortibus unreliable, but the castle was a key to the Isle of Wight, and the island to the security of the south coast. Indeed, on most occasions when the king took possession of a private castle, it was for reasons of defence. His frequent occupation of the Bishop of Durham's castle of Norham has been mentioned. In 1255 the king claimed the castle of Wark, close neighbour of Norham on the river Tweed, the reason given being 'the present business in the March of Scotland'. Robert de Ros, its owner, seems to have been intimidated by the king's action and 'lent [the castle] to the king on his journey to Scotland'.[69] The castle was subsequently entrusted to Robert de Neville, sheriff of Northumberland, with the promise that it would be returned to Robert de Ros at the end of the war. Meanwhile, it was provisioned with 'victuals and other necessaries'.[70] At about the same time he 'unexpectedly required' Pontefract Castle from Alice de Lacy.[71]

The king had many ways of using a baronial castle to his advantage. He might abruptly demand that it be handed over to one of his servants, as was Pontefract Castle in 1265,[72] or he might billet a company of his household knights on the castle, as at Berkeley.[73] In 1246 William de Warenne was ordered to hand over his castle of

Oswestry to the Justiciar of Chester, and the reason given was that the castle had been an intermediary in the supply of food from England to the Welsh.[74] Corfham Castle, in Shropshire, was held by John de Braose 'peaceably and in fealty to the king, which castle, like other castles in those parts is built for the security of the country',[75] when it was attacked and held by the Mortimers. The king took possession of the castle, ostensibly to preserve it as a stronghold against the Welsh. Tonbridge Castle, in Kent, was held as hostage for the good behaviour of Gilbert de Clare, lord of the honour.[76]

The king might also place restrictions on the use or alienation of a baronial castle. John de Ripariis was, for example, authorised to let and farm the manor and hundred of Ongar in Essex, but was obliged to retain the castle, which might otherwise have fallen into the wrong hands.[77] Normally a tenant-in-chief required royal permission before he could convey or alienate a castle. John de la Warre was thus authorised to entrust his castle of Ewyas Harold in Herefordshire to another member of his own family.[78] The number of such permissions tended to increase. The king clearly kept a close watch on the castles of his realm, but one has at least a suspicion that the reason lay more in the fines which he could extract when occasion offered than in any fear for the military situation.

If royal licence was necessary for the construction of a castle, it follows that the king could properly order the demolition of a castle built without it. But this right was seldom exercised.[79] The case of Nafferton Castle provides the clearest instance of this, but even here baronial jealousies played as significant a role as the king's devotion to law and order (p. 104).

Similar cases arose during the troubled later years of Henry III's reign when, it might have been thought, the king was too preoccupied to be aware of the activities of minor barons.[80] Not at all. In 1260 he wrote that the report had reached him that Roger de Layburn was fortifying his seat at Leybourne in Kent.[81] He was firmly ordered to desist; otherwise *dictum castrum prosterni faciat*. Two years later the king learned of an even more serious breach of custom. His letter began with the assertion that *nullus castrum vel fortelicium formare debeat in regno nostro sine licencia nostra speciali*. Notwithstanding, Roger de Somery had presumed to fortify two castles, at Dudley (Staffordshire) and Beaudesert (Warwickshire).[82] He was ordered to desist under threat of dire but unspecified consequences. In all three instances, the fortification which offended the king must have been a *re*fortification. Dudley Castle had played a minor role in the wars of Stephen, and both Beaudesert, which overlooks Henley-in-Arden, and Leybourne had been motte-and-bailey castles dating from before the accession of Henry II.

It happened not infrequently during the periods of baronial opposition to the Angevin kings that the king assumed possession of the lands of a hostile baron. Lands were generally returned but a castle might well be retained for an indefinite period, as happened to the minor barony of Kilpeck in Herefordshire.[83]

An alternative to the demolition of an illicit castle was its emasculation to the point of military impotence. In 1228 the sheriff of Devon was ordered to overthrow

Henry de Tracy's castle at Torrington, and to level its ditches, but the walls of Tracy's other castle, at Barnstaple, were to be reduced only, to a height of ten feet. Within this protection Henry de Tracy might retain his dwelling – *edifica sua et mansionem habere possit.*[84] The comparable destruction of Bedford Castle has already been mentioned (pp. 119–20).

The king was quick to destroy unimportant castles which had been crenellated without his licence. He was no less ready to subsidise others. Such was Pain's Castle, held by Ranulf de Tosny. It lay in that strategically important area, known as Elfael, between Hay and Builth (see p. 37). It played an active role in resisting the Welsh and its long defence by Matilda de Braose had earned it the name of *Castra Mathildis.* In 1233 the king paid the wages of mercenaries serving there, and later saw to it that the castle was properly victualled and munitioned.[85] At about this time the king also granted 12 marks to Eva de Braose to strengthen the baronial castle of Hay, across the hills from Pain's Castle.[86] Humphrey de Bohun similarly received the considerable sum of 100 marks to strengthen and munition Richard's Castle, to the south of Ludlow,[87] and Corbet, for the defence of Caus Castle.[88] The FitzAlan castle of Oswestry was always a matter of concern to the king, since here the Welsh mountains came very close to the English plain. John FitzAlan had evidently spent heavily 'about the munition of the castle after the commencement of the present war in Wales' on orders from the king.[89] After his death his widow was allowed the truly large sum of £668..10, which her husband had spent, such was judged to be the importance of Oswestry Castle. The king was often generous with building materials. In 1241, for example, he allowed the constable of de Warenne's castle of Reigate to take timber from the royal wood at Dorking.[90]

In 1285 Edward I excused a debt of £57 which Walter Hackelutel owed to Aaron le Blund, a Jew of Hereford, because Walter had built and crenellated a house in the Marches.[91] The house probably lay in Radnor, where he held land and owed service to Cefnllys Castle.[92]

The cost of keeping them probably deterred the king from taking many baronial castles into his own hands. But he not infrequently sent directives to their constables, instructing them to be vigilant. In 1234 garrisons in the March of Wales were instructed to stand fast, so that no harm might result.[93] The unimportant castle of Stogursey in west Somerset was to be munitioned,[94] and similar orders were issued to numerous castles on the Welsh Border. Disturbances in and around the castle of Oswestry were ordered to cease, 'since Oswestry is in the Welsh March'.[95] Farnham Castle, which belonged to the see of Winchester, was to be 'provisioned locally',[96] which probably meant that this obligation devolved on the estates of the bishop.

Building and maintenance

Little is known from the records of the cost of building and maintaining baronial castles. One assumes that the rates of pay of servants and craftsmen would have been similar to those prevailing in royal castles, but the wage of constables may have been lower, because they tended to be equated with manorial reeves rather than with sheriffs and other highly placed servants of the crown. The constable of Carmarthen Castle received 20s a year, but this was a highly responsible post and it included the wage of an interpreter.[97] Evidently the constable had frequently to deal with Welsh-speaking servants and others. On the other hand the constable of Carreg Cennen Castle received the considerable, if somewhat odd, sum of £7..16.4½,[98] the keeper of Snodhill Castle in Herefordshire, only 39s,[99] which was below the level of a castle chaplain. Even the constable of Monmouth Castle got only 20 marks, and this was in an area of considerable danger. The slender evidence suggests that those who kept private or baronial castles received a wage close to the bottom of the range for this office.

The reasons are not far to seek. Although some baronies (see p. 147) were immensely rich, the majority were poor, and the cost of staffing a castle, even at a minimal level, was beyond their means. The king was able to munition his castles without difficulty. He had a manufactory for crossbow bolts at St Briavels. His household included craftsmen who made bows and could – and did – travel from castle to castle repairing them, and he could get the timber and ironware necessary for the engines of war. The barons, even some of the more richly endowed, had none of these advantages. Their castles *must* have been poorly equipped as well as inadequately manned. This is the reason why the king provided munitions and made small monetary grants to the lords of castles along the Welsh Border. They could not otherwise have offered an effective resistance to the Welsh.

It might be thought, from the growing number of licences which the king issued, that there was a conspicuous increase in castle-building (Figure 10.3). This was far from the case. It will be shown (pp. 260–2) that many such licences were not acted upon, and that in others the 'crenellations' were insubstantial. One can only assume that in these cases the cost of acting on the licences they had received was beyond the financial means of a large number of the recipients.

Some idea of the cost in monetary terms of building a castle can be obtained from the royal records of expenditure on them. This must be matched with baronial incomes. These varied very greatly. A small number of earldoms, each an agglomeration of baronial honours, could afford to garrison and maintain a considerable number of castles. But their resources arose only from taking over a series of honours and, as it were, 'stripping their assets'. In other words, they closed down castles they found to be unnecessary and concentrated their resources on the remainder (see p. 104). Baronial incomes fluctuated because, in addition to fixed sums in the form of rent and commuted services, they received a highly variable revenue from fines imposed in their courts and the sale of farm produce.[100] Whereas the royal income can be known with some degree of accuracy from the Pipe Rolls and other records, there is no surviving set of accounts for most of the barons. For only a few of the earldoms, notably those of Cornwall and Lancaster, is there any series of accounts. Most studies of manorial economy and income have in fact been based upon estates of monasteries and cathedral chapters.

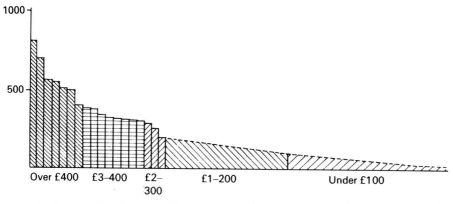

6.5 The income of the baronage about 1200. Based on S. Painter, *Studies in the History of the English Feudal Baronage*, Baltimore, MD, 1943.

Painter has calculated the income of about a third of the members of the baronage in the period 1160–1220.[101] There were at this time about 160 barons, with a gross income of about £32,800, an average of about £200. The data for a sample of fifty-four of them can be broken down:

Table 6.1

Baronial incomes over	£400	7
Baronial incomes	£3–400	8
Baronial incomes	£2–300	3
Baronial incomes	£1–200	16
Baronial incomes under	£100	20
	Total	54

A century later the range in baronial incomes was incomparably greater, and, with the creation of the inflated earldoms of Cornwall, Lancaster and Arundel, it became larger still. Painter provided data for twenty-seven barons within the period 1260 to 1320.[102] Their average income had risen to £668, owing in large measure to the concentration of honours in the hands of a small number of greater barons.[103] The income of Richard of Cornwall approached £4,000, and Isabella de Fortibus, the wealthiest widow of the century, lived in luxury at Carisbrooke on about £2,500 a year. Gilbert de Clare had about £1,800 a year from his English lands alone, and Altschul put his total income at about £3,700,[104] second only to that of the Earl of Cornwall. The last Earl Ferrers had £1,500–1,700 and William de Forz, earl of Albemarle, about £1,000.[105] But most of the barons, who were conspicuous in political life in the later thirteenth and subsequent centuries, received a great deal less than this.

The barony of Coupland, or Egremont, in Cumberland was worth about £537, and the Courteney honour of Okehampton, later to become the nucleus of the earldom of Devon, £489.[106] Even Mortimer of Wigmore was worth no more, and Bardolf of Wormegay, Marmion of Tamworth, Tregoz of Ewyas, and Mohun of Dunster, a great deal less. The Umfraville honour of Prudhoe had an income, *after* it had been absorbed into the estates of Percy of Alnwick of about £130.[107] The earldom of Warwick was comparatively unimportant throughout the thirteenth century, the reason being that it had not the resources to support a prominent role until it was inherited in 1268 by Beauchamp of Elmley Castle.[108] Within a few years, however, acquisition of the baronies of Tosny, Elmley, Ewyas Lacy and part of the de Clare holdings in South Wales, raised the income of the earldom to more than £5,000.[109]

Any estimate of baronial incomes has to take account of the 'steady drain on their resources through the prolonged survival of widows'.[110] It was the baronial practice to allocate manors and castles to the wife as dower, to be enjoyed should she outlive her husband, as frequently she did. The dower lands and the income from them, could not be touched as long as the dowager lived, though the king occasionally fastened his grip on any military assets she might hold.

It is convenient here to examine the assessment of wealth made in 1436 and studied by H. L. Gray, although it lies well outside the period covered in this chapter.[111] Gray's figures have been criticised as too low, since they omitted income from lands in Wales and from those held in dower or used to endow younger sons, most of which eventually returned to the honour.[112] Nevertheless, it is agreed that totals given for the lesser baronies are not wide of the mark. A breakdown of the totals given by Gray is:

Table 6.2. *Baronial incomes,*
1436

Incomes of over	£3,000	2
Incomes of	£2–3,000	1
Incomes of	£1–2,000	12
Incomes of	£500–1,000	18
Incomes of under	£500	33
	Total	66

The level of wages of porter and watchman, craftsmen and mercenary soldiers has already been discussed (p. 90). A mounted and armoured knight cost up to 2s a day, and if a castle were to be defended the most modest garrison required more than the total income of many a small barony. Over and above this was the cost of building and, once built, of keeping a castle in a fit condition to inhabit and use. Masonry defences were costly. At Wark and Chilham, baronial castles temporarily in royal hands, Henry II built tower-keeps and perhaps other structures at the cost of, respectively, £357 and £419.[113] A castle built in the thirteenth century was not likely to require a tower-keep, but curtain walls, mural towers and gatehouse, with portcullis and drawbridge, did not come cheaply, and even then a hall, domestic apartments, kitchen, stables, workshops and store-rooms would have been needed. Painter has claimed that 'a baron who wanted a stone castle had to be able to spend a minimum of about £350'.[114] It has been suggested above that for this he got only an economy model. It is not surprising that one can point to comparatively few castles built *ab initio* after the reign of Henry II and before the Hundred Years' War, when 'windfall profits' turned some humble knights and obscure barons into very rich men (see p. 260).

Baronial building consisted, by and large, of the selective development of castles which already existed. Wooden defences were rebuilt in masonry; walls were made thick enough to support a wide fighting platform. Mural towers, at first rectangular in plan, as at Framlingham, and then half- or three-quarters-round as at Hadleigh, were added and so placed to command the intervening wall space. The gatehouse, from being a simple entrance tower, again as at Framlingham, began to assume the form of two D-shaped towers with an elongated entrance passage between them as at Tonbridge and Rockingham. At White Castle (Monmouthshire) a small tower-keep was swept away and its materials doubtless used in the walls and towers of the early thirteenth century, which still survive. These developments were accomplished piecemeal and were spread over a period of many years. Not only was building a slow and seasonal process; no ordinary baron had the income to pay for an intensive building campaign or the means to borrow capital on the scale required.

Henry II built Orford on the Suffolk coast, and John the castles of Odiham and Sauvey. Henry III initiated no new military building except in the March of Wales. Baronial castle building was on a similarly modest scale. Of course, there was a degree of rebuilding, but the number of fresh starts was small. Indeed, new castles were greatly exceeded by the number of those which were destroyed or allowed to go out of use and fall to ruin. The loss of baronial castles started early, with the documented destruction of almost fifty between 1154 and 1216, and this 'certainly falls short of actual contemporary numbers'.[115] Archaeological investigation can be expected to add to the list, but, with that imprecision which characterises archaeological evidence, is unlikely to throw much light on the number of castles in use in any given year.

Documentary evidence becomes more varied and more abundant in the thirteenth century. Indeed, there is at times a kind of richness about it. But it leaves a lot to be desired. References to an 'old castle' or a 'castle worth nothing' really tell us little. One does not expect a castle to be worth anything in the sense of yielding an income. It might be just inhabited by a watchman or steward. It might be crumbling into ruin, then refurbished for a year or two before being allowed to resume its process of decay. And this was the condition of many castles during the century. One cannot say when they passed out of use, when the process of decay became irreversible. An examination of baronial castles in the thirteenth century shows us that some twenty-five which were in use at the beginning of the century had, for practical purposes, passed out of use before its end. Among them were such baronial *capita* as Skipsea, Haughley, Lavendon, Rayleigh[116] and Barnstaple, as well as other castles of significance during the previous century, like Topcliffe, Holdgate, Dorchester and Hanslope. In a very few instances, Castle Bytham for example, the site appears to have continued to be occupied by a manor house. In others, it was refortified, sometimes with a licence to crenellate, after a considerable lapse of time. This happened, for example, at Dudley and Harptree.

Only a handful of baronial castles in England were built after the reign of John. Prominent amongst them were Beeston in Cheshire, begun by Ranulf de Blundeville, earl of Chester, in 1220, and paid for, according to Ranulf Higden, by a levy on all his tenants.[117] The castle itself consisted of an irregularly rounded enclosure with a powerful gatehouse, on the summit of a steep crag which breaks the level of the Cheshire Plain.[118] When the castle passed into crown possession with the end of the earldom in 1237 its construction appears to have been largely completed. Minor additions were made by Edward I, for which building accounts are in part extant.

Comparable in some ways with Beeston Castle and of similar date was Hadleigh Castle, on the Essex coast overlooking the Thames estuary.[119] It was built by Hubert de Burgh while he was still in favour with Henry III but, on his fall from power, was surrendered to the king and, like Beeston, remained in royal possession. Unlike Beeston, however, it underwent considerable rebuilding in the following century, so that it is not always possible to distinguish the work of de Burgh from that of later date. Hadleigh Castle was oval in plan, covered about half a hectare, and contained a hall, solar block, kitchen and stables. The castle was maintained both for coastal defence and as a royal residence.

Bolingbroke Castle, Lincolnshire, as we see it today, was contemporary with Beeston and Hadleigh, but was probably preceded on the site by some form of ringwork.[120] Its builder was probably that Ranulf de Blundeville who had built Beeston Castle and inherited the earldom of Lincoln. His castle was an irregular hexagon in plan, with massive half-round towers and a strong gatehouse. Little is known of the domestic arrangements, though there must have been a hall and solar for the entertainment of its distinguished visitors.[121]

Acton Burnell Castle was built a half-century later than the three castles just discussed.[122] Bishop Burnell of Bath and Wells was given licence in 1284 to crenellate his manor house of Acton, Near Shrewsbury. What he built was, in fact, a castellated first-floor hall and solar with projecting square corner towers. It probably stood within an enclosure, probably palisaded, in which there was a free-standing kitchen, as well as stables and agricultural buildings. A castle could not be less military than Acton Burnell, 'a crenellated manor house, not a castle', and it is evident that by the closing years of the thirteenth century a crenellated building might have nothing more than a few battlements to hide its domesticity.

What the builders of all four castles had in common was their great wealth. Ranulf de Blundeville was Earl of Chester and Lincoln; de Burgh was Earl of Kent,

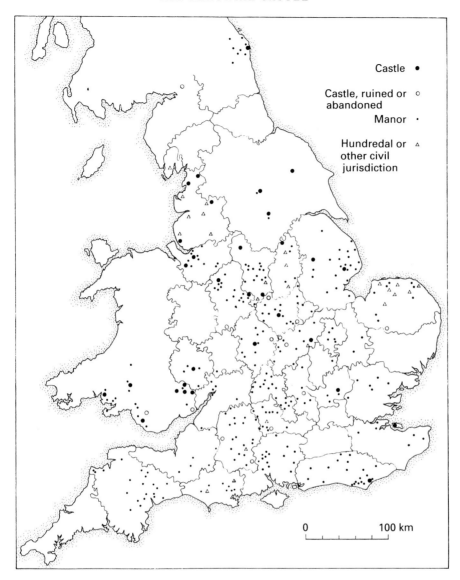

Castle •

Castle, ruined or ○
abandoned

Manor ·

Hundredal or △
other civil
jurisdiction

0   100 km

6.6 Lands and castles of John of Gaunt, Duke of Lancaster. Based on S. Armitage-Smith, *John of Gaunt*, Westminster, 1904.

and Robert Burnell Chancellor of England and one of the most notorious pluralists of his age. Other castles which were built, or extensively rebuilt at this time, were also the work of wealthy men: Chartley, Dudley, Halton, Bridgwater, Codnor and Red Castle. These were not altogether ineffective militarily, but the increasing attention given to hall, kitchen and domestic apartments shows how the balance was gradually tipping from defence to domesticity. And this will be the theme of Chapter 10.

CHAPTER 7

The frontier regions of medieval England

> And the saied lordes, att their first coming to those lordships by conquest, espyenge
> out the fertile parkes in ech countrye, builded their castles for themselves, and
> townes for their owne soldiors and countryemen who came with them to remayne
> neere about them as their guarde, and to be allwayes ready to keep under such of the
> countrye inhabitantes as wold offere to rebell.   Owen, *Pembrokeshire*

All English kings were concerned for the security of their frontiers during the
Middle Ages. The danger of invasion from continental Europe receded after 1217,
but never disappeared. The threat of Welsh raids into the English plain was present
into the fifteenth century, and that from Scotland remained long after the union of
the two crowns. And so Border castles continued to be maintained in fighting order
until the end of the Middle Ages, and coastal defences even longer.

The coastal defences of England

The Conqueror himself had demonstrated how a small force could land unopposed
on the English coast, and the lesson was reinforced at intervals during the next
century. English kings were always concerned for the security of the south-eastern
coast, and, as a general rule, were careful to keep the coastal castles in safe hands. The
castles themselves were a legacy from the early years of the Conquest, and the
scheme of coastal defence was not significantly modified before the end of the Middle
Ages. Some coastal castles of the Conquest, like Hastings, were allowed to decay;
others remained in baronial hands, but expenditure on Dover Castle continued at a
high level even after the completion of the great tower keep. Carisbrooke was taken
into royal possession when the security of the realm required, and increased
attention was given to Southampton, Porchester and Corfe castles. A feature of this
development was that proportionately less care was taken of castles designed to repel
invaders, and more of those which protected havens from which expeditions could
sail to France. Coastal castles were assuming an 'offensive' role, more in line with
England's growing political and commercial importance. Porchester Castle, on the
very edge of Portsmouth harbour was held by Mauduit until the rebellion of 1173,
after which it passed into royal hands.[1] Its great tower-keep has been dated to the
Mauduit period, but Henry II continued to spend on the defences of the inner
bailey.[2] Southampton Castle was in being when Henry II came to the throne, its

motte rising beside the navigable Test.[3] Expenditure on it was small under Henry II, but became very considerable indeed under John. Carisbrooke came only intermittently into crown possession,[4] but there can be no question that its occupants, the family of the de Redvers, earls of Devon, were closely watched, and orders were issued not infrequently for its safe custody.[5]

Wales and the March

Of all external sources of danger to the Norman state Wales seemed to contemporaries the most dangerous, the most menacing and the one against which the most careful defence seemed necessary. The Welsh threat had long been felt. In the eighth century Offa of Mercia had built a dyke from near Prestatyn in the north to a point on the Severn near Chepstow. It was less a defensible line than a permanent and visible boundary, and in the popular imagination it serves this purpose today. The root of the problem lies in the terrain. Wales, like Greece, was born divided. It is made up of a number of hilly or mountainous masses, separated by rivers most of which discharge eastwards towards the English plain. The valleys of the Dee and upper Severn, of the Teme, Wye and Usk and their tributaries opened avenues into the heart of Wales. They facilitated invasion and conquest from England. They provided, no less, routes by which the Welsh could raid the English plain.

There is, however, an important distinction between the northern third of the March, north approximately of the great bend of the river Severn, and the rest. In the former (Figure 7.2) the transition from mountain to plain is abrupt, and the Welsh mountains present a continuous front from the Clwyd range to the Berwyn. Beyond them lie the Cader Idris massif and the mountains of Snowdonia. Good cropland was scarce, except in Anglesey; resources were few, and population small. Such a region held little attraction for the Normans and their effective penetration of the region came late.

South of the Severn, however, the terrain was different. Out in front of the hills of central Wales – Radnor Forest, Mynydd Epynt, the Brecon Beacons – lay isolated hills, fragments of Wales thrust forward and rising like islands from the softer, richer soil of the English plain[6]: Long Mountain, Stiperstones, Long Mynd, Clee Hills, Malvern Hills, Forest of Dean. The gaps between these hills lay wide open and inviting, and behind them were extensive areas of lowland: the Vale of Montgomery, the valley of the Teme, the plain of Hereford, Archenfield, and the tract of rolling country which stretches from the Wye near Monmouth westward towards the Usk. It was in these valleys and lowlands that the Norman favourites of Edward the Confessor settled, and where they built the first castles to be seen in this land, and it was here that no less than twelve of the castles named or alluded to in Domesday Book were located.[7]

The Conqueror was well aware of the threat posed by the Welsh to the security of his realm. The creation of the Marcher earldoms of Chester, Shrewsbury and

Hereford and the organisation of compact tenures within them has already been discussed (pp. 34–9). The earldoms, except that of Chester, lapsed, to be replaced by baronies, small but compact and strong, poised on the edge of England. The barons were an unruly people; 'violence was a pleasure for its own sake, and [in Wales] they indulged their taste for it with little restraint'.[8]

The condition of Wales gave them every encouragement. Its several principalities rose and declined in political importance. On the eve of the Norman Conquest the princes of Gwynedd, the mountainous north of Wales, were in the ascendancy; Gruffydd ap Llewelyn extended his authority over central Wales and into Deheubarth, the extreme south-west, and controlled the whole country except Morgannwg and Gwent, which bordered England in the south. It was this advance that so aroused the Anglo-Saxons under Edward the Confessor, but it was shortlived. Harold led an expedition into Snowdonia; Gruffydd was murdered, and the Welsh state broke up into its component princedoms.

The internal organisation of Wales facilitated invasion and conquest. The country, below the level of the kingdoms of Gwynedd, Powys and Deheubarth, was divided into cantrefs and their subdivisions, commotes.[9] Each centred in an area of low-lying and cultivable land. At the head of each commote was the *tywysog* or chief, and his home, the *llys*, was generally a timber-built hall where he held his court and ruled over his small patrimony.[10] The conquests of one Welsh 'kingdom' at the expense of another consisted essentially in attracting the loyalty of the *tywysog* and his 'clan'. When the Normans began to conquer Wales their procedure was the same; they occupied commotes, one at a time, so that these units remained the building blocks of which feudal Wales was made.

The Domesday Survey gives some indication of the extent of Anglo-Saxon and later of Norman rule in the Borders of Wales. The survey covered the whole of modern Cheshire, Shropshire, Herefordshire and Gloucestershire and locally, as in Flint, Denbigh and the valleys of the Severn and Wye, reached into Wales.

In this Border region King William encouraged his barons to build castles. William himself established Chester Castle;[11] Shrewsbury Castle was mentioned in Domesday Book,[12] and Hereford Castle was almost certainly built by Earl Ralph, nephew of the Confessor.[13] In addition there were castles at this time at Rhuddlan (Flint), and at Clifford, Ewyas Harold, Monmouth, Richard's Castle and Wigmore; and also at Montgomery, Oswestry and Stanton Holgate in Shropshire and at Caerleon and Chepstow. These are shown in Figure 2.4, together with other castles for the existence of which there is compelling evidence at some time before the death of the last of William's sons. These formed a springboard from which the Normans embarked upon the invasion and conquest of much of Wales.

The course of these events was dictated by the available routes. In the north it was possible to follow the narrow coastal plain westward to the river Conwy and beyond. This had been the route of the future King Harold in 1063 when he dealt a fatal blow to the pretensions of Gruffydd ap Llewelyn. From their base in the earldom of Chester, the Normans, led by Robert of Rhuddlan, a vassal of Earl Hugh

4 Caldicot Castle (Monmouth). A round tower-keep stands on a low motte in the corner of a large bailey. Photo: the author.

d'Avranches of Chester, advanced into Caernarvon and even reached Anglesey. They established castles at Rhuddlan, where its motte, Twt Hill, still remains south of the Edwardian castle; at Deganwy, Caernarvon, where the motte was encapsulated within the later masonry castle; Bangor and at Aberlleiniog, near Beaumaris in Anglesey.[14] The Norman occupation of North Wales was shortlived. The Welsh recovered, regained some degree of internal unity, and drove the Norman forces back beyond the river Conwy, and eventually back to the estuary of the Dee. Rhuddlan was lost and even areas included within the Domesday Survey passed into the hands of the Prince of Wales. Castles built at Prestatyn and Basingwerk to protect Cheshire were lost, and Ewloe Castle (Flintshire) was actually built and held by the Welsh themselves.

To the south, an early advance up the Dee valley and into the Vale of Llangollen

155

was checked and the invaders eventually driven back. The commotes of Bromfield and Ial (Yale), within 12 km of Chester itself, became a frontier zone. The earldom of Chester in the early thirteenth century lay on the frontier with Wales and a line of castles guarded the border. To the south, Oswestry, with Ellesmere, Knockin and Whittington, protected the northern boundary of Shropshire until, late in the thirteenth century, the danger had ended.

South of the upper Severn valley the situation was different, both physically and politically. The mountains were lower and broken into discrete masses, by wide valleys which followed the 'grain' of the country from north-east to south-west. The Wye and Usk cut across this grain, creating a chequer-board pattern of mountains in central and South Wales. From their bases near Shrewsbury and Montgomery the Normans pressed up the Severn valley into the commote of Arwystli, and from here into the valley of the Teifi and the lowlands which bordered Cardigan Bay.

The upland mass of Clun and Radnor forests separated the upper Severn from the Wye valley. To the south-east routes led from northern Herefordshire and Shropshire past Radnor and Knighton, Colwyn and Pain's Castle, to converge on the Wye at Builth. From here a valley continued to Llandovery, Carmarthen and the coast. Yet farther to the south, beyond Mynydd Epynt, valleys linked the middle course of the Wye with the upper Usk, where Brecon served as a meeting point of routes. South of the Usk and Towy the terrain rose to the Black Mountains and Brecon Beacons, south of which, almost pinched out between the mountains and the sea, the lowlands extended from Gloucestershire through Glamorgan and Gower to Carmarthen. This pattern of highland and lowland, of hilly masses and intervening valleys, guided the Norman adventurers, providing cropland for their villages and critical points where valleys converged, as at Builth, Brecon and Abergavenny, from which to dominate the region.

The land through which the Normans moved was made up of cantrefs, which they occupied one by one, replacing the chieftain's *llys* with the lord's castle, taking over the obligations of the native Welsh, and transforming them into feudal dues. Each length of valley was the focus of a cantref, whose somewhat indeterminate boundaries ran through the intervening higher ground. By 1100 de Braose had advanced from northern Herefordshire into cantref Elfael, where he erected the first castle of Radnor.[15] From here the route ran southwestward, never climbing much over 600 ft, to the Wye at Builth. Cantref Buillt, which was next occupied by de Braose, was one of the most important, not only because it embraced a considerable area of good cropland, but also because it lay at the crossroads of mid-Wales.[16] The road from Gwynedd toward the south ran down the upper Wye valley before continuing through Bronllys and Tretower to the lower Usk. The road from the plains of Herefordshire and Shropshire continued up the Irfon and down the Towy to Carmarthen and west Wales. If ever the course of invasion, conquest and settlement was dictated by the terrain, this was in central and South Wales. The

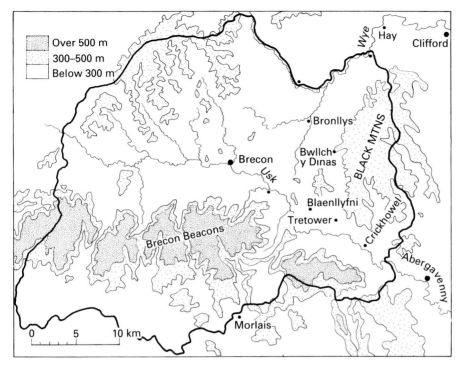

7.1 The lordship of Brycheiniog (Brecon), corresponding very closely with the Welsh Cantref Selyf, Cantref Mawr and Talgarth. After W. Rees, 'The Mediaeval Lordship of Brecon', *Tr Cymm*, 1915–16, 165–224.

capita of lordships were established where routes met, and their subsidiary castles were built on the roads which led to neighbouring cantrefs.

No event illustrates the nature of the Norman conquest better than the formation of the lordship of Brecon. Bernard de Neufmarché was settled in northern Herefordshire after 1086.[17] From this base he advanced south-westward along the Wye, through the gap which his successors were to defend with the castle of Bronllys, and descended into the Usk valley at Brecon. Brecon Castle had been built by 1093. The land which he seized was made up of Cantref Selyf, lying north of the Usk, and Cantref Mawr, to the south and reached into the Brecon Beacons (Figure 7.1). Bernard allocated land within the two *cantrefs* to the knights who had followed him, to each a compact territory, with the obligation to build a castle to defend it and to provide military service in their lord's castle of Brecon. In 1094–5 the Welsh revolted, but 'again [the Normans] came into Brycheiniog [Brecon] and built castles there'.[18] War threatened for the next two centuries, and the castles were manned until the Edwardian conquest.

The Black Mountains of western Herefordshire and the Brecon Beacons set a southern limit to the cantrefs occupied by Bernard de Neufmarché. Their peat-covered summits were a barrier to movement and settlement. South of the mountains the land was one of rolling hills and richer soil, more attractive to the Normans of Herefordshire and Gloucestershire than the hilly country of mid-Wales. Even before the Conquest the Normans had built the castle of Ewyas Harold on the southern edge of the Black Mountains. By the time of Domesday they held Monmouth and Chepstow (Striguil) castles beyond the Wye, and from these bases they progressed with remarkable ease and speed through the lowlands of Wentloog (Monmouthshire) and Morgannwg (Glamorgan). Petty lordships were established on the fringes of the Black Mountains – Snodhill, Dorestone, Kilpeck, Ewyas Harold, Ewyas Lacy and, above all, Abergavenny. At all these sites, and at many others they built motte castles with strong, compact baileys. These became centres for administering territories which were, as far as practicable, transformed into manors on the English model.

The slow advance of the Normans along the flanks of the Black Mountains contrasted with the sudden swoop of Robert FitzHamo from his Gloucester base into the Vale of Glamorgan. About 1090 he established Cardiff Castle within a Roman fort. From here his followers fanned out over the low country, occupying the fiefs allocated to them, building castles and contributing to the defence of Cardiff.

The lordships of Glamorgan reached from the coast up to the foothills of the mountains.[19] The land above about 600 feet was 'Welshry'. The Anglo-Normans did not settle or even build castles there. They exercised lordship over it and by their ring of castles strove with indifferent success to exclude its inhabitants from the Englishry of the Vale. Their limits coincided approximately with the boundaries of cantrefs or of their subdivisions, the commotes. The castles at Llanblethian, Tal-y-van, Dinas-Powys and Ogmore were organised early in FitzHamo's occupation of the region.[20] Some of these lordships became almost independent of their lord in Cardiff, but always the Welsh threat imposed an unwilling unity upon the turbulent lords of the March. The subjugation of the hill country to the north was little more than nominal until late in the thirteenth century. Towards the west the hills came close to the sea, and here, in the cantrefs of Nedd (Neath), Afan and Kenfig, the danger to the Norman lords was greatest. This was a frontier within a frontier. The castle and lordship of Neath – an 'isolated and perilous lordship' – lay at the tip of the Norman advance through Glamorgan.[21]

Pressure on western Glamorgan was relieved at the beginning of the next century by the conquest and colonisation of Gower. Henry I, unlike his brother and father, took a personal interest in the campaigns into Wales.[22] He made an expedition into west Wales and assumed directly the lordship of Carmarthen. It was Henry I who granted Gower which, strictly speaking, was not his to grant, to Henry de Newburgh, who about 1106 invaded Gower, almost certainly by sea, and founded a castle at Swansea.[23] Gower, which coincided with the traditional cantref of Gwyr, was, like the plain of Glamorgan, mostly granted as fiefs to the knights who accompanied de Newburgh. The lordships were smaller, but each centred in a castle:

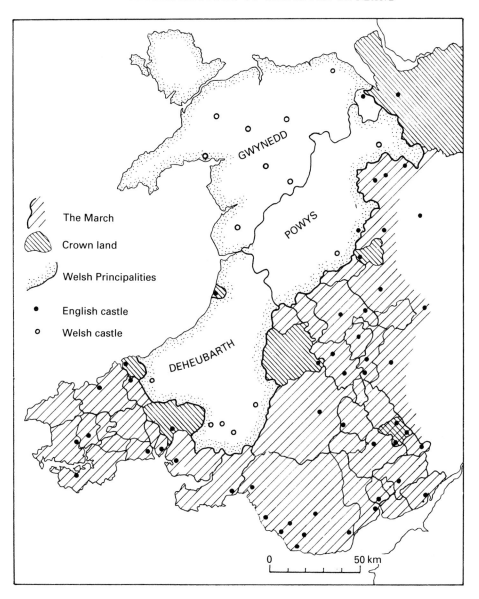

7.2 Wales and the March on the eve of the Edwardian Conquest.

Oystermouth, Oxwich, Penrice, Scurlages and so on. The occupation of the next cantref of Cydweli (Kidwelly) followed almost at once.

Yet farther west another adventurer, William FitzBaldwin, sheriff of Devon, came by sea to the Towy estuary and there built the castle of Rhydygors on the east bank of the river.[24] Within a few years FitzBaldwin had disappeared and his castle was replaced by that at Carmarthen. This remained, except for very short periods, in royal hands and constituted the centre of administration and seat of the Justiciar of the Western March.

Beyond the lordship of Carmarthen lay Pembroke. Unlike the rest of South Wales, Pembroke was reached by Normans coming from the north. They had crossed from Arwystli, and had reached the shores of Cardigan Bay.[25] Their numbers appear to have been sufficient to control the whole of Ceredigion – the later county of Cardigan – and to build a castle within each of the cantrefs. Under Arnulf of Montgomery, younger son of Roger of Montgomery, they advanced beyond the Teifi into Pembroke. Here, over the next decade, a radical change was made in controlling conquered territory. A body of Flemings, who were apparently already in England, was moved to the Western March and was settled around Haverford and Wiston. They were neither knights nor mercenaries, but farmers and craftsmen, who displaced the native population and made this region an island of English, or at least of non-Welsh culture. 'It was thus', wrote Sir John Lloyd, 'that southern Dyfed lost its Welsh character; the Welsh language ceased to be spoken there, and, English having gradually taken the place of Flemish, it became "Little England beyond Wales"'.[26]

In the areas of Flemish settlement the traditional division into cantrefs disappeared, but elsewhere in Pembrokeshire the native land units were with modifications taken over by Norman lords and held as fiefs of the earls of Pembroke: Cemaes, Kilgerran, Narberth, St Clears, each centred in a castle. Only the cantref of Pebidiog, in which lay the religious centre of St David's, was without a lay lord with his castle.

Thus the March of Wales, from Shropshire to Pembroke, came to be occupied by Norman lords and divided into lordships, each with a castle both to carry on its administration and to symbolise the power and authority of the lord himself. Lordship in the March differed fundamentally from that found in England. It was concentrated; it was a single, compact tract of land, not a wide scatter of manors. It tended to conform with the pre-existing Welsh territorial unit, the cantref. Even in Cheshire, Shropshire and Herefordshire, which were not within Wales, lordships were small and compact, though this owed nothing to Welsh institutions and everything to planning at the time of the Conquest.

The Marcher lordships, secondly, lay outside the realm of England, and their relations with the king were ambiguous. He claimed to be their lord, and occasionally he visited the March, asserting his authority and receiving the homage of the barons. But in taking over the Welsh cantrefs the latter also adopted Welsh law and customs.[27] English shrieval organisation was not extended to Wales until

1536, and itinerant justices went no farther than the English counties which bordered Wales. Within the March, as in all frontiers and at all times, authority was exercised locally and according to the exigences of military conquest and occupation. The lords were a law to themselves. They made war and built castles as they chose. The king in England claimed the right to license, to confiscate and to destroy castles, but in Wales he made no such claim, and certainly could not have enforced it if he had. Nevertheless, the king might inherit or acquire through escheat one Marcher lordship or another, as he did for example that of Builth in the thirteenth century.[28] But in doing so he became as one of his barons, and his 'liberty' extended only as far as his lordship.

Lordships within the March of Wales differed from those in England also in their durability. In England feudal jurisdictions and obligations were divided between heiresses, traded among barons, taken into the king's hands and regranted in different forms. Fractional knights' fees abounded and, in some instances, became gradually smaller until they lapsed. In the March, lordships passed from one family to another. They were concentrated in the possession of a de Clare, a Mortimer or a de Braose. They passed into the king's hands and were returned to those of his barons, but they remained territorially intact. Each represented, as it were, a quantum of baronial power, below which it was impossible to conceive of feudal units.

There were very few Marcher lords who did not also hold land in England, and many had possessions just across the border from the March, in Herefordshire and Shropshire. FitzAlan and Mortimer, indeed, had their *capita* in England, at Oswestry, Clun and Wigmore, while most of their landed possessions lay in Wales. It would not be surprising if they tried to extend to their English lands the freedom which they enjoyed in Wales, and in fact, some were successful in doing so.[29] Clun had been an integral part of Shropshire, yet in 1306 John FitzAlan was able to make good his claim that the king's writ did not run in the lordship of Clun.[30] The lordship of Oswestry, which was also held by FitzAlan and lay in Shropshire, was excluded from the jurisdiction of the local sheriff, and William de Braose, lord of Brecon, claimed in 1199 that 'neither the king nor the justiciar nor the sheriff' should interfere in an affair on land in Herefordshire, which was held of his lordship of Brecon.[31] The boundary of the March came to be obscured as lands on the English side of the line were assimilated to the Law of Wales.

The Marcher lordship thus emerges as a small, relatively compact territory, its boundaries imprecise only because they ran through land of little value.[32] At its central-place was a castle, of earthwork and timber in the first instance, but increasingly thereafter of masonry. In the perception of the local population it had succeeded to the *llys* of the local clan leader. It was the meeting place, 'at the castle gate', of the court of the lordship.[33] The surrounding land had been subinfeudated, allocated in fees to the followers who had helped their lord to conquer this land. Knights' fees probably existed in most lordships, and guard duties continued to be performed long after they had become obsolete in England.[34] A list of fees tributary to Cardiff Castle has survived from about 1260, and certain knights were obligated to maintain 'houses' within the castle bailey.[35]

The native population was made to supply timber for fuel, to quarry stone and to perform other services.[36] As far as practicable a castle was provisioned from its own cantref, but necessarily there were exceptions. The demands of a large garrison exceeded local resources of supply, and food had to be brought in. This was far from easy in the disturbed conditions of the March. In 1244 a Welsh force under Dafydd ap Gruffydd lay between Chester and the castle of Dyserth, and a letter from the Justice of Chester complained that his strength was insufficient to break through with supplies.[37] Again, Roger Mortimer wrote of his difficulty in obtaining supplies for his castles in the Middle March and appealed to the sheriffs of Shropshire and Hereford for help.[38] He complained – an interesting comment on his priorities – that the supply of wine was particularly difficult. The uncertain supply of foodstuffs led to an order at Hereford that castles be 'double-provisioned'.[39] Food had to be seized wherever it could be found, and the only way of depriving a castle of supplies was to ravage its cantref. There was a movement of food, clearly irregular and dependent on the exigences of war, from the West Midlands to the castles of the March, from Bristol and the West Country to those of South Wales, and from Chester to Rhuddlan, Deganwy and those castles in North Wales that were accessible by sea.

There was an advantage in siting a castle close to a navigable waterway, though the Normans were somewhat slow in learning it. The fact was that readily defensible sites were rarely coastal or besides navigable waterways. But Pembroke Castle, the only castle within the March never to have been taken by the Welsh, combined all the advantages of site. Swansea, Cardiff and Kidwelly castles were built close to the sea, and Carmarthen Castle was relocated on a site overlooking the navigable Towy. In the course of the thirteenth century greater provision was made for the seaborne supply of provisions. The second castle at Rhuddlan virtually embraced a small port on the river Clwyd, well adapted to the twelve-oared boats in use. The third castle at Aberystwyth was sited on a low bluff overlooking the sea and all the new Edwardian castles of North Wales were integrated from the first with port facilities.

In the larger and more important lordships the central castle was far from being the only one. Subsidiary castles formed a screen and commanded the roads leading to it. To what extent these conformed to a preconceived plan is difficult to say. Those that ringed the castle of Brecon suggest that there was conscious planning. A not dissimilar arrangement appears to have been made around Builth, strategically the most exposed in the March. But in the lordship of Glamorgan the pattern of subsidiary castles was more nearly random. Here, and also in the lordship of Gower, the holders of knights' fees built small castles wherever they had the resources to do so.[40]

The plain of Hereford, the Vale of Montgomery and the Cheshire plain were all ringed, at least along their western margins, by 'barrier fortresses', and it is all too easy to see in their pattern, especially if represented on a small-scale map, some controlling hand. In all probability there was none. Land was allocated without clear knowledge of where it lay and what it contained. The feoffees were encouraged to build castles, and each did so in accordance with his perception of *his* land and of the risks and dangers to which it was exposed. He was more likely to build a castle if it lay close to 'Welshry' than if he were protected by distance. Even so, what he built, even in exposed areas, often fell short of the contemporary concept of what a castle should be. The lordship of Gower, not one of the least exposed, developed, like Glamorgan, a scattered pattern of knights' fees and castles, one of which, at Weobley, could only be described in an inquest *post mortem* as *manerium batellatum vocatum Webley*.[41] Perhaps for this reason a later jury felt compelled to add that it was *destructa per diversas accessus rebellium Wallicorum*.[42]

The building of castles below the level of the lordship – and Weobley was held *of* lordship of Swansea – depended as much on resources as on the will of the tenant. It is difficult to say how far down the feudal hierarchy the practice of building masonry castles extended. It seems that it was far from general even among the knightly subtenants of the Marcher lords. On the other hand the Marches, especially the Middle March which overstepped the counties of Shropshire and Herefordshire, were strewn with earthwork castles of which there is, in most instances, little documentary record. Dozens of motte castles and ringworks, many of them apparently without a bailey, lie up and down the valleys which open to the Severn, Wye and Usk. One must conclude that most of them never evolved beyond an earthen bank or motte and palisade, that they were located within the manor which they served, that they never played any strategic role, and at most gave slight protection to the household that lived within.

The Welsh Wars

The Norman penetration of Wales occurred at a time when the Welsh princes were more than usually disunited and powerless. But this condition of weakness could not be expected to last, and was, indeed, followed by a recovery which coincided with disunity and war in England. The wars between the Welsh and the English intruders comprised an immense number of petty wars both among the Welsh princes and between them and the Marcher lords. These events are chronicled in the several versions of the *Brut y Tywysogyon*, or Chronicle of the Princes.[43] It is not easy to see, beneath this interminable and repetitive account of siege and destruction, the real pattern of events, for there was an ebb and flow in the Norman penetration of Wales, and the success of one side or the other reflected the rise and decline of princes and the unity and disunity of their respective countries. On the English side, the wars of Stephen and the Barons' Wars of the reigns of John and Henry III were times when the Normans and their successors showed little unity of purpose and even called in the help of the Welsh in their intra-baronial struggles. For their part, the Welsh princes, by a combination of mortality and astute management, were brought together at intervals in the acceptance of a prince of Wales as overlord.

Defeat and invasion at the hands of the Normans was followed, after the death of

Henry I, by recovery and the re-establishment of Welsh rule over much of the March. Until the wars of independence late in the thirteenth century the three principalities – Gwynedd, Powys and Deheubarth (Figure 7.2) – maintained their independence, and, despite periodic inroads by barons of the March, they even expanded the area under their control. In this they were aided by the acceptance of the Norman institution of the castle. Some castles they took over in the course of conquest; others they built themselves. The castles of the Welsh in some respects perpetuated the plan of the earlier Anglo-Norman castles, with tower-keeps, sometimes apsidal in plan. But the quality of their masonry was poorer, and they often seemed to be somewhat inelegant copies of those met with in the March.[44]

Dominance during the first part of this period was held by Rhys ap Gruffydd, prince of Deheubarth, who eliminated his rivals and even secured recognition by Henry II. From his castle of Dinefwr (Dynevor) in the Towy valley, with its outlying fortresses of Dryslwyn, Llandovery and Newcastle Emlyn, he threatened the Anglo-Norman hold on south-west Wales, even overrunning Dyfed to the gates of Pembroke Castle. But like every other ascendancy it was short-lived. His death (1197) was followed by division within Deheubarth, and the Anglo-Norman barons again nibbled at his territory, strengthening their lands and reoccupying castles on the borders. De Braose, lord of Abergavenny, Brecon, Builth, Elfael and Radnor, threatened from the east, and from the north-east came Roger Mortimer, reoccupying the hilly country of Maelienydd and threatening southern Powys as well as Ceredigion. Powys itself broke into two parts, Powys Wenwynwyn and Powys Fadog, neither of which was able to put up sustained resistance. English barons built castles within Powys and eastern Gwynedd, at Mold, Mathraval, Pool (Welshpool) and elsewhere.

It was, however, from the ruins of Rhys ap Gruffydd's princedom that the next – and last – unification of Wales emerged. Its architect was Llewelyn ap Iorwerth, and its basis was Gwynedd, rugged, poor and backward and an unlikely foundation for hegemony. He was, however, able to profit from disunion in England and brought Deheubarth and Powys under his control. He raided deep into the March, and attempted to regulate the succession and ensure the permanent unity of the principality. But the death of Llewelyn in 1240 was followed by a disputed succession and, in England, by the restoration of harmony between the barons and the crown. The work of Llewelyn was largely undone. The English extended their authority in North Wales as far as the Conwy and began the rebuilding of the castles – Deganwy, Dyserth, Rhuddlan and others – intended to make this occupation permanent. Farther south, they re-established their castle at Llanbadarn (Aberystwyth), re-occupied Cardigan and detached the rulers of Deheubarth and Powys from their loyalty to the princes of Gwynedd.

In less than twenty years the dialectic of Welsh history had taken another turn. Llewelyn ap Gruffydd, grandson of Llewelyn the Great, established himself in Gwynedd (1255) and, by a combination of persuasion and force, brought

Deheubarth and both parts of Powys under his control. His success was due in part to the contemporary turmoil in England, where events were moving towards the Barons' War. The English barons, even those of the Marches, were divided amongst themselves and, far from presenting a common front to Welsh expansion, even allowed Llewelyn to enlist the support of some of their number. The high point of Welsh success was reached in 1267 when the English king, unable to deal both with the 'Disinherited' within England and the Welsh along its borders, accepted the Treaty of Montgomery. Llewelyn was recognised as Prince of Wales and overlord of the principalities of Powys and Deheubarth. The English withdrew from North Wales, and the boundary of Gwynedd was extended to Cheshire. Farther south the territories of Ceri, Maelienydd, Elfael, Builth and Brecon fell under his control, a castle was built at Dolforwyn, across the Severn from Montgomery, and the Marcher lords were put on the defensive as at no time since the early years of the twelfth century. There was a flurry of activity along the March. The castles built or strengthened in recent years at Cymaran, Cefnllys, Colwyn, Rhayader and Builth and in Elfael and Brecon, had clearly not sufficed to hold the Welsh advance. Further protection was necessary. From Oswestry to Pembroke constables, royal and baronial, were ordered to look to their defences. Hasty surveys were carried out of the fabric of the castles, and stores of food and munitions were checked in anticipation of farther Welsh advances.

The most momentous development of these years, however, was in Glamorgan. Here, in the mountains that separated Brecon from the Vale of Glamorgan, lay a thinly peopled region which had accepted Marcher domination but had remained in essential respects part of 'Welshry'. Here was a soft point in the ring of Marcher lordships. Llewelyn attempted to detach the ruler of Senghenydd, essentially the valley of the Taff, from his reluctant loyalty to de Clare. Gilbert de Clare acted quickly.[45] In 1268 he began the building of Caerphilly Castle where the Rhymney valley begins to open out towards the plain, but the unfinished work was destroyed in a Welsh raid of 1270. De Clare's response was to push ahead with the rebuilding of Caerphilly and to build a second castle at Morlais, high up above the Taff valley on the very borders of Brecon.

The building of Caerphilly was a turning point in the history of the castle in Britain. It was the first to be built *ab initio* on the concentric plan. Dover, Kenilworth and the Tower of London were in process of being adapted, but here the newest ideas were incorporated from the start. A roughly rectangular court, with two gatehouses and massive drum-towers at the corners, was surrounded by a concentric outer bailey. The siege of Kenilworth Castle in 1266 had demonstrated how effective a defence a lake could be, and at Caerphilly a heavily fortified dam was built to hold back a very large lake. When it was finished in 1277, Caerphilly Castle was the strongest in Britain. It was immune to tunnelling and its water defences kept 'engines' at a distance. Only a baron of immense wealth and supreme confidence could have undertaken such a work, and Gilbert de Clare (see p. 147) possessed both. Building accounts have unfortunately not survived but its construction could not possibly have cost less than any one of Edward I's castles of North Wales (see p. 176), and probably appreciably more, since the hydraulic engineering here was on a scale not met with elsewhere.

Edward I and the conquest of Wales

Caerphilly was still incomplete when, in 1272, Henry III died. His son, Edward I, was on crusade, and did not return to England for his coronation until 1274. Llewelyn, Prince of Wales, was summoned to the ceremony and was expected to do homage to the king for his principality. He did not come, and gave further evidence of his hostility by proposing to marry the daughter of Simon de Montfort. The First Welsh War quickly followed. Once again political unity within England coincided with growing discord not only between Llewelyn and the princes of Powys and Deheubarth, but also within his own family. Royal forces attacked from three directions. In the south, they moved from Carmarthen up the Towy valley, taking the castles of Dryslwyn, Dinefwr and Carreg Cennen. From Montgomery in the Severn valley they struck into central Wales, and, lastly, the main attack was mounted from Chester both along the coast to Anglesey and through the forests of Clwyd and Perfeddwlad to the river Conwy. During the following summer Welsh resistance crumbled, and the Prince of Wales was compelled to accept a treaty which, in effect, restored conditions much as they had been after the death of Llewelyn ap Iorworth. The princes of Deheubarth and of the principalities of Powys severed their dependence on Gwynedd. In North Wales the English extended their control to the river Conwy, thus regaining the castles of Deganwy and Rhuddlan, as well as the territories of Bromfield and Yale. Farther south they regained Llanbadarn and acquired, for the first time since the early twelfth century, its hilly hinterland of northern Ceredigion. Cantref Bychan, with its castles of Dryslwyn, Dinefwr, Carreg Cennen and Llandovery, was regained, and served to link Carmarthen with the lordship of Builth.

The First Welsh War was followed by intense building activity, for no one could have regarded the settlement reached at Aberconway in 1277 as permanent. Building was mainly in central and northern Wales. The castles in the south, Carmarthen, Cardigan and others, were made ready, but there was no lavish expenditure on them. In the spring following the Treaty of Aberconwy a surveyor was sent to review the condition of the castles within the March.[46] Builth Castle, regained from the Welsh, was refurbished. As a temporary measure, a wooden palisade was built round the outer bailey, replaced later by a masonry wall. Building continued until the end of the century, and overall more than £1,666 was spent on developing Builth Castle.

Even larger sums were expended on Aberystwyth Castle. The first castle at Aberystwyth – the Llanbadarn of the records – lay beside the Ystwyth river, 2 km from the sea.[47] This was destroyed by the Welsh, who themselves appear to have built a castle to the north, perhaps at Plas Crug.[48] This too had been destroyed when,

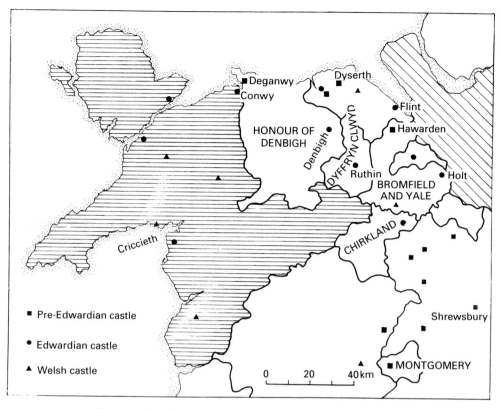

7.3 Castles and political–administrative organisation of North Wales about 1300.

in 1277, Edmund of Lancaster, brother of Edward I, came with an army to re-establish a castle in northern Ceredigion. He chose a site on the low cliffs that border Cardigan Bay, and here, at the cost of nearly £4,000, he built the Edwardian castle. It was diamond-shaped with strong round towers at the corners and a massive gatehouse, the whole contained within a concentric outer ward. In plan it showed the influence of Caerphilly, begun nearly ten years before. The castle, along with the town that was growing up beside it, appears to have been raided and severely damaged[49] and the task of restoring the situation, architecturally at least, was entrusted to Master James of St George. He was at the time *magister cementarius*, an office which combined the functions of architect and master of the works, at Flint and Rhuddlan. He was almost certainly a Savoyard, brought to England by Edward I, to work on his fortifications in North Wales.[50] There can be no question also that his creations 'constitute, as a group, one of the most impressive monuments of military architecture in Britain'. The plan of Aberystwyth Castle bears a close similarity to that of Rhuddlan, and, since Master James' 'restoration' was on a massive scale, it is not unlikely that he adapted his Rhuddlan plan to the Aberystwyth site. Payments for work on Aberystwyth Castle appear to have terminated in 1289, when it was for practical purposes complete. In 1294–5 it successfully withstood an assault by the Welsh.

A third important royal castle in mid-Wales was Montgomery. Though its keeping had been marked by parsimony and neglect, it stood upon its rock above the Severn Plain and needed only to be refurbished. This was all the more necessary because Llewelyn ap Gruffydd had recently built the castle of Dolforwyn on a similar site beyond the Severn. The threat which the latter posed was ended when the men of Montgomery attacked and took it, but danger continued in the Middle March, and it was not until the next century that Montgomery Castle ceased to play a dominant role in its protection.

It was, however, in the north that most money and the greatest effort were expended. Until the middle years of the thirteenth century the princes of Deheubarth and Powys had constituted the greatest threat. Gwynedd was mountainous and remote, and thus no threat to the March. The approaches to Cheshire appeared to be sufficiently guarded by a line of castles, from Rhuddlan to Oswestry. The castles of Deganwy and Rhuddlan were long in dispute between the Earl of Chester and the princes of Gwynedd, and were several times destroyed and rebuilt. They were taken by Llewelyn ap Iorworth, but lost again during the period when his successors disputed the rule of North Wales. It was then that Henry III began the rebuilding of Deganwy and the erection of Dyserth Castle, which was intended to supplement or replace the first castle of Rhuddlan.[51]

The rebuilding of Deganwy began in 1245 and was completed in 1254. The cost of its re-occupation must have amounted to some £10,000. At about the same time a castle was begun at Dyserth at the northern end of the Clwyd range and in a position of considerable natural strength.[52] Both castles were attacked and destroyed by Llewelyn ap Gruffydd in 1263, and appear never to have been reoccupied.[53]

The First Welsh War of 1276–7 ended with the English reoccupation of the coastal strip of North Wales as far as the Conwy river, and the replacement of the castles destroyed by Llewelyn. The approach of Edward I to the administration of his castles and the preparations for war differed fundamentally from those of his father. A rudimentary office of works was established in London with a branch office in Chester, which had responsibility for the finance and construction of the North Wales castles.[54] First to be built were Flint and Rhuddlan. Their purpose was to hold the disputed cantref of Tregeingl (Englefield). They marked a departure from the practice of the previous reign. They were built wholly of masonry, and conformed with the newest thinking on military architecture. Their construction was a national undertaking in so far as much of the country was called upon to supply labourers and materials. Above all, both (and also the castles built subsequently in Gwynedd) were established on the tideway, capable of being supplied by boat from Chester, or Ireland.[55]

Both castles were begun in the summer of 1277. Work was interrupted during the winter months and was not always actively pursued even during summer. The record of payments to masons ends in 1284. Work on the two castles ran

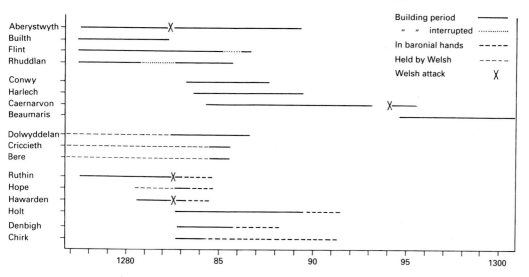

7.4 The timetable of castle building in North Wales. The evidence for a timescale is slight when the castles were in the possession of either Welsh princes or of English barons. This graph gives no indication of the extent of building at any one time or of the sums expended.

concurrently, and workmen were moved between one and the other. Unfortunately their building accounts were also, in part, conflated, so that it is difficult to estimate the cost of each. They appear to have been completed in 1285, despite a Welsh attack in 1282.[56] Flint Castle consisted of a square court with three-quarter round corner towers and, at the south-east, a detached round tower – a sort of keep – of immense size and strength. This court lay against the river Dee, with, on its exposed or southern side, an outer ward protected by a moat. Rhuddlan Castle, which replaced the abandoned motte known as Twt Hill, lay on the high east bank of the Clwyd. It was closer in plan to Caerphilly than to Flint Castle, with a diamond-shaped court, corner towers and two massive gatehouses. This inner ward was completely enclosed by a less strongly fortified outer ward, whose walls ran down to the Clwyd to give protection to a small quay.

An army of almost three thousand workmen was brought in for work on the two castles. There were 1845 *fossatores*, employed to dig foundations and water defences, 320 *cementarii* or masons, and 790 woodworkers of all kinds.[57] The task of organising so vast an operation overshadows anything that had gone before. The efforts of these years were not confined to building the two castles of Flint and Rhuddlan. Several of the castles which protected the approaches to the Cheshire Plain had been destroyed by Llewelyn ap Gruffydd, and were in varying degrees restored after the Peace of Aberconwy. Indeed, the Second Welsh War began with what can only be called a pre-emptive strike by the Welsh against the castle of Hawarden. Caergwrle (Hope) Castle was restored after its destruction by Llewelyn,[58] but the task of building and restoring so many castles at the same time strained both financial resources and the manpower available. A partial solution was reached at Caergwrle, where Edward I gave £100 to Sir Richard Siward 'towards his maintenance and the charges and expenses' of putting it into a state of defence.[59]

A similar procedure was adopted at this time in the castle of Ruthin. Ruthin lay near the head of the Clwyd valley and commanded a road through the hills to the Dee. It was part of the Four Cantrefs of Perfeddwlad which Edward I had entrusted to David, Llewelyn's brother, after 1277. But in 1282 David returned to his allegiance to Llewelyn and the Justice of Chester, Reginald de Grey, took possession of Ruthin Castle, and its cantref of Duffryn Clwyd. The Greys of Ruthin were henceforward its lords.

At Denbigh, down the Clwyd valley from Ruthin, one of the more powerful castles of North Wales was built, not by the king, but by Henry de Lacy, earl of Lincoln, to whom Edward I had granted the cantref of Rhufoniog. At the same time the territories of Bromfield and Yale, which bordered Cheshire on the west, were granted to John de Warenne, earl of Surrey. They contained the Welsh castle of Dinas Bran, on high ground above the Vale of Llangollen. De Warenne chose to leave Dinas Bran in ruins and to begin a new castle at Holt, close to the river Dee.[60] The land of Chirk which lay immediately south of Yale was, lastly, granted to Roger Mortimer, younger son of Roger Mortimer of Wigmore, who thus founded the house of Mortimer of Chirk. It is uncertain when he began the construction of Chirk Castle, but it belongs to the later years of the thirteenth century, and, like others named, was conceived as part of a defensive curtain from the sea to Oswestry and Montgomery.[61]

The effect of these changes was to create in northern Powys and eastern Gwynedd a new breed of Marcher lords, whose task it was to protect the approaches to the Cheshire Plain. The motte castle of Hawarden was restored after the raid of 1282, but the Welsh castles which passed into the hands of the English, including Ewloe and Dinas Bran, were not rebuilt. Instead new castles were established. There is some reason to believe that the king's master craftsmen from Chester may have played a role, if only advisory, in their construction, and at Ruthin workmen with experience at Rhuddlan were employed.[62] The plans adopted in the newly built castles at Chirk, Holt, Ruthin and Denbigh lacked the regularity of those erected by the king's engineers. Chirk was a square court with drum towers at the corners. At the others the court was polygonal, with round towers at the angles. All had large and strong gatehouses and were located on commanding sites. At Chirk Castle, the most regularly planned of them all, three-quarters of the enclosing curtain survives, the southern face of the castle having been demolished and rebuilt. The entrance differs from that met with in all royal castles of this period in not being deeply set between drum-towers. This fact alone would suggest that royal builders made little contribution to Chirk.

Such, however, was not the case at Denbigh. Here the summit of the steep hill above the Clwyd valley, was enclosed by a polygonal wall, with projecting D-shaped towers, and integrated with the walls of the town. The castle was taken –

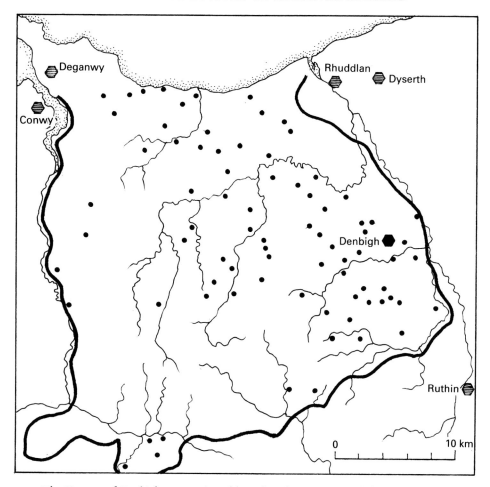

7.5 The Honour of Denbigh, as constituted by Edward I. It comprised the Welsh cantrefs of Rhos and Rhufoniog, and centred in the castle of Denbigh. It represented, along with Holt and Chirkland, a revival of the earlier concept of a territorial honour.

perhaps still unfinished – by the Welsh in 1292, and then retaken by the English. The north and west walls, which separate the castle from the town and include a massive gatehouse, differ from the rest in the quality of their masonry, which is reminiscent of that of Caernarvon Castle, built a few years earlier. This is not the only evidence that the king interested himself in the building of Denbigh Castle. He made a monetary contribution towards its cost; tools were supplied from Rhuddlan, and royal master craftsmen were on occasion present during its construction. The territory granted to the de Lacy lord of Denbigh consisted of the cantrefs of Rhos and Rhufoniog, and extended up to the Conwy valley. It was organised as a Marcher lordship would have been a century earlier, with manors held in demesne (Figure 7.5) and the obligation of military service in the castle imposed on the lordship generally. A garrison of thirty men-at-arms and 120 archers, large by contemporary standards, was maintained.[63]

David ap Gruffydd's abandonment of the cause of King Edward and his attack on Hawarden and other castles in 1282 opened the Second and decisive Welsh War. It lasted little more than a year. English forces from Carmarthen and Cardigan advanced respectively up the Towy and northwards through Ceredigion. Dinefwr, Carreg Cennen, Dryslwyn, Emlyn and Llanbadarn were retaken. In Mid-Wales, forces from Montgomery attacked and destroyed Llewelyn's castle of Dolforwyn. But the centre of Welsh resistance was in Gwynedd. Here the English forces overran the Four Cantrefs, reached the Conwy, and then moved to isolate the mountain stronghold of Snowdonia. From Chester and the Dee, English forces moved by sea along the North Wales coast and invaded Anglesey. Under these circumstances there was a grave danger that the princes of Powys and Deheubarth would make their peace with the English. Llewelyn went south to rally his forces, and near Builth he was met by an English force and killed. The Welsh in the north put up a brave but fruitless resistance. Their castles – Dolwyddelan, Criccieth and Bere – were attacked and taken, and by the summer of 1283 the war was over. The whole principality passed to the English king, and was parcelled into shires, each consisting of 'an aggregation of old cantrefs, and commots'.[64] There was, henceforward, a threefold division of Wales. Throughout the Marches, to which was now assimilated the territory of Powys Wenwynwyn, the land continued as semi-independent lordships. Their lords, now relatively few in number and proportionately more powerful, continued to exercise their quasi-sovereign powers, to settle their mutual disputes by warfare among themselves, and to reject English law and the justice of the itinerant English courts. To these lordships Edward I had just added those of Holt, Chirk, Ruthin, Denbigh and Hawarden-Mold.

Secondly, there were the lordships, such as Montgomery, Builth, Cardigan, Emlyn and Carmarthen, which the king had long held or claimed to hold. They were attached to the crown, and, appearances to the contrary, were not strictly a part of the March. Lastly, lands of the Welsh princes, taken during the recent wars, were claimed absolutely by the English king. In addition, there were relatively restricted lands held by the church, of which the cantref of Pebidiog, belonging to the see of St David's, was the most important. It is against this division of the country that we must set the building and maintenance of castles during the remainder of the Middle Ages.

The cessation of the Second Welsh War and the Statute of Rhuddlan (1284) governing the constitutional position of the principality were followed by a campaign of castle building, the most ambitious and costly ever known in British history. Its purpose was to isolate the mountainous core of the principality, together with its dependency of Anglesey, from the rest of the country.

The castle of Deganwy had, before its destruction by Llewelyn ap Gruffydd, stood upon a crag, east of the Conwy. It lay a kilometer from the tideway, was ill-suited to English needs, and was never rebuilt. Instead, Conwy Castle was built on

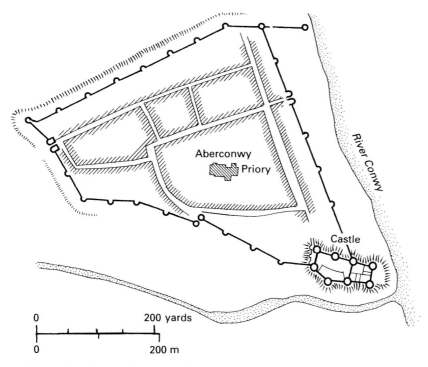

7.6 The castle and town of Conwy. The town walls were contemporary with the castle.

the opposite bank of the river. It occupied a rocky ridge, washed by the waters of the river. The site was a strong one with the added advantage of direct access to shipping and supplies. The work was begun in 1283 and continued into the next century. In the next year a town was established below the castle (Figure 7.6), and in the process the Cistercian house of Aberconwy, burial place of Llewelyn ap Iorworth, was moved up the valley to Maenan.[65] Late in the next year the castle received a permanent garrison, and the castle, together with the town walls, was effectively completed by 1291–2.

The English advance into Gwynedd was both along the coast from Conwy and, by the upper Conwy valley and Dolwyddelan, to the west coast. Here a castle was begun in 1283 at Harlech.[66] Its site, one of the most scenic and formidable in Britain, was a crag which then rose directly from the sea and had access to a small port.[67] At the same time the Welsh Castell y Bere was occupied by the English, who spent a considerable sum on it and then abandoned it. Its site, high on the flanks of Cader Idris, was eminently defensible but it could not be provisioned by sea, nor did it fit into Edward I's strategic plan. This, however, was not the case with Criccieth, a castle probably built by Llewelyn ap Iorworth on a crag beside the sea and only a few kilometres south-west of the mountain fastness of Snowdonia. It was occupied by the English, put into a state of defence and garrisoned.

But the crowning achievement of Edward I's castle-building was Caernarvon. It was, apart from Beaumaris, the last to be commenced and probably the most expensive to construct. The building was probably begun in the summer of 1283, and was sufficiently advanced by April of the following year for Edward of Caernarvon, the first English Prince of Wales, to be born there. It incorporated in its upper ward the motte put up by Earl Hugh of Chester some two centuries earlier. In his building of Caernarvon Castle the king made significant departures from the style of earlier construction. It lay beside a navigable waterway, and was integrated with a planned and walled town.[68] Like Conwy, it consisted of two elongated wards set end to end. But its style marked a new departure. Its towers and turrets were not round, but polygonal, in this resembling the somewhat later work at Denbigh. The masonry, secondly, shows a banded structure, created by the use of contrasted stone. This was an expensive device, and its use must have been carefully considered. A model for this, it is claimed, lay in the Theodosian Wall of Constantinople, which had possibly been seen by some of Edward's entourage. It added in any case to the imperial concept which the castle represented.[69] It may, furthermore, have been not unimportant that the castle lay close to the remains of Roman *Segontium*.[70]

The Edwardian castles of North Wales were nearing completion when the revolt of 1294–5 broke out.[71] Their garrisons were depleted by the king's expedition to Gascony. Several, including Cardigan and Caernarvon, were besieged, but the English control of the sea restricted the spread of the revolt: 'Castles held out as long as provisions could be brought . . . by ship'.[72] Aberystwyth, Conwy and perhaps Criccieth and Harlech were provisioned from Bristol and Ireland. During the winter – not a usual time for campaigning – the king's forces pressed into Gwynedd. Caernarvon was relieved, and in the spring of 1295 work began on the last of Edward's castles, Beaumaris.

The revolt had shown the weakness of the English grip on Anglesey, important as a source of food. The purpose of Beaumaris Castle was to ensure the king's control both of the island and of the coastal shipping routes. The events of the previous months are reflected both in the location of the castle on the shore of the Menai Straits and in the provision of a fortified flour mill and dock, capable of taking the small craft used in the coastal trade, within its fortified perimeter.[73] Beaumaris was geometrically the most perfect of the Edwardian castles, and the skilful engineering of its towers, gates and water defences have never ceased to astonish. Its cost was immense, almost as great as that of Caernarvon, and even so it was left unfinished.

The castle-building of Edward I represented in part an extension and completion of the scheme which he had inherited from his father, in part a well-conceived strategic plan of his own. Over much of Wales and the March he was content to hold and strengthen a relatively small number of strategically placed castles, of which Cardigan, Carmarthen, Aberystwyth, Builth and Montgomery became the most important, but his expenditure on them was small. North Wales was seen to present the greatest danger, and it was here that he concentrated his investment and his efforts. All castles west of Chester, both royal and baronial, had suffered in some

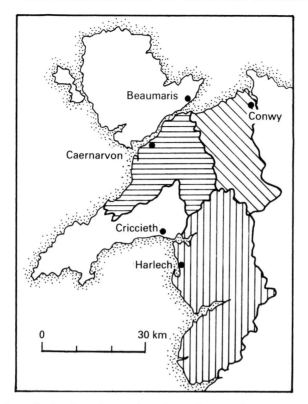

7.7 Areas supplying foodstuffs to the North Wales castles. Based on W. Rees, *An Historical Atlas of Wales*, Cardiff, 1951 and E. A. Lewis, *Medieval Boroughs of Snowdonia*, London, 1912.

measure from Welsh attack. The king's plan was to repair and rebuild where possible and, where not, to build new, more scientifically designed and more carefully located castles. Two of his father's more important castles, Dyserth and Deganwy, were not repaired. Instead, they were replaced respectively by Rhuddlan and Conwy. Flint, in effect, took the place of Hawarden and Mold, but the four great castles of North Wales were built by him *ab initio*.

Edward experienced the greatest difficulty in paying for his building programme. Its true monetary cost cannot be known. For some individual years no record of payments has survived, and for others there are only abbreviated accounts in which expenditure on several is conflated in a single total. A significant part of the cost, furthermore, was borne by the sheriffs who recruited and despatched workmen to the building sites.[74]

Relatively little was paid for building materials beyond the cost of quarrying and transporting them. The quarries themselves were deemed to be regalian, and, since most lay close to the buildings in which their stone was used, transport constituted only a small part of total costs. Out of 2,940 employed at Beaumaris in 1295, only about 160 are estimated to have been carters. This contrasts with the very high transport costs for most important ecclesiastical buildings. The reason lay in the fact that in most instances local stone was used. The masonry was, in the main, roughly coursed rubble, most often of carboniferous limestone or older gritstones, all of them abundant in North Wales. In very few instances is it possible to identify the particular quarries that provided the stone, though in the case of Conwy there can be little doubt that it came from Silurian gritstone quarries on the edge of the town.[75] Caernarvon Castle appears to have drawn much of its limestone and sandstone from quarries in Anglesey, possibly from Penmon, whence it could be taken by boat to the site.

Sir Goronwy Edwards has made a brave attempt to compute the expenditure of Edward I on his Welsh castles. Table 7.1 shows both recorded and estimated expenditure over the whole building period:

Table 7.1. *Recorded and estimated expenditure*

	Recorded	Postulated[a]
Aberystwyth	3,889	
Beaumaris	11,289	13,000
Builth	1,666	
Caernarvon	12,286	16,000
Conwy	13,690	19,000
Criccieth and Bere	571	
Flint	7,022	
Harlech	8,185	
Rhuddlan	9,506	

Note:
[a]Figures have been rounded to the nearest £1,000.

'In short', wrote Sir Goronwy Edwards, 'we may almost certainly take £80,000 as a safe notional figure for the total sum expended by Edward I on his castle-building in Wales'.[76] By contrast, the total royal expenditure from 1154 to 1189 was of the order of only £21,500. Even if one makes allowance for the small degree of inflation during the intervening years, this was an immense outlay within a fairly short period. How was it paid for?

Local resources were quite inadequate for so vast an investment, and the resources of the crown were stretched to the limit. A letter of 1299 reported that workmen were unpaid and that, unless money was made available, they would abscond.[77] In 1296–7 the burgesses of Beaumaris prayed the king for payment of £600 for 'carts and carriage of stone and for ale' owed them.[78] Building workers were at this time paid in coin week by week.[79] Coin for the North Wales operations came in part from Ireland, in part from the incipient government department known as the Wardrobe. The Wardrobe received money from the Exchequer, into which were paid the many and varied receipts of government. It had long been the practice of the crown to earmark certain sources of revenue for specific purposes. A windfall revenue which the crown could occasionally expect to receive was that from episcopal estates during vacancies in the sees. The issues of the see of York went in 1279 to finance the building of Rhuddlan, and those of Winchester in 1280–2 supported work at Flint. The crown derived over £11,000 from the see of Winchester; 'Harlech castle was probably built for less than this, and . . . Conwy for less than twice as much'.[80]

Recruiting workmen was only a degree less difficult than finding money to pay them. Castle construction called for less fine masonry than a church, and there were proportionately more workers whom we can describe as unskilled or semi-skilled. A high proportion of those at Harlech in 1286 were described as *minuti*, and are likely to have been semi-skilled.[81] The king clearly regarded the building as urgent, and very large numbers were employed. Work was, of course, seasonal. Most was done between April and November and, on the evidence of the Harlech account, the winter workforce was less than a fifth of that employed in summer. In the years 1285 to 1287, when work was advancing fairly rapidly, the total employment on Conwy, Caernarvon and Harlech was between 2,200 and 2,700, with the number reduced to around 400 in winter. At Beaumaris in 1295 the numbers employed in summer rose almost to 3,000.

Such a workforce had to be drawn from as far away as Dorset and Devon. Most travelled overland to Chester and were despatched from there to the building sites. Men from the South-west gathered at Bristol, and were taken by sea to Carmarthen, Cardigan and Aberystwyth. There were masons from the stone-belt of the West Country, carpenters from the wooded Midlands and diggers (*fossatores*) from the Fens of Lincolnshire.[82] We do not know what they did during the winter; probably they returned home. Nor do we know how they lived on the sites — probably like other building workers in roughly made 'lodges'. One is surprised that the king was able to obtain so large a workforce. It was large enough 'to constitute a noticeable draught upon the total pool of mobile labour that was available in the England of [the] day'.[83]

The king's representative in North Wales was the Justiciar of Chester, whose base was Chester Castle. Except when the king was present, he had overall charge of operations, and it was from him that constables and master-masons took their instructions. After the Statute of Rhuddlan the Principality ceased to be dependent upon Chester, and acquired a royal representative of its own, the Justiciar of North Wales, whose seat was Caernarvon Castle.[84] The chain of command in the construction of the Welsh castles is far from clear. On each site there would have been a *magister cementarius* who combined the duties of supervisor of the works with that of architect. In the latter respect, however, he was far from having a free hand. Every master-mason received instructions, more or less detailed, from his employer. His task was to translate these general instructions into more detailed plans. But who gave these general instructions to the master-mason? In the case of the North Wales castles it was Master James of St George. He is well documented, but remains a somewhat enigmatic figure. He is variously described as 'mazun' (mason) and 'ingeniator' (engineer), which in this context means maker of military works.[85] It has been convincingly argued that he was the same as that *Magister Iacobus latomus* who was employed by the Count of Savoy on his castle and town of Yverdon and other works in Savoy and Vaud.[86] Count Philip of Savoy was a relative and friend of the English king, and Edward had himself visited the Count's newly built castle of St George-d'Espéranche on his return from crusade in 1273. Whether Edward met Master James on this occasion is not known, but James, along with other Savoyard craftsmen, followed him to England where they were employed from 1278 on the king's castles in mid- and North Wales. His status is measured by the fact that he received 1s a day with an additional shilling when travelling. We first find him at Flint and Rhuddlan where he appears to have served as master-mason. It was from here that he made an expedition to Aberystwyth apparently to advise on its rebuilding after the raid of 1272 (see p. 167).

It was after the Second Welsh War of 1282–3 that his greatest work began, the planning and construction of the four castles of Conwy, Caernarvon, Harlech and Beaumaris. These, with the exception only of Caernarvon, display a uniformity of concept and style which strongly suggests a single controlling authority. Furthermore, Arnold Taylor has demonstrated that stylistic traits found in these castles can be seen also in the Savoyard castles associated with Master James. All consist of a roughly square ward with round corner towers and a massive gatehouse. There was, indeed, nothing unusual in such a plan at this date, but the same building tricks: helical putlog holes in round towers, oblique putlogs in curtain walls, a belated use of round arches, the style and size of windows, and the placement of garderobes, all betray the hand of the master. In detail Caernarvon Castle differed significantly from the others, but there is no reason to doubt that it was designed by Master James. Its stylistic features were 'a deliberate and conscious adornment, introduced at the royal will, of a building intended from its inception to become the principal seat of English power in North Wales'.[87]

The Scottish Borders

The third source of danger to the English realm lay in Scotland. But the nature of this threat was radically different from that posed by Wales, and the organisation of defence followed different lines. The Borders were remote from the centre of power in England. English kings rarely travelled north of the Trent, and when they did so their journeys were more like military expeditions than their peaceful perambulations around England. They were generally content to leave northern England to its local barons, who were, well into the thirteenth century, more backward-looking, more feudal and economically less developed than their contemporaries in the South. The barons of the Welsh March may have been a law to themselves within their lordships, but they were English barons; many held land in England as well, and they participated fully in English affairs. This cannot in general be said of the northern barons.

The border with Scotland was, in physical terms, far less clearcut than that with Wales. The Pennine uplands formed a spine through northern England. They had few perceptible gaps other than those guarded by castles like Brough, Bowes and Skipton, and for much of their length they interposed a formidable barrier between the lowland routes to west and east. The former, furthermore, was blocked by the Lake District fells, and only to the east, from Yorkshire, through Durham and Northumberland, was there a relatively easy route between England and Scotland. In late Anglo-Saxon times the Scottish kingdom of Strathclyde had reached south of the Solway as far as Rere or Rea Cross on Stainmore, below which Brough Castle was later built. On the other hand the Saxon kingdom of Northumbria had reached beyond the Tweed and the Borders as far as the Lothians.[88] On the west Rufus had advanced his authority to the Solway and founded the castle of Carlisle (see p. 43). East of the Pennines, the Conqueror had himself advanced into Scotland, made the earldom of Northumberland dependent on himself and built the first castles at Newcastle and Durham.

A line approximating to the present Anglo-Scottish boundary came to be accepted by both sides, probably in the early twelfth century. When in 1138 King David of Scotland reoccupied both Cumberland and Northumberland he held these lands as a vassal of the English king. In 1157 Henry II forced Malcolm IV to give them up. This involved no expedition or military conquest; merely a change in feudal obligation. In the meanwhile the idea had taken hold of a firm boundary between England and Scotland, whatever the feudal loyalties might be on each side. The line ran up the Tweed from Berwick to a point above Coldstream and thence along the summit of the Cheviot Hills to the Solway Plain. The Bishop of Durham built his castle of Norham beside the Tweed on the border between the two kingdoms,[89] and when the Treaty of York was negotiated between the two kingdoms in 1237 the Tweed–Cheviot line was 'by then an old established institution'.[90]

But the presence of a generally known and mutually acceptable boundary did nothing for the peace of the Borders. Underlying social conditions made warfare endemic.[91] This was a poor land, capable of supporting its population only at a low level of welfare. Political authority in the shape of English and Scottish kingship was distant and ineffective, and the Borders were by and large left to themselves. The constant raiding and pillage within the Borders masked a fundamental unity. The barons who had been granted lordships in northern England were, as a general rule, small men, and with few exceptions, of which Percy of Alnwick became the most significant, they held no lands in the south of England, as the barons of the Welsh March did. They did not feel drawn into English affairs. Instead their 'frontier' lay to the north, and it was into Scotland that they spread when, in the twelfth century, they felt the need for more land.[92] The Scottish lowland families of Stewart, Lindsey and Oliphant all derived from south of the Border, and England's most important contribution to Scottish history was the families of Brus and Balliol, which long bestrode the boundary between the two countries.

Kings, both Scottish and English, could afford for much of the time to leave the Border lords to their own devices. Indeed, the English court seems to have known very little about local political and social conditions, and its directives sometimes seem to have been thoroughly ill conceived. Yet there were similarities to the March of Wales. Lordships may, with few exceptions, have been small, but they were compact, easily managed and to that extent politically more powerful. Beyond northern Yorkshire and Lancashire they were established later than in the South.[93] The barony of Liddel was established astride the Scottish boundary in the middle years of the twelfth century, and its great motte – Liddel Strength – presumably built at this time. The barony of Langley on the high ground of the northern Pennines came even later.[94] Lordships in northern Lancashire and Cumbria were established after Rufus' foundation of Carlisle Castle.[95] East of the Pennines a 'line of baronies running to the Tweed' was established.[96] They lay along the belt of lowland between the Pennines and the sea: Prudhoe, Morpeth, Mitford, Warkworth, Alnwick, Ellingham, Embleton, Bolam, Bothal, to end with the Ros honour of Wark-upon-Tweed, each with its stronghold on the invasion path most often used by the Scots.

To the west the 'great waste' of the Cheviot Hills and northern Pennines gave an uncertain protection to the lordships in the lowland region of Northumberland. Their population and resources were slight, but they offered a route, secure because it was unobserved, from Teviotdale and the Merse into Northumberland. Here the Norman lords pushed up the valleys of the Coquet, Rede and North Tyne, attracted, not by the resources of this region, which were small indeed, but by their need for castles from which raiders might be controlled. Such castles as Harbottle, Elsdon, Wark-in-Tynedale were small, but remarkably strong. At no time was the failure of the English government to comprehend conditions in the North more conspicuous than in the early years of the thirteenth century, when Hubert de Burgh attempted to apply here his policy of reducing the number and strength of baronial castles. Richard de Umfraville, lord of Prudhoe, was ordered to destroy his castle of Harbottle, high up in the Coquet valley. He replied 'that the castle was usefully planted on the Marches of Scotland towards the Great Waste'.[97] At about the same time the same Richard de Umfraville, who showed himself so jealous of his castle of Harbottle, lodged a complaint against his neighbour, Philip de Ulecotes, who had, without licence, begun to fortify his castle at Nafferton.[98] The king, in total ignorance of the local situation, concurred and the castle was destroyed;[99] the masonry tower which now occupies part of the site was built in next century (see p. 104).

Protection of England from Scottish raids devolved, by and large, on the castles which had been built throughout the Borders region. Even churches – in particular church towers – were built for defence against a sudden raid.[100] Yet the role of the king in occupying or building castles was, in comparison with Wales and the March, relatively small. Newcastle was established about 1080 by the Conqueror, and Carlisle by Rufus. Durham Castle was established by the Conqueror about 1072 and at once entrusted to the Bishop of Durham. Bamburgh was taken by Rufus after a siege in 1095, and remained a crown possession. Only one castle, Bowes, in the south-west corner of County Durham, was subsequently built by the English king north of Yorkshire and Lancashire. For the rest defence was left to the local barons, who on the whole performed their task well.

The settlement of northern barons within Scotland meant the early introduction of elements of feudalism there.[101] Lowland Scotland became dotted with castles, and one can discern 'in simpler and looser form, a lively and vigorous replica of the system which prevailed in England'.[102] The Scottish kings had occupied Cumbria and Northumberland from 1138 to 1157, and until 1237 cherished a vague claim to all lands north of the Tees. Even after this the Scottish king held the honour of Tynedale with the castle of Wark-on-Tyne, as well as the manor of Penrith. Northern barons intermarried with Scottish, and Henry III's daughter, Margaret, had married Alexander III of Scotland. Alexander died in 1285, and was succeeded by his granddaughter, Margaret of Norway. The English kings had long claimed to be overlords of Scotland, a pretension which was grudgingly admitted. At this juncture it seemed that a union of the two crowns might be effected without invasion or conquest. In March 1290 a marriage was arranged between the young Queen Margaret and Edward of Caernarvon, Edward I's eldest son, even though both were still children. In the course of the haggling which preceded the agreement Edward I demanded that the chief Scottish castles be placed under his control, and the Scots countered with a demand that nothing be done to strengthen castles on the English side of the Border. It is evident that holding castles was still seen as the only way to control territory. For the rest, the boundary was left unchanged; English overlordship was to continue, but the two crowns were to remain separate. A form of 'dual monarchy' was envisaged.

In the autumn of 1290 the young queen died and the Scottish succession was wide open. The contenders were the descendants of the three daughters of Earl David of Huntingdon, brother of King William 'the Lion'. They were John Balliol, Robert Bruce and John Hastings of Abergavenny, all of them with close English ties.[103] A commission, in part nominated by the English king, opted for John Balliol, who did homage for his kingdom and assumed the rule of Scotland. But differences between the two kingdoms continued and were exacerbated by the growing closeness of their relations. Most were matters of feudal jurisdiction and obligation, but in 1295 Balliol rashly allied himself with the king of France, and Edward I, outraged by his conduct, set about asserting his rights as 'overlord' and invaded Scotland. Scottish castles, including those of Edinburgh, Roxburgh and the Merse, surrendered. Lowland Scotland was overrun and Balliol found refuge in exile.

The English king began to strengthen the Borders, placing garrisons in the more important castles. But English control was short-lived.[104] In 1297 a Scottish rising under Wallace not only defeated the English and drove them from Scotland but even led to an invasion of England. The castles of Roxburgh and Berwick, which Edward had garrisoned, held out, and became the foci of his second invasion. Again Scotland was overrun but never subdued. Some effort was made to repair and garrison castles. But work on them was hurried, and much of the construction was in wood. The castle of Dumfries was strengthened; small sums were spent at Edinburgh and Linlithgow was turned from a sumptuous manor house into a castle. It was in this context that James of St George was summoned from Wales to the Borders to advise on construction.[105] The king's plan at first included a masonry-built gatehouse, with twin towers, such as he was accustomed to build in Wales. This plan was not pursued, and in the end Linlithgow Castle came to depend on a wooden palisade and water defences.[106] At the same time the castles of Selkirk, Kirkintilloch and Dumbarton were strengthened, and the Scottish fortresses at Bothwell and Stirling taken, after prolonged sieges. New castles were built in the Lowlands at Tullibody, Inverkeithing and Polmaise but they appear to have been feeble structures. In the building accounts which survive there is record of payments to diggers and carpenters but of very little to masons.[107] Despite the presence of James of St George and of other experienced craftsmen, Edward's programme in Scotland and the Borders was poorly conceived, badly executed and technically backward looking. In the course of the next Scottish rising most of the castles which the English had strengthened and garrisoned were lost, and it became the policy of Robert Bruce so to destroy them that the 'English might never again be able to lord it over the land through holding its castles'.[108] The last attempt of Edward I to reimpose his will on Scotland ended with his death at Burgh-by-Sands as he was about to cross the boundary.

Edward II led an invasion in 1310 and a more serious attempt in 1314 ended in disaster and humiliation. Bruce continued to mop up castles in the Lowlands and the Borders until in 1328 the English king abandoned his claim to overlordship. Nonetheless Edward III, in 1333, attacked Berwick and again attempted to put his protégé Edward Balliol on the Scottish throne. He won a battle outside Berwick, but failed to make Balliol king or to suppress Scottish resistence. His resources were barely adequate to holding the more important castles. In 1337 his attention was diverted by the more attractive lure of the French crown, and he turned his back on Scotland. English garrisons were one by one reduced and the boundary restored more or less to its traditional line.

But warfare between the English and the Scots did not end. Only its character changed. It ceased to be a war between two kings, and became one between their peoples. Previously Scottish incursions into northern England had been led or at least authorised by the kings of Scotland. Henceforward raids in both directions were by small bands, acting wholly on their own. Their purpose ceased to be the assertion of sovereign rights; rather the acquisition of booty. The era of the moss-trooper had dawned and was to continue even after the personal union of the two kingdoms in 1603. With the change in the character of war came a shift in the structure and function of the castle.

The king of England was, however, able to retain for most of the Middle Ages two significant castles lying north of the Tweed. The castle of Berwick had been first built by the Scots on a steep bluff above the north bank of the Tweed. Together with the town, it fell into English hands in 1296. Frantic efforts were made to put the town into a state of defence and to strengthen the castle, which lay to the west of the town and separated from it by a deep gully. In 1318, however, it fell to the Scots. Edward III retook the town and castle after the battle of Hallidon Hill in 1333. After this the Scots ravaged the town and even took the castle, but were eventually driven back.

The other castle which the English kings strove to keep in their own possession was Roxburgh. It had been held for a few years by Henry III, but remained in Scottish hands until the attack by Edward I in 1296. By this date it was a strong, masonry-built castle with a tower-keep, and Edward does not appear to have found it necessary to make any significant changes or additions. Nevertheless, it fell to Bruce in 1314 and was, according to the Lanercost chronicler, destroyed.[109] After his reoccupation of Berwick in 1333 Edward III moved on Roxburgh, which he refortified with a wooden peel or tower which he had brought in pieces from Newcastle-upon-Tyne.[110] A large sum was spent on rebuilding it, and the fragmentary remains seen today belong mainly to this period. Work continued through the fourteenth century, and, although still incomplete at the beginning of the fifteenth, it was able to repel Scottish attacks in 1417 and again in 1436. At last, in 1460, when England was preoccupied with its own internal strife, Roxburgh Castle fell to the Scots.

The English failure in Scotland contrasts with the success of the Welsh campaigns of the 1270–80s, and the contrast is difficult to explain. Scotland was distant. Even from Newcastle-upon-Tyne it was a very long journey to the Scottish Lowlands. Furthermore, Scotland, even southern Scotland, was much larger than Wales, and the lie of the hills and valleys, which in Wales had opened the country to the invader, presented in Scotland a far more formidable barrier. Less was spent on the Scottish wars than on the Welsh, and the former came late in the life of Edward I, the only king who might have prosecuted them with success. It has been pointed out that in Wales the key to the English success lay in expensive castle-building. No such expenditure was ever made in Scotland. Most of the castles were taken over from the Scots and refurbished. When a castle was extensively rebuilt, as was Roxburgh, the cost was only a fraction of what was spent on the least of the Edwardian fortresses of North Wales.[111]

It has already been noted that only a relatively small part of total construction costs was expended on masons and masonry. By contrast, the cost of hauling timber and the wages of carpenters were high. The Edwardian castles in Scotland were, by and large, of wood, and their ability to resist the onslaught of the Scots was limited. 'In Wales', in Colvin's words, 'he had built in stone on sites carefully chosen for their strategic value: but in Scotland he built chiefly in timber in places already marked by tower and moat'.[112]

CHAPTER 8

Castle and community

I seigh a tour on a toft trieliche ymaked,
A deep dale bynethe, a dongeon therinne,
With depe diches and derke and dredfulle of sighte
A fairfeeld ful of folk fond I ther bitwene –
Of alle manere of men, the meene and the riche,
Werchynge and wandrynge as the world asketh

Piers Plowman, B Text, Prologue, §§14–19

No castle ever stood in isolation. It was always part of a community. Indeed, there were two communities: the one within the castle, the other surrounding it and forming its milieu. Their mutual relations were marked by both interdependence and animosity. How did the people of the town or village view the castle? Was their fear of it modified by their dependence on it for protection and employment? Above all, what were the institutional relations between community and castle? Was the former obligated to perform services or to provide goods? What kind of jurisdiction did the lord of the castle claim over the community, and how did the latter, as it strove for some kind of independence, come to define both its boundaries and its rights? These questions are not easy to answer, and they can be addressed with some degree of assurance only for well-documented royal castles.

The community of the castle

Much is known of those who lived and worked within royal castles, because their duties were defined and their wages paid by exchequer, wardrobe or sheriff. The castle, whatever its size and status, served three purposes. It was home to its lord, or his constable. There were often guests, welcome or more often not, who had to be accommodated and entertained, and there were servants who formed the least visible part of the castle community. The castle, secondly, was a protected place. It was capable of being defended, and for this purpose had, or could call on, soldiers of some kind. The third function which the castle fulfilled was adminstrative. It is difficult to point to any castle, before the construction of coastal defences in the later years of the fourteenth century, which did not control, in a legal rather than a military sense, some area of land. Edward III's building of Queenborough Castle, Kent, in 1361 may be said to mark the beginning of the purely military castle (see p. 256).

The relative importance of these functions varied greatly. Among the Edwardian castles of North Wales the military function predominated, but a castle such as Denbigh was also the centre of an important lordship,[1] and Caernarvon was the seat of the Justiciar and centre of administration of the Principality.[2] These castles, and others built at this time, were 'home' to the constable and other officials during their tenure of office, as well as to servants, retainers and garrison. In royal castles in the heart of England, such as Northampton, Cambridge, Oxford and Norwich, the administrative function was the most important. They were the centre of county government, where the sheriff presided, the county court met and itinerant justices held their assize. But most castles belonged to the baronage, and were home for at least part of the time to a baronial or knightly family. All private castles, however, shared in the other functions. They provided protection and they were the centres of manorial control, where the manorial court was accustomed to meet 'from three weeks to three weeks'.

The internal arrangements of a castle reflect the functions which it was intended to serve. Where the military risk was great, as it was in the Marches, North Wales and the Scottish Borders and along much of the eastern and southern coasts, the walls were proportionately more substantial; mural towers more numerous and carefully located; and entrances more jealously protected with portcullis, *meurtrières* and 'turning' bridge. Greater provision was made for storing food and weapons and for milling grain and procuring water during siege.

But, whatever the paramount functions of a castle, it invariably contained domestic apartments and facilities. There had, in the first place, to be a hall, the focus of life within the castle, where the community ate, and a significant part of it was accustomed to sleep. At the two ends of the hall and accessible from it there were respectively private apartments for the lord, and a kitchen, buttery and pantry where food could be stored and prepared. Our concept of these domestic apartments may have been coloured by what we know of the unfortified manor house. Castle and manor house are, indeed, likely to have been broadly similar, since this was the way in which the upper classes were accumstomed to live. In a castle, however, there were constraints on space. The hall *may* have been smaller than in an unfortified manor house, the kitchen facilities less generous, and private apartments less numerous.

In early motte-and-bailey castles these buildings are likely to have been of wood, which has perished, leaving at most anonymous postholes. If the defences were of wood, it is extremely unlikely that masonry would have been used for domestic buildings except, perhaps, as sills or pads for the uprights.[3] Unfortunately, very little has survived of the domestic arrangements in the earlier castles. One needs to know how and to what extent life was divided between the building on the summit of the motte and those scattered around the bailey. Did the lord sleep, eat and attend to manorial affairs in the security of his wooden tower or did he enjoy somewhat more spacious surroundings in the bailey? To this archaeology has supplied no answer. It can only be said that in the very few instances where the motte has been excavated little evidence for domestic life has been found. On the other hand, the description of the collapse of the wooden bridge leading to the motte at Thérouanne as the bishop and his retainers were crossing, suggests that the motte was intended for more than occasional use.[4] More to the point is the description of the house built on the motte of the Count of Guisnes at Ardres in Flanders.[5] It was of wood and consisted of three storeys. On the ground floor 'were cellars and granaries, and great boxes, tins, casks and other domestic utensils'. Above were the living rooms and chambers and on the second storey the children and retainers had their sleeping quarters. Adjacent to the wooden tower was a kitchen. This must have been an unusually elaborate structure, and could have been built only on a motte of considerable breadth. But this account was written late in the twelfth century, when expectations had been greatly raised above the level of a century earlier. Most mottes would have been far too small for so ambitious a 'house', but there can be little doubt that in many of them a house was to be found.

The masonry tower-keep gave greater scope for domesticity. Indeed, most appear to have been organised rather like the wooden tower at Ardres. On the ground floor, protected by thick walls, were stores, even though most keeps lacked a ground-floor entrance and the basement had to be reached from above. At Goodrich Castle, the first-floor entrance, reached by some kind of wooden steps, was at a later date closed up and replaced at the ground level. The first floor was, as a general rule, the hall. It had windows, albeit narrow ones; it may, if large enough, have been divided by a cross wall into hall and solar. There was some sophistication in the decoration at this level. In Norwich Castle the entrance was by a decorated arch of several orders. At Castle Hedingham both the first and second storeys – there are altogether four floors in this lofty tower-keep – have a grand, oversailing arch and both window openings and fireplace are finely decorated with chevron mouldings.[6] At a number of other such keeps the principal apartments have elaborate decoration.

Except on the largest mottes, and in the most generously proportioned tower-keeps, life tended to gravitate towards the bailey in the course of the twelfth century. There can be no doubt but that buildings within the bailey at this time were timber framed.[7] The casual finds of sherds, nails and other metal work give a faint indication of the quality of life lived here. At Hen Domen, the bailey proved to have been crowded with timber-framed buildings. They were not all contemporary, for the castle was occupied from soon after the Conquest until the latter part of the thirteenth century. There is a presumption that one of the more massive structures was, in fact, a first-floor hall.

Fortunately a masonry-built hall was erected at some castles at an early date, and has survived. First in point of time must be Scolland's Hall in Richmond Castle. It was built before the end of the eleventh century and was contemporary with or even earlier than the great tower gatehouse. It was a first-floor hall and was built, presumably for greater protection, on the very edge of the steep cliff which drops to the river Swale. At Christchurch (Hampshire), a somewhat similar first-floor hall was built freestanding *within* the bailey. At both Leicester and Oakham an aisled hall

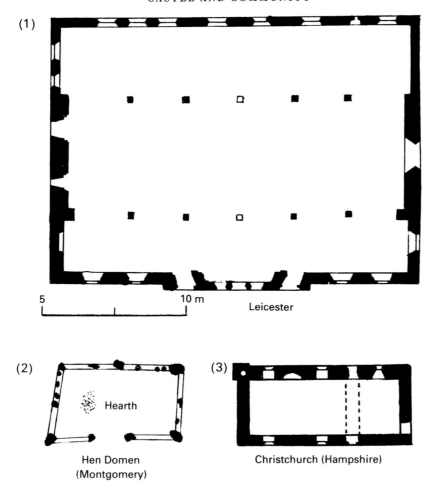

(1)

5   10 m   Leicester

(2)   (3)

Hearth

Hen Domen   Christchurch (Hampshire)
(Montgomery)

8.1 Examples of freestanding castle halls. These may be regarded as typical respectively of (1) a large royal or baronial castle, (2) a minor masonry baronial castle, (3) an earthwork and timber castle.

was built in the bailey during the twelfth century. Enough of the former survives, though in mutilated form, to show how large and magnificent a structure it was.[8] It measured 25.5 m by 17.6 m, and its roof, which is claimed to be original, was supported by a double arcade of timber pillars. The Oakham hall has survived more nearly intact. It is an aisled hall but smaller than that of Leicester. But the finest surviving castle hall is, without question, that of Winchester Castle. It was built 1222–35 and replaced an earlier hall.[9] Its overall measurements are 33.8 m by 16.8 m, making it the largest hall of this date after Westminster Hall.

During the thirteenth century the restricted accommodation within the keep or on the motte was increasingly supplemented or replaced by more generously planned apartments in the bailey. In the earliest instances, including those already

187

cited, the hall was freestanding, perhaps because the perimeter wall was of timber supported by an earthen rampart. But with the building of a masonry wall around the bailey it became the practice to build the hall against it and even to light it by means of windows cut through the outer wall. Space does not permit any listing of such halls of the thirteenth and fourteenth century, and a few examples must suffice. That at Carisbrooke Castle was built before 1200, and at Brough in Westmorland the earliest hall in the bailey must have been built very soon after the tower-keep at the other end of the castle. This was in turn replaced by a first-floor hall.

One must ask whether the keep or motte was abandoned with the building of apartments in the bailey, and to this there is no ready answer. At Winchester Castle the hall in the 'tower' continued to be used long after a hall had been built in the bailey.[10] On the other hand, there are frequent references in official records to the decayed condition of the 'great tower'. At Newcastle, where the sheriff had recently spent a large sum on the hall in the bailey, the keep was roofless, and he sought instructions on what to do with it.[11]

On the other hand, there were castles where a separate hall seems never to have been built in the bailey. At Castle Rising life appears always to have been focussed in its huge and highly decorated keep,[12] and at the Earl of Cornwall's castle of Restormel domestic buildings were concentrated in the shell-keep.[13]

The building of a hall in the bailey faced certain problems. As a general rule the bailey was too small for a freestanding hall–solar–kitchen block, and the hall was built *against* the perimeter wall. Since this was rarely straight the hall itself was likely to be curved in plan. The single-aisled hall at Conisborough Castle, Yorkshire, is also skewed in this way[14] as is the hall at White Castle, Monmouthshire.[15] But the extreme case is provided by Restormel Castle, where hall, kitchen, solar and chambers form an almost perfect circle. At Grosmont, Monmouthshire, the earliest masonry building was a first-floor hall which largely survives and is well known for its highly decorative chimney. The polygonal court was later grafted on to the south-west side of the hall, whose other walls thus came to constitute the outside walls of this important little castle.[16]

The hall would have been lighted by windows on one or both sides. Even when built against a bailey wall there were often windows on this side, small and raised as high above the ground as possible. Those opening into the bailey were commonly more generous. But much depended on whether they were glazed. Before the sixteenth century, glass was relatively expensive and sparing use was made of it in secular buildings. Generally speaking, large glazed windows are found only in the halls of royal and important baronial castles, and it is, by and large, only these that have survived. Ludlow Castle hall has large windows facing into the inner bailey and smaller ones towards the field. At the nearby castle of Stokesay the hall has large windows, low to the ground even in the outer wall, which seem almost to invite an intruder, but Stokesay was rather a pretentious manor house than a castle. Most halls, especially if they were timber framed, would have had small window openings, unglazed, but capable of being closed by wooden shutters or grills.

Most castle halls would have been sparsely furnished. An inventory of the goods in the hall of Haverford Castle in 1334–5 listed only a table, three pairs of trestles and six forms.[17] A similar inventory of 'dead stock' at Narberth Castle listed amongst hall furniture only tables, trestles and benches,[18] and at Pembroke Castle there were 'three tables in the hall' together with trestles and benches.[19] The Chamberlain of Chester's accounts show payment for repairing the 'benches of the great hall with stone'. These must have been along the walls of the hall, like the stone benches sometimes found in churches.[20] The floor was strewn with rushes, regularly renewed. At Windsor Castle two cartloads were taken to the castle each week.[21] There would have been a central hearth, the smoke escaping through louvres in the roof. The roof trusses supported a covering of slate, stone, lead or, towards the end of the Middle Ages, clay tiles. But in humbler castles great use was made of thatch, which had the grave disadvantage that it could readily be set alight.

By the end of the twelfth century it was becoming the practice to build a fireplace into the wall of the hall, replacing the central hearth. The earliest surviving fireplace is probably that in Colchester Castle. Here the flue ascends obliquely in the thickness of the wall for only about 4.3 m before discharging through a loop in the exterior wall. When a fireplace was built in the keep of Conisborough Castle, late in the twelfth century, the flue was made to rise in the wall to the fighting platform at the top and to terminate in a chimney.[22] Twelfth-century fireplaces, some with a high degree of decoration, survive in the keeps of Rochester and Hedingham.

The hall rarely stood alone. It was linked closely with both the kitchen and the private chambers of the lord. An independent kitchen was a relatively late development, and was in military architecture a feature more of the thirteenth than of the twelfth century. At Hen Domen the only evidence for cooking was a hearth in the middle of the hall floor, and this arrangement must at first have prevailed universally. Doubtless cooking was also done in the open in the bailey. In the course of the thirteenth century the preparation of food, in all except the humblest castles, moved to a separate kitchen. On a manor it might have been freestanding, owing to the danger of fire. In the restricted space of a castle this was rarely possible, though an oven was sometimes built separate from other buildings. The oven was, as a general rule, dome-shaped and round. It was heated by burning brushwood within it. This was raked out, and the prepared dough was placed on the hot oven floor. The oven was a serious fire hazard, which explains its frequent isolation from the hall–kitchen complex. In larger castles, and it is to these that most of the evidence relates, a bakehouse and brewhouse began to be separated from the kitchen. A list of work carried out at Montgomery Castle about 1250 included repairing the kitchen and bakehouse, in the latter of which a new oven was constructed.[23] The context suggests that these structures were of masonry, and at Chester also the kitchen, together with an adjacent chamber, was of stone.[24] Kitchen equipment was very restricted, consisting of little more than cooking pots – *olla enea* (cauldron) and *cacaba* (cooking pot) – which could be set amid the ashes of the hearth, and large spoons doubtless for serving the gruel which was the chief ingredient of a meal.[25] At

Chepstow Castle a list of household gear included *3 ollas eneas cum 1 broche de ferro* (spit).[26] Though rarely mentioned in inventories, some form of spit must have been present in every fireplace and on every hearth. Most inventories, however, show a marked poverty of movable goods.[27]

The private chambers of the lord were, as a general rule, placed near the 'head' of the hall, but practice varied with the configuration of the space available. In a hall keep, as at Castle Rising, they were beside the hall, separated from it by the cross-wall of the keep. In a tower-keep they were more likely to be placed on the floor above the hall. But once this accommodation had been moved to the bailey it was generally possible to adopt the position familiar in medieval manor houses. At Ludlow Castle, the thirteenth-century hall was built against the north wall of the inner bailey, with a solar block of two storeys above a vaulted undercroft at the east end of the hall. And this plan is repeated in dozens of castles built or remodelled during the thirteenth and fourteenth centuries. At Newcastle-upon-Tyne, about 1338, one of the king's clerks petitioned for the settlement of an account of over £100 expended on rebuilding the hall and roofing it with lead, retimbering 'a chamber abutting the hall, heighten[ing] and lead[ing] [roofing] a kitchen . . . retimbering the Queen's chamber . . . [building] a new chamber at the end of the hall . . . [and] a new chamber above the postern gate . . . with a chimney and garderobe chute'.[28] By this date, early in the fourteenth century, a fireplace had become normal in the private chambers of the rich as well as in their halls.

Once the preparation of food had been relegated to a separate kitchen, the hearth served only to provide warmth, and was, in an increasing number of cases, moved to the side wall. The thirteenth century was marked by the construction of fireplaces, with chimneys in the thickness of a wall, in the solars where the lords came increasingly to enjoy some measure of privacy.

The provision of toilet facilities, euphemistically termed 'garderobes' in the literature, assumed a greater importance in the confined space of a castle than in a manor house or village. How they were contrived in timber-built castles can only be guessed; no evidence has been found for cesspits or soakaways. In a masonry-built castle the garderobe was a small room within or projecting from an outside wall, with a chute usually corbelled out over the ditch or moat. Occasionally, as in the keep of Orford Castle, they merely discharged excreta into the bailey, from which, one hopes, it was collected at frequent intervals. The provision of such facilities was often surprisingly generous, and a garderobe was sometimes built *en suite* with a chamber. In the course of extensive rebuilding at Nottingham Castle about 1230 the queen's wardrobe was ordered to be enlarged, 'a privy chamber to be made by the queen's chamber where the privy chamber, of the long chamber by the hall now is . . . [with] another privy chamber [and] a privy chamber between the said house [. . .] and the chamber of the king's chaplains'.[29] At about the same time a fireplace and a privy chamber were ordered to be built at Winchester Castle.[30] Garderobe chutes remain amongst the most numerous and conspicuous excrescences on the external walls of a castle.

8.2 The garderobe outlet in the keep of Orford Castle, Suffolk.

All castles found an internal source of water necessary. Most often this was a well lined with masonry. Most of the great hall- and tower-keeps had a well reached from the basement. In some cases, Rochester for example, the well shaft was carried upwards in the thickness of the cross-wall, so that water could be obtained at each floor level. Building accounts show small but frequent expenditures on repairs to the well and on renewing the bucket and rope.[31] The Justice of Chester was ordered in 1242 to provide a well in Rhuddlan Castle, 'so that the water in the castle cannot be taken away'.[32] At Sarum a house was erected over the well, with a wheel to draw water;[33] at Flint a 'trendell' (windlass?) was installed;[34] and at Abergavenny a wheel required mending 'above the water pit'.[35] One wonders how sanitary this source of supply was. At Bamburgh, it was reported, two of the three wells ran dry in summer, and the garrison was then accustomed to draw water from a third, which lay outside the walls, within the hospital of Le Maudeley,[36] and was reached by a postern.[37] In more elaborately constructed hydraulic systems water was conducted by pipes to various parts of the castle. At Chester Castle there was a leaden conduit from the well in the outer bailey to a cistern 'in the small kitchen on the east side of the great hall'.[38] At Windsor Castle the water-supply system was far more elaborate. A cistern was made within the motte so that *totam pluviam cadentem super eandam motam circumquaque recipiat*.[39] It was from here, presumably, that water was supplied to a

8.3 Rochester Castle, the cross-wall of the keep, with (centre) the opening to the well shaft. The latter was accessible from each floor of the keep.

cistern (*puteum*) in the upper bailey whence 'it was fed to the kitchen'.[40] At about the same time water from a spring in the 'court by the tower' was ordered to be conducted to the 'door of the king's hall' where it was supplemented by water from the cistern in the great tower.[41] Few water-supply systems can have been as complex as that introduced by Henry III at Windsor Castle, though the same monarch had a piped water supply in his palace at Westminster.[42]

The business of storing and preparing food in a castle differed from that in a manor house only in the need to feed larger numbers and to hold bigger supplies in store. There was, at least in the larger castles, a bakehouse and brewhouse separate from the kitchen. Bread grains constituted the principal food. Since they could not be kept for any long period after milling, it was necessary to be able to grind at frequent intervals. There were thus few castles that did not possess in their close vicinity a water-driven corn mill.

The castle mill constituted a perennial problem. It was a flimsy construction, almost certainly of wood,[43] liable to rot or be swept away by floods. At Abergavenny a carpenter was paid only 5 marks for building a mill on the river Usk below the castle. The 'king's mill below the castle'[44] at Nottingham required frequent repairs,[45] and the Castle Mill at York was a never-ending burden because it suffered from the floods of both the Ouse and the Fosse.[46] At Colchester there was 'a mill under the castle called "Midelmelne"' as early as 1100,[47] and at Ludgershall, Marlborough, Bristol, Oxford and almost every royal castle there is record of a castle mill nearby. The difficulty of maintaining a castle mill, coupled with the fact that only rarely could the castle make full use of it, led to its being 'farmed' to a miller who paid a rent and made what profit he could. That at Marlborough Castle was, for example, let at 40s a year and the mill by the castle of Hereford was worth 20s.[48] At Windsor there were mills in the Great Park, for which two millstones were ordered.[49]

The castle mill was, of necessity, outside the limits of the castle, and no reliance could be placed on it in time of danger. It was therefore supplemented by other and generally simpler devices within the castle. There is some evidence for the use of a windmill mounted on the walls.[50] Occasionally a horse-mill was used. At Pembroke Castle 'the house of the horse-mill [*molendini equinii*] . . . through defective roofing has decayed to the extent of 10s 8d'.[51] There was a horse-mill in the castle of Deganwy, which could not conceivably have had access to a water-mill.[52] At Nottingham Castle a horse-mill supplemented the water-mill, but was ordered to be demolished to make way for other buildings.[53] At Windsor Castle, where Henry III seems never to have left anything to chance, there were, in addition to the mill in the Park, 'a horse-mill and four hand-mills'.[54] Hand-mills, or querns, were the most important supplement to the water-mill, and were a necessary furnishing of castles exposed to danger. In 1301–2, the Chamberlain of Chester acquired 'five pairs of hand millstones' at the cost of 7s for the castles under his charge.[55] A quern was provided for Dryslwyn Castle, which, like Deganwy, can have had no access to a water-mill.[56] A *mola manuali* was bought for Carmarthen Castle for 1s 6d *quia in partibus walliae difficili huius modi mola inuenitur*.[57]

An inquest found in Scarborough Castle ten 'querenstones' which had become valueless with age. A good millstone retained its rough surface, but many became smooth with wear, and had to be discarded. Millstones were expensive – the best of them were brought from the Rhineland, and at Porchester Castle 40s was paid for one.[58] On the other hand only 20d was paid for two at Cambridge Castle;[59] they must have been of inferior stone.

In a very few cases it was possible to enclose a water-mill within the defended area. Such a mill was built into the dam which held the lake around Caerphilly

Castle. At Leeds Castle was a defended mill close to the gatehouse,[60] and at Beaumaris a mill was built close to the well-protected dock.[61]

The structures already discussed by no means exhaust those found in the bailey. Surveys conducted in response to royal inquisitions give some idea of their range. An extent of Fotheringhay recorded a castle 'well built, walled and crenellated [with] a stone tower [i.e. the tower on the motte] and a moat; there are therein a great hall, two chambers, two chapels, a kitchen and a bakery of stone'.[62] These would all appear to have been within the bailey which lies south-east of the motte; 'without the castle there is another plot within the walls [i.e. of the outer bailey, see plan] built over with houses and called the manor, where are a grange, a granary, a great stable, a long house used for oxhouse, cowhouse, dairy and larder; a forge and a house for the outer gate with a chamber above'.[63]

At the same time the neighbouring castle of Oakham was surveyed and found to be 'well walled, and within are a hall, four chambers, a chapel, a kitchen, two stables, a grange for hay, a house for a prison, a chamber of a gatekeeper'.[64] Although Fotheringhay was head of an important barony, both it and Oakham were of slight military importance. It was otherwise at Bamburgh. Here a survey noted each of the many towers which strengthened the walls. The names of some of them – 'Smethy' (Smithy), 'Horsemylehousse', 'kynggis Chaumbre', 'Tylour toure' and 'Cole toure' – give some indication of the purposes to which they were put. Within the castle were the 'Kynggishall', pantry, buttery, kitchen and bakehouse; three chambers for the knights harbinger (*harmegerii*, probably from *haubergerius*, armed with a hauberk); chambers of the officials; wardrobe buildings, 'dedehouse' (for 'dead' stock), a 'madynchaumbre' (presumably for unmarried women) and three stables.[65] In Devizes Castle, an important royal residence, there were separate chambers, with their respective wardrobes (= garderobes) for king and queen, as well as kitchen, 'a bakehouse with two ovens [*fornicibus*] and two furnaces [*fornassibus*] and *garnerium* [pantry]'. In a sheriff's castle space was provided for the officials of the county, and in those royal castles which the king might be expected to visit there were separate suites for the king and his consort.[66]

Unfortunately these miscellaneous buildings were all too often designated merely as 'houses' (*domi*) and it becomes impossible to identify their purpose. There was, however, continuous building and rebuilding within the walls of comparatively unimportant castles, as new needs arose and older buildings decayed. Buildings were converted from one use to another. The hall might be enlarged or rebuilt on a different site, the kitchen expanded, and a bakery, buttery or pantry added.

Little was wasted in the course of rebuilding. Stone was re-used, roofing materials transferred from one building to another, and lead carted across country wherever it could be profitably used. At Rochester, the hall and chambers which had suffered by fire were taken down and the materials re-used,[67] and at Cambridge stone from a ruinous curtain wall went to the rebuilding of the county gaol;[68] at Sauvey, where a stable had collapsed, the roofing stone was used on the chapel,[69] and lead from the roofs of collapsed buildings in Oxford Castle was taken all the way to Clarendon

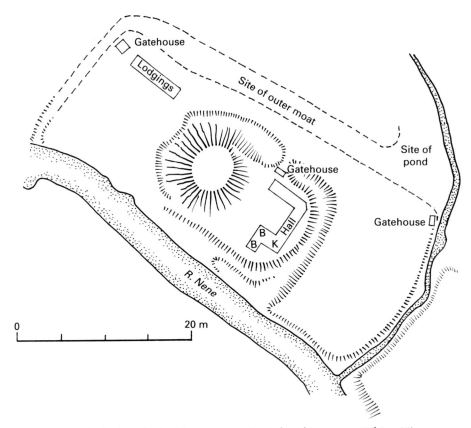

8.4 Fotheringhay Castle. The reconstruction is based in part on Cal Inq Misc.
B, B = bakehouse, brewhouse   K = kitchen

Palace, near Salisbury.[70] Material from ruined houses in the city of Winchester was absorbed into construction within the castle[71] and, conversely, rubble for which there was no immediate use could be given to the church, as at Sarum, to the benefit of the king's soul if not also of his purse.[72] Stone from the unfinished castle of Nafferton was used in Bamburgh and Newcastle[73] (see p. 104) and at Rayleigh, Essex, the king gave the local people 'the foundation of an old castle that used to be in that town [together with] licence to explore the foundation and take away stones'[74] for their own church. Perhaps the supreme instance of the economy in building materials is found at Marlborough Castle in 1260, where the constable was told 'to take straw off the roof of the outer chamber ... and roof it with shingles from the kitchen, and make a roof of lead for the kitchen'.[75]

Amongst the miscellaneous 'houses' which cluttered the bailey were stables, workshops and various tenements occupied by guests of the lord and by those working about the castle. The stables were clearly of great importance, for the horse was essential to feudal society. Stables were large; the 'great stable' at Chester Castle required 21,000 Welsh slates to roof it.[76] In the course of the extensive rebuilding of

Newport Castle, early in the fifteenth century, 'houses' were demolished to make way for the stable[77] and reference to the repair and rebuilding of stables are legion; at Wallingford Castle the very considerable sum of £20 was spent on stables,[78] and at Corfe Castle a stable was built to accommodate twenty horses.[79]

The term *domus* was used for any habitable quarters within a castle. It included tenements over which the lord or his constable had little or no control. Some were associated with the performance of castle-guard. In Northumberland, where this obligation lasted longer than elsewhere (see p. 49), the baronies of Bolbek, Gaugy, Gosford, Bailiol, Hadston and Vale each held tenements within the bailey of the New Castle. An inquest found them liable to build and maintain a 'house'[80] though these were generally poorly kept. At Bamburgh Alexander de Bradeford, who had commuted his guard duties, nevertheless continued to have a 'house in the said castle of his own',[81] and the same was true of William de Sey in Dover Castle.[82] In 1121–2 land was granted to Bernard the Scribe within Launceston Castle 'for his lodgings'.[83] Of course Bernard may have been a clerk of the constable for there is indication that the tenement was not his to occupy in perpetuity. At Rochester Castle the situation was similarly ambiguous. The archbishop was granted lodgings (*hospicia*) in the bailey, but this may have been to enable his servants to do their military duties.[84] Even earlier (1102) Robert de Lacy granted to Ralph le Rous lands at Clitheroe which included *messuagia illa . . . infra le Baille et deorsum*.[85] At Bristol, about 1150, John son of Odo gave *domum et terram . . . in castello de Bristollia* to Margam Abbey.[86] The occupation of houses in Cardiff Castle was clearly related to the obligation to defend it,[87] but in Swansea Castle a century later such duties had atrophied, and the houses appear to have been held and exchanged in fee simple. Indeed, there appears from the charters to have been a row of cottages and farm buildings *in forinseco ballio castri*[88] which changed hands with some regularity. In Sarum Castle *quamdam domum* was actually sold.[89]

Such 'houses' generally lay elsewhere than in the innermost court of the castle. Some are precisely located in the outer bailey, which in some cases seems almost to have passed out of the control of the lord and to have been absorbed into the local community (see pp. 211–14). The limit was reached at Bridgnorth Castle, where, in 1242 the inner bailey was declared to belong to the king, but the 'outer bailiwick of the castle is parcel of the town, and the men and tenants hold of the king'.[90] A last instance of the passage of land from the possession of the castle to that of the town is provided in Norwich.[91] Here the north-east bailey was probably the last to be created and remained militarily weak until in 1345 it passed formally into the possession of the city.[92]

To those who occupied houses within a castle on a more or less permanent basis must be added visitors who at times descended upon it. They must, according to their rank and retinue, have created quite a stir. The steward of the Duchy of Cornwall was ordered in 1354 to put Restormel Castle into a fit condition for its prince.[93] Least frequent and perhaps most dreaded was a visit by the king. Several royal castles had suites of chambers designated for the use of the king, queen and their retinue. At Windsor, Winchester and the Tower, these were kept in repair and were wainscoted and painted with considerable care (see pp. 83–4). But at many, a royal visit was rare, and the royal apartments were neglected. A writ directed to the sheriff of Yorkshire in 1361 complained of the condition of York Castle, adding that 'if the king or the queen or any of their ministers had to dwell in the castle, they would have no dwelling place except their chambers', which were ordered to be renovated,[94] and repairs were hastily made 'to that part of Lancaster Castle devoted to the accommodation of the king ... upon the occasion of a visit of the court'.[95] At Gloucester Castle an apartment for the queen was built in 1250 at the cost of about £215,[96] and on another occasion 'the king's chamber [was] cleaned against his coming'.[97] Elaborate preparations had usually to be made before the king's arrival, and large stores of food accumulated. Edward I's enforced stay at Lanercost Priory before his invasion of Scotland in 1307 proved to be so burdensome that the house never recovered.[98]

Other visits than those of the king called for careful preparation. When, in 1248, the queen of Scotland visited Rochester, the sheriff was called upon 'to clean and decently prepare (*mundari et decenter preparari*) the king's chambers within the castle'.[99] The royal apartments seem not infrequently to have been made available to members of the aristocracy. In 1282 the constable of Winchester Castle was directed to allow Amice, Countess of Devon, 'to lodge in the queen's great chamber adjoining the chapel towards the hall and in the adjoining houses'.[100] Beatrice, the wife of Aymer de Valence, was similarly allowed the use of the king's apartments in Marlborough Castle.[101] Evidently the royal apartments spread over a considerable area of the castle. Countless less exalted persons dwelt in the castle, most often the families of barons and knights who were absent on the king's service.[102] These guests evidently placed a heavy burden on the constable. At Scarborough they were to be entertained only if they in no way jeopardised the military effectiveness of the castle,[103] and at Rockingham it was specified that the privileges of the guests did not extend to the keep, which remained the exclusive domain of the constable.[104] At Sherborne it was made clear that the sheriff was not to be crowded out of his castle.[105]

Most constables had also to entertain guests of a different kind. There were, in addition to criminals awaiting trial, the hostages taken in the course of the wars. The former may have stayed only until the next gaol delivery (see pp. 98–9), but there were also those arrested by the lord's officers and awaiting the next session of the court baron. Private jurisdictions were however of diminishing importance, and the use of baronial castles for this purpose was ceasing. Hostages, however, were a different matter. They were not criminals. They were being held as a security for the good behaviour of their compatriots or until a ransom had been produced. They were mostly of gentle birth and their demands must sometimes have taxed the resources as well as the patience of the constable.

Amongst the castle's community there would have been servants, retainers and at least a handful of fighting men. Its garrison has already been discussed (see pp. 122–3). The servants, grooms and retainers, on the other hand, are an almost unknown quantity. Except when their wages were handled by the Exchequer or Wardrobe — and this was rare indeed — their numbers and functions are unknown. One assumes that they were recruited locally and were paid out of the personal resources of the lord or constable. Craftsmen who served within a castle are somewhat more visible, because most were engaged in the making and repair of weapons. At many castles there was a smith, and at the Tower he was regularly supplied with iron and charcoal. In larger castles, where the task of maintaining the fabric posed considerable problems, there would have been building craftsmen permanently resident within the castle. Windsor Castle seems regularly to have had a complement of such workmen.[106] There was a master carpenter, with doubtless his assistant, a chief plumber,[107] and a 'chief rough mason' whose task it was to lay stone to stone. Dover Castle was no less well appointed in the later Middle Ages,[108] and at Rochester Castle the forge and 'plomerie' each occupied separate buildings.[109] For the castles of North Wales, built later than others and with a more unified system of control, there were a master-mason and a master-plumber who had overall supervision, no doubt recruiting whatever workmen were necessary for a specific task.[110] But it was in the Tower of London that one finds the greatest number and variety of craftsmen. There were armourers, fletchers, *attiliatori* who made crossbows and engines, as well as smiths;[111] there was even a *'joignour* [joiner] to serve the king in his trade'. They were expected to produce work of a very high standard, and one smith was recorded as a Florentine, employed only to make breastplates. They seem to have lived within the Tower, and their letters of appointment even specified the 'houses' which they were to occupy. There were also the officers and workmen of the royal mint, and a host of grooms, servants and retainers. Together they must have run to hundreds, especially if their families lived with them within the castle.

A rural castle — and even some urban ones — might be expected to include a garden and even a tract of grazing land within an outer bailey or just beyond. At Castle Rising there was a gardener at 2d a day,[112] at Windsor was 'a great garden on the south side of the Castle'[113] enclosed by a wall, and also a vineyard.[114] Even in the little castle of Torrington (Devon) there was a garden beside the castle.[115] The gardener of the Tower of London, where a garden might have been least expected, was paid the relatively high wage of 6d a day,[116] and a palisade was ordered around the garden at Nottingham. In Gloucester Castle there was a herb garden with trellises (*treilarum*) over which presumably plants were trained.[117] Like the apartments, the garden was also cleaned up in anticipation of the prince's coming. At Chester Castle three grass plots were made because the Lord Prince (the future Edward II) was expected, and men were paid for 'digging and carrying of green turves'.[118] The same castle garden later yielded fruit to the value of 6s..8d[119] and somewhat later its apples were valued at 9s.[120] The garden also produced vegetables for the lord's table. That the Chester garden actually lay within the castle is shown by the fact that in one year the wall of the inner bailey collapsed and the masons were working 'in the same garden in the fruit time of the same'.[121] At Cardiff Castle there was a garden in the bailey, which probably means somewhere within the perimeter of the Roman fort.[122] In 1388 a survey found nothing of value in Oakham Castle except two gardens, whose fruit respectively was worth 12d and 10s.[123]

The castle garden, like the enclosed garden plot of any other manor house, produced vegetables as well as fruit for the lord's table. The garden at Chester Castle was a source of *caules* (cabbages) and leeks, and at Lancaster Castle a gardener held land by the service of providing pot herbs.[124] It would appear that in these instances the duty of providing vegetables was a serjeanty imposed on certain lands of the manor. Only in the most spacious of castles could the garden have been included within its walls.

Not unrelated to the produce of the garden was the grazing afforded by the 'herbage' which grew over the motte and the earthen ramparts. In some instances it was worth several shillings a year, as at Haverford,[125] where there were also complaints that its value had been reduced by the recent extension of the castle ditch. At Hastings Castle the herbage *within* the bailey was worth 6s..8d, and at Barnstable the grazing on the abandoned motte brought in 6d.[126]

A castle frequently had under its direct control an area of meadow, a fish stew and an area of parkland and forest.[127] All called for careful management, and usually the constable was directly responsible. The pond, or fish stew, was possibly the least of his problems. It called for periodic cleaning, and at intervals the fish stock was replenished.[128] The constable of Northampton was, for example, supplied with twenty live bream (*bretnias vivas*).[129] At Cranborne Castle, a small motte castle located high on the chalk downs of Dorset, fifty bream were supplied for the castle moat [*fossatis castri*],[130] while the Bishop of Worcester was given fifty bream from the king's *vivarium* at Kenilworth Castle.[131] At Windsor, the capacity of the stew which lay in the Great Park, was much larger, and 300 pike and 300 dace and roach were ordered for it.[132] In 1241 the king sent his own fisherman to Oxford *ad piscandum in fossatis castri*.[133] At York the river Fosse was in some way converted to a fish pond for the castle, at Marlborough the stew was held back by sluices which required repair, and at Knaresborough the fishery would appear to have been in the mill pond.[134] A value seems rarely to have been placed on a fish stew, but its contribution to the food supply of the castle was not necessarily of little importance.[135]

The meadow, which sometimes lay beside the stream near the castle, was very much more highly regarded. Meadowland was, during the Middle Ages, more valuable than arable because it provided much of the winter feed for animals. Every castle had its hay barn which complemented the stables. At Newcastle-upon-Tyne the king's meadow was worth 50s a year,[136] at West Derby, 20s,[137] and even at Bamburgh Castle it was valued at £4..13..6.[138] At Hope Castle, in Flintshire, the constable mowed 15½ acres of meadow, spread and gathered the hay and had it taken in carts to the castle at the cost in wages of 27s..2½d.[139] At Dudley the obligation was placed on certain tenants to carry hay to the castle.[140]

Park, meadow and warren played an important role in the economy of the castle.

Not only did they supply building timber, fuel and a certain amount of fresh meat; they served also for the principal recreation of king and aristocracy, the hunt. Frequent visits to such castles as Marlborough, Devizes and Ludgershall are explicable entirely in terms of the facilities that they offered in this respect. But parks and forests were immensely varied. They ranged from extensive areas of open woodland, like New and Sherwood forests and the Forest of Dean, to small parks, one of which survives as Windsor Great Park. Sometimes the constable had charge of a neighbouring tract of woodland, receiving an additional fee for his pains; sometimes the office of forester or 'parker' was separated from that of constable. The frequent changes in these respects can have arisen only from the king's desire to reward or reprimand one individual or another. One forest seems never to have been separated from the constableship, that of Dean.[141] The reason is clear. This was not a forest in which the king was accustomed to hunt. Instead, its purpose was to provide the wood and metal for the munitions that were fabricated at St Briavels, though the constable was at intervals called upon to supply venison to this castle or that. Another which seems regularly to have been attached to the office of constable was that 'between Oxford and Rockingham', perhaps because Rockingham Castle was as much a rural retreat as it was a military fortress. The cluster of Wiltshire castles – Devizes, Ludgershall, Marlborough – owed much of their importance to the proximity of the forests of Chippenham, Clarendon and Savernake.

Few castles had large forests within their purview, but most had jurisdiction over a small extent of woodland or warren. These may have provided sport, but their chief purpose was as a source of building timber and fuel.[142] At Colchester wood was taken from non-royal forests – there were no royal forests nearby – for fuel, but constructional timber was brought over a much greater distance from royal woodland.[143] Guildford Castle drew wood for its furnace from its nearby park;[144] and Bristol Castle from north-east of the city in Kingswood Forest, over which the constable usually had jurisdiction.[145] But good oaks for constructional purposes were less easy to come by, and much of the timber used for joints and rafters, and even for simple palisading, had to be transported considerable distances. Gloucester Castle was allowed by the constable of St Briavels to draw on the resources of the Forest of Dean,[146] but for work on Corfe Castle it was necessary to turn to the broad woodland which still covered much of the Vale of Blackmore,[147] as well as to Hampshire,[148] and Sarum Castle, on the treeless downs of Wiltshire, also had timber brought from Blackmore and Clarendon.[149] Long four-wheeled wagons were used, but the building and repair of castles, which were extravagant of timber, must have placed a severe burden on both forest resources and transport facilities.

In 1305 Queen Margaret, who had received Marlborough Castle as part of her dower, had Savernake Forest added because 'the forest is necessary for the frequent repairs of the castle and town'.[150] The care of a major forest was doubtless too large a task to be undertaken by a constable, but the lesser forests were not infrequently left in the care of the constables, who made the greatest use of them. The constable of

Porchester, for example, was entrusted with Porchester Forest.[151] The minor Marcher castles of Blaenllyfni and Bwlch y Dinas each had a forest and chase, though their extent and value must have been small.[152] The castle of Newcastle-under-Lyme had a small royal forest, with a forester who was subject to the constable,[153] and attached to Devizes Castle was a forest and a park with deer.[154] The forest or park must be distinguished from the warren. The latter was small in extent, and was an area of waste in which small game animals, notably the hare and the newly introduced rabbit, bred and were hunted. It was an asset of marginal importance. In 1275 the warren belonging to Cambridge Castle was said to be in the king's hands 'because no one was willing to keep it'.[155]

The castle and rural community

Most castles lay in rural areas and were closely associated with the communities which supplied labour and services as well as food. The castle was in fact the manor. The records speak consistently of the 'castle and manor', as if the two were virtually synonymous. The manorial court met in the castle, or before its gate, and here were resolved the petty disputes and problems inevitable in a small, tightly structured, agricultural community.

The castle had demesne land amid the fields of the villages, cultivated with local labour, and into the castle were taken hay from the meadow and crops after harvest. The castle was almost inseparable from its lands. They gave a monetary value to the castle.[156] Repeatedly one finds from an inquisition that the castle itself had no value, and that its income derived from demesne, mill, the services of tenants and the profits of courts.[157] On rare occasion the *corpus* of the castle was separated from its lands, but usually for a particular and temporary reason. Not until Edward I built his fortresses in North Wales do we find castles wholly divorced from the life of the land. The profits from manorial land were sometimes reckoned to be sufficient to cover the maintenance of the castle.[158] Even a castle as dangerously exposed as Pain's Castle — *Castellum Matildis*, in Radnor — was, as indeed it still is, a farm. An inventory of its goods, made in 1397, included amongst 'dead stock': 'a cart with furniture, an iron-bound 'trokell, 5 loads of hay, straw, 3 iron-bound wagons, 2 bodies of wagons, worn; 2 harrows with iron teeth, 2 harrows with wooden teeth, 2 flails, 3 ploughs with furniture, a measure called a "trug", a saw, a mattock, an axe, a bill-hook, 2 horse shears (*ceras equinas*), a hammer, 2 iron forks and an old chest'.[159] There were, in addition, oxen, cattle and sheep and a considerable store of wheat and oats. This, of course, was after the subjugation of the Welsh Principality, but Kilgerran Castle in Cardiganshire was in 1274 under threat from Llewelyn ap Gruffydd, and castles in these parts were on constant guard.[160] Its constable was, none the less, ordered to have 'oxen and plough horses . . . brought and . . . the demesne lands . . . tilled'. At both Dinefwr and Dryslwyn castles there was no monetary income from the sale of the castles' hay since *remanet in castro in garnestura*. There was, in this unsettled region, a disposition to neglect the cultivation of land belonging to a castle; hence the repeated injunctions to plough and sow.[161]

It was, indeed, essential to cultivate the demesne and tend the meadow. In the Marches each castle housed a contingent of men-at-arms and retainers. The movement of food and supplies across country was difficult and dangerous, and each castlery in the border country had to be largely self-sufficing; 'a major purpose of direct demesne exploitation [being] to provide food supplies for the castle garrisons, although there is no way of calculating exactly how much of the total was consumed in this way'.[162]

In the peaceful heart of England it became increasingly the practice, at least in royal castles, to 'farm' the castle with its lands and other perquisites. The castle itself had little value. The 'body' of Tattershall Castle was in 1306 said to be worth 40s a year.[163] Very few would have been valued at more. Yet their maintenance was far more costly than that of a simple manor house. In most cases the perquisites would have been adequate to keep the castle in peacetime and even to leave a small surplus. The 'farmer' took the castle and its lands at a rent, managed and maintained them and hoped to make a profit. The amount of farm sometimes paid shows how valuable could be the miscellaneous items of revenue which accrued to a castle.

On rare occasions, as at Ongar, the king saw fit to let the manorial lands and appendages, while retaining possession of the castle;[164] at Corfe Castle the king granted 'the keeping of the *corpus* of the castle' at a fixed fee, while retaining in his own hands 'the warren, forest and all other things without the walls',[165] and at Horston (Horsley) in Derbyshire, the *corpus* was similarly retained by the sheriff while the rest was let at farm.[166] But such arrangements were rare and shortlived. More often a package deal was arranged by which the lands and profits supported the castle and 'farmer', and left a small margin for the king.

We have no means of knowing whether the 'farmer', intent on making a profit out of his undertaking, was a harsher master than the constable who received a fixed income. It is inherently probable that he was, but the constable claimed certain rights which he used and abused, that were denied to the 'farmer'. He managed his lord's gaol, in which, even in a baronial castle, there always seemed to be a few inhabitants. Indeed, the abuses of the constable were almost legendary.[167] Many and varied were the complaints made before the commissioners who compiled the Hundred Rolls. Most prominent were accusations of extortion and wrongful imprisonment and for this there is no lack of confirmatory evidence. Cattle were seized unjustly and released only on payment of a fine. Illicit tolls were charged by the constable on passing carts[168] and on business at the local market;[169] crops and farm animals were raided and taken to the castle.[170] An inquisition of about 1395 reported that the keeper of Bolsover Castle 'is so great a maintainer and extortioner that no poor man dwelling in those parts can live well if he is not attendant on him and his servants and their commands',[171] and an inquiry into John Tauny's management of Chepstow Castle reported that 'he was not guilty of any extortions against the tenants',[172] as if this were something unusual. William Isely and Benedict Saleman, clerks of the sheriff of Kent, who was also constable of Canterbury Castle, arrested and imprisoned a man for forty-one days in the castle, and no one could replevy (bail) him 'by reason of the terror and threats of . . . William and Benedict'.[173]

The cases cited are known only because they were revealed by judicial inquiry. How many went unnoticed by the courts we have no means of assessing. Their number would have increased in times of war or civil strife, when the constraints of the judicial system were relaxed. At such times castles were provisioned, often hurriedly and ruthlessly. In 1268 the king learned that 'many enormities have been committed [in] the munition of [Pevensey] castle',[174] and worse was to follow during the siege of Kenilworth in 1266.[175] Under Richard II an inquiry was instituted into the 'extortions and oppressions by the king's ministers' in Northampton Castle.[176] In the March of Wales conditions were worse, for here the king's writ did not run and royal justice was not done.[177] Even a castle as well managed as Dover was not above reproach.[178]

The practice of using a castle, or at least its outer bailey, as a place for folding or impounding cattle led to numerous abuses. Stray animals were rounded up; they were distrained for debt, and even placed within the castle for security.[179] It was claimed before the court of King's Bench that at Hereford 'there is no other pound save only within the walls of the castle'.[180] The management of such animals was commonly left to a porter, who made what profit he could from the operation. At Exeter the family of John Ianitor had a hereditary right to 'the . . . custody of the gaol . . . [and] of all beasts taken in distraint for debts to the king',[181] and was accustomed to receive a payment of no fixed amount on their release. From demanding an extortionate fee for the release of animals legitimately impounded it was but a short step to seizing animals and charging their owners. None, however, was as ingenious as the janitor of Scarborough Castle, one Walter of Dodemore. The jurors at the Hundred inquisition declared that he made a practice of scattering oats over the banks and ditches of the castle, and thus of attracting the pigs of the local community. These he then impounded, *et sic extorsit ab hominibus pecuniam injuste*.[182]

Most castles relied on their local communities for labour and services. No doubt these were eventually paid for, but there were in the early years of English feudalism numerous and varied unpaid obligations. These can be summarised as work on the fabric of the castle, garrison duty and various and sometimes curious serjeanties. The Norman kings had inherited from their Anglo-Saxon predecessors the right to exact labour in the *fyrd* and on bridge and roadwork – the *trinoda necessitas* (see p. 20). In some degree the Normans continued to exercise this right, but how far it translated into labour on fortifications is an open question. It must be assumed that the earthwork castles of the Conquest were raised with forced labour. There would otherwise be little point in the Conqueror and his successors granting to favoured religious houses an immunity from such work for their tenants.[183] The canons of several Yorkshire houses were specifically freed from '*fyrd*-service and castle work', the two being clearly linked.[184] The list of exemptions granted to monastic houses is so long, and repeated so many times that one is obliged to assume that the monastic rights were sometimes violated.

Illicit though such demands may have become, they continued to be made into the reign of Henry II.[185] In some places, particularly in the Marches and Borders, such obligations were placed on a quasi-legal footing. At Aldford, one of the castles which guarded the northern March, land was held 'by the service of making 2 perches (48 feet) of hedging (*hircheti* – palisade?) round [the] castle as need might arise'.[186] This case came to light only when the tenants refused to fulfil their obligation, claiming that the 'hedge' had been replaced by a mud wall. Local labour was probably inexpert and unreliable. At the neighbouring castle of Oswestry, which was held by the FitzAlan earls of Arundel, four named persons were obligated 'whenever the lord orders work on the walls of Oswestry Castle [to] make and maintain a furnace for lime-burning'. The lord provided the fuel and the men might have the waste of the trees and also permission to smoke a side of bacon in the furnace. 'But if the fire goes out through their negligence . . . then these four must remake it.'[187] A further obligation placed on a manor of the Oswestry honour was to 'cart all the timber needed . . . into the castle as far as the outer guard of the inner bridge', but it was stated specifically that their duties did not extend beyond the limits of the lordship. At Corfe Castle those who owned carts were obligated to carry wine to the castle as well as bread and beer for the constable, but for this they were to receive a small payment.[188]

It has already been argued that knight service and castle-guard were in some measure interchangeable. Could castle-guard be extended to work on the fabric of the castle that was being guarded? There is some evidence that it could. More than twenty fees of the honour of Bramber were in the mid-thirteenth century excused, not only from their duties of castle-guard, but also from maintaining the castle wall – *ad wardam castri . . . et ad muragium ejusdem castri*.[189] Pevensey Castle was owed 'heckage' by a number of manors in the vicinity, which is said to have denoted 'the obligation of repairing and keeping up a certain portion of the palisade upon the ramparts'.[190] At Dunster Castle, Somerset, there seems to have been a similar obligation *ad firmandum castrum* which was reinforced by a directive from King John, adding that *id libenter facere debitis quia hoc fiet pro vobis et securitate vetra*.[191] A curious fact here is that the duty was commuted for a payment of 12 marks by each tenant, in order to pay for building the lower bailey. The obligation had been to repair the walls of the upper castle, which can only have been the shell which enclosed the broad summit of the motte. Have we here an instance of the abandonment of the motte in favour of the more spacious bailey? And, since this agreement was acknowledged before the king's justices, have we not also an instance of informing the king of changes that could affect the security of the realm?

It did not often happen that the local community was called upon to defend the castle which dominated their lives. Indeed, it would almost seem that they were not welcome within it. The court was often held, not within the castle, but at its gate. At

Pembroke Castle the court seems to have been held in this way, and it was noted in 1290, with evident surprise that 'the gates of Haverford Castle had been opened and everyone went in and out as he pleased'.[192] The community of Bamburgh even petitioned the king for the right of 'free access to the castle',[193] but what they meant here was probably the right to take refuge from Scottish raiders (see p. 206). All attempts, found by this writer, to exclude the local community from a castle related to the larger and militarily more important of them. In 1389 one Thomas Fort was indicted for treason in that he showed to John de Ispania 'the secrets of all the castles of South Wales'.[194] Nine castles, including Pembroke, Haverford, Cardigan and Carmarthen, were mentioned by name, and two more were subsequently added.

At Corfe Castle 'the tenants of the town, when there is war in the neighbourhood ... should be at the castle for forty days at their own charge for the defence thereof as service for the tenure of their lands'.[195] But at other times, if they wished to present a petition regarding their local privileges, they might only 'come to the castle gate'. At Castle Rising, also a coastal fortress, the constable was in 1386 instructed 'to compel men of the parts adjacent to remain in the castle upon its safe keeping whenever and as long as danger threatens, as they were wont to do in times past'.[196] These instances are strongly suggestive of the Anglo-Saxon *fyrd*, and can probably be regarded as part of a general obligation to defend the realm rather than as the enforcement of a peculiarly feudal right.

What contribution did the castle make to the well-being of the community? It is reiterated in the records that the castle was for the security of the country and region. Repeated injunctions from the king's chancery called for the secure defence of castles against invasion which, to judge from the records, was always seen to be imminent. But the castle was a protection against civil strife; it was a place where the local community could withdraw in an emergency and thus gain some degree of protection. In many communities where there was no castle, the local church, and especially its tower, served the same purpose.

During the first century of English feudalism the village was often intimately linked with the castle, being enclosed by ditch, rampart and palisade, and forming in effect an outer bailey. Numerous instances can still be traced. It is doubtful, however, whether such enclosed villages continued to be created after 1154, except in frontier regions. Though, in theory, the castle in England continued to offer protection, there is little evidence that use was made of it in this way.

In frontier regions things were different. Here it was assumed that one of the functions of a castle was to serve as refuge in time of invasion or war. At the end of the fourteenth century, during one of many invasion scares, the inhabitants of the region were ordered to withdraw into Dover Castle, but there is no evidence that they did so.[197] More threatening was the danger from the North. In 1323 letters were sent to all northern sheriffs, as well as to the constables of the castles of Knaresborough, Pontefract, Scarborough and Tickhill, announcing that invasion was imminent, and that all in Cumberland should take their animals into Yorkshire, and 'their victuals, stock and all other goods to castles and walled towns for safety, so that the enemy . . . may not have any sustenance . . . all constables of castles . . . on this side of Trent [were] to permit such persons to bring in their victuals, stock and goods'.[198] This was, of course, a panic measure, and could not possibly have been implemented. Nevertheless, certain castles, such as Carlisle, served as 'a defence and refuge of the adjacent parts against the Scots'.[199] In Ireland the Archbishop of Dublin sought from Henry III a grant of land in order 'to build a castle [at Castlekevin, County Wicklow] on the frontier of the whole march for the relief and defence of the common people'.[200] Permission was given on condition that it was kept in order, but a century later a jury found it 'utterly destroyed'.

In England a comparable case was Bamburgh Castle. The castle itself occupied a steep-sided outcrop of the Whinsill, and covered almost two hectares. Elaborate precautions were taken for its defence and those northern baronies which owed castle-guard were obligated to maintain 'houses' for use when on duty.[201] Nevertheless, there must have been considerable space for the country folk in time of danger. There seems little doubt but that they were accustomed to seek refuge in the castle and had come to regard this as a right. In 1315 the people of Bamburgh complained to the king of the losses they had suffered at the hands of the Scots and petitioned for confirmation of their right of 'free admission to Bamburgh Castle where they lodge at their own expense and help with watching duties'.[202] It is evident that they were not always made welcome, and on one occasion they complained that the constable 'charged them 12d for each plot of ground within the castle where they could store their personal belongings'. Furthermore 'the gate-keepers demanded fees for their access and exit'.[203]

The castle of Dunstanburgh occupied a similar site some 15 km along the coast. It was begun soon after the defeat at Bannockburn left northern England exposed to Scottish inroads, and was designed both to hold a large garrison and to receive the people of the surrounding countryside. It embraced within its walled perimeter about 3.6 ha and its vast space was uncluttered by buildings. Indeed the only permanent structures, including the massive gatehouse, lay in the south-west corner.[204] It has been described as a 'gigantic cattle pound'; it served, in the words of Sir Robert Bowes in 1550, 'as great refuge to the inhabitants of those partes, if enemies came to annoy them, either arriving by sea or coming by land out of Scotland'.[205]

The castles of the Welsh March were rarely called upon to serve this function because the Welsh themselves seldom made deep incursions into England. In England itself castles were used to store valuables, but rarely can they have been used as places of refuge. Indeed, they seem often to have been used as if they were a bank vault. In 1400, for example, Thomas Eylong had thirteen silver dishes put away in Bristol Castle,[206] and others also stored their valuables there. A chest worth 7s was in safe keeping at Dunster Castle,[207] and the sheriff of Hampshire was called upon to assign a safe place in Winchester Castle 'for Taldus Valoris to keep his goods; and to have ingress and egress, provided no peril to the castle'.[208] There is no record of payment for such services, but it is not improbable that some recompense was counted among the profits to which the constable was entitled.

On the other hand there were the occasional acts of pious generosity. A hermit was supported at 1d a day in the Tower of London,[209] and Emma the recluse in Dover Castle.[210] There was an almonry in Rochester Castle,[211] and at Windsor it was customary on certain feasts of the church to fill the great hall of the castle with the poor of the vicinity, and feed them.[212] But this appears to have been a quirk of Henry III, and is not mentioned after his death. There were also occasional gifts, but always to religious institutions. Stone from the ditch of Exeter Castle was given to the Friars Preachers for their building,[213] and at Shrewsbury fifty loads of lime were given to the same order from the store accumulated for work on the castle.[214] But overall the charitable acts for which constables were responsible amount to very little. The hermit and the recluse were just curiosities, like the elephant and the royal lion, which were their neighbours in the Tower.

The urban castle

No less than forty-eight castles were built by the Conqueror or his followers within the limits of pre-existing towns (p. 57). Eighteen of these were in towns of Roman origin, and the rest were established within burhs of Anglo-Saxon or, in the cases of Nottingham and Stamford, of Danish origin. Norwich, Northampton and Guildford were not technically 'burhs', but had developed as commercial towns late in the Anglo-Saxon period. Another category of urban castle was that which, though established in the countryside, became the focus of urban development. The castles in this category constituted a very varied group, which will be discussed later.

When a castle intruded into an existing town, the choice of site was all-important. If one of the tasks of the castle was to overawe and control the local populace, then a site against the perimeter defences, with access to the open country, was desirable, and where there already existed a town wall this was generally speaking the location adopted, the only conspicuous exception being Colchester, where the *podium* of the temple of Claudius was too attractive a foundation to be ignored (Figure 8.5).[215] Even so, it appears likely that the bailey of the castle did extend to the north wall of the Roman town. At Winchester, London, Exeter, Gloucester, Chester and Worcester, where the Roman town had been angular in plan, a corner site was adopted. Elsewhere, as at Canterbury and Chichester, it was built *against* the curved line of the wall. At Rochester the first castle was just outside the line, but was rebuilt within. In a few instances – Gloucester and Winchester, for example – the castle lay astride the wall, and it is impossible now to say what use may have been made of the Roman fortification.

At Wallingford and Wareham, both planned towns of Anglo-Saxon origin, the Norman castle was built into a corner of the rampart. At Norwich, Thetford, Stamford, Nottingham, all of them unplanned towns of Scandinavian or late Anglo-

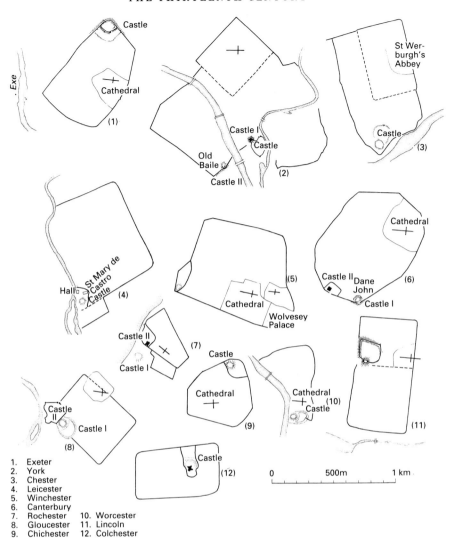

8.5 Early urban castles in relation to the earlier walled perimeter of former Roman towns.

1. Exeter
2. York
3. Chester
4. Leicester
5. Winchester
6. Canterbury
7. Rochester   10. Worcester
8. Gloucester   11. Lincoln
9. Chichester   12. Colchester

Saxon origin, the castle would appear to have been on the edge of the populated area. At Norwich (see p. 211) it later came to be enclosed within the expanding town.

A castle could not have been established within the limits of a walled town without causing some damage to property. Domesday records ten towns in which damage and destruction are specifically attributed to the building of a castle, and eight further castle towns in which there was recorded destruction. The most extensive was at Lincoln, where 166 *domus* were destroyed. At Norwich ninety-eight *domi* were *in occupatione castelli*; at Shrewsbury fifty-one were *vastae* on account of the castle; at Warwick four; at Stamford five and at Cambridge twenty-seven. At Wallingford, eight *hagai* were destroyed to make way for the castle, and at

Gloucester and Huntingdon fourteen and twenty-one *domi* respectively were said to be *modo desunt* or *modo absunt*.

London and Winchester are not fully accounted for in Domesday, but it is unlikely that no houses were destroyed in these relatively prosperous towns to make way for the castle. At Canterbury, Dorchester (Dorset), Leicester, Northampton, Oxford, Wareham and Worcester, as well as the marginal site of Lydford (Devon), there was also destruction of houses, but the reason is not specified. There is no mention of destruction at Chester, Colchester, Chichester, Hereford, Nottingham and Rochester. At the last-named the castle was at first built outside the walls, and at Nottingham the rocky site of the castle lay well outside the Danish borough.

One cannot say whether any compensation was made for land taken and houses destroyed, but at Gloucester, in 1105, the abbey church of St Peter was given certain manors by Henry I in exchange for a garden in which the king's tower was built.[216] The castle itself had been built as a motte and bailey a generation earlier. Did this exchange represent an extention of the earlier castle, and was the *turris* in question the tower-keep which replaced the motte?[217] The extension of existing castles and the construction of new continued for the next two centuries to bring damage and destruction to urban buildings. The documentation, however, is slight before the thirteenth century, when the problem was, in any case, becoming less acute. Churches were removed or destroyed to make way for a castle at Bedford and Hereford;[218] at Nottingham a certain Isolda de Maydr received compensation for the loss of a house when the ditch of the barbican was dug about 1236,[219] and at Leicester a rent was paid to Leicester Abbey for land also taken for the barbican.[220] At Windsor the castle ditch was enlarged at the expense of local property holders and compensation was given,[221] and at Newcastle-upon-Tyne a rent of £5..10..6 was owed to the citizens 'to be distributed proportionately to those who have lost their rents by reason of the dyke and new work constructed under the castle on the side towards the water'.[222] Castle-works must have wrought havoc on nearby land. In 1299 it was complained that land in the London parish of St Olave, 'near the Tower, has been occupied from the time when the king caused the ditch of the Tower to be made until now by earth raised from the ditch and thrown upon the said land'.[223] It would appear that at long last the builders had cleared their debris, and the land was returned to its previous occupant. Damage extended far beyond the building operations themselves. At Windsor the digging and carting of sand for the king's works caused damage to the property of the local burgesses.[224]

The defence of a castle called for a clear space around its walls. In Newcastle-upon-Tyne a messuage worth 4 marks a year was demolished because it overlooked the castle.[225] The siege of Bedford in 1227 must have caused very extensive damage to the town and surrounding countryside, and small amounts of compensation continued to be paid throughout much of the century.[226] Gloucester suffered similarly during the Barons' War, when houses were demolished because they were thought to endanger the castle's defences.[227]

In a few instances houses continued to be demolished into the fourteenth century and even later. Structures in Newport (Monmouthshire) were removed as late as 1402 to make way for stables,[228] but, except in North Wales, urban castles had long since reached their greatest extent, and some had begun to contract, to abandon their outer ditches and allow a civil population to invade their outermost baileys. The process was twofold: the encroachments, licit or otherwise, of town properties on the castle and the dumping, generally illicitly, of the town's waste on the land of the castle; and secondly, of the formal leasing of plots within the castle for the occupation of townsfolk. For the latter we have the cases of Bridgnorth, where the outer bailey was surrendered to the town, and Lincoln, where the Baile, between the castle and the cathedral precinct, gradually passed from the control of the garrison to that of the townspeople.[229]

More often it was a simple case of trespass, condoned because the townsfolk stood to gain and the sheriff or constable was not interested. In 1400 a commission at Shrewsbury enquired into 'the building without licence of divers houses in the king's . . . ditch . . . between the castle and the town',[230] and at Colchester a plot was 'occupied with filth of men and animals and with other foul-smelling accumulations . . . above the ditch of the castle'.[231] In 1364 a fine was instituted for throwing offal into the castle ditch.[232] At Norwich a citizen had in 1345 'usurped and inhabited to the king's prejudice a plot . . . parcel of . . . le Castil ditch . . . of the fee of the castle'.[233] A generation earlier 'a void place' in the castle ditch had been formally granted to a citizen of Norwich to build on. As the plot measured 100 feet long and only 8 feet wide it probably *was* the castle ditch.[234] No longer did it seem necessary to keep an open tract of land around the castle. At Newcastle-upon-Tyne a burgess was allowed a tenement which fronted onto the road before the castle but extended 'to the castle moat behind'.[235] In 1348 there was a 'cottage *upon* the ditch of [Liverpool] castle'.[236]

The case of Worcester Castle, already mentioned (p. 96), is more straightforward but no less intriguing. The royal castle had usurped part of the cemetery of the cathedral-priory and had thus earned the hostility of the bishop.[237] The castle figured prominently in the wars of William II and Stephen, and continued throughout the twelfth century to be a seat of the Beauchamps as hereditary sheriffs. Their principal castle, at least until they acquired the earldom of Warwick in 1268, was at Elmley, 20 km to the south-east of Worcester. Worcester Castle, dominated by the cathedral only 200 m to the north, can have held little military value, and the cathedral priory seems never to have relinquished its claim to the land taken from it.[238] Henry III made restitution in 1217, ordering the bailey – *ballium castri nostri* – to be given back to the priory,[239] and the motte – *motam castri* – to remain with Walter Beauchamp. This partition of the castle was vaguely drawn, and in 1217 a jury was empanelled to determine who had jurisdiction and where. A line was drawn from the great gate of the castle to the postern gate beside the Severn, separating the precinct from the castle.[240] The latter, thus emasculated, lost all military value. What remained of the bailey served to accommodate the county gaol while the motte became overgrown and was abandoned.

A town had by definition some degree of self-government. It had a court and officers chosen from among its burgesses, but it had no jurisdiction over the 'fee of the castle'. That usually constituted an enclave within the urban area, and might even claim some vestigial rights over the town itself. The 'fee of the castle' must have originated in the needs of defence. Instances have already been given of the removal of buildings that were seen as a threat. But, from the middle years of the thirteenth century, the probability that an urban castle would be attacked became remote, and, in so far as the castle clung to its rights over the surrounding land, it was for the monetary gain that accrued. Profits came from the use of the soil and from legal jurisdiction. There are many instances in municipal records of the lease to burgesses of plots within the castle ditch, but if one of those burgesses committed an offence on his plot, then the constable would have both jurisdiction and the profits of court that arose. Such a case occurred in Newcastle-upon-Tyne about 1320. A prisoner, held in the *town* gaol for an offence committed in the 'franchise of the castle', petitioned for release, and succeeded because the case was actionable only in the constable's court.[241] Felons and lawless persons, it was claimed by the city of Norwich, 'took refuge [in the Castle Fee] and avoided justice, being screened by the Sheriff of the county and the bailiffs of his liberty'.[242] There is no evidence for a 'protection racket' exercised by the constable, but it is clear that the profits of court were worth striving for. In 1345 the king surrendered to the city the whole of the Castle Fee, except the castle and *le Shirehouse* which remained attached to the county.[243] It seems probable that the fee embraced not only the motte and two baileys but also an extensive area around.[244]

The existence of the Castle Fee at Norwich may have been little more than a local irritant; at Chester it raised more serious problems. As at Norwich, it was subject to the Earl of Chester and thus to his local officer, the Justiciar, but it was considerably larger than the Norwich fee, and thus gave scope for greater abuse. It embraced a considerable area to the north and east of the castle, and was known as the hamlet or township of Gloverstone.[245] Traders who had failed to gain admission to the franchise of the city were allowed to settle here, paying, it must be presumed, some small fee to the constable.[246] This independence of a significant part of intra-mural Chester continued into the nineteenth century, and in the census of 1801 Gloverstone was credited with thirty houses and 122 inhabitants.

As a general rule little precision was shown in delimiting the respective spheres of castle and town. At Ludlow the burgesses were allowed the whole town 'except the site of the castle and a meadow called Castelmede'.[247] At Reigate Castle, the castle ditch was used to mark the boundary, and this became the usual practice.[248] But at Rochester the king seems to have abandoned all claim to what lay beyond the crumbling walls of the castle, allowing the citizens not only *le Boley*, site of the first castle, but also 'the profit of the grass and pasture growing outside the walls of the . . . castle and in all the ditches belonging to the castle'.[249] And so it was in most urban castles; the castle relinquished its jurisdiction over areas which had ceased to be of value to it. It is an interesting comment on the vested interests involved that when

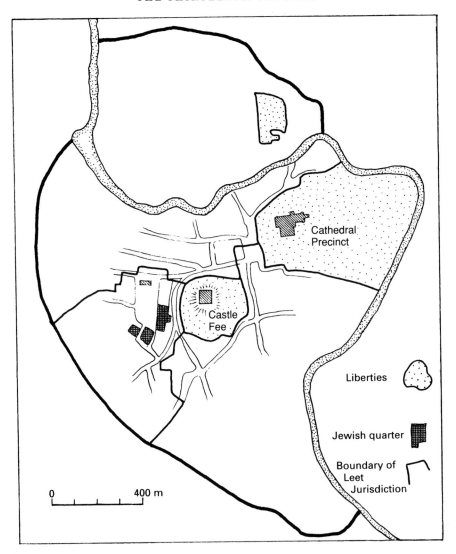

Cathedral
Precinct

Castle
Fee

Liberties

Jewish quarter

Boundary of
Leet
Jurisdiction

0   400 m

8.6 The city and castle of Norwich, showing the 'Castle Fee', and the area of the city settled
predominantly by the Jewish community.

the king transferred most of the Castle Fee of Norwich to the city, he increased the
fee-farm of the latter by £2..14..4, approximately the amount which the lands
involved were worth in rents and fines.[250] Leicester was a baronial castle which
became attached to the Duchy of Lancaster, and thus to the crown in 1399. Here the
earl, or his constable, maintained a tight grip on the town. It was the porter of the
castle who executed the judgments of the court leet of the city and collected rents due
to the earl.[251]

It is of some importance to know where the principal gate of the castle was placed

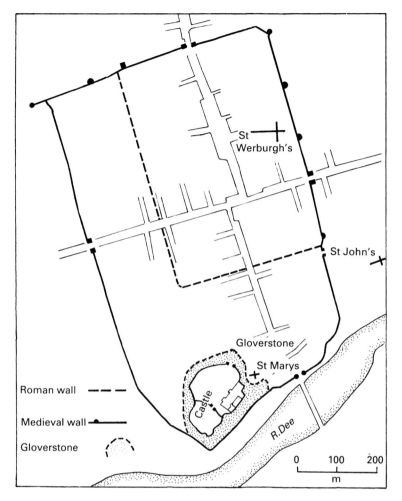

Roman wall — — —

Medievil wall —•——

Gloverstone

8.7 Chester, showing the castle and the liberty of Gloverstone.

in relation to the town. It might be expected to have opened, not into the town, but towards the open country, so that access could be gained to the castle without going through the town. Such, however, was not generally the case. The main entrance was usually from the town. A possible reason was that the castle was, in most instances, built against the perimeter wall of the town which would have had to be breached to make an entrance on this side. The Tower of London is the most complete of urban castles, and here the principal entrance, covered by an elaborate barbican, was on the west towards the city. In 1233 repairs were made to the barbican of Bristol Castle *que est versus villam.*[252] At Exeter the eleventh-century gate-tower looks over the city, and at York, the bailey was accessible only from the street within the city known appropriately as 'Castlegate'.[253] Northampton Castle was built between the Anglo-Saxon town and the river, but had its great gate opening northwards *into* the Anglo-Saxon town.[254] The great gate of Nottingham Castle survives on the gentler eastern slope of the castle rock, towards the town; at Leicester the bailey was entered from the town beside the church of St Mary de Castro, and the main gate and drawbridge of Rochester Castle lay to the north-west of the cathedral, towards the High Street.[255]

There seems always to have been a secondary point of exit, free from observation and control by the town. It was commonly known as the postern, and its chief protection lay in its narrowness and difficulty of access. At Lincoln, where the surviving main gate faces the west front of the cathedral, a postern was cut in the west wall of the main courtyard. This wall was Roman in origin, and thus pre-dated the castle. In the early years of the twelfth century Henry I gave permission to the bishop, 'to make an exit in the wall of the king's castle for his house, provided that he does not weaken the wall'.[256] The location of this particular postern is unknown. The palace lay to the south of the cathedral and would have been approached from the east wall of the castle. There is no reason to suppose that the bishop's postern was that which played so significant a role in the siege and battle of Lincoln Fair (see p. 116).

Of all the important urban castles of medieval England only two, Warwick and Winchester, show signs of ever having had a main entrance facing away from the town. And when Edward I came to build his integrated castles and towns in North Wales, the castles were in all cases entered directly from *within* the walls of the town.[257] The king and his engineers might well regard the burgesses as on the same side as the garrison, since they had been recruited in order to help resist the Welsh. But we have good reason to know that the Conqueror gravely mistrusted the citizens of both Exeter and London, and when he established Rougemont Castle at Exeter, the tower-gatehouse looked down the gentle slope of the 'red mount' into the Anglo-Saxon town. One can only suppose, topographical arguments aside, that his object was to dominate the town, to allow his garrison easy access to its streets to suppress any incipient revolt.

The shadow of the castle must have loomed large over the town. Its physical presence must have been overpowering, especially as most of the royal urban castles were very large structures. The castle was also a source of petty annoyance to the townsfolk: pre-emptive buying by the constable's staff in the local market, the control exercised from the castle over the communal oven, the price of beer owed to the castle, and the rights asserted by the castle court.[258] The town of Abergavenny owed a fraction of the beer from each brew to the castle, but the steward 'exceeded at his will the amount due . . . and transferred the [surplus] to his own dwelling . . . instead of to the use of the castle'.[259] In this case, a jury found for the steward, but one wonders how impartial was a jury drawn from the tenants of the honour.

On the other hand, the urban community stood to benefit from the presence of the castle. Its crafts and commerce are likely to have been stimulated by the demands of the castle. Its citizens held land by serjeanties performed in the castle.[260] The office of janitor at Bamburgh Castle was held in this way,[261] and serjeanties in Lancaster

Castle included not only the office of carpenter, but also that of smoking venison and bacon for the castle.[262] In many small ways there must have been some economic gain to the community from the courts and other happenings within the castle. And as the military importance of the castle declined, so its role as a centre of administration increased.

There was one segment of the urban community which was, more than any other, indebted to the castle for its safety – the Jews. They had come to England in the years following the Conquest and had settled chiefly in the cities of the South-east, where they became craftsmen and dealers in all sorts of commodities.[263] The Jews stood in a special relationship to the king. He was their protector; his courts heard their suits, and the task of watching over them devolved inevitably on the sheriff. They formed permanent colonies only in the larger towns, principally in the county towns where the sheriff had his seat. He became their local protector and, though there was never a legal ghetto, they tended to live fairly close to the castle, and in an emergency sought refuge within it. In 1189 the York community withdrew to the castle which was, during the absence of the constable, stormed by the citizens.[264] At the same time the Lincoln community retreated to the castle in the face of a citizenry enflamed with crusading zeal, and were saved.[265] In Norwich the Jewry lay close to the castle,[266] and at Oxford at no great distance.[267] The king, of course, profited from the Jews, but the burden of protecting them from their fellow citizens always fell on the sheriff, who admitted them to his castle and heard suits between them and their fellow-citizens. At times his patience must have been sorely tested. In 1264, when the Northampton Jews were attacked, they retreated to the castle from which they refused to be dislodged, 'whereby the king is suffering no small loss'.[268]

The castle-gate town

The second kind of castle-town is that described by Beresford as the 'castle-gate' town.[269] It differed from the towns and castles already discussed in that the castle was the primary feature. It antedated the town and was the nucleus around which the town grew. Sometimes the town developed quickly. There were incipient boroughs at several of the castles named in Domesday Book. At Tutbury, in Staffordshire, there were forty-two *homines de mercato* who lived *in burgo circa castellum* by 1086.[270] In the Edwardian castle-gate towns of North Wales the construction of the town and its defences began long before that of the castle had been completed, and the two were tightly integrated, each satisfying the needs of the other. But as a general rule, there was a lapse of many years between the establishment of a castle and the foundation of its dependent borough.

It would be simplistic to assume that the castle-gate town developed by the gradual attraction of craftsmen and traders to the site. The process was immensely varied and never simple. Even in the late eleventh century there was little virgin land in England, and no knight or baron who built a castle could have done so far from an inhabited place. There was always a castle-gate village (see pp. 222–4) which

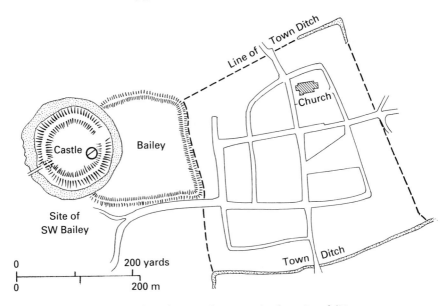

8.8 Castle and town of New Buckenham (Norfolk).

supplied labour and services to the castle and for which the castle served as manor house. The question is: how did a castle-gate village transform itself into a town?

A borough was both a legal and a functional entity. It enjoyed a legal status which distinguished it from the surrounding country. Its burgesses enjoyed a greater degree of personal freedom than the rural population; they had a court to settle their disputes; they each paid a fixed rent – a burgage rent – for their tenements, and they had a right to hold weekly market and perhaps an annual fair. This legal status was matched by a higher economic standing. The relative freedom of the borough attracted craftsmen who found little to hinder the pursuit of their· trade, and there arose a class of men in some degree divorced from the life of the land.

It was to the advantage of the lord to attract such a population to the vicinity of his castle. The creation of a castle-gate borough *could* become profitable through burgage rents and market tolls, but there was a limit to the number of boroughs that a primitive and nearly self-sufficient economy could sustain. Hope may have sprung eternal in the minds of lords, but all too often their hopes were dashed, and their incipient borough wilted and failed to grow. Many new towns were brought into being from the time of the Conquest until the mid-fourteenth century. Some grew up at the gates of monasteries; others at a river-crossing or a cross-roads.

It is impossible in many instances to date the rise of a borough. The first evidence we have of it is the grant of a charter to the would-be burgesses. This might be done by the king or by any of his barons for the settlements that they controlled. The charter defined and guaranteed the liberties of the borough. The terms and conditions of charters varied. The incorporation of towns was new in the late

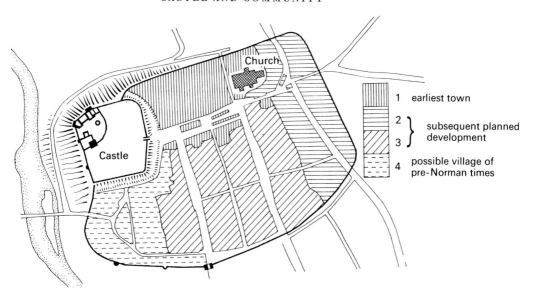

Church

1 earliest town

2 } subsequent planned
3 } development

4 possible village of
pre-Norman times

Castle

8.9 Ludlow: a planned town added to a castle-gate town.

eleventh century, and the model set by one apparently successful borough was
copied by countless others. The example of the 'liberties' of Breteuil, in Normandy,
was followed throughout the Welsh Border as one lord after another attempted to
establish a borough and thus to profit from its rents and tolls.[271]

The older boroughs, those which the Normans found in England when they
arrived, already had corporate institutions, however inchoate these may have been.
It was into these towns that the first category of urban castle had intruded. The castle
could not easily dominate and control a town, and the long struggle between them
ran through much of the Middle Ages. Such towns held their liberties by a kind of
prescriptive right. They none the less found it desirable to obtain and to renew
charters – almost always from the king – as a guarantee of their privileges. The
castle-gate town was, by contrast, the creature of its lord, who, as a general rule,
retained some degree of control over it. The royal officers, for example, maintained a
tight control over the towns of North Wales,[272] where the constable often served as
mayor.

Their long history was an indication of the economic success of the older castle-
towns. They had weathered successfully their early period of trial and difficulty. But
the castle-gate boroughs were new, untried and in some way experimental. A very
large number of the 'new towns' of the Middle Ages never achieved a condition of
sustained growth; some were still-born. In this sense, the country was over-
urbanised. Too many boroughs were incorporated without the economic basis for
sustained growth, and among these were many in Wales and the Marches. Mary
Bateson made the unkind remark that these 'planted' towns were most numerous in

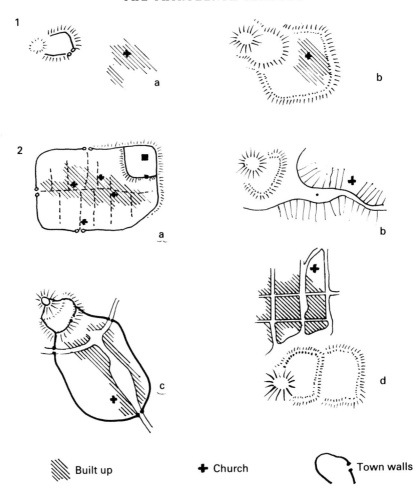

8.10 Castle and community; a simple model of the spatial relationships in (1) a village community; 1b shows a fenced village annexed to a castle; (2) the several patterns assumed by urban castles.

the more 'primitive' parts of this land.[273] The reason is that there was less need for them in the more developed areas, which had inherited a network of towns of Roman, Anglo-Saxon or Danish foundation.

About a third of the 'new towns' enumerated by Beresford were castle-gate towns. Even if many of these played no significant economic role, the importance of the castle in urban formation remains significant. Castle-gate towns had a form which clearly distinguished them from older boroughs. Limitations on space were less pressing; the town had usually little by way of defences – the North Wales boroughs constitute a significant exception – and it tended to straggle along a road. In a few instances the borough was located *within* a castle bailey, as at Trematon,[274]

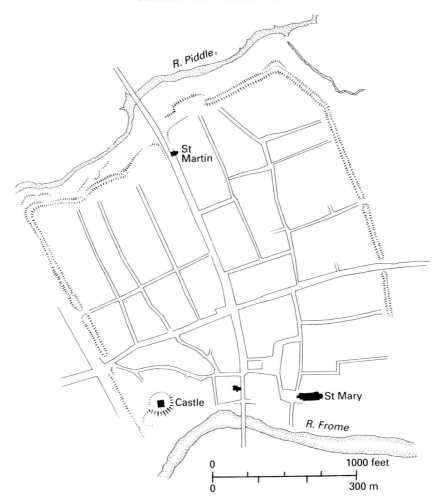

R. Piddle

St
Martin

Castle

St Mary

R. Frome

0				1000 feet

0			300 m

8.11 Wareham, fortified town and castle. The town was fortified late in the ninth century. The castle was established at an indeterminate date but soon after the Conquest, in the south-west corner of the town.

Richard's Castle, Skipsea, Oswestry and Caus. In general it was close by, consisting of little more than a broad street which stretched away from the castle-gate, widening sufficiently to constitute a market-place and bordered by the burgage plots which reached back to the edge of the surrounding fields. The borough of Tregony is typical of such towns, but similar town-plans can be seen at Pembroke, Totnes and elsewhere. At Devizes and Pleshey the main street of the town follows roughly the curvature of the castle ditch. In some instances, notably the Edwardian towns of North Wales, the urban settlement was built on a grid-iron plan, far more convenient if it was to be walled. Even in England such castle-gate towns emerged, as at Chipping (Saffron) Walden in Essex, Castle Acre and New Buckenham in

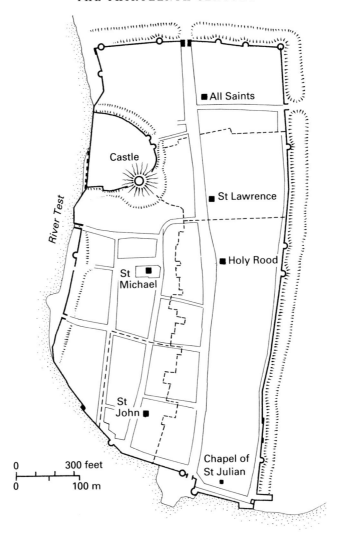

8.12 Southampton town and castle. The motte castle was built on the western edge of the Anglo-Norman settlement, between it and the River Test. The town walls were built later, and after a period of relative neglect the castle was greatly strengthened late in the fourteenth century as part of a system of coastal defence.

Norfolk, and Lostwithiel in Cornwall. When the castle of New Montgomery was founded in the 1220s, a town of straight, intersecting streets was laid out on the flat land below the rock on which the castle was built.

Nor was the town always at the castle-gate. When the de Cardinhams founded the borough of Lostwithiel they did so a kilometre and a half to the south of their castle of Restormel, beside the river Fowey, which was navigable up to this point. The town of Newport, Isle of Wight, lay even farther from Carisbrooke Castle, the seat of its founder, Richard de Redvers, and the boroughs of Montgomery, Dryslwyn and Dinefwr all lay below the crags on which these castles had been built.

The degree of control exercised over a castle-gate borough by the lord who had created it varied. In some instances the burghal liberties were little more than nominal; in others they amounted to a degree of freedom as great as that enjoyed in any royal borough. Frequently their burgage rents were commuted for an inclusive *firma burgi*; sometimes a fee was paid in lieu of the profits of courts and market tolls. But usually there remained some residual evidence of their dependent status: the obligation to bake in the lord's oven or to grind at the castle mill. In the borough of Trematon, in addition to all the obligations, the burgesses owed suit to their lord's court, and 'in time of war for the fortification of the castle they will carry two boat loads of stones . . . And they shall sell to the constable . . . 1 gallon of unshelled oysters for 1d'.[275] Such was the level of petty obligation that survived: too little in most instances to be burdensome but enough to be irritating.

The diagrams in Figure 8.10, attempt to represent the types of relationship that existed between castle and both borough and church. The latter relationship was of great significance for both the community of the castle and that of the castle town, and is examined in the next chapter.

CHAPTER 9

Castle and church

Thenne the moder of Parys shewed hir al the castel, and ledde hir in to an halle, al ful of armes and abylemens of warre for to fyght in battayll . . . And the chambre of Parys where that he slept . . . [and] on a syde of the chambre . . . they fande a lytel dore, of Whyche henge a lytel key by a thwonge, and anon they opened the dore and entred therin. And there was a lytel chambre whyche was xii fote large, and was an oratorye wherein was the majeste of our Lorde Jhesu Cryst upon a lytel aulter, and at eche corner was a candelstyke of syluer.

Storye of the Knyght Parys and of the fayre Vyenne, Caxton 1485

In the medieval view there were three orders of society: the feudal classes, the church and the peasantry, from which gradually emerged the fourth estate of traders and craftsmen. In the last chapter the relationship of the feudal class, as represented by its castle, to the peasant and commercial classes has been discussed. It remains to explore the relations of castle and church. These were especially close. The more exalted members of the church's hierarchy came, for the greater part, from the feudal and landowning classes. The church was itself a great landowner, holding about a quarter of the area surveyed in Domesday Book. Many bishops possessed fortified residences, and there were monasteries which surrounded themselves with crenellated walls.

The feudal aristocracy was, in its own estimation, dependent upon the church. It was the church which could provide atonement for their rumbustious and violent lives. The masses said for their souls could alone save them from eternal damnation, and they were prepared to buy their future salvation at a very high price. One is constantly amazed at the extent of the lands with which knights and barons were prepared to endow a church, at least until the Statute of Mortmain (1279) set limits. But at the same time the laity was always watchful of its interests; it would endow a monastic house with land and yet cavil at paying tithe on the corn ground at the castle mill.

Castle and parish

The parochial system of this country was taking shape when the first castles were established. Much of lowland England was already divided into parishes, though little precision had yet been given to parochial boundaries. By 1086 there was a more or less uniform system of parish churches over much of England, each endowed with

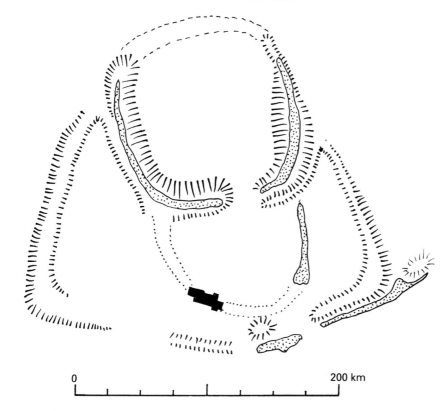

0   200 km

9.1 Castle Camps (Cambridgeshire). The outer bailey of this large ringwork of the de Veres
appears to have been enlarged to form a village enclosure. The parish church was sited
approximately over the ditch of the original outer bailey.

a field or two (the glebe), demanding tithe of the yield of nature, and receiving fees
and oblations for marriage and burial. In many instances the church belonged to the
local lord; it was his *Eigenkirche*; he appointed and paid a priest and received the
profits of the 'living'. It was a profitable business, like establishing a market or
creating a borough, but it was one which the lords could be induced to forgo in the
interests of their future salvation.

In the course of the twelfth century the parochial system acquired the shape which
it was to retain throughout the Middle Ages. It had grown out of the large and
inchoate minster parishes of the Anglo-Saxon period. Its churches were either
mission centres, established by and served from minsters, or private churches,
founded and endowed by a thegn for himself, his family and his dependants. Indeed,
possession of a church was one of the features which distinguished the thegn from
the ceorl.[1] The thegn had built the church and had endowed it with a small tract of
land, and to his successors it was a source of income. The Norman lord who took
over the lands of the Saxon thegn inherited also the latter's church. The church
already served a small community, and the three – lord, church and parisioners –

223

formed a discrete whole. If a castle replaced the thegn's burh, as it did in very many instances, it was absorbed into this microcosm. The thegn's church became the church of the Norman lord, and castle and church, symbiotically linked, became a common feature of rural England. In a few instances the church even lay within the bailey of a castle (Figure 9.1). In a majority of cases the castle was built within half a kilometre of the church. One cannot be sure in every instance that the ownership of the church was vested in the castle which had been built nearby. There are instances of a single parish being divided between two lords, each, as for example at Ascot (Oxfordshire), having his own castle. But in many instances Domesday shows the church as a dependency of the manor.

The first wave of castle-building in England and the Marches coincided with a period of reform within the church. At the heart of the latter was the eradication of lay control. Kings and princes were denied the right to nominate and control the higher dignitaries of the church, while, at a lower level, the local lord was induced to give up his rights over his *Eigenkirche* and to entrust them to a religious institution. The latter henceforward received the revenues, of which the tithe was by far the most important, and deputed a 'vicar' to minister to the spiritual needs of the parishioners. In return the prayers of the religious house, so much more effective than those of a humble parish priest, would be offered for the souls of the lord's family. The nexus between the castle and its local church was in a sense broken. Members of the lord's family might continue to be buried in the church or its cemetery, and later in the Middle Ages a chantry might be added both for their interment and for the masses that would be said for their souls. But the lord no longer controlled the church and its priest ceased to be *his* man.

The castle chapel

There were many reasons why a private chapel should be established within the walls of a castle, not least of them the fact that in many instances the lord had lost control over the local church. At a time when the mass was assuming an ever greater importance in the lives of laymen and clergy alike, and when altars were proliferating around the apses and transepts of great churches, the lord desired his own private chapel, where daily masses could be said on his behalf. In the earliest masonry-built castles, Colchester and the Tower of London, a chapel of generous proportions was incorporated in the plan from the start, the eastern face of the keep being made to protrude in order to contain its rounded apse. The possession of a private chapel called for the services of a private chaplain. Since the priest was likely to be the only literate member of the castle community, he was called upon to keep the records and return the writs. These activities were of little significance before the mid-twelfth century, but thereafter every royal castle and every baronial *caput* required some form of secretariat, and, as the volume of business and administration mounted, so did the demand for the services of the domestic clerk.

It is difficult to determine how far the ministrations of a parish priest were

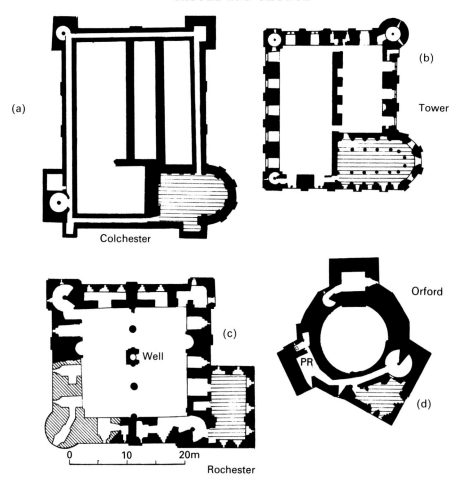

9.2 The location of the chapel (shaded horizontally) in four tower-keeps: (a) Colchester, (b) Tower of London, (c) Rochester, (d) Orford. Orford had in addition what appears to have been a priest's room (PR).

replaced by those of a domestic chaplain. A chapel was expensive to build; the priest demanded a salary, and there were also the incidental expenses of vestments, mass books and sacramental materials, as shown in the quotation at the head of this chapter. A knight or lord of two or three manors could not, in all probability, rise to such an outlay, and the symbiotic relationship between castle and parish church may have continued as long as the castle remained habitable. It was probably a matter of cost. A chapel was built within the *capita* of most baronies, but almost certainly not in the simple wooden defences of a small motte-and-bailey. There is no evidence for a chapel even in the castle of Hen Domen, though there was one in the masonry castle which succeeded it.

During the thirteenth century the evidence, both documentary and archaeologi-

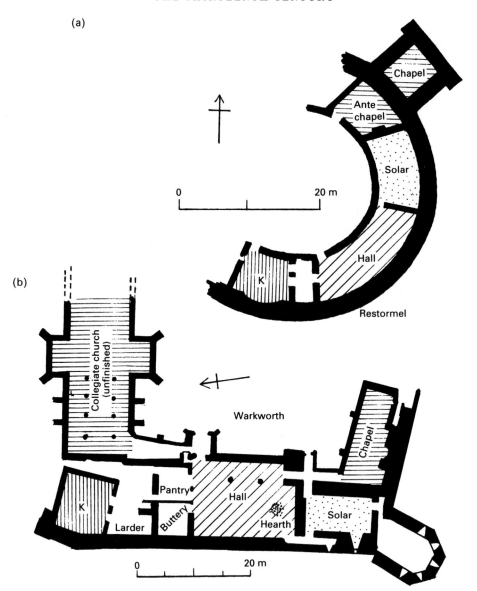

9.3 Chapels as part of the hall–kitchen–solar complex at (a) Restormel Castle (Cornwall) and (b) Warkworth Castle (Northumberland). At Warkworth the earlier chapel to the east was intended to be replaced by the large collegiate church, to the west, which was left unfinished.

cal, is overwhelming for the existence of chapels in royal castles and the more important baronial ones. The public records show from quite early in the century not inconsiderable expenditures on the equipping and repair of chapels. In 1243 order was given to build *unam capellam magnam de plaustro in castro regis* of Hertford.[2] This was evidently a timber-framed structure with walls of wattle and daub. In 1237 timber was provided for the chapel of St Jude (Sancti Judoci) in Winchester Castle,[3] and order was given at Rhuddlan to make 'a wooden chapel' and engage a chaplain to say mass three times daily.[4]

It is unlikely that the chapel would have been of masonry when the outer defences of the castle were still of timber. Large hall-keeps had space for a chapel; the smaller tower-keeps probably had not. One looks in vain for a chapel within the restricted space of most masonry-built shell-keeps. That at Restormel (Cornwall) was added later, and was made to project into the ditch.[5] It might not be an exaggeration to say that the proliferation of castle chapels really began when the life of the household began to spread from the tower- or shell-keep to the greater space of the bailey. The chapel of Orford Castle was perhaps the last to be built within a tower-keep. It was constructed above the entrance passage in the forebuilding.[6]

When, in the thirteenth century, castles began to be built on a courtyard plan and older castles to be remodelled, the chapel was generally built, along with hall and chambers, along the sides of the bailey. The Edwardian castles of Harlech and Conwy show this development, and at Conwy there is evidence in the building accounts of Llewelyn's Hall, that hall and chapel were conceived as a unit and built at the same time.[7] In earlier cases, where the chapel was not incorporated into the keep, it was built as a freestanding structure within the bailey, as at Pevensey, Pickering and probably Richmond, where it was later moved to the side of the court.[8]

During the later Middle Ages the diocesan bishop claimed some control over private chapels, licensing them and recording them in the episcopal register. But bishops achieved only a limited success. They could, and did, deny the right to have a baptismal font and a cemetery, the prerogative of parish churches, but could not otherwise prevent the appointment of priests to say mass and carry on secretarial duties within a castle.[9] Indeed, when the Bishop of Lichfield advanced a claim over the chapel of St Michael in the castle of Shrewsbury, he was rebuffed with the words that it was 'exempt from all ordinary jurisdiction'.[10] And when chapels were built at the new castles of Sauvey,[11] Horston,[12] York,[13] Hertford[14] and at the North Wales castle of Dyserth[15] in the thirteenth century, there is no suggestion that the bishop was in any way involved.

The constitutional position of some castle chapels, however, was more complex than this. The building of a castle chapel and the appointment of a priest was analogous to the thegn creating his own *Eigenkirche*. The relationship of landholder to church had almost come full circle. It remained only to endow the castle chapel with land so that it would continue to have an income, thus making it independent of the castle. The chapel of St George within Oxford Castle was endowed in this way.[16] The chapel of Chilham Castle enjoyed an income of one mark a year,[17] and at

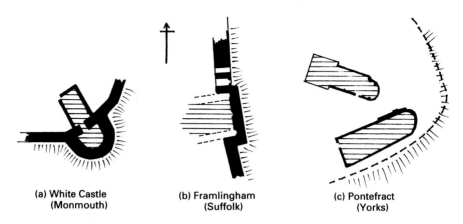

(a) White Castle
(Monmouth)

(b) Framlingham
(Suffolk)

(c) Pontefract
(Yorks)

9.4 Chapels in relation to the curtain wall at (a) White Castle and (b) Framlingham. At Pontefract (c) there were two freestanding chapels in the bailey, one perhaps replacing the other.

Farnham Castle, which belonged to the Bishop of Winchester, an endowment was set up to support the chaplain.[18] At Ludlow Castle the chapel was worth 40s a year,[19] and at Pleshey Castle, £6..13..4.[20] St George's Chapel in Windsor Castle was unusually well endowed,[21] as were the chapels at Wallingford, Hastings, Bridgnorth, Pontefract and at several others. At Barnard Castle land was given to support two chaplains serving the chapel of St Margaret;[22] at nearby Richmond Castle an income of £25 was designated for the support of six chaplains, enough to allow them to live in some comfort,[23] and at Nottingham the chapel was allocated the tithe of the Castle Mill.[24] At the relatively unimportant castle of Snodhill (Hereford), its owner, Sir John Chandos, retained the advowson – the right to present a priest who would serve the chapel and receive its emolument – after he had alienated the castle without having first obtained royal consent.[25]

A castle chapel, once it had acquired an independent income, became an asset which any monastic house would have desired, especially if the cost of supplying a priest was less than the income of the chapel. The chapel of St George within Oxford Castle was thus given to Oseney Abbey[26] and to it were later added the tithes of the castle mill.[27] The canons of Oseney became accustomed to crossing a small bridge when they went to celebrate in the castle. When, in 1324, the bridge was removed by the sheriff for the security of the castle, the king ordered its restitution for the convenience of the canons.[28] In 1130 Henry I confirmed to the canons of St Mary of Huntingdon the chapel of Huntingdon Castle.[29] The castle was destroyed after the revolt of 1172, but the grant of its chapel was confirmed by Henry III more than a century later;[30] evidently the priory had continued to enjoy the emolument while its obligations had evaporated. Henry I also gave to the canons of Launceston Priory 'the portion and alms of his chapel in the castle there which Bernard the priest and Hamelin held. The canons shall serve the chapel by one priest as Hamelin did'.[31] Stephen of Brittany gave the church of Richmond, together with the castle chapel

9.5 The chapel of Ludlow Castle, unique among castle chapels in Britain in having a round nave. The drawing shows the west door. There was an apsidal chancel to the east.

and the tithes of the whole castlery within Yorkshire (*decimas de dominio castellariae suae . . . in Eboracshira*), to St Mary's Abbey, York.[32] Other instances could be cited: the canons of Leeds Priory celebrated in Leeds Castle;[33] the chapel of Scarborough 'has been time out of mind . . . annexed to' the church of St Mary of Scarborough,[34] and the chapel in the 'Old' castle of Basing (Hampshire), worth 40s a year, was held by an alien priory,[35] and for that reason was in 1349 held in the king's hands.[36] In the end all such advowsons (*advocationes*) passed to the king when the monastic houses were dissolved.

The opposite happened at Farleigh Hungerford (Somerset), where Sir Thomas de Hungerford built a castle about 1383. At first it had no chapel, but was separated only by its ditch from the parish church of St Leonard.[37] Some forty years later a second ward was added by his son, Sir Walter de Hungerford, enclosing the parish church, which was transformed into the castle chapel. This was followed by the building of a new parish church 300 m to the west. The original parish church became a chantry, served by a staff of priests who lived in the surviving priests' house, built into the eastern curtain of the outer ward (Figure 10.7).[38]

In thus becoming separately endowed many castle chapels assumed quasi-parochial functions. Did any of them, one may ask, ever become fully parochial? There is the curious case of the chapel, built in all probability by Roger of Poitou in his castle of Clitheroe (Lancashire).[39] The castle lay in the parish of Whalley, whose church was some 10 km from the castle. According to a history of the de Lacys, probably written at Whalley Abbey, the chapel was not only endowed with land and tithes, but came to serve the community gathered round the castle because of the distance from the mother church. The castle chapel became something more than a chapel-of-ease; it enjoyed the tithes of the quasi-parish of Clitheroe, an arrangement that was confirmed in 1185–7 by Pope Urban III.[40]

Castle chapels did not, as a general rule, have fonts, since these were a mark of parochial status. Nevertheless, when the parish church of Farleigh Hungerford was brought within the castle and a new church was built elsewhere (see p. 229), the font was retained, and remains within the castle today. There is also a case recorded in an inquest *post mortem*, of a baptism in the chapel of Caerphilly Castle.

Clitheroe was not the only castle whose chapel assumed parochial functions. It is even likely that some castles assimilated a pre-existing church and used it for their own purposes. The representation in the Bayeux Tapestry of the building of Hastings Castle (Figure 9.6) shows, beside the earthwork, the tower of a completed church which may have served some parochial functions, and the college of canons which was founded on the site is assumed to have derived from this pre-Conquest church.[41] At Pevensey also there was a pre-Conquest church within the walls of the Roman fort of Anderida, performing presumably parochial functions. It was enclosed within the inner bailey of the Norman castle, where its ground plan remains visible today.[42] In 1152 Stephen gave *capellarium de Pevenesel*, together with all that belonged to it, to the Bishop of Chichester.[43] It appears to have continued to serve as a parish church until, about 1250, permission was given to build another church for the parish outside the walls of the castle.

A not dissimilar situation arose at Hereford. Here the Anglo-Saxon church of St Guthlac was enclosed within the limits of the castle, where its foundations have recently been excavated.[44] It appears to have been abandoned only when its parish was merged with the urban parish of St Martin. The church of All Saints, Warwick was, it is claimed, built within the bailey of the castle by Henry de Beaumont early in the twelfth century. It was parochial, and for this reason was later moved outside the castle. Both the parish and its tithes were then merged with those of the collegiate church of St Mary.[45]

Even though the parochial system was at the time of the Conquest still in process of formation, it is not improbable that a castle, especially an urban castle, would incorporate a church within its limits. It is arguable that the castles of Oxford, Norwich, Colchester and Leicester incorporated earlier churches and thus inherited some kind of parochial status and function. At London and Dover this process is clearer. The building of the Tower of London in the south-eastern corner of the Roman enceinte led to the blocking of a road which ran from Eastcheap, along Great

Tower Street, to a gate in the Roman wall near the river.[46] Close to this road lay the church of St Peter ad Vincula, its parish occupying this corner of the walled city and stretching eastwards beyond the walls. The outline of the early *castellum*, as revealed by Davison's excavation, shows that the church was left outside, but very close to the perimeter of the castle.[47] Only with the construction of Henry III's circuit of walls was the church taken into the castle and handsomely rebuilt.[48] The acquisition of a new baptismal font is evidence that its parochial functions continued, even though the church itself became like the chapel of St John within the Tower, a 'free' chapel, subject only to the king and the Pope.

Of the antiquity of the church of St Mary within the castle of Dover there can be no question. It was a masonry-built church of cruciform plan, annexed at its western end to the surviving Roman *pharos*.[49] It probably lay within whatever fortifications had been erected by the last of the Anglo-Saxon kings, but was outside the first Norman castle.[50] It was not until the thirteenth century that the castle wall was extended and a deep ditch cut to bring the church within the castle. There can be little doubt that St Mary's was and remained a parish church. In 1251 the sheriff was instructed to buy copper and tin to cast three new bells for the church – a mark of parochial status.[51] The church was listed in the *Taxatio* of Pope Nicholas IV of 1291, and during the next century St Mary's was repeatedly referred to as a 'parish' church. But the parish was evidently small and poor, and in 1380 a fee of £10 a year, given to the priest, was raised because the 'oblations and other obventions of the parishioners are of little value'.[52] The chapel within the great keep of Dover was a royal peculiar, but the parish church of St Mary was, like any other, subject to the jurisdiction of its own diocesan.

Many castle chapels, particularly those located in royal castles, were, indeed, crown peculiars, exempt from the jurisdiction of the bishop, and subject only to the king and the pope. It was customary to refer to them as 'free' chapels. The extent to which baronial castles enjoyed this privilege is obscure. The great majority of castles built before the thirteenth century had no private chapel and were fully a part of the parishes in which they lay. Demesne and castle paid tithe to the parish church or to a monastery to which it had been impropriated. It is in the castles of the richer and more powerful barons that one finds private chapels, and it was just these lords who were best placed to flout the jurisdiction of their bishops. Nevertheless, this writer has found evidence for a 'free' chapel in only a handful of castles, among them Pleshey,[53] Skipton,[54] Old Basing,[55] Stafford,[56] Oswestry[57] and Oakham.[58] There were doubtless some where the baronial claim was accepted and, probably, others where the matter was never put to the test.

The castle and the religious orders

The Norman conquerors exhibited an intense religious fervour, by which they compensated for the ferocity with which they lived and fought. Their munificence to the church was not restricted to the endowment of private chapels and the gift of advowsons. They established monasteries and endowed them with lands and revenues. They upgraded minster churches into houses of regular canons, and this practice continued until Edward I set limits to it.[59] An *Eigenkloster* was a more exalted possession than an *Eigenkirche*, and doubtless the spiritual gains were proportionately greater. The monastery was expected to offer prayers for the pious founder and his family, and the latter became the 'patrons' of the house. They expected to be consulted on important matters and to continue to use the monastic church as a kind of dynastic mausoleum.

The church which they founded was commonly close to their principal castle, though it might be wherever they had land to give. Michael Thompson has published a tentative list of castles whose lords founded and endowed a house of monks or canons in the vicinity of their castles. Foundations varied greatly in the scale of their endowment. Monastic houses rarely came into being spontaneously, because there was no land without its lord who alone could allocate it to whatever religious order he favoured. An income was generated, and a church and conventual buildings were erected. The size and elaboration of the buildings depended upon the scale of the endowment. Amongst the largest were the Cluniac houses founded by William de Warenne within sight of his castles at Lewes (Sussex) and Castle Acre (Norfolk). Amongst the smallest was the priory of Penwortham (Lancashire), founded by William Bussel, a short distance west of his castle of Penwortham, on the south bank of the Ribble.[60] The priory was so poor that it became a cell to Evesham Abbey, and the castle appears to have been abandoned at an early date.[61] Some such foundations were cells of alien houses in France, and thus suffered a premature dissolution early in the fifteenth century. Amongst them were the diminutive priory of Brimpsfield, a cell of Fontenay in Normandy, founded by the Giffards beside their motte castle in Gloucestershire,[62] and also Beaulieu (Beadlow) Priory, established by Robert d'Aubigny of Clophill (Cainhoe) Castle (Bedfordshire), as a cell of St Alban's.[63]

Barons were most active in founding religious houses from the time of the Conquest until the mid-twelfth century. Thereafter there was a lull, followed by renewed activity in the fourteenth and fifteenth centuries. The following table, derived from Thompson's statistics, shows the dates of foundation of castle-related houses.

Most of the early foundations belonged to the established monastic orders. A third were Benedictine or Cluniac and almost a quarter Augustinian. About 18 per cent were cells attached to alien houses, most of them set up during the very early days of the Conquest, when the Normans still retained close ties with Normandy. Only eleven houses out of 124 were secular colleges. After about 1200 a change took place in the nature of the houses established. Out of forty-six foundations only eight belonged to the regular monastic orders. The rest were houses either of friars or of secular canons. This must have reflected changed attitudes towards the church. Gone was respect for the monk who withdrew from the world. Instead, lands were used to endow Augustinian canons, the orders of friars, and, above all, secular

Table 9.1. *Monastic foundations
related to castles*

Eleventh century	45
Twelfth century	79
Thirteenth century	9
Fourteenth century	23
Fifteenth century	11
Sixteenth century	3

canons, who lived in the world and became in varying degrees the social workers of their age.

Colleges of secular canons were set up, each consisting of a group of priests, their number varying with their endowment and 'linked more or less closely to the patron's household, the service of his chapel, and perhaps the staffing of his secretariat'.[64] The college was a more flexible body than a community of monks. The lord could 'present' the prebends who made up the college, and thus he had a means of rewarding those who served him. The canons were not tied to the cloister, and were free to undertake other services on his behalf, and, on the spiritual side, he had no reason to suppose that their masses were less effective than those of cloistered monks.

Some such colleges appear to have been founded soon after the Conquest. One of them was the college of secular canons established within the bailey of Hastings Castle. Its surviving foundations, according to Taylor, contain pre-Conquest features.[65] This college was founded and endowed by Robert d'Eu, the first Norman lord of the Rape of Hastings, who must be presumed to have taken over and adapted an Anglo-Saxon structure. The castle lay on the edge of the cliff which has since receded, so that it is now impossible to say how extensive was the original bailey. The canons' church, together with their conventual buildings, may have occupied a considerable part of it, thus reducing its military effectiveness.[66] An inquisition of 1273 found that the income of the college amounted to 4 marks in tithes, 10 marks in offerings and £5 in rents. At the same time there were eight prebends, whose individual stipends ranged from $3\frac{1}{2}$ marks to 50.[67] The latter sums derived from lands that were attached to individual prebends. The college was thus as wealthy as many a small monastery. The king retained the right to nominate prebends in spite of the attempts of the Bishop of Chichester to limit his choice and control their induction. The canons occupied 'houses' within the bailey, where their relations with the constable and garrison were, at the least, somewhat troubled. In 1322 the constable was accused of expelling the canons from their dwellings and of seizing the keys of the vestry, treasury, chapel and belfry.[68] The castle was then increasingly neglected, and the canons complained that the walls were inadequate to give them protection from intruders.[69] Indeed, the college outlived the castle. It appears to have enjoyed

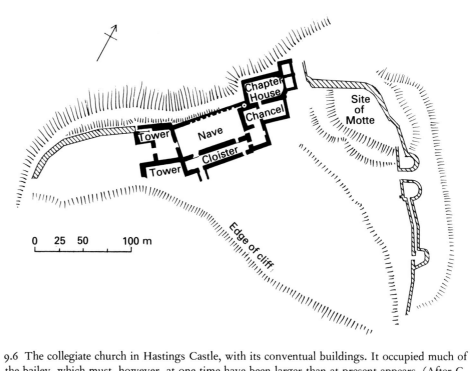

9.6 The collegiate church in Hastings Castle, with its conventual buildings. It occupied much of the bailey, which must, however, at one time have been larger than at present appears. (After C. Dawson, *History of Hastings Castle*, London, 1909.)

parochial status, though its parish may have amounted to little more than the castle site, and was in the sixteenth century merged with that of St Andrew-sub-Castro, whose church has also in its turn disappeared.

West of Hastings lay the Rape of Bramber, where William de Braose founded Bramber Castle and established a college of canons, claiming for it parochial rights. The latter was located, not within the castle, but on the steep slope below its gatehouse tower. The remains of the present church suggest that it was a cruciform building, and surviving sculpture provides evidence of an early Norman date.[70] It appears to have tried to usurp parochial rights over the Steyning district, and was resisted by the Normandy abbey of Fécamp to which the parish had been impropriated. A judgment of 1086 went against de Braose, and bodies had to be dug up from the Bramber cemetery and reinterred at Steyning, Fécamp, of course, receiving mortuary dues.[71]

More familiar are the collegiate foundations established in the castles of Bridgnorth and Shrewsbury by members of the de Montgomery family. The chapel of St Michael within Shrewsbury Castle had parochial rights and an endowment of 150 acres.[72] Its site is unknown, as is the constitution by which it was governed.[73] In the later fourteenth century its buildings, like the castle as a whole, were in disrepair, and the list of chaplains or deans ends early in the next century.[74]

The collegiate church at Bridgnorth has a longer and fuller history than most others. It was, like St Michael's, Shrewsbury, founded by Roger de Montgomery in or very close to his castle of Quatford, above the steep, *eastern* bank of the Severn.[75] Nothing is known of it, but the parish church, which adjoins the castle site, has some splendid Norman arches. At the end of the eleventh century the castle was abandoned by Robert of Bellême, Roger's son and successor, in favour of a hilltop site at Bridgnorth, 3 km distant and on the west bank of the river.[76] The collegiate foundation was moved along with the castle, and was established in the outer bailey. It came eventually to be staffed by a dean and six prebendaries, who were mainly non-resident. The college was a 'free' chapel, and the prebends were in the gift of the king, who used them to reward his friends and servants. The college was dissolved in the sixteenth century, but its church continued in use until, late in the eighteenth century, it was torn down and replaced by the present classical building. Eighteenth-century drawings of the medieval church show a nave and large chancel, together with a west tower.[77] Though free of episcopal jurisdiction, the college was clearly parochial. It appears to have had some authority over the town in which the church of St Leonard was only a chapelry of St Mary's in the castle.

There were collegiate foundations at an early date at other royal and baronial castles. At Pontefract there was a college comprising a dean and four canons, quite independent of the nearby priory which had also been founded by de Lacy.[78] It was given the tithes of a number of parishes and was relatively well endowed. The case of Alnwick Castle formed a close parallel to that of Pontefract. In addition to a priory, founded by the lords of Alnwick, there was also a chantry within the castle served by four priests, who must have constituted a small and somewhat informal college. Their church, 'between the ravine and the Constable's Tower', was relatively large, and was subject to the jurisdiction of the *Arch*bishop, whose register records the induction of the chaplains.[79] The chantry certificate submitted at the Dissolution recorded three priests, who were given pensions, but no landed endowments. Subsequently, a 'parcel of concealed land', valued at one mark, came to light.

The college of St Mary in the castle of Leicester is said to have been founded by Robert le Bossu early in the twelfth century, but in 1143 it was given as part of its endowment to the newly founded Leicester Abbey.[80] It continued, however, to exist as a semi-independent college, 'probably on the ground that thus a staff of priests, living on freehold benefices of their own, was secured to the castle'.[81] The college had parochial status and enjoyed privileges rarely granted to such an institution. Henry IV granted it a court leet for residents of its precinct, 'notwithstanding part of the site being within the view [of frankpledge] of the castellward of Leicester and part within the view of the town'.[82]

The college which Robert d'Oilly founded within his castle of Wallingford attracted considerable endowments[83] and was able to support six chaplains, six clerks and four choristers.[84] In 1445 the priests and clerks, who already received 10 marks a year from the king, were given an additional 10 marks 'in consideration that for lack of choristers the dean and chaplains . . . must needs hire children elsewhere on every feast day'.[85] In 1389 the church of All Saints, Wallingford, was appropriated to the college, and presumably the parochial functions of the two were merged.[86]

After about 1300 chapels and religious foundations within castles fell upon less fortunate times. The records emphasise their ruinous condition and the non-residence of their canons and chaplains. The chapel of St George at York Castle was in 1446 'long desolate for non-residence of chaplains and owing to its small value'.[87] The slender endowment of many others must have made it difficult to maintain good order and to pay a serving priest. At the same time popular views on the role of the church were undergoing a change. If the ideas expressed, for example, in *Piers Plowman* were at all widespread, as they were, there would have been a growing reluctance to support castle chapels. Furthermore, the castles themselves were increasingly neglected. Many were rarely used; their administrative functions, which had been closely linked with the support of clerics, declined, and the great lords who journeyed from one castle to another were likely to take their ghostly retainers with them as part of their entourage.

Yet interest in establishing both chapels and colleges within or in close proximity to castles did not wholly disappear during the last two centuries of the Middle Ages. New castles were established and in most of them chapels, some of them very splendid, were built. In several, plans were laid – not all of them fulfilled – for establishing colleges of canons. When Sir John Fastolfe built Caistor Castle (Norfolk), his intention was to found some form of religious community within one of its spacious wards.[88] This he did not do during his lifetime, but at his death in 1459 he left lands to his executors to carry out his wish. His will was disputed, and no attempt was ever made to found the college. What happened at Thornbury Castle (Gloucestershire) was similar. In 1510 Edward Stafford, Duke of Buckingham, secured licence to 'fortify, crenellate and embattle' his manor house. The resulting structure had little military pretension, but it contained a chapel, and it was intended to establish a college of canons. This was anticipated by the Duke's execution in 1522.[89]

The great college in Warkworth Castle (Northumberland) was yet another abortive attempt to establish a college of canons *within* a castle. It was planned, in all probability, by Henry Percy, the first earl of Northumberland, at the end of the fourteenth century. As originally conceived, it consisted of an aisled nave and chancel, with transepts and a tower at the crossing. It was placed *across* the bailey, completely blocking access to the motte and keep (Figure 9.3) so that a vaulted passageway had to be constructed beneath the chancel to connect the two.[90] It was never finished, only the foundations giving some idea of its size and probable splendour. It is likely that Northumberland's involvement in the rebellion against Henry IV and his flight in 1405 put an end to his schemes.

At the same time Richard, Lord Scrope, was building his castle at Bolton in Wensleydale, and had obtained from Richard II leave to have in it a chantry for six priests.[91] A few years later his plans were changed. Instead of a small college within his castle, he now established a collegiate foundation in the village of Wensley, 6 km down the dale, stipulating that it provide a chaplain to serve in the chapel of St Anne within the castle.[92]

Of approximately the same date was the college set up at Fotheringhay (Northamptonshire) by Edmund of Langley, earl of Cambridge and younger son of Edward III. No attempt was made to locate it within the castle. Instead, a tract of land was set aside for it 'between Fotheringhay Castle . . . the rectory . . . the churchyard . . . and the river Nene'.[93] The college consisted of a master, twelve fellows, eight clerks and thirteen choristers, but today only its nave and west tower remain.

Another such foundation was that which Lord Treasurer Ralph Cromwell established beside his towering keep at Tattershall. Permission for the foundation was given in 1439, but it was another ten years before the buildings were erected and the warden inducted.[94] The cloistral buildings, which lay to the south of the church, followed but were not complete until long after the death of their founder.

One feature of all these late medieval collegiate foundations was the large scale on which they were conceived and the fineness of the workmanship that went into them. They were, without exception, creations of the aristocracy. Why, one may ask, did they lavish their wealth on such foundations which could have been of little practical use to them? The answer may, perhaps, be found in the biggest, grandest and most richly endowed of all colleges established within or close to a castle: St George's, Windsor. Windsor Castle, as one of the principal residences of the kings of England, was well equipped with chapels and priests. Until late in the twelfth century there was a chapel, served by a single priest, probably in the Great Tower. A second chapel was then established in the lower ward, and a third close to the Queen's lodging, and the number of priests was increased proportionately with the amount of royal business.[95] A 'great new chapel' of St Edward was then built in the lower ward, and additional chaplains hired.[96] Early in the next century a chapel was established near the south gate of Windsor Great Park. The spiritual establishment of Windsor Castle was thus widely diffused and expensive to maintain, and Edward III rationalised the system by drawing its disparate elements together into a single chapel dedicated to St George, and freestanding in the lower ward.

The king's motives were not only to reduce expenditure, which he may not have done, but also to create a proper home for the new order of chivalry which he had created, the Order of the Garter. The collegiate foundation was established by royal patent in 1348. It consisted of twenty-four canons, later raised to twenty-six, one of whom was to be warden, and a similar number of poor knights and others who had earned this elegant retirement by their service to the king. All lived within the castle, received a wage and were fed and clothed. The patent rolls record the appointment of both the priestly and the lay members of the college. The earlier chapel of St Edward was adapted to the new requirements, and an additional cloister was built, together with houses for the priests and pensioners.[97] The college of St George, when completed later in the century, consisted, in addition to its chapel, cloister and lodgings, of bakehouse, brewhouse and horse-mill.[98] A latrine was constructed for

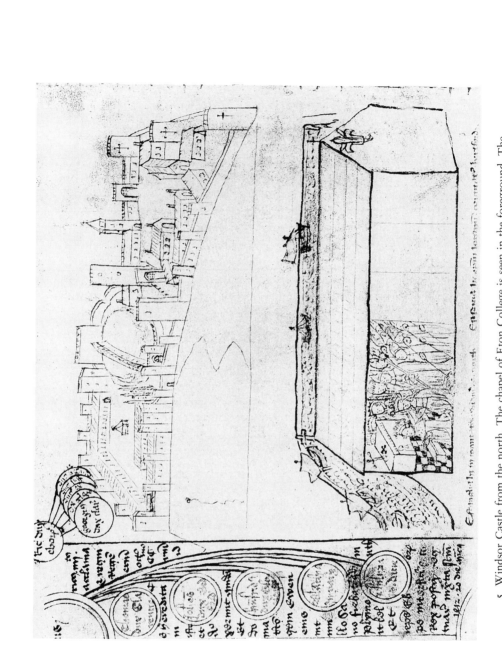

5 Windsor Castle from the north. The chapel of Eton College is seen in the foreground. The motte and great tower appear between the upper (left) ward and the lower. Freestanding in the latter is Edward III's chapel, predecessor of the present St George's Chapel, in which the Order of the Garter was initiated.

the canons in a tower of the north wall of the bailey, and their cemetery, beyond this wall, was reached by a postern cut for the purpose.[99] The feast of St George was celebrated here with great splendour in 1358, by which date, it is to be presumed, the college was complete. The college of Edward III lay in the north-east corner of the lower bailey, with the two cloisters of the canons between it and the bailey wall. It is shown in a drawing (Plate 5) in the library of Eton College. It must have been a splendid structure, making a profound impression on the Garter Knights who gathered here to celebrate the feast of their patron. Several of those who founded, or attempted to establish, colleges in their castles, must have participated in the ceremonies of the Order in this very chapel.

Edward IV, nevertheless, set out to build a chapel even grander than that which he had inherited. The new chapel – the present St George's – was built to the west of Edward III's chapel, which was demolished and its site occupied by the new Lady Chapel.[100] Construction was begun in 1477, but was far from complete when the king died in 1483. His successor contributed nothing, and it was left for the early Tudors to finish the building.[101] St George's, Windsor, became at once the grandest of all castle chapels and, indeed, of all collegiate foundations outside the universities. It was the Yorkists' reply to the Lancastrian chapel of Henry VI at Cambridge. It dominated the lower ward of the castle and shows how completely the military functions of this – one of the strongest of English castles – had been subordinated to other considerations.

The castle chapel

Very few stone-built castles lacked a chapel. A few still maintained their symbiotic relationship to the church of their parish, but most had succeeded in distancing themselves from it and had established a private chapel for the lord and his household. For many castle chapels there is neither unambiguous documentation nor surviving remains. But if a lord had the means to build a substantial masonry castle he might be expected also to maintain a chapel and its chaplain. Pride, piety, convenience and even profit called for no less. In royal castles and the greater baronial ones the size of the clerical staff was as likely to be determined by the volume of writs and records to be handled as by the spiritual needs of the castle's community. Even in small baronial castles there were court rolls to be kept and accounts to be enrolled. *Piers Plowman* gives us a picture of the priest who was better at handling his master's manorial court than at saying mass.[102]

In most tower-keeps of the later eleventh and twelfth centuries a chapel was incorporated into the original plans. Most often it opened off the main hall and was readily accessible from the principal living quarters. Most splendid and also one of the earliest is the chapel of St John the Baptist in the Tower of London. It occupies a significant part of the lofty upper floor which contained the king's state apartments.[103] It is an aisled structure with a triforium, and terminates in an apse which projects from the east wall of the Tower.

At Colchester Castle, begun a year or two before the Tower and conceived on an even grander scale, the chapel occupied a similar position in relation to the keep as a whole. Unfortunately the upper floor of the castle, and with it the chapel, has been destroyed. It appears, however, to have been a little shorter than that of St John, but had a similar apsidal termination.[104] It is likely to have had an arcade, and, opening off it, in the thickness of a buttress, is a side chapel, also with an apsidal termination.

In no other keep did the chapel assume so prominent a role, and in some of the smaller tower-keeps it was little more than a small apartment contrived in the thickness of a wall or in a corner tower (Figure 9.4a). At Norwich Castle it occupied the south-east corner at the first or principal floor level, and here too it appears to have been aisled on one side. In several keeps the chapel was built into the forebuilding which protected the first-floor entrance. Quite exceptionally, at Newcastle-upon-Tyne the chapel is at ground level *beneath* the entrance passage and accessible from the basement.[105] It is more often found *above* the entrance, in a space that was, in a sense, superfluous. Such was the position of the chapels in Dover Castle, for there were two, one opening off the vestibule at first-floor level and the other, twice as large, above it and reached from the main hall of the castle.[106] At Rochester also the chapel was located in the forebuilding above the entrance and on the same floor as the principal hall.[107]

In the two late twelfth-century castles of Orford and Conisbrough, both of which have round or polygonal keeps with massive protruding towers, the chapel was, in the former, built above the vestibule,[108] and in the latter in the thickness of the wall, with the chancel inserted into one of the buttresses.[109] It is rare to find a chapel in the restricted space of a shell-keep, and at the Earl of Cornwall's castle of Restormel the chapel was made to project into the surrounding ditch. In many castles a chapel was built in the bailey at a relatively early date. One finds, for example, a freestanding chapel in the inner bailey or loosely attached to a hall at Pevensey, Berkhamsted, Pembroke, Ludlow, Carisbrooke and many other castles.

In the course of the reorganisation that took place in many castles in the thirteenth century it became increasingly common to place the chapel at the side of the bailey and against an exterior wall. Here it tended to form a single complex with the hall and the principal chambers. There was, however, the small matter of orientation. Though the rule in this regard was never observed with great precision, the chancel was always made to point in a direction between north-east and south-east. This was observed in the early keeps, which seem almost to have been built on an east-west axis. This orientation was less easily achieved in an irregular bailey. At Framlingham the correct orientation was obtained by containing the altar within a projecting square tower in the eastern curtain, and allowing the body of the chapel to extend at right angles into the bailey.[110] A similar plan was used at White Castle (Llantilio), where a mural tower became the chancel, leaving a timber-framed nave to extend back into the court.[111] At Goodrich Castle, where space was limited, the chapel was built on an upper floor of an eastward-facing gatehouse,[112] and a similar position was adopted at Newark.

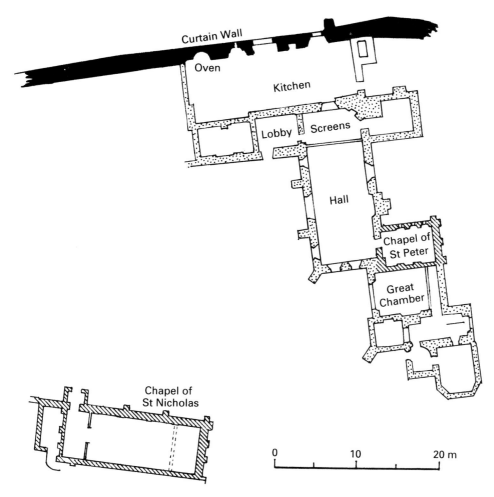

9.7 The chapels of St Peter and of St Nicholas, the latter later and freestanding, in the bailey of Carisbrooke Castle (Hampshire). After P. G. Stone, *The Architectural Antiquities of the Isle of Wight.*

More often than not, however, an orientation within permissible limits could be achieved by building against a curtain wall. Figure 9.4 shows the location of the chapel in relation to both curtain-wall and hall-chamber complex at several thirteenth-century castles. In most Edwardian castles of North Wales and in those built in the fourteenth century it was a relatively easy matter to place the chapel against a curtain wall. One begins to sense in some of these castles – the episcopal castle of Llawhaden in South Wales, for example – an approximation to the academic plan met with in the older Oxford and Cambridge colleges and in certain hospitals and schools, such as Eton and Winchester.

During the thirteenth century there was a marked increase in the number of chapels in the more important castles, and especially in those regularly used by the king and his entourage. Not only did the king have his private chambers and chapel away from the crowd that thronged his court, but in the course of the thirteenth century separate suites were built for the queen as well. The records make this very clear at Windsor Castle. If we can assume that the chapel in the Great Tower was the earliest, then that established in the lower ward in the twelfth century must have constituted the second.[113] By 1246 there was a third chapel for the queen, adorned with pictures.[114] A year or two later four chaplains were engaged for the king's new chapel,[115] which presumably replaced that in the lower ward and was destined to serve as the first chapel of the Order of the Garter. It was over 21 m long and $8\frac{1}{2}$ m wide, and may well have been the most splendid castle chapel built to this date. There appear at the mid-century to have been seven chaplains in the castle, and, even though they received only 50s a year each, together with their keep, the cost of maintaining the chapels must have constituted a not inconsiderable drain on the royal finances.

The situation at Winchester Castle was similar, and again it was Henry III who was responsible for this explosion of spiritual activity. There had, of course, been a chapel since the earliest days of the castle. In 1252 the sheriff was required to provide altars for the king's chapel of St Thomas and also for the 'chapel by his bed'.[116] There was also a private chapel for the queen and a chapel of St Katherine 'at the top of the castle'.[117] Whether the tower of the king's chapel 'in the upper part of the castle which threatens to fall'[118] belonged to St Katherine's is not clear. In 1241–2 a chaplain was appointed to serve the chapel of St Mary,[119] and in 1237 the round chancel (apse) of the chapel of St Josse was pulled down and made square. Its walls were raised, and two chapels 'with fine windows made there, one above for the queen and one below for the king'.[120] These were presumably intended to replace their earlier private chapels. The 'apse' of St Josse's chapel suggests a twelfth-century chapel in the bailey. We thus have a record in the thirteenth century of at least five and possibly six chapels at one time. In 1241–2 four chaplains were employed in the castle.[121]

Beside Windsor and Winchester the Tower of London appears peculiarly ill-provided with spiritual comforts, with only the chapels of St John the Baptist in the Tower and of St Peter ad Vincula in the ward.[122] In 1354 a complaint was made that a single chaplain was quite inadequate for the Tower, and three more were ordered to be appointed, though the context suggests that the need was more administrative than spiritual.[123]

There is evidence for two or more chaplains, with separate chapels for king and queen, at a number of castles: Nottingham, Northampton, Gloucester, Hertford and probably at others.[124] If both king and queen had their own private chapels, it can be assumed that there was also a 'public' chapel for the castle community. How far down the social scale one can find more than a single chapel it is impossible to say. The smaller private chapels are sometimes difficult to locate. The king's and queen's private chapels were, generally speaking, close to their private chambers. Henry III had, as has been seen, a chapel beside his bed. One has to visualise, in a well-appointed royal castle like Winchester, Northampton or Nottingham, where all architectural evidence has been destroyed, two or more private chambers with *en suite* chapel and garderobe.[125]

Such luxury was not restricted to the king and his consort. At Beverston Castle (Gloucestershire), built about 1225 by a junior and far from well-endowed member of the Berkeley family, there were two chapels. The larger was on the first floor of the south-west tower of the castle (Figure 9.8) and is a very fine example of a thirteenth-century domestic chapel. Above it, however, on the second floor, is another and smaller chapel, with piscina, but without the sedilia which are so conspicuous a feature of the lower chapel. But what makes this upper chapel so interesting is the two squints by which a view of the altar could be obtained from each of the adjoining rooms.[126] The larger of these rooms is described by Parker, probably correctly, as the lord's chamber, but can the other fairly be called the 'priest's room'? Would the priest need to have such a view of his own altar? It seems more likely that we have here the separate chambers of the lord and his lady, sharing a single oratory. Henry III had a chapel beside his bed; so had Maurice de Gant of Beverston, and he too could lie in bed and view the mass being said on his behalf. At Compton Castle (Devon) also there is a pair of squints from, in this case, the ground-floor solar into the chapel (Figure 9.9).

The chapel might be *en suite* with the lord's chamber; it was no less closely linked with the priest's chamber. At Orford a priest's room is clearly identifiable in the thickness of the wall of the keep near the chapel. At Northampton Castle provision was made for a 'privy chamber' adjoining the priest's room.[127] The chaplain's chamber could sometimes be a great deal more than a simple hole-in-the-wall; at Winchester Castle it was ordered to be lengthened by 15 feet, and at Sherborne Castle the chaplain had a 'house' of his own.[128]

The maintenance of a chapel and the performance of its daily services called for no small expenditure. Although some chapels were timber-framed, the great majority were not only masonry-built but were elaborately carved and decorated. The two twelfth-century chapels at Dover and those at Newcastle-upon-Tyne, Rochester and elsewhere were exquisite miniatures, while the chapel of St John the Baptist in the Tower of London remains one of the most impressive ecclesiastical buildings of its age. The gothic chapels of the thirteenth century were no less elaborate, and the best surviving example, that at Beverston, shows a wealth of detail met in only the finest of parish churches. At Marlborough Castle one of the chapels had a belfry with two bells, and there were bells also in Dover Castle, probably in the tower of St Mary in the Bailey.[129]

The interiors of most chapels were wainscoted or painted, the windows were glazed, and the floor tiled. There were stalls for the priests and always the vessels and vestments for mass. The records show the occasional purchase of a missal,[130] a censer or a thurible[131] and there were frequent expenditures on vestments. Even the bread and wine for the daily mass could be expensive. At Windsor Castle these were provided by the constable, but in some other cases a specific sum was allocated for

SECTION OF TOWER, SHEWING THE TWO CHAPELS

A, the vaulted Lower Chamber. B, the Chapel. C, the Oratory or Upper Chapel.

9.8 An east–west section through the Great or Berkeley Tower at Beverston Castle (Gloucester), showing both chapel and, above it, the oratory. The drawing was curiously reversed: east is to the left. From J. H. Parker, *Domestic Architecture*, 1857.

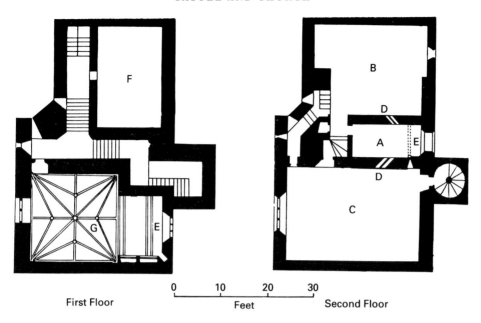

First Floor   Feet   Second Floor

9.9 Plans of the first and second floors of the Berkeley Tower of Beverston Castle. There is a marked unevenness in the floor levels of the third floor. (A) oratory, with squints; (B) priest's room; (C) lord's room; (D) squints; (E) altars; (F) parlour; (G) main chapel.

their purchase.[132] At Belvoir Castle 2s a year was set aside for bread, wine and candles.[133] Then there was payment for the chaplains themselves. Throughout the thirteenth century the going rate was 50s a year together, of course, with a room, food and, as was specified in some instances, sufficient fuel.[134] The slight evidence for the twelfth century suggests a somewhat lower rate, and higher payments were made in the fourteenth century. In 1355 the Black Prince paid his chaplain in Trematon Castle (Cornwall) 5 marks (66s..8d),[135] but this was in the years immediately following the Black Death. The news must have got around, for nine months later the chaplain at Tintagel Castle, on the opposite coast of Cornwall, quit 'on account of the smallness of his fee' of 50s.[136] The constable was ordered to appoint another with an increment of 16s 8d. Evidently the post-Plague rate was tending to be 5 marks. But there continued to be exceptions, and one must assume that chaplains were sometimes paid extra for unusual skills or special responsibilities. Thomas Tredynton was, in the later years of the fourteenth century, paid a very high fee of £10 a year as chaplain in the newly built tower of Southampton Castle, but he appears to have been also an engineer of no mean competence.

PART III

The castle in the later Middle Ages

CHAPTER 10

The changing role of the castle

> The south side is fully finished with curious works and stately lodgings. The said
> west side and northside be but builded to one chamber height; all these works being
> of a fair ashlar, and so covered with a false roof of elm, and the same covered with
> light slate. The east side, containing the hall and other houses of offices, is all of the
> old building, and of a homely fashion. The outer ward was intended to have been
> large, with many lodgings . . . a goodly garden to walk in, enclosed with high walls,
> embattled.   Thornbury Castle, *Letters and Papers of Henry VIII*

In 1295, following the Welsh rising of 1294, Edward I began the building of
Beaumaris Castle. It was the last of his North Wales castles, and it was left
unfinished. It marked symbolically a turning-point in the history of the castle in
England and Wales. Castles continued to be built for exclusively military purposes,
as was Queenborough in 1361 and Cooling (Kent) twenty years later, but more and
more they were becoming well-protected homes. They were, for lack of any better
term, semi-fortified. They still bore what Michael Thompson has called a 'martial
face', but in reality they spoke more of domestic comfort than of military strength.
They belonged to an England in which there were deep social divisions, but where
disputes were settled in the courts or on the battlefield, rather than by holding and
besieging castles. During the Wars of the Roses, which dragged on intermittently
for nearly forty years, there was not a single siege of more than local significance,
and most of them were in Wales or the northern Borders. Warfare had become a
matter of movement, of conflict in the field, not of using castles to hold territory.

The changes in the role of the castle had many causes: social, political and
technical. The introduction of gunpowder and the adoption of artillery not only
influenced castle design but rendered many smaller castles virtually useless
militarily. The disappearance of the feudal obligation to provide knight service and
castle guard made it ever more necessary to use mercenary soldiers. No longer were
fighting men in their lord's service for the short term – forty days or whatever they
owed; they became available on a permanent basis. They could participate in
military campaigns which might last many months and include pitched battles. The
defence of a castle became less important; the ability to command forces in the field
assumed a far greater significance. The Barons' War had involved pitched battles but
ended with a full-scale siege – that of Kenilworth Castle. The Edwardian conquest
of Wales was secured by means of castles, and castles played an essential role in the

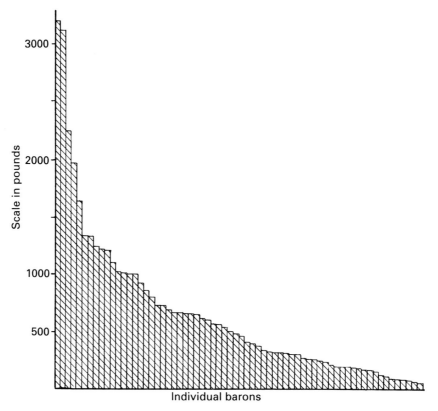

10.1 Baronial incomes in England in 1436, based on H. L. Gray, 'Incomes from land in England in 1436', *EHR*, 49 (1934), 607–39.

Edwardian attempt to hold southern Scotland. But in the baronial struggles of the reign of Edward II the seizure and defence of castles was significant only in the so-called 'Glamorgan War'.[1] Thereafter they played no military role of importance and the Wars of the Roses, which occupied much of the period from 1455 to 1485, were fought by marching armies in a few set-piece battles and many random skirmishes.

'Feudalism still existed formally intact', wrote McFarlane, 'but was becoming for all practical purposes a complex network of marketable privileges and duties attached to the ownership of land, with little or no importance as a social force ... the new order of patronage, liveries and affinities occupied the front of the stage ... Its quintessence was payment for service'.[2] The feudal host ceased to be summoned after 1385, and its place was taken by bodies of retainers whose loyalty was as much to their captain as to their employer. The change occurred slowly. It was most apparent in the first half of the fourteenth century, when the class of mercenary soldier was finding employment and profit on the fields of France. It was preceded by a period when the 'money-fief' began to replace the fee in land, the loyalty and service of the knight being guaranteed by a regular pension.[3] This in turn led to the indenture system, by which the knight was bound to his lord by a written contract, enforcable at law, which defined his obligations and rates of remuneration. Indentured retinues became a social problem during the fourteenth century, and in 1390 Parliament legislated against them.[4] It was not easy, however, to draw a line between resident household staff: indentured men, bound to serve their lord for a prescribed period, and the more fluctuating body who wore their master's badge and served him as long as it suited them. The last were outlawed and the indentured retainer became the mainstay of armed forces in the fifteenth century. It became normal to garrison castles on the coast and in Wales with indentured soldiers, and there is no reason to suppose that their loyalty was any less than that of knights who held their fees by military service.[5]

At the same time the ranks of the baronage were greatly reduced. The hazards to which they had been exposed have already been mentioned. The numerous barons of the thirteenth century had 'been replaced socially and politically, by a peerage which seldom exceeded about sixty families'.[6] And with their reduction in number the peerage had grown richer. The numbers able to build masonry castles and raise bands of indentured retainers had become small indeed. Below the barons were the rich knights and gentry, with incomes of over £100. Their numbers were estimated by Pugh:

Table 10.1. *Knights and gentry, fifteenth century*[7]

	Income (£)	Number
Richer knights	over 200	c. 183
Prosperous gentry	40–100	c. 750
Lesser landowners	20–40	c. 1,200
Poor gentry	10–20	c. 1,600

At this time archers were receiving about 6d a day, and men-at-arms and knights considerably more. A couple of archers and an armed knight could not have been hired for much less than £100 a year.[8] The maintenance of a band of armed retainers was effectively beyond the scope of knights and gentry, without the income from war. Many of those who obtained licences to crenellate their manor houses could not possibly have afforded to do so, and few of those who had inherited castles from an earlier age could have paid a garrison to defend them.

It is against this background that we must see the semi-fortified manor house with its crenellations and gatehouse. They were the gentry's answer to the castles and the retinues of the aristocracy. But a few of the gentry were determined to become relatively rich overnight.[9] Some acquired wealth by trade, like the de la Pole earls of Suffolk. Others gained profits from war and spent it on castles beyond the wildest dreams of their forebears. A few grew rich on public office and the law, and, lastly, there were those who married into the families of the landed nobility. These were the men who built the castles of the later Middle Ages, designed more to assert their wealth and rank than to repel any potential enemy.

Castles and cannon

The importance of cannon in the changing role of castles has often been stressed.[10] Their walls, it is said, could not stand up to bombardment by the new artillery which fired a missile far more deadly than any propelled by trébuchet or mangonel. The use of guns did, indeed, become widespread in Western Europe during the later years of the fourteenth century, and cannon of very considerable size and range began to be made during the fifteenth. But their role in castle warfare has perhaps been exaggerated.

The discovery of the explosive qualities of a mixture of sulphur, saltpetre and charcoal must be credited to the alchemists of the thirteenth century. The adaptation of this discovery to weaponry came at some time early in the fourteenth. The ingredients of gunpowder were already being used as a kind of 'Greek fire'; in 1304 the king ordered 'cotton thread, quick suphur and saltpetre' and 'arrows well feathered and ironed [tipped]' for the siege of Stirling Castle.[11] The earliest illustration of a cannon shows a bulbous pot with a touch-hole and arrow-like projectile. It would probably have been of bronze, since cast iron did not become available in Western Europe until late in the fifteenth century, and in England not until the early sixteenth. But bronze was costly and gunmakers turned to wrought iron, forming the barrel of the gun by welding together pieces of bar iron like the staves of a barrel – hence its name – and securing the whole with iron hoops.[12]

Such guns were produced in the later fourteenth and early fifteenth centuries in a variety of sizes. The smaller, which would have been of the greatest importance in the defence of a castle, were mainly of cast bronze. Larger guns of welded iron became more numerous late in the fourteenth century, and tended to replace those of cast metal, which often cracked when fired.[13] Very large pieces were set up in the Tower of London under Richard II, some weighing up to 600 lb. The effectiveness of early guns was reduced, not only by their liability to burst, but by the quality of the powder, which was difficult to transport and store without losing its effectiveness. A further problem was the supply of spherical missiles of iron or stone; too large and irregular, and they jammed the gun barrel; too small, and much of the explosive force was dissipated. The barrels of early guns were uneven, and this added to the uncertainty of their use. Not until late in the fifteenth century did it become usual to finish the barrel by drilling it out with a steel bit.[14]

The question at issue here is how effective were early cannon in the siege and defence of castles. There can be little doubt that they were employed at the Battle of Crécy (1346) and in the siege of Calais which followed,[15] but it is unlikely that they had any effect on the outcome. The traditional weapons maintained their ascendancy throughout the fourteenth and, indeed, the fifteenth century. The king's engines continued to be built and maintained at the Tower and elsewhere, and hand-guns in no way replaced the traditional crossbow before the sixteenth century.[16] Nevertheless, the number of cannon in the possession of governments began to increase in the later decades of the fourteenth century. Gunpowder first became important in the 1360s, and castles were first equipped with small cannon during the few years of peace following the Treaty of Brétigny (1360). In 1365 cannon, fabricated in the Tower, were sent to Queenborough Castle and later to Dover, Carisbrooke and Southampton. At the same time the control over cannon exercised by the Wardrobe of the Tower was relaxed. Guns began to be made by private individuals, who offered both themselves and their weapons for hire. Richard II ordered the manufacture of no less than seventy-three pieces, most of which weighed more than 300 lbs and could be transported only on carts or wagons. Such artillery was effective against fixed fortifications, but only over short distances. The gun was, in consequence, exposed both to fire from the walls and to damaging sallies by the defenders. Chroniclers picture the early cannon as almost completely ineffective in both defence and attack.[17] Only towards the end of the fifteenth century, when they became more accurate and more manoeuvrable, did they become significant in siege warfare. One wonders whether, in the fourteenth and early fifteenth centuries, the importance of cannon was not largely psychological. The gun was a frightening weapon, and it was not necessary for it to do great damage in order to instill fear in the enemy.

Nevertheless, from the reign of Richard II the number of guns owned by the king and kept usually in his principal castles slowly increased,[18] but the retention of traditional terms tends to hide the fact that the weapons were guns and not mechanical engines. In 1379 the keeper of Carisbrooke purchased two cannon and a supply of saltpetre, which suggests that the powder was made on the spot.[19] Three years later a cannon was purchased for Southampton Castle, and guns were also provided for Corfe, Porchester and Dover castles, as well as for Berwick-on-Tweed and Roxburgh. Even 'so unimportant a castle as Trematon', wrote Tout, was supplied with gunpowder. Trematon was, in fact, a significant guardian of Plymouth Harbour. More surprising, perhaps, was the supply of powder to a baronial castle like Holt. Queenborough Castle, on the Isle of Sheppey, was built in 1361, and in 1365, 'two great guns and nine small ones' were sent there. The castle was, however, not designed with the use of guns in mind, and castles built much later than this usually had only a small gunport or two, contrived where least inconvenient. At Kirby Muxloe (see p. 266), built towards the end of the fifteenth century, the gunports were low down, only about two metres above the water of the moat (Figure 10.2). Their range from this position must have been short.

All early references to the deployment of guns relate to coastal defence, and without a threat of French invasion it is doubtful whether they would have been installed. As it is, some older castles, such as Dover, Saltwood, Carisbrooke and Corfe, were adapted to the use of guns. At castles newly built, like Bodiam, Cooling

10.2 Gunports in the gatehouse of Kirby Muxloe Castle (Leicester). They were pierced through blocks of limestone set in the brickwork of the castle.

and Herstmonceux, provision was made from the start for gunports, and at Southampton Castle 'an expert in guns and the management of artillery' was retained for much of the fifteenth century.[20]

The only castles, apart from those near the south-east coast, to have been equipped with cannon before the late fifteenth century were in the Scottish and Welsh Borders. Pontefract may have served as a northern base of supply for *all* weapons, as the Tower of London did in the South-east. In 1400 Robert Walys was given the office of 'maker of bows, springalds, crossbows and gear and the *arraying of the king's guns within the castle [Pontefract] and elsewhere*'.[21]

The documentary evidence lends little support to the view that the use of cannon greatly influenced the security of castles or displaced traditional armaments in any significant way. There is, nevertheless, growing evidence for structural changes in both castles and urban defences in order to accommodate cannon. Arrow slits, which served the needs of the crossbowmen, were ill suited to artillery, and a battlemented parapet gave little protection for a gunner and his gun. From early in the second half of the fourteenth century gunports, designed to accommodate contemporary guns, began to be incorporated into newly built fortifications. The commonest form was a circular opening, some 215 mm in diameter, with a vertical slit above it for sighting the gun – the so-called 'keyhole' gunport (Figure 10.2). It was intended for handguns, and would have been 'the most effective type until the appearance of the large rectangular gunports in the later years of the fifteenth century'.[22] Such loops were incorporated in Bodiam and Cooling castles, and were added at Dover, Carisbrooke and Saltwood. Lord Cobham's instructions to his mason, who was working on the gunports of Cooling Castle, have survived: *x arket holes* [harquebut holes] *de iii peez* [feet?] *longour en tout saunz croys* [without cross-slits].[23] In addition, loops of this or other patterns were incorporated into urban defences, and can still be seen in the west gate of Canterbury, at Southampton[24] and in the precinct wall of Quarr Abbey in the Isle of Wight.[25]

In the course of the fifteenth century greater provision was made for the use of guns. Gunports, most of them of 'key-hole' pattern, were not only inserted into existing castles and incorporated into new, but were also built into manor houses of relatively humble standing. Minor castles like Berry Pomeroy in Devon, Baconsthorpe in Norfolk, and the unfinished castle of Kirby Muxloe in Leicestershire, were all equipped.[26] Monastic buildings, such as the gatehouses of Titchfield and Tavistock abbeys, had gunports, as also did a number of castellated manor houses like Cotehele and Oxburgh. In some instances the number of gunports was very small, often merely covering the entrance. There is, of course, no proof that the owner of a house with a gunport actually possessed a gun. The construction of the port may have been wholly precautionary, and at most could have given some protection against an intruder. Many of the 'houses' equipped with gunports in the later fifteenth century were neither capable of withstanding a sustained attack, nor were they intended to do so, but one or two guns might give some advantage against local raids of lawless bands.

Although the fifteenth century was notable for its lawlessness, there was no instance of prolonged siege warfare within England. Only in the Scottish Borders and in Wales during Glyndwr's rising and the Wars of the Roses were castles attacked and defended. When the king built up a park of artillery and accumulated a store of powder and missiles, it was either to take on campaign in France or to defend the coasts and frontiers. Their location, in the Tower of London or at Pontefract, is evidence of this. The cost of artillery that could be used in defending a castle put it beyond the range of all except the wealthiest of the king's subjects. Others could afford at most a hand-gun or two, and this is what the frequency and distribution of gunports suggests. One must conclude that the small, hand-held 'bombard' may have made the castle and manor house safer for the owner and his family, but the coming of the great gun did not herald the decline of the castle. For that one must look for changes in society.

A classification of late medieval castles

We are here caught in a semantic dilemma. The term 'castle' is applied generally both to a fortified home and to one which merely has some of the superficial trappings of crenellation. This confusion is increased by the very wide spectrum of buildings which resulted from the issue of licences to crenellate. In earlier centuries castles had varied greatly in both structure and in their ability to withstand attack, but there can be no question that they were intended to be defensible. This cannot be said of castles in the later Middle Ages. There were castles which continued to proclaim their military role. Such were Cooling, Bodiam and Edward III's creation at Queenborough. Then there were castles which were palace-fortresses, defensible if necessary but adjusted more to the gracious living of the higher ranks of the aristocracy. Amongst these castles were Pleshey (Essex), Kenilworth (Warwickshire) and perhaps Alnwick (Northumberland), which did, however, withstand a siege by Edward IV. At a lower level was the semi-fortified house, no more defensible than any one of the moated sites which proliferated on the clay lands in the later Middle Ages. There were 'castles' for all seasons, for every variety of circumstance, and for all levels of society. The castles of England and Wales during the last two centuries of the Middle Ages can nevertheless be said to fall into four, far from exclusive, groups. In the first were those already abandoned before the death of Edward I, and which remained in ruin. Some had been dismantled soon after building; a few, indeed, had never been completed. A considerable, though rather indefinite, number had been destroyed deliberately under Henry II, and others were torn down during the following century. But most such castles had been abandoned for no such identifiable reason. Their owners had, in all probability, left their cold, cramped and uncomfortable quarters for more spacious manor houses nearby, or they had been taken by heiresses to husbands who felt no need for them.

No place illustrates the changes that took place more aptly then Tretower Castle and Court in Brecon.[27] The castle — a small motte-and-bailey — must have been built in the early years of the Norman penetration of this region. Masonry replaced the palisade, and in the early thirteenth century a round tower-keep was added to the motte. The castle figured in the Welsh wars, but in the more peaceful conditions of the next century was abandoned in favour of a more spacious manor house, built 300 m away. By the end of the Middle Ages the latter had developed into a courtyard house with a gatehouse which offered a degree of protection. Meanwhile the castle was not wholly neglected. It appears to have served as a refuge as long as conditions remained disturbed, and was even patched and repaired, before its final abandonment at the end of the Middle Ages.

For whatever reason, at least half the 1,500 castles built since the Conquest had been deserted by the early fourteenth century. They continued to be mentioned in the records as 'sites', worth little or nothing beyond the grazing they provided. Liddel Strength, for example, was in 1349 'the site of the castle . . . destroyed . . . worth 6d'.[28] The earthworks and ruins of such castles remained into the sixteenth and seventeenth centuries and, in some instances, until today.

There was, secondly, a considerable number of castles which continued to be inhabited and used, but which were imperfectly repaired and maintained. Many royal castles, at least in England, belonged to this category. The sheriff continued to hold his court in a hall with a leaking roof and windows open to the weather. The defensive walls were crumbling and of no military value, and occasionally someone appeared before the Hundred court charged with stealing lead or timber or stone from the half-ruined structure. Slow decay might be interrupted by a half-hearted attempt to patch the gaps and repair the roofs, but decline was usually continuous, and John Leland[29] in the sixteenth century could report only the 'shape of a fair castle, now decaying'[30] (Blaenllyfni, Brecon); 'a castle of 7 towers, now decaying for lack of coverture'[31] (Ruan Lanihorne, Cornwall) and at the de Clare castle of Caerphilly he found 'ruinous walls of a wonderful thickness, and tower kept up for prisoners'.[32] Indeed, in a great many castles only a hall for holding courts and a house for keeping those who appeared before them remained in adequate condition by the end of the Middle Ages.

A third group of castles consisted of those which continued to be inhabited and kept in a decent state of repair. Some were, in fact, extended by the addition of a court, the rebuilding of a gatehouse or the erection of a chapel. Some were frequented by king and court, like Windsor and Winchester, and had a great deal of money lavished on them. But such castles were comparatively few, and most, like Arundel, Alnwick, Warwick, Ludlow and Pontefract, were the seats of the richer members of the aristocracy. By the beginning of the fifteenth century the crown could afford to be selective in what it maintained in habitable condition, and what it allowed to slide into delapidation and ruin. The Second Duke of Lancaster and his descendants came to hold more than thirty castles, including Hertford, given him by Edward III, and Pevensey, Tickhill, Knaresborough and the Peak, all of which he received in exchange for Richmond Castle, which the king wished to restore to Earl John of Brittany.[33] His income was adequate to maintain this vast panoply of power, 'a power which no other feudatory . . . could rival . . . To each castle he appointed a constable, a knight or esquire who was entitled to the wages of his office . . . [He] was responsible for the military efficiency of his castle; he stocked it with artillery and saw that his garrison had bows and sheaves of arrows enough; he superintended the repairs of its walls and the new works planned by his master – the most lavish and inveterate builder of his age'.[34] John of Gaunt was no less a traveller, and his *Register* shows him travelling from one castle to another, ordering repairs here, extensions there. The great hall of Kenilworth Castle, one of the most princely in any English castle, was his work. He stayed long and frequently at Hertford, Tutbury, Kenilworth, Bolinbroke, Tickhill and Pontefract.[35] But when some thirty Lancastrian castles came, in 1399, to be merged with the crown estate, there was little need for most of them. They remained centres for the administration of segments of crown land but, it would appear, little was done to keep them in repair, and many must have lapsed into the second category of castles. The royal castles of Bolsover and Sauvey were probably allowed to decay. That of Hastings ceased to provide adequate protection even for the college of canons established within its walls. Hadleigh Castle, on the Essex coast, was refurbished during an invasion scare in the 1360s, but was then allowed to resume its process of slow decay. Even the Tower of London, foremost arsenal of the English kings, received no significant addition or modification after Edward I had completed its outer enceinte.[36] Winchester Castle, upon which Henry III had lavished so much, suffered relative neglect, and less than a dozen royal castles can be said to have been fully maintained. First and foremost among them was Windsor, unquestionably the favourite residence of Edward III. Leeds Castle, in Kent, was retained as a sort of dower house for widowed queens, and Rockingham and the castellated manor of Moor End (Northamptonshire) as royal hunting lodges. Nottingham and York castles, the keys to national security in the North, and Chester, Gloucester and Bristol in the West were maintained at least into the fifteenth century, but by 1480 the hall of Bristol Castle was in ruins and the rest of the castle little better.[37] Expenditure on such once-important castles as Cambridge, Oxford, Exeter and Colchester was negligible, little more, in fact, than was necessary to keep a roof over the hall and bolts on the door of the gaol.[38] The preservation of a royal castle in usable condition depended essentially on local conditions and circumstances. Many, like Orford, built to control the Bigods in the late twelfth century, were no longer necessary. Others were duplicated by more recent acquisitions of the crown and became redundant.

Only along the south coast, repeatedly threatened with invasion from France, and in North Wales and the Scottish Borders, was there even an adequate expenditure on the fabric of the king's castles. Here, at all royal castles and some private, there was a flurry of activity in the third quarter of the thirteenth century, as the French threat intensified. Even private castles, like Bodiam and Cooling, were built or strengthened. Dover Castle had reached its maximum extent during the previous century, and thereafter received only 'adequate maintenance'.[39] Indeed, it was one of the very few significant castles whose history was not one of gradual decay, punctuated by hasty repairs. Porchester Castle, which commanded the waterways around Portsmouth, was kept in repair and its inner bailey strengthened.[40] The French threat to the sheltered waterways behind the Isle of Wight was not taken lightly. The king's master mason, Henry Yevele himself, was sent to Southampton to advise on the building of a great tower on the 'Old Castell Hill'.[41] This must have been one of the most ambitious building projects undertaken for a purely military purpose in late medieval England. Speed's plan shows a round or polygonal tower enclosed within a stone-built mantlet, crowning the steep motte of the earlier castle.[42]

Expenditure on Corfe was in general very small, but here, as at Dover, the work was complete before the death of Edward I.[43] The care bestowed on Dover, Porchester, Southampton and Corfe contrasts with the almost total neglect of Pevensey, which was first settled on Queen Philippa as dower and then turned over to the Duchy of Lancaster.[44] A reason may possibly have been the fact that Pevensey protected only an open beach, and not the sheltered waters likely to be needed by an invasion fleet of the later Middle Ages, with its deep-draught vessels.

The royal castles in Wales had been built more recently than those along the south coast and may be presumed to have been in better condition. Furthermore, the king employed itinerant masons and carpenters, based in the castles of Chester, Caernarvon and Carmarthen, whose task it was to inspect and keep the works in good shape. Nevertheless, those castles which were regarded as of small importance for security, like Aberystwyth, Bere, Builth and Criccieth, were allowed to decay in the years following the conquest of Wales, and most others suffered neglect during the fifteenth century.

On the Scottish Borders the situation was similar. The royal castles whose purpose it was to guard England from invasion were essentially Carlisle, Bamburgh and Newcastle-upon-Tyne. These were supplemented by a number of castles in the Scottish Borders, which were intermittently in English hands.

In the heart of England, where the threat of insurrection or invasion was minimal, the king was content to offload many of his redundant castles, and leave them in the uncertain care of his barons. Orford Castle was in 1336 entrusted to Robert de Ufford, Earl of Suffolk; Odiham and Leeds became for much of the time part of the queen's dower, and numerous other castles were temporarily held by other members of the king's family or by newly ennobled members of the aristocracy in order, as their patent was apt to put it, 'to sustain the dignity of an earl'. Possession of a major castle may have lent prestige, but probably did little to improve the baron's finances.

Despite grants and alienations, the king retained a number of castles in his own hands, and Henry VI probably held as many as Henry II. But there were important differences. No longer were letters sent to the constables whenever danger threatened, ordering their safe custody. They included a few favoured residences and the county castles used by the sheriffs, but, with few exceptions, their condition left much to be desired. They were kept in being only by periodic doles for their repair. The sheriff might spend up to £10 or £20 on roof or walls, and this, in a climate like that of England, was quite insufficient. The records are full of reports of collapsing walls, leaking roofs, deteriorating lead, tiles torn off by the wind, and gaping cracks in the walls of great towers. The sheriff and constable were fortunate if they could keep even essential quarters in some usable condition. Often they did not, as is shown both by repeated complaints and the escape of prisoners. And so, even the best maintained of the sheriffs' castles slowly decayed during the later Middle Ages, until they reached the condition described by William Worcester and John Leland.

Nor were baronial castles necessarily in better shape, and the brief review of baronial finances serves to show that few of the barons could afford the luxury of a well-maintained and well-equipped castle. But again there were exceptions. There were barons and even knights who built with the express purpose of supplementing the royal system of fortification and protecting the realm. The motives of the Percys and Nevilles in the North; of the de Lacys, Mortimers of Chirk and Herberts on the Welsh Border, and of Cobham, Dalyngrigge, Chideock and Courteney in the south were far from selfless, but their role in this respect was an important one.

The last category of late medieval castles consists of those built *ab initio* after the death of Edward I. They were, with the exception only of Queenborough Castle, exclusively baronial. By and large, they conformed with the castle plan that had evolved in the thirteenth century. They were rectangular, with corner towers and a gatehouse. They commonly made considerable use of water defences, but some were not otherwise particularly strong or easily defended. Their walls were relatively thin, and in an age when cannon were beginning to be employed, their sites would appear in many instances to have been singularly ill chosen if their purpose was primarily military. Their military pretensions were generally slight, but they presented, almost without exception, a very bold front. Care was lavished upon their gatehouse towers, and their displays of heraldry could on occasion be overwhelming.

All this reflected the class of men who built them. They were, in the main, 'new men'. Their wealth derived in part from land. Their ancestors had been the tenants, even the sub-tenants of great lords. But death had taken its toll of the latter, allowing these men to rise to the surface of politics. Some had prospered in trade. When Sir John Fastolf built Caistor Castle he was able to use his own ships to carry building materials to the site. Yet others had profited from the French wars, and returned to England to use their booty and the ransom money they had gained to build castles as much like those they had known in France and the Low Countries as was practicable. They moved, lastly, into a society in which obligation was no longer based upon land. Except in the Borders and Marches – and this is an important exception – landholding was no longer predicated upon military service. Castle-guard had been transformed into rent, precisely known and regularly collected. Honourial courts had largely disappeared. There was no certain body of retainers, tied to their lord by tenurial obligations. A cash nexus was replacing the obligation to serve at court and in the field, and even in the close vicinity of the castle, the demesne was likely to be leased at a cash rent to a 'farmer'. The castles built in the fourteenth and fifteenth centuries reflected these conditions. They adopted new forms, learned in part in the wars in continental Europe, and, in their internal arrangements, they were adjusted to a structuring of society which was radically different from that of earlier times.

Licence to crenellate

The theory that only the king could authorise the building of a castle continued to be observed in practice throughout the later Middle Ages. Formal grants of permission to fortify and embattle a home are few before 1200. Thereafter their number increased, and they become very numerous indeed during the middle years of the fourteenth century (Figure 10.3). The practice of requesting (and paying for) such licences diminished during the fifteenth century, but is met with as late as the second half of the sixteenth. Charles Coulson's calendar of licences enumerates considerably more than 500. Some of these represent the renewal of earlier grants and no less than fifty-eight were granted to religious institutions, either to build a defensive tower or to enclose their precinct with a crenellated wall. But even if these are eliminated, we are still left with some four hundred licences to build something which could have amounted to a castle. There are no extant licences to crenellate *castles* in Wales, since

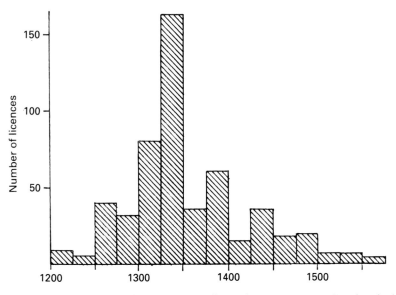

10.3 The distribution of grants of licence to crenellate. This in no way implies that the licences were acted upon. Based on the manuscript list compiled by Charles Coulson.

the 'law of the March' was deemed to confer this right on all Marcher lords,[45] nor in the palatinate earldoms.

The number of licences is completely at variance with the archaeological and documentary evidence for castles built in the period. In a very few instances (see p. 104) a castle was built without licence, and its owner compelled either to compound for his transgression with a fine, or to have his castle torn down. The opposite, however, was the more usual situation; the licence does not appear ever to have been acted upon, or the resulting structure was merely a protected house with no military pretension. A careful examination of the identifiable sites where the erection of a castle was authorised shows that in about forty cases – 13 per cent of the total – a castle was actually built, and that in about 180 (60 per cent) cases nothing of military significance ever resulted. About 20 per cent of the structures may have had some slight military pretension but can at most be described as semi-fortified. The rest of the licences relate to towns or religious foundations. Le Patourel has distinguished between true castles on the one hand and fortified and semi-fortified manors on the other. The criterion of a castle was 'provision for flanking fire and . . . multiple towers considered necessary . . . for genuine military purpose'.[46] The fortified manor had 'stone walls with crenellations and wall walks' and perhaps a moat; the semi-fortified had significantly less by way of protection, and formed 'a class not sufficiently defensible to interest the central authority'. Le Patourel equates the category of 'fortified manors' with those which had received a licence to crenellate, and the 'semi-fortified' with those for which no such permission was asked for or required. In other words, there was a threshold, below which a kind of 'planning permission' was not required. This simple correlation, however, does not work out in practice.

A number of licences was granted for places which had been and still were the sites of castles. The licence granted in 1309 to Robert de Clifford to crenellate his castle of Brougham (Westmorland) ignored the fact that a masonry castle had existed here since the later twelfth century.[47] The same was true of the Bishop of London's castle at Bishop's Stortford (Hertfordshire) of Bungay (Suffolk), Dudley (Staffordshire), Saffron Walden (Essex) and Sherborne (Dorset). Licences were granted for Bampton and Torrington (Devon), Stansted (Essex), Harptree (Somerset) and Tattershall (Lincolnshire), all of which possessed earthwork castles of the early twelfth century. Then, too, licences were often repeated. John de Chideock obtained a licence for his house at Chideock, near the Dorset coast, in 1370, and had it renewed ten years later. The fortified house at Rotherfield Greys (Buckinghamshire) was licensed in 1346 and again two years later. The Bishop of Carlisle's licence for a castle at Penrith of 1397 was later amended, and his predecessor similarly obtained permission to fortify Rose Castle in 1336, and had it renewed in 1355.

We sometimes find permission in a single charter for more than one castle. In 1333 John de Beauchamp obtained leave to build castles at Stoke-sub-Hamdon[48] and Hatch Beauchamp, both in south Somerset. The former he built; the latter he did not.[49] Bishop Wyvill of Salisbury obtained licences for his house in Salisbury, for four manors in Wiltshire, two in Dorset and one in Berkshire, and at none of them did he erect anything that could have been described even as 'semi-fortified'. His Berkshire manor of Sonning, rebuilt in the fifteenth century, was 'an irregular group of buildings surrounding a court', and protected by nothing more secure than a ditch.[50] Another manor which the bishop had permission to crenellate was Potterne, near Devizes. The manor house has disappeared completely but a survey of 1640 represented it as no more than a large manor house with dependent farm buildings.[51] In 1447 the Bishop of Chichester obtained licences for no less than twelve of his manors. These included Aldingbourne, a motte castle in which excavation has revealed the foundations of a large tower-keep,[52] and Amberley, the only castle to have resulted from this wide-ranging grant.

Licences were especially numerous under Edward III, when the king was able, through his sheriffs and justices, to keep a close watch on events in the provinces. It is possible, therefore, that those who built manor houses would play for safety and obtain permission to erect a structure that might in fact fall short of crenellation. It is likely also that some did not know what they wanted or could afford, and, like Bishop Adam of Chichester, obtained a blanket permission that might cover any eventuality. There may also have been an element of social competition. The calendar of licences to crenellate may tell us much about aspiring members of the gentry class. It tells us nothing about the structures they built.

Kings, bishops and the greater barons were in constant motion. They moved

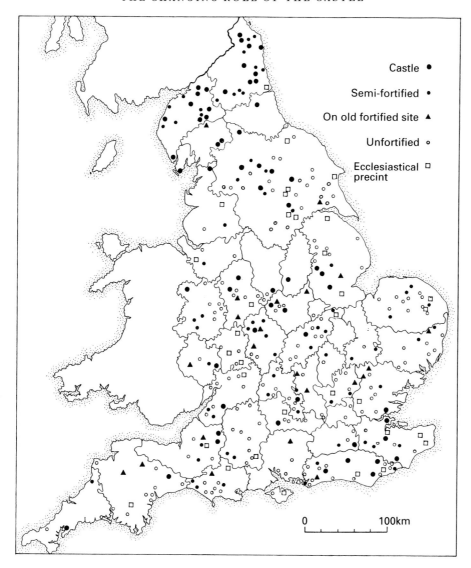

10.4 The spatial distribution of licences to crenellate. Urban houses have been omitted. The Bishop of Durham exercised the right to grant licences within his palatinate, as did the lords Marcher within the March of Wales. Based on C. Coulson's list.

between fixed points at each of which some form of accommodation awaited them, together with a store of food. Some of these points were, of course, castles *sensu stricto*, but many were manor houses, without any significant provision for defence.[53] The king had Clarendon, Woodstock, Silverstone, Clipston, at each of which he was likely to make prolonged stays, and if no castle or manor lay conveniently to hand, he was always ready to trespass on the hospitality of a monastery. Fortunately the itineraries of English kings are broadly known. This cannot, however, be said of their barons, who were no less peripatetic than the king himself. They too travelled between fixed points within their estates, punctuated by stays in London or with the king wherever he might be.[54] The detail of their movements is hidden, in most cases, by the failure of their accounts to survive.[55] The Percys, with estates in Scotland, Northumberland, Yorkshire and the south of England, needed many intermediate stops on their interminable travels. Houses were acquired in Newcastle-upon-Tyne, York and London, and at Wressle in Yorkshire they built, late in the fourteenth century, a large castellated house,[56] which was, however, occupied by a junior branch of the family.

All the greater barons kept a number of manors in their own hands, and visited them frequently if not regularly. The Bigods continued to hold a dozen East Anglian manors in demesne. They held a castle, probably ruinous, at Bungay, but among the demesne manors there was 'only one moated manor . . . as far as can be determined from the accounts [and this is confirmed by field work], and no fortified manor, nor was there any [inhabited] castle'.[57] Much of the time the manor, hall and chambers, large and numerous enough for an earl's retinue, stood idle. The travels of the bishops around their dioceses are better documented. They too kept a number of demesne manors in their own hands, in most dioceses one or two of these were fortified. It is clear that not every bishop bothered to obtain a royal licence when he crenellated his palace or one of his rural manors. The Bishop of Lincoln, with a diocese which stretched from the Humber to the Thames, had castles of some significance at Newark, Sleaford and Banbury, and in the fifteenth century Bishop Rotherham added the semi-fortified manor house of Buckden in Huntingdonshire for which no licence seems to have been requested.

This was a lawless age. There was everywhere a striving for wealth and power, and, since wealth no longer consisted largely in the possession of land, it too became transportable. As people acquired more tangible possessions, so the need developed to protect them. Earlier ages were not intrinsically more law-abiding; there was less excuse for lawlessness. As one reads the records of gaol deliveries and local sessions, one is impressed not so much with the scant regard for human life, but with the greed for property. Barbara Hanawalt, in the most exhaustive study of medieval crime to have appeared, has demonstrated that larceny, burglary and robbery together made up almost three-quarters of the crimes handled by the courts.[58] Furthermore, since larceny was one of the most under-reported of felonies, its extent was probably far greater than appears. Most rewarding of the several forms of theft was burglary, the act of breaking into a building for the purpose of removing property. Most burglars were unskilled, as they are today, content to break open a door or window or to climb through any opening. Those able to build even semi-fortified manors had much to lose in the later Middle Ages. Their manor houses were often left unoccupied, and their only insurance was to make entry as difficult as possible.

To some extent the degree of protection found in such houses was intended to safeguard against such crimes as burglary. But protection went farther than this. There had always been feuds within the landowning classes, deriving in some cases from disputed inheritance but more often from personal rivalries and animosities. The petty skirmishing which resulted involved at most small bands of men. They may have been armed retainers who followed great lords about the country or footloose adventurers looking for casual employment and gain.

In 1322 the castle of Bowes, in County Durham, was entered, during the absence of its lord, by a band which 'partly burnt a hall . . . consumed four tuns of wine . . . of the price of 20s and other victuals, carried away his armour, springalds and engines and other goods, and left the castle without guard while the Scots were in those parts'.[59] One marvels at the mobility of a band after such heavy consumption. The Bishop of Lincoln's castle at Sleaford was broken into and animals and documents taken.[60] Gerald de Barry claimed that certain persons had 'besieged his castle [Manorbier], broken the doors, and carried away his goods'.[61] Similar complaints were made of intrusion and theft at Naworth,[62] Sheffield,[63] Lewes,[64] Trematon,[65] Haywra,[66] Workington[67] and Sandal, where goods to the value of 5000 s. were removed.[68] It would appear from these instances that theft was as much the objective of armed bands as the prosecution of family feuds. Even a castle as strong as Sandal was vulnerable; how much more so was an unprotected manor house is demonstrated in the gaol delivery and sessional rolls. It was, in part, to deal with such cases that the Court of Star Chamber was established in the late fifteenth century. Fortification afforded no complete protection, but it was a great deal better than no protection at all. It is in this light that we must see the use of fortification in the later Middle Ages.

The typology of the late medieval castle

Considerably more than a hundred castles, in the sense of militarily defensible structures, were built *ab initio* after the death of Edward I. One cannot be precise because many have vanished, and it is difficult, without early plans and descriptions, to assess the strength of their defences. In the last resort, judgment must be subjective. Any building could be defended if the will to do so were present, and some of the 'castles' held by the royalists during the Great Civil War had certainly not been built with defence in mind. At the top end were indubitable castles, like Nunney, Bodiam, Bolton and Farleigh Hungerford, but with Binamy (Cornwall), Boarstall (Oxfordshire) and Thornbury (Gloucestershire) we pass into a grey area, in which defence was very far from dominant.

These late castles have certain features in common. Most were rectangular or subrectangular in plan, with corner towers and gatehouse. The latter was designed as much to impress as to deter. The corner towers, most often round in the South, rectangular in the North, were equipped with loops and designed to given enfilading fire. Where the terrain permitted, a moat gave further protection. Within the court were domestic buildings: hall, chambers, kitchen and chapel, which were in some castles duplicated. These were the structures found in any well-appointed manor house, and at Farleigh Hungerford their arrangement suggests that walls and towers had merely been built to encompass a pre-existing house. At Compton Castle (Devon) (Figure 11.4) the hall and solar block of c. 1340 preceded the crenellated walls of c. 1500. But more often walls and domestic buildings were conceived as a unit, the curtain serving as the outer wall of hall, chamber block, chapel and domestic offices.

This courtyard plan was not restricted to late medieval castles. It was, with endless variations, the plan of unfortified manor houses, of colleges and hospitals.[69] In plan, there is little difference between a castle such as Caistor or Maxstoke,[70] a late medieval hall like Oxburgh or Halnakar,[71] a school such as Winchester or Eton, and the earlier colleges at Oxford and Cambridge. With the growing need for space, an additional court could be added on one side or another. It was usually less strongly protected and its structures less elaborate, and it contained stables, grange and storage space and commonly accommodation for retainers.

Typical of such castles was that which Sir John Fastolf began at Caistor in Norfolk in 1432.[72] He had become rich in the French wars, and, according to William Worcester, invested £6,000 in his castle. The building accounts are incomplete, but during three of the years when building was in progress the expenditure was almost £1,500.[73] For comparison, the building of Herstmonceux Castle cost about £3,800 and Ampthill Castle (Bedfordshire) was sold for 5,000 marks. Fastolf's castle consisted of two wards, a roughly rectangular inner ward, around which were ranged in regular order the domestic buildings of the lord, and against it a more lightly protected outer ward. Construction was in brick, made close to the site, with dressings of limestone imported into this region of clay and peat. The walls were thick, but the corner towers, except that on the south-west, were slight. The latter was the dominant feature of the castle, a slender round tower rising nearly 30 m above this flat land. This innovation, it has been claimed, was introduced from the Rhineland, where Fastolf may perhaps have seen it. The court was surrounded by a wide moat, beyond which lay the outer ward, protected by a thinner wall and a secondary moat. The castle withstood a short siege by the French in 1458, and again in 1469 in the course of a dispute with the Duke of Norfolk regarding Fastolf's inheritance.[74]

Caistor followed the plan of numerous castles of the fourteenth and fifteenth centuries. Codnor (Derbyshire), begun before 1300, ended as a castle of similar plan to Caistor.[75] Farleigh Hungerford (Somerset) was begun about 1380 by Sir Thomas Hungerford, Speaker of the House of Commons, who was in 1383 pardoned for having begun it without licence.[76] It was rectangular in plan (Figure 10.7) with a polygonal outer court, less strongly defended, added about 1425 (see p. 229).[77]

At Kirby Muxloe (Leicestershire) a rectangular castle, of perfect regularity, was begun by William, Lord Hastings, in 1480, but never finished. As at Farleigh Hungerford, the walled perimeter enclosed a free-standing hall block. An outer court, to the north-west of the main frontage, was planned but barely begun.[78]. Baconsthorpe Castle (Norfolk) followed the same pattern. A rectangular court, with gatehouse and corner towers of 1480–6 was first enlarged on its northern side, and

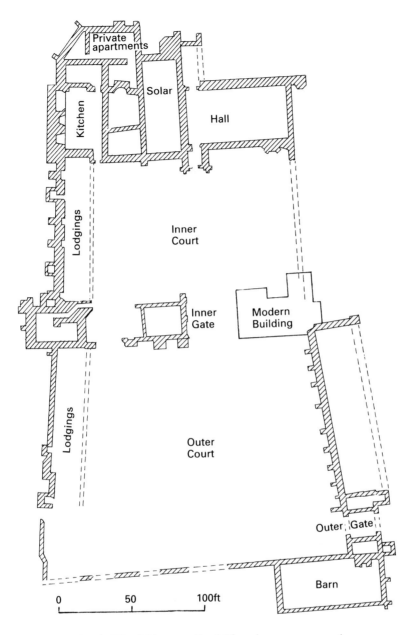

10.5 South Wingfield, a castellated fifteenth-century manor house.

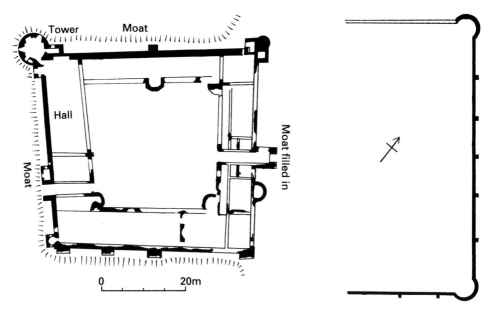

10.6 Caistor Castle (Norfolk). The large, weakly defended outer court probably contained lodgings and stables and barns.

then given an outer court, of which the gatehouse survives, covering the main entrance.[79]

The same plan, but without the towers and crenellations, is apparent in Lord Treasurer Cromwell's protected house at South Wingfield,[80] Ralph Boteler's Sudeley Castle, and John Holand's Dartington.[81] The last, and potentially the grandest of all these late medieval castles, was Thornbury Castle (Gloucestershire), began following a licence to crenellate, granted in 1510 to Edward Stafford, Duke of Buckingham, and left unfinished at the time of his execution in 1522.[82] The valuation of his estates contained an unusually full account of the castle:

The manor or castle stands to the north of the parish church, and has an inner and an outer ward, forsquare . . . The south side is fully finished with curious works and stately lodgings. The west side and north side be but builded to one chamber height . . . The east side, containing the hall and other houses of offices, is all of the old building, and of a homely fashion. The outer ward was intended to have been large, with many lodgings, where of the foundations on the north and west side is taken and brought up nigh to laying on a floor . . .[83]

The valuation goes on to describe the quality of the masonry and the disposition of the garden and orchard.

Was the Duke of Buckingham's great house a castle or merely a very sumptuous manor house? Those who conducted Henry VIII's inquisition were uncertain, as have been most writers on architecture since that date. It clearly incorporated an earlier house – the 'old building' – constructed in 'homely fashion', but in plan it resembled Fastolf's Caistor or Hasting's Kirby Muxloe.

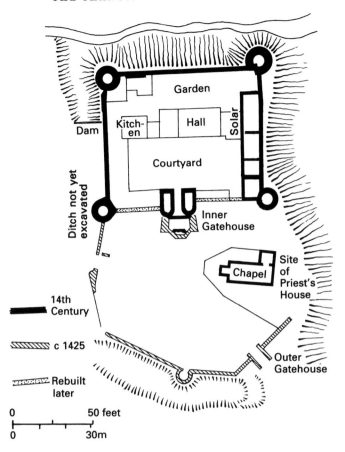

Garden

Kitch-
en

Hall

Solar

Dam

Courtyard

Ditch not yet
excavated

Inner
Gatehouse

Chapel

Site
of
Priest's
House

14th
Century

c 1425

Rebuilt
later

Outer
Gatehouse

0   50 feet

0   30m

10.7 Farleigh Hungerford Castle (Somerset). The main court was built *c*. 1380, and contains a
hall–kitchen–solar block. The outer court of *c*. 1440 enclosed the local parish church, which
became the castle chapel.

Return to the tower-keep

Most of the castles and fortified manors built during the fourteenth and fifteenth
centuries conformed broadly with the courtyard plan, but from the later years of the
fourteenth century a new element intruded into its simple and regular outline. There
was a renewed interest in the tower as the principal accommodation within the castle.
Square tower-keeps had ceased to be built in England in the later years of the twelfth
century, though round or polygonal keeps continued into the early decades of the
thirteenth. Interest in such structures survived longer in Wales and Ireland, but
thereafter, it is generally assumed, the keep went out of fashion and was forgotten,
although existing keeps remained in use. In many sheriffs' castles a tower-keep was
kept in being and in repair, and the idea of a free-standing tower of great strength can
never have been far from the minds of those lords who built and inhabited castles

269

during succeeding centuries. The major emphasis during the thirteenth century was on the gatehouse, which was developed in some of the Edwardian castles of North Wales into the principal structure in the castle. Masonry gate-towers of about 1100 at Ludlow and Richmond were converted to tower-keeps by closing the entrance tunnel. The same happened in the fourteenth century at Dunstanburgh, where a very strong gatehouse was made into the castle's strong point,[84] and at Llanstephan in South Wales,[85] and at nearby Kidwelly a very large gatehouse was built, incorporating hall and chambers on its upper floor.[86]

Clearly the idea of a large, tower-like building as the focal point of a castle was far from dead. But to build a freestanding tower-keep in the fourteenth century might seem a case of atavism, of returning to the forms of more than a century earlier. As far as England is concerned one can point to tower-keeps in the Marches, erected long after the fashion had changed in much of the country. The keeps at Hopton,[87] Wattlesborough and perhaps also at Alberbury (Shropshire) belong in all probability to the thirteenth century, and in 1284 Bishop Burnell began his keep-like house at Acton Burnell, in the words of West, 'as the most appropriate symbol of authority'.[88]

In Wales the tradition of the tower-keep was more persistent, and several of the castles built by the Welsh themselves were dominated by a tall and rather crudely built tower, but Flint, with its remarkable detached tower, was exceptional among the castles of Edward I. In the North of England also a tower tradition lived on, and flowered in the tower-houses of the later Middle Ages and sixteenth century. But in England itself it appears by and large to have succumbed, and was revived only in the fifteenth century. One can, perhaps, see in the castles of France the prototype of the fifteenth-century tower, just as the origins of Fastolf's tower at Caistor may have lain in the *Wasserbürgen* of the Low Countries. But one can nevertheless claim that in England the tower-keep tradition, though moribund, was never dead.

The number of tower-keeps built in the last century of the Middle Ages was not large. They were very expensive and only the greatest of noble households could afford the elegant living to which they were adapted. There was a certain consistency in the plan of keeps in the twelfth century. There was no such uniformity in those built towards the end of the Middle Ages. They varied greatly in design, and it is to be assumed that they derived in some degree from castles which their masters had seen in France. They were all of three or more storeys and embraced a great hall, usually on the first floor, as well as private chambers, kitchen and other domestic offices. All represented craftsmanship of a very high order, and were designed to allow very rich men to live in luxury and splendour.

Dudley (Staffordshire), the earliest of them, was built by Sir John de Somery early in the fourteenth century.[89] It was placed upon the summit of a large motte which had belonged to an earlier castle, and consisted of four round towers built so close together that the space within formed a rectangle only 15 m by 8.5 m. A comparable but considerably larger tower was built in the course of the fourteenth century on the motte of Stafford,[90] and at Nunney (Somerset) a tower of closely similar plan was built on a virgin site and surrounded with a wide moat.[91] At the end of the century Henry Percy, first Earl of Northumberland, built a great tower on the motte of Warkworth Castle (Northumberland).[92] It was much larger than the towers at Stafford or Dudley, and lacked their distinctive corner towers. Instead it had apsidal projections in the middle of each side. Its internal arrangements were extraordinarily complex, and included great hall, chambers, kitchen, buttery, pantry and store-rooms, all skilfully arranged around a central well which culminated in a tower-like lantern. Indeed, most of these great towers of the later Middle Ages displayed an extremely complex and ingenious internal planning, with interlocking halls and apartments, which contrasts with the relative simplicity of the hall- or tower-keep of the twelfth century.

There was clearly an affinity in the minds of builders between the great tower and the gatehouse tower. The one could be converted into the other, and the gatehouse was sometimes planned, as at Kidwelly, Beaumaris and Harlech, to embrace the suite of rooms commonly found within a tower-keep. At Hylton (Durham), an elaborate tower was built as if it were a gatehouse leading to something even grander.[93] In fact, it seems never to have led to more than a manorial courtyard. Above the entrance passage and rooms for the porter were the hall and, at its respective ends, the solar block and kitchen – in effect, a very elaborate first-floor hall. On a second floor were further chambers.

At about the same time John, fifth Lord Lovel, built Wardour Castle in Wiltshire, after having been given a licence in 1393.[94] It is pentagonal in plan, and displays the same elaborate organisation of space met with at Warkworth. And, again as at Warkworth, its state rooms and chambers were built around a minuscule court, less than 15 m across, which served only to light some of the inner rooms. Here, as at Hylton and in the gatehouse-keeps, the great hall was built above the entrance.

The largest and grandest of all these late medieval keeps was Tattershall, built by Ralph, Baron Cromwell, Lord Treasurer of England and a man of immense wealth.[95] The date of its erection is uncertain, and has been put by Anthony Emery between 1445 and 1454. It was built on the site of a motte-and-bailey, and preserved in part the curtain wall and mural towers of the latter. It was constructed of brick with limestone trim, and consisted of four floors above a basement. Its bold machicolation suggests a building of great strength, belied by the large windows, even on the ground floor, and its undefended entrance. It was 'first and foremost . . . a splendid mansion',[96] but one, nevertheless, which gave a degree of protection to its lord.

It is difficult to say how far Tattershall provided a model for other such tower-houses. The similarity of the Bishop of Lincoln's tower at Buckden in Huntingdonshire, cannot be wholly accidental,[97] and Bishop Fox's Tower at Farnham Castle, though much smaller, bears a superficial resemblance.[98]

In the 1460s William Herbert, Earl of Pembroke, greatly extended the castle which his father had begun at Raglan (Monmouthshire) by building a polygonal, freestanding tower, surrounded by a mantlet. It lay, as at Flint, outside the main court of the castle, commanding its principal entrance. It provided self-sufficing accommodation for its lord as well as a degree of protection not met with in other late medieval towers.[99] Its construction by Herbert must be seen as a step in the consolidation of Yorkist power in South Wales by one of Edward IV's strongest supporters.

One other elaborate tower-house calls for mention, that at Ashby-de-la-Zouche.[100] Ashby was merely a rather modest manor house before its acquisition and development by William, Lord Hastings. In 1475 he received licence to fortify his enlarged house and added the perimeter wall and the tower which bears his name. It was built into the line of the wall and rose 27.5 m and four storeys above the ground. It was, like most of these towers, strongly machicolated but, unlike the others, had an entrance protected by a portcullis. Hastings was a Yorkist, and his tower, like Herbert's at Raglan, must be seen in the context of the consolidation of Edward IV's rule.

No other castle is known to have been built with a tower-house of such size and elaboration as those mentioned, though a polygonal tower, with far greater military intent, was built on the motte of Southampton Castle (see p. 245). In many lightly fortified homes of the later Middle Ages there was commonly a less pretentious tower. That at Caistor Castle has been mentioned, and there were minor towers – solar towers in fact – in the perimeter walls of Sudeley, South Wingfield and Cotehele (Cornwall). They could have had no significant military value, but remained a part of the tradition of a protected home. The tower lent prestige rather than protection, and was a feature both of the later medieval castle and of its more romantic successors of modern times.

Late medieval feudalism

Much has been made of the alleged lawlessness of the bands of retainers who served the great lords of the fourteenth and fifteenth centuries. This was, indeed, a lawless age, when disputes and feuds were likely to be settled by raids and skirmishes. Magnates had bands of retainers, bound to their service by indented agreement.[101] Such contracts may have been difficult to enforce in the courts, but there is absolutely no reason to suppose that these bands were untrustworthy or disloyal. The argument, deriving from Victorian speculation and pursued with vigour by W. Douglas Simpson, that these late medieval tower-keeps were designed to protect the lords from their own insubordinate retainers, dies hard, but is completely without foundation. Retainers wore their lord's badge with pride and were, as a general rule, absolutely dependent on him.

If the separate suites – hall, solars and kitchen – were not intended to isolate the lord from his rebellious dependant, what in fact was their purpose? Such suites of apartments, sometimes with individual kitchens, had begun to appear in the greater castles, both royal and baronial, early in the thirteenth century. With increasing wealth and deeper social cleavages in the fourteenth and fifteenth, they increased in

10.8 The *manche* of the Hastings family represented in burnt headers in the brickwork of Kirby Muxloe Castle.

scale and in number. Piers Plowman complained that the lord was, in the later fourteenth century, no longer willing to eat in the common hall along with his servants.

> Elyng is the halle · uche daye in the wyke
> Ther the lord ne the lady · liketh noughte to sytte
> Now hath uche riche a reule · to eten bi hym-selve
> In a pryve parloure · for pore mennes sake
> Or in a chambre with a chymneye · and leve the chief halle
> That was made for meles · men to eten inne[102]

The inference is that this was in a simple manor house. Social distance would have been far greater in the households of the magnates. Indeed, there are likely to have been more than two social levels, as reflected in the arrangement of halls and suites of chambers. Between the lord's suite, usually fairly small but elaborately decorated, and the common and doubtless boisterous hall of servants and retainers, there was, at least in castles developed in the later Middle Ages, an intermediate hall and suite of apartments for, perhaps, the knightly or gentry class. In Warkworth and Tattershall the chief suite would have been in the tower; others in the bailey, dependent on an older, ground-floor hall. In a castle of the courtyard plan, the several halls and related chamber blocks were arrayed against the curtain wall.

The resulting social segregation is best demonstrated at Castle Bolton. This is, in reality, only a further refinement of that met with at Chepstow and Goodrich (p. 141).[103] The difference is that Scrope's castle was newly built on a virgin site, and was conceived as a series of suites and lodgings, each focussing on its appropriate hall. The castle is rectangular in plan, with square corner towers which are carried up for a further two floors above the rest of the building. The ground floor is occupied by guardrooms, stables, stores and lodgings for, doubtless, the more menial members of the community. The main hall and kitchen (now destroyed) were on the first floor, linked with a series of suites and lodgings, and on the second is a chapel and more suites. The total accommodation 'can be broken down into no less than eight major household units and some twelve lesser lodgings all integrated into one unified conception'.[104]

Bodiam Castle was built at about the same time as Castle Bolton, by Sir Edward Dalyngrigge, who had made a fortune in the French wars. Its concept was similar: a series of suites and lodgings, built around an open court and integrated with one another. The presence of a second kitchen suggests that there was also a second hall.

In these two castles the social stratification, which first became apparent at Chepstow and in the royal castles of Winchester and Windsor, was carried to its extreme. Scrope and Dalyngrigge and, for that matter, Hastings, Fiennes, Lovel, Percy and Cromwell expected to entertain lavishly, and anticipated that their noble guests would come each with his household and retinue. Accommodation had to be abundant, and adjusted in its location, size and embellishment to the status of each. The fine gradations in rank were advertised by the hierarchy of noble titles and the conceits of heraldry. Never, perhaps, in the course of English history has rank been demarcated quite as outrageously as by the gradations in the accommodation within the late medieval castle.

The retinues that these castles were called upon to accommodate could be very large, their size depending on the ability of their lords to pay them. They included knights and esquires as well as men-at-arms, craftsmen, cooks, menial servants and clerics who doubled as clerks. Cases are known of entourages which numbered more than a hundred. If such numbers were permanently retained, they must have cost considerably more than £1,000 a year, beyond the means of most even of the aristocracy to support or of their castles to house.

Earlier centuries saw only two social classes, the 'warring noble and the cultivating peasant'.[105] Increasing wealth, the rise of a middle class of merchants and craftsmen, the extinction of the older baronage and the fragmentation and reconsolidation of their estates all contributed to a social mobility such as this country had never previously known. There was an upward striving at all levels of society as each reached for the symbols of that which it saw as higher in the social scale. And the highest levels struggled to keep the lower orders in their proper place. Sumptuary legislation regulated dress, the foremost symbol of rank, and a great lord, especially if his own origins would not bear close scrutiny, took good care that no egalitarian ideas prevailed within his castle. All, in the words of the Parliament Roll, should 'be led and governed in his estate and degree'.[106] The architecture and style of a castle, no less than the dress and the diet of those who lived within it, was adjusted to this rank and standing.

CHAPTER 11

Tower-house, pele and bastle

. . . a vertical range of rooms . . . There was no thought of spreading, of walking,
from one room to another. One went upstairs or down; no other route was possible.
S. Cruden, *The Scottish Castle*

The great towers, put up by the magnates during the closing centuries of the Middle Ages, were not the only tower-houses built at this time. The country was strewn with little towers erected by the humbler orders, the knights and gentry, to protect their families and possessions. With the abandonment of the motte, the tower-house became the simplest, the most functional and the most cost-effective means of defending the small man against his neighbour and enemy. Tower-houses were built in the cities; they were put up near the coasts, and they proliferated in the Marches and Borders. Like a small motte castle, the tower-house served only for local protection. It was never part of a broadly conceived plan of defence, and if tower-houses were more numerous in some areas than in others, this was only because the dangers were perceived to be greater.

The origin of the tower-house, as it was built in the later Middle Ages, is obscure. Clearly it bore a certain relationship to the tower-keep of the twelfth century, but it differed in major respects. It had no forebuilding; it was entered at ground level; it was more lightly built, and it was not, as a general rule, a part of a larger fortified area, though it often had an enclosed yard for holding stock. It was a secure house, a 'house of fence'. There was a world of difference between a tower-house and a small motte, but in *function* there was a remarkable similarity, and the former deserves no less than the latter to be subsumed under the term 'castle'.

Although the need for protection, especially in the Borders and along the coast, may have been an important factor in building tower-houses, the desire for conspicuous consumption was, over much of the country, very far from absent. The later Middle Ages were, as has been noted, an age of ambition and social emulation. A tower was a status symbol. It suggested power and rank, and it implied that its owner was well able to look after himself. It suggested, further, that its contents were worth protecting, as, indeed, they probably were. However slight its military pretensions, the tower-house was designed to give security and to make entry as difficult as possible.

The urban tower

The urban castle, apart from the sheriff's castle in the county town, was rare in England. The Italian, and indeed the Mediterranean city generally, bristled with '*turri*': over 100 in Viterbo; almost as many in Tuscania, and large numbers in almost every other city of medieval Italy.[1] Dozens of them survive to show their internal arrangements. Many were extremely tall, 50 m and even more. Their groundplan was usually small, with a maximum dimension not more than 10 m. They consisted of room piled upon room, until the whole structure became so unstable that few of those surviving today retain their original height.

In 1248 Brother Salimbene observed, while watching a royal procession in the town of Sens, that in northern Europe 'burgesses only dwell in cities, whereas the knights and noble ladies dwell in the villages and on their estates'.[2] In southern Europe, by contrast, the nobility had moved to the cities where they pursued their quarrels and built their towers in a kind of unbridled feudal anarchy. The origin of the Italian towers is less obscure than that of the tower-house in England. They were too numerous to represent centres of any kind of feudal jurisdiction, but their function is clear. They formed strong points in the interminable private and party warfare which was subsumed in the struggle of Guelph against Ghibelline.[3] In the congested conditions of the medieval Italian city there was little scope for building a court around the tower. At most there was a small enclosed yard. The *turri* achieved the floorspace they needed by piling room on room.[4]

Northern Europe in general escaped the anarchy which at times prevailed in Italian cities. Yet there was a trend towards the urban tower-house, halted in part by royal control of fortification, in part by the development of urban self-government and the rule of law. As the constitution of English towns evolved, some degree of immunity from urban jurisdiction became necessary for a castle. The sheriff's castle generally stood within its own 'liberty' or 'fee'. What evidence, then, is there for the existence of other such feudal enclaves within English towns? Little indeed, and most of those for which there is evidence were ecclesiastical. There is evidence in London for two castles in the western part of the city. One of them, known as Montfichet from the baronial family which presumably held it, disappeared early.[5] The other, Baynard's Castle, lasted longer, but in the thirteenth century its site was given to the Dominicans, who have left their name there until today.[6] In the *Quo Warranto* proceedings before the London Eyre, Robert FitzWalter claimed 'to have a soke [jurisdiction] . . . from the wall of the canons of St Paul's . . . to the Thames, and . . . along the walls of the said city to Ludgate . . . he says that formerly he had a certain castle in London [Baynard's] pertaining to his barony which he holds from the king in chief'.[7] There is an early twelfth-century reference to Ravensger's Tower, close to the Tower itself,[8] but it disappeared early and nothing is known of it. There were other tower-houses in London. About 1300 Nicholas de Cokfeld was granted 'a certain tower' (*turellum*) on the east side of Bishopsgate 'on condition that he keep it in good order.[9] This could have been one of the city's mural towers, but other city towers were certainly not. In the next century a tower was built 'opposite to the one to be erected at the expense of John Phelipott',[10] and there was another *turellum* on the south side of Aldgate within an enclosed garden.[11]

The Patent Rolls record the licence given to John le Molyns to 'crenellate his dwellingplace' in the west of the city,[12] and permission was later given both to fortify a *mansionem* within the precinct of the Carmelites[13] and to crenellate the Palace of the Savoy which lay outside the city's west gate.[14] A tower was even built by Richard II 'at the corner of his private palace of Westminster'.[15] Nor does this exhaust the list of urban towers which *could* have been built. Coulson's list catalogues no less than a dozen licences granted for crenellated houses within London, as well as grants in Beverley (Yorkshire), Hull, Maidstone and Shrewsbury.

The handful of tower-houses that are known to have been built within London did not constitute a threat to public order, and it is very doubtful whether, apart from Baynard's, they enjoyed any immunity from civic jurisdiction. In many of the older cities there were 'liberties', but little evidence that they ever became the sites of castles, beyond the reach of civil jurisdiction. Winchester, with the bishop's castle of Wolvesey, is an exception. This was, in effect, a palace clustered around a small tower-keep of the early twelfth century.[16] There were other areas within the city in which the mayor's writ did not run.[17] They were sources of disorder through their lack of effective urban authority, but none ever became the site of a castle.

In Lincoln there was an immunity, the Hungate fee, which was feudally held, but its lords seem never to have asserted themselves.[18] In the lower part of the medieval city and close to the Witham there was, however, a castle which briefly appeared in the records as Thorngate. It had, together with certain lands, been pledged to King Stephen, who turned over his rights in it to Bishop Alexander.[19]

In a few instances an urban tower was erected by the citizens themselves for their own protection. At Harwich, for example, a tract of land 160 feet square was acquired in order to erect a 'castle of stone'.[20] A tower, perhaps not dissimilar, was built on the cliff edge at Rye (Sussex), and survives as the Ypres Tower.[21] At Melcombe Regis, on the Dorset coast, the Dominicans were allowed to build 'a tower for the fortification of their house'.[22] A number of ports were in the fifteenth century protected by stone-built towers. At Fowey, where they survive in part, they protected the ends of a boom which was used to close the harbour mouth. Here, however, we are passing from the castle as a fortified home, and into the very different realm of fortification erected by public authority for the nation's protection.

The tower-house in England and Wales

Tower-houses were few in lowland England, though some have been destroyed and others probably await discovery.[23] They were far more numerous in the northern counties and the Borders, where Barley claims that there were at one time some 150. Pevsner claims thirty-two in Westmorland and fifty-eight in Cumberland.[24] They were, however, notably rare in Wales.[25] No inventory of tower-houses appears ever to have been made for England. The tower was part of a house, and suffered the rebuilding and destruction common to all early houses. Houses, furthermore, are in general poorly documented, and without archival or archaeological evidence it is impossible to demonstrate the former existence of a tower-house. Barley has, for example, recently shown that there were tower-houses at four unsuspected sites near Nottingham, only one of which, Halloughton, near Southwell, still stands to its full height. The others were revealed only by the groundplan of later buildings or by a thickening in a wall.[26] Many such towers must survive, in part at least, encapsulated within later building, in other parts of the country.

The tower-house was commonly rectangular in plan, and rose three storeys and, on rare occasions, four.[27] The tower was commonly plain. The mouldings of windows and doorways were simple, and on stylistic grounds the tower is usually very difficult to date. The northern tower-houses showed little development in style over a period of two centuries and more.

The ground floor was often used for storage, and sometimes had a separate entrance. It was unlikely, especially in northern England, to be vaulted in stone as a precaution against fire. The first floor usually served as hall or living-room, and chambers occupied the upper floor. A winding staircase was likely to have been contrived in the thickness of a wall or in a projecting corner tower, just as in a contemporary church. There was often a fireplace on the main floor, and sometimes also in the solar above, with chimneys enclosed within the wall, but there is often little evidence for a kitchen or for other rooms for the storage and preparation of food. It is possible that these activities were carried on elsewhere, in buildings, possibly of wood, which have since been destroyed.

The tower was often battlemented, with a wall-walk. Sometimes two of its four sides were gabled. There were, as might be expected in architecture which approached the vernacular, regional variations in design, and tower-houses in Scotland and the Borders differed significantly from those met with in the rest of Britain.

In England most towers were at one time annexed to a hall, thus raising the important question whether they were added to a pre-existing hall or, on the other hand, a hall was added to an earlier tower. This problem remains in many instances insoluble. At Stokesay (Shropshire) the earliest structure is the northern tower, against which the hall was built by Lawrence of Ludlow late in the thirteenth century. Then, many years later, the more southerly tower was added, and was linked to the hall block by a covered passage. The licence to crenellate, granted in 1291, may have related to this tower. The structural history of Stokesay may have been more complex than that of most tower-houses. In England, it may perhaps be postulated, the hall came first, and the tower represented a lofty and pretentious solar block at its upper end. In numerous cases a crease on the face of the tower shows

6 Stokesay Castle (Shropshire). On the left is the north tower, the earliest part of the present structure, and at the right the south tower which was added after the grant of a licence to crenellate. Between lies the hall. The site was surrounded by a moat, invisible in this photograph.

where the gable-end of the hall had once butted against it. In the North, where the tower was built more for protection than from pride, the hall may have been added to the tower as both security and wealth increased.

This raises the question of how defensible was the tower and whether it could be cut off from the hall and held separately. The northern tower was, generally speaking, a unit in itself. The southern communicated more readily with the hall, to which in very many instances it can have served only as a solar block.[28] It is difficult to determine the balance in the minds of the builders of tower-houses 'between the dual aspects of prestige and defence'.[29] Perhaps they were themselves unsure of their own motivation. In retrospect one can perhaps claim that in certain instances

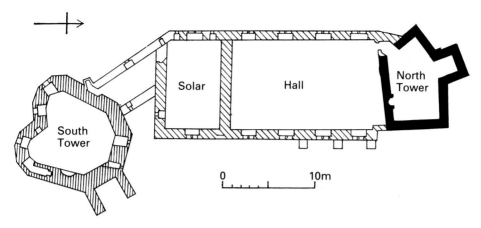

11.1 Stokesay Castle (Shropshire). The original tower is shown in black. The more impressive tower at the south end appears to have followed the grant of a licence to crenellate in 1291.

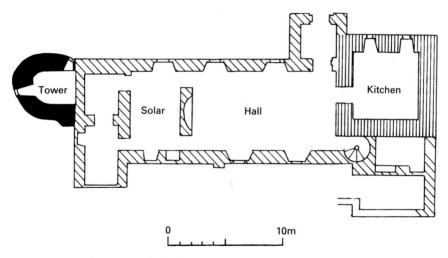

11.2 Lympne Castle (Kent). The half-round tower at the west end was added to a hall–solar block.

protection came before pride, and that in others the situation may have been the reverse.

Lympne Castle (Kent) is an instance of the addition of a tower to an earlier manor house (Figure 11.2). It stood on a low bluff, looking across the coastal marshes, then much narrower than today, towards the French coast. A ground-floor hall, with kitchen and solar at its respective ends, was built in the thirteenth and fourteenth centuries. About 1420 a tower of irregular, horseshoe plan was added to the solar block and was carried up for four storeys.[30]

Closely similar, but of somewhat earlier date, is Godlingston Manor in Swanage

11.3 Pengersick Castle (Cornwall). The entrance to the tower, showing the machicolation-like device above the doorway.

(Dorset), also lying within a short distance of the sea. Here too a manor house of conventional plan had a rounded tower added at one end.[31] A last example from the south coast is Pengersick Castle (Cornwall), built within a half kilometre of the shore of Mount's Bay, by a well-to-do member of the local gentry.[32] It is a rectangular granite tower of three storeys, with a newel staircase built within a projecting corner turret. It was probably the solar block of a hall house which has vanished, leaving only the crease of its gable on the face of the tower. It was nevertheless entered by a lightly protected doorway on the ground floor (Figure 11.3) which communicated by the newel stair with the upper levels. There is no evidence that it ever communicated directly with the vanished hall.

The three tower-houses just mentioned all lie very close to the sea, and it is evident that they were intended to give some protection from seaborne raiders. That this fear was not altogether fanciful is shown by the numerous raids by the French on

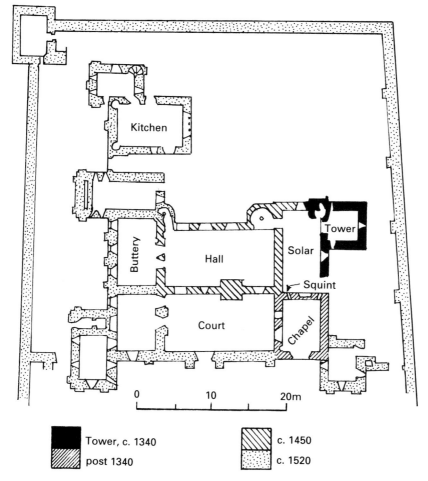

Kitchen

Buttery

Hall

Solar

Tower

Squint

Court

Chapel

0   10   20m

▮	Tower, c. 1340	▨	c. 1450
▨	post 1340	▨	c. 1520

11.4 Compton Castle (Devon). The hall and solar, as they exist today, were grafted on to an earlier tower. The enclosing wall is much later.

the south coast and by pirates who raided the shores of the North Atlantic. All such towers were intended to give short-term protection against a small force, intent more on seizing booty than on controlling territory.

In the interior of England there was less need for such protection, and one can point to very few towers that appear to have been built primarily for defence. Security from intruders was almost certainly an objective, but that is very different from protection against an armed raid. It is likely that many of those who sought a licence to crenellate their homes contemplated nothing more than a strong tower at the end of their hall. The tower at Kyme (Lincolnshire) survives from such a 'castle'. It was built about 1340–50 by a member of the northern family of Umfraville which had inherited the notional barony of Kyme. The house has been destroyed, but the tower, of four storeys and 23.5 m high, still stands.[33] One tends to think of Kyme Tower as a cultural borrowing from Northumberland.

There is a cluster of tall tower-houses in Lincolnshire and the East Midlands, which appear to have derived their inspiration ultimately from Ralph Cromwell's tower at Tattershall. The Tower-on-the-Moor at Woodhall Spa may have been built by Cromwell himself, and still rises 18 m from the ground. Broadly similar, but of a somewhat later date, are Hussey and Rochford Towers, near Boston. Hussey Tower, of which a substantial part remains, has been dated to about 1460. It is of brick and formerly had a hall attached to it.[34] Rochford Tower is also of brick and of three storeys, with battlemented and corbelled corner turrets.[35] At Creslow (Buckinghamshire) is a tower of mid-fourteenth-century date, attached not to the end but to the side of the hall.[36] There are also towers surviving at Southwick (Northamptonshire), Astwell[37] (Northamptonshire) and Ayscough, near Spalding (Lincolnshire).

A tower-house which can have had no military pretentions is Chesterton Tower, built near Cambridge during the fourteenth century.[38] It is of only two storeys and has a vaulted ground floor, so that it is in effect a first-floor hall. It is of rubble masonry, of local origin, with quoins of superior oolite. Its machicolations are pretentious, but could have served no military purpose. The building was, in fact, wholly domestic. Shute Barton (Devon)[39] and Little Wenham (Suffolk)[40] are also impressive solar towers in which domesticity predominated over defence. There are remains of two domestic towers at manorial sites in Kent: Nurstead[41] and Greenhithe,[42] and more are likely to come to light as older structures are examined more carefully.

But the best surviving tower-house in lowland England is probably Longthorpe Tower, near Peterborough. It was built early in the fourteenth century by Robert Thorpe, a local man, said to have been of villein origin, who had risen in the service of Peterborough Abbey.[43] His humble origin may help to explain why his building was so pretentious. He added a tower to a hall house which in the main survives. The tower itself consists of a vaulted basement and first floor, which served as its master's principal apartment, and an upper floor. The basement has a separate entrance from without, and there is no direct access from it to the main floor, which was reached originally only from the hall. Longthorpe Tower is far better preserved than most such towers. Its internal walls were plastered and painted with a series of religious and morality motifs. 'No comparable scheme of domestic mural decoration of such completeness and of this early date exists in England', wrote Clive Rouse,[44] and it gives some idea of the nature and sophistication of the decoration that must once have existed in royal castles and other secular buildings.

All in all, the number of tower-houses of which some fragments survive in the heart of England is far greater than is suggested by the map of such structures in *Houses of the Welsh Countryside*.[45] But the more one considers them the more apparent does it become that they were an affectation of the rising gentry, intended to impress but never to give protection against anything more than the casual intruder.

Tower-houses are very few in Wales and the March, despite the prevailing insecurity of the region. Neither the first-floor hall nor the solar block was part of the local building tradition, and they are found in numbers only in the southern and most English parts of Pembrokeshire.[46] In the Marches the motte castle appears to have continued in use longer than in England. There was a tradition of building small square or round tower-keeps, which continued through the thirteenth century and even later,[47] but it never merged into a tower-house tradition. The solar tower at Stokesay is probably the earliest in the March,[48] though the so-called Forester's Lodge at Millichope on Wenlock Edge is effectively a small tower-house of about the same period.[49] The only other examples within the Welsh Border are in Flintshire. At Lyseurgain is a late-fifteenth-century tower-house, much restored, and at Mold is another of, perhaps, somewhat earlier date.[50]

Northern England and the Borders

Only in northern England and the Border regions of Scotland did the tower-house become a common feature of the landscape. Its origin lay in the prevailing insecurity. The failure of Edward III's invasion of Scotland and his subsequent distraction by the lure of the French crown was followed by centuries of uneasy peace. The English king was content to leave control over the Border counties to the Wardens of, respectively, the Western and the Eastern March, and these, with few exceptions, were Nevilles or Percys, *les seigneurs marchers del north*, as they were termed in the Parliament Roll.[51] It was to their advantage to maintain an uneasy relationship with the Scots and to encourage raiding and skirmishing, which brought them profit and excused their private armies. 'The king's justice was remote and ineffectual in the three most northern counties [and] the local lord commanded more respect than the distant King.'[52]

In the absence of effective royal control, local authority devolved on the Marcher lords. No more than half a dozen families dominated the northern counties of England, and a similar group, most of them ultimately of English origin, controlled affairs on the Scottish side. At a lower social level was the northern equivalent of the gentry. These formed kinship groups, locally known as 'surnames', each of which supported this magnate or that, and feuded amongst themselves. Agriculture was as backward as society itself. The land was poor, and scarcity, even famine, far from rare. The sparse population was driven to make the most of the grazing which became available on the high ground during summer, and transhumance was regularly practised. Under these circumstances raiding was normal, the Scots seizing flocks and herds on the English side of the Border, and vice versa, and one 'surname' riding off with the possessions of another.

After Edward III's abortive invasion of Scotland the powers in Westminster lost interest in the Borders, content merely to pay a fee to the Wardens of the March to hold some half-dozen royal castles. For their part, the Percys, Nevilles, Dacres and the rest were happy to allow this state of low-level anarchy to continue, secure in the knowledge that it provided justification for their own local powers and for the bands of armed retainers whom they employed. Raiding became a way of life. Villages and homes suffered at the hands of small armed bands, and family feuds were pursued with fire and sword. Recourse to the courts was often impossible, since these were controlled by the great men of their districts.[53] And so the individual was thrown back on his own resources. He protected himself as well as he was able by building a tower, capable of defence for at least a short period. There is little evidence that artillery was used against tower-houses, except in the course of a military expedition. It is doubtful whether most raiders possessed even hand-guns. In 1523, an invading English force, equipped with guns, made very short work of the tower-houses that resisted.[54]

The term 'peel' or 'pele' was increasingly used in the fourteenth century for what was in effect a lightly fortified homestead.[55] It appears at first to have denoted little more than a palisaded enclosure. Later a tower, perhaps of wood, was built within the enclosure. Many of the fortifications which were erected or repaired in the course of the Edwardian invasions of Scotland were of this kind. Then, towards the end of the Middle Ages, the wooden tower was rebuilt in stone, but still retained the popular name of 'pele'. Eventually popular usage restricted the term to the stone-build tower alone.[56] On the other hand, the Scottish practice was to call the masonry tower-house a 'tower', while the term 'pele' or 'pelehouse' denoted a much humbler structure with a great deal less military pretension.[57] In this chapter the nomenclature recommended by Dixon is used, and the masonry tower-house is known by that name. The term 'pele' is reserved for the humble, protected house of later centuries.

The spread of tower-houses through the northern counties took place mainly in the later fourteenth and fifteenth centuries with the growing insecurity of the region. Existing castles were strengthened; some new castles, among them Ford, Naworth, Penrith and Rose, were built, but chiefly it was existing manor houses that were strengthened by the addition of a tower. The scale and elaboration of the tower varied with the wealth of the builder and his perception of the danger faced. This was clearly greatest along the traditional invasion routes – the plain of Northumberland and, west of the Pennines, the Eden valley. Here tower-houses became almost as numerous as motte castles had formerly been in the Welsh Marches.

It is not always clear whether here the tower was added to a pre-existing hall, or whether it existed first as a free-standing structure to which others were added. Curwen claims that in Cumberland and Westmorland the latter was generally the case.[58] In Northumberland, on the other hand, there are many instances where a tower was butted against an earlier hall, forming an extended solar block, as was commonly the case in lowland England. Edlingham Castle is typical. A late-thirteenth-century hall-house with octagonal, but probably only decorative corner

11.5 Yanwath Hall (Westmorland). The tower-house to the right and the hall–kitchen to the
left appear to have been of one building phase.

turrets, was contained within a moated enclosure.[59] About 1360–80 a square tower
with diagonal buttresses was built close beside it, and the whole complex was
enclosed within a curtain wall. Halton Castle seems to have had a similar
development. A lightly protected hall-house of the thirteenth century was
strengthened by the addition of a four-storeyed tower-house.[60] Other comparable
examples are to be found at Featherstone,[61] Shortflatt and Welton in Northumberland, and at Burgh-by-Sands (Cumberland).[62] But at Yanwath (Westmorland) at
least the ground floor of the tower is contemporary with the adjoining hall.[63]

On the other hand there were throughout northern England tower-houses which
were complete in themselves, without ever having had an attached hall or kitchen.
Such were Dacre and Shank castles (Cumberland)[64] and Belsay[65] and Chipchase
(Northumberland).[66] In each there was a hall on the first floor, usually with a
kitchen, as well as a series of chambers on the second floor and higher.

The northern tower-house was typically rectangular in plan, with little external
embellishment. The ground floor was in almost every instance vaulted in stone, and
its entrance further protected by an iron grill, or 'yett', on to which oak boards had
been fastened. A newel staircase, either in the thickness of the wall or in a corner
turret, led to the upper floors. Walls were thick – up to 3 m at the ground-floor level,
diminishing upwards by internal offsets. Everything was done to make entry as
difficult as possible and to protect the tower from the danger of fire.

The first floor served generally as a hall, and above it were chambers. In the more
elaborate tower-houses fireplaces were built into the wall at each level, and there was

287

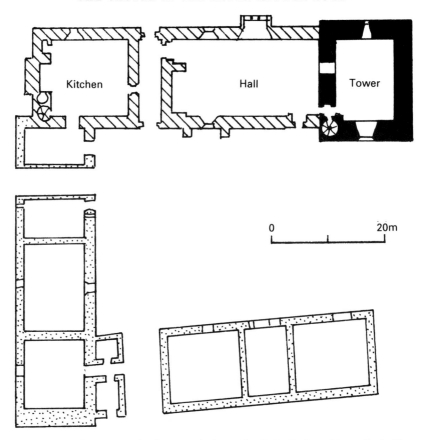

11.6 Yanwath Hall (Westmorland), ground plan. After J. H. Parker, *Domestic Architecture*.

a garderobe in its thickness at most levels, with chutes projecting from the exterior wall. The parapet was commonly battlemented, protecting a narrow wall-walk, and in the more sophisticated it was machicolated out from the wall. At the corners there might be corbelled bartizans of the kind that became common in Scotland.

The tower-house rarely stood entirely alone. In some instances there was an adjacent hall block; in most there was an enclosing wall or fence, and sometimes also a ditch. The enclosed yard, often called a 'barmkin', served many purposes. Stock could be penned here, tools stored and even a kitchen built. In the most elaborate examples there was also a simple gatehouse. But the barmkin was rarely defensible, and when danger threatened the household would be likely to retreat into the tower.

A similar development occurred on the Scottish side of the boundary, which was no less exposed to raiders.[67] Indeed the frequency of towers was even greater, they lie thick along the valleys of the Esk, Liddel, Teviot and Jed Water.[68] Their construction was broadly similar to that of English tower-houses: a basement for storage and two or more upper storeys to provide living accommodation, the whole enclosed by a fenced yard. But there were subtle differences, reflecting the different

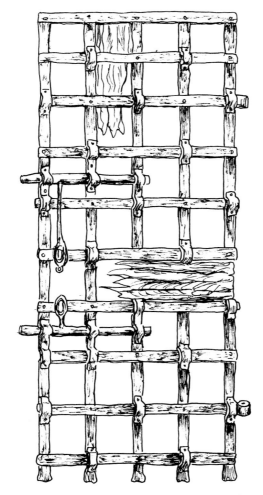

11.7 An iron 'yett' protecting the entrance to the tower of Naworth Castle (Cumberland).
Wood was fixed between the bars of the iron grill.

social structure and cultural influences.[69] While some were extremely plain and simple, many showed a high degree of elaboration. There was a tendency, especially in the sixteenth century, for the battlemented parapet and rampart walk to be abandoned in favour of a steep ridge-roof and gables, with, at the corners, corbelled bartizans, a cultural trait of French origin.[70] Greater attention was given to comfort in such towers, with a more generous provision for fireplaces and latrines, and there might even be a gunport covering the entrance.[71]

At the same time the plan of the Scottish tower-house became more complex than in England.[72] It was common, first, to add a projecting wing at one corner of the tower, producing an L-plan. In Scotland this was carried farther, with a second wing at the diametrically opposite corner, giving the so-called Z-plan. Other adaptations of the original plan followed. They satisfied an increasing demand for space within

11.8 The Vicar's Peel, Corbridge (Northumberland). It is of three storeys, and the ground floor is vaulted. There were originally corbelled bartizans at the corners. A garderobe chute opens from the top floor.

the tower, for in Scotland the tower-house seems rarely to have been accompanied by a separate hall or solar block, as in many instances in northern England. The Scottish tower-house did not evolve from the private accommodation built at the end of a traditional hall. It was, and remained, a freestanding and isolated tower. Its greater size, in many cases, and more elaborate decoration reflected not so much greater wealth than in England, as a different distribution of wealth.

Dixon has shown that the builders of tower-houses within the Border region of both countries were men of substance. One can only guess the monetary cost of raising a tower-house; it would have been high. Wealth was largely in flocks and herds and was essentially mobile. It shifted between the Scottish and the English Borders, and on balance Scotland gained and England lost. This, however, is insufficient to explain the very considerable differences in tower-house construction. There were also fundamental contrasts in the structure of society. In England the foremost people, with very few exceptions, were 'themselves manorial tenants, either of the crown or of absentee landlords, and their tenements were only of moderate size'.[73] By contrast society on the Scottish side of the boundary was more hierarchical. Many of the lairds and headmen had been enriched by 'good husbandry and the proceeds of full rentals'.[74] In a sense the English Borders remained more 'feudal' than the Scottish, and, paradoxically, more egalitarian, because the peaks of their landholding hierarchy lived elsewhere and drew rents and revenues from the Borders. The simple fact that in Scotland the rich and powerful tended to be the local lairds meant that their raiding was better organised and more successful, and the tower-houses that they built were proportionally larger and more elaborate. And so the balance of the Borders tipped ever more in their favour. This alone can explain the very great number of tower-houses in the Scottish Borders and the relatively high quality of their construction.[75]

The map, Figure 11.9, shows the distribution of known tower-houses in northern England and the Borders. They cluster around the invasion routes from Scotland, and lie along the Pennine dales to give protection to isolated settlements from the reivers who came down from the fells. They continue, more and more widely dispersed, into Yorkshire. To the west, they lie along the valleys of the Kent and the Lune, where there had previously been a succession of motte castles, and they end on the flanks of Rossendale, where Turton Tower is almost the last.[76] Tower-houses are, as a general rule, poorly documented, and their lack of architectural detail makes it extremely difficult to date them. Their simple plan continued with little modification for well over two centuries. The map attempts to show only those built before 1500, but there can be no assurance that some were not built during the following century, for security came slowly to these northern fells and dales. Even the union of the crowns of England and Scotland in 1603 brought no lasting peace, and men continued throughout the seventeenth century to protect themselves from armed bands of freebooters and cattle thieves. The increasingly wide dispersion of tower-houses, as one moves south from the Borders, is a rough measure of the growing sense of security. Nor can the map be regarded as complete. Lost tower-houses and those awaiting discovery have of necessity been omitted. Nevertheless the map conveys an impression of their general distribution.

Bastles and pelehouses

Below the level of the tower-house there developed within the Borders a humbler type of protected home, variously known as pelehouse, bastle and stonehouse. Tynedale, in the words of a visitation report of 1828, 'is full of uncouth but curious old houses which betoken a state of constant insecurity and of dubious defence, in which the inhabitants of the Border were so long accustomed to live.' The ordinary house, without fastened windows and locked doors, lay throughout the Middle Ages

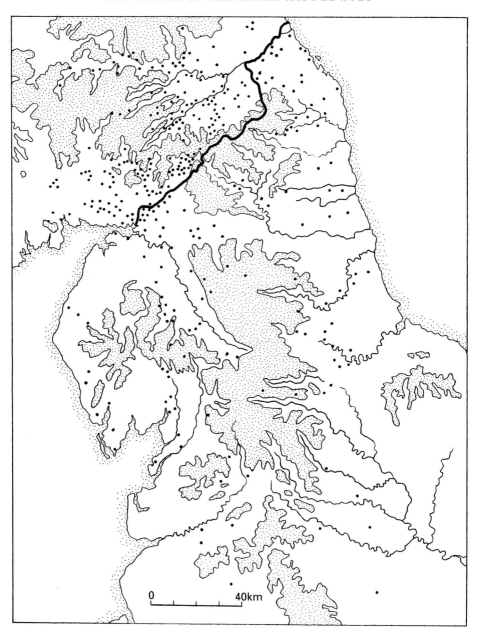

11.9 Tower-houses in northern England and the Scottish Borders, built mainly before 1500. Their greater density north of the Border probably indicates greater wealth rather than insecurity.

11.10 A pelehouse, now destroyed, in Haltwhistle (Northumberland). The entrance, shown here, was secured by drawbars, and there was probably no other opening to the ground floor. The turret on the left appears to have been more decorative than useful. After a photograph by Philip Dixon.

and early modern times, open to the intruder. The bastle or pelehouse was merely a safe house, masonry-built, proof against fire and with some kind of protected entrance. It lacked the height and thick walls of a tower-house, but could none the less give some degree of protection. To such houses Dixon has reserved the term 'bastle'.[77] They were comparatively few on both sides of the boundary, since all who could afford it extended their building to a tower-house. Far more abundant was the 'pelehouse', in Dixon's nomenclature. These were 'small, roughly built, barn-like houses with thick drystone walls'. They were formerly as numerous on the English side of the Cheviots as tower-houses were on the Scottish.[78] They reflected the lower general level of wealth, and their weakness ensured that their owners were victimised yet more by raiders from across the Borders. The pelehouse, roughly built and generally without mortar, is a disappearing feature of the northern landscape. Its purpose ended when the Border ceased to be raided by freebooters and cattle thieves, and that was not until the eighteenth century.[79]

And so the history of the castle as a fortified and protected home came full circle. It had begun in the eleventh century with ringworks and mottes, with wooden towers and palisades. It ended with houses crudely built of roughly hewn stone. It ended as it had begun, as a protection for the small man, the laird or the lord of the manor, in times of insecurity and unrest. Between these extremes lay five hundred years of development and decay, from motte, through keep, curtain wall and gatehouse, back again to the simple tower and ramshackle pelehouse. This history has a peculiar symmetry. It forms an arc, which begins and ends with the humblest structures, and shows at the peak of its development the complex structures of a Caerphilly or of a Kenilworth.

CHAPTER 12

Conclusion

Knouwyth that beth and schul be
That I am mad in help of the cuntre
In knowyng of whyche thyng
Thys is chartre and wytnessyng

Inscription of *c.* 1381 at Cowling Castle

The castle belongs to a particular phase in the development of Western society. It came between the decay of tribal society in the early Middle Ages and the emergence of the centralised state in modern times. It marked a period when the organs of government were immature, and many of its functions had necessarily to be delegated to those in local areas who could perform them. This phase in social development has come to be known generally as feudalism.

In Britain the transition from a tribal to a feudal society had begun under the Anglo-Saxons, and a feudal phase in British social history may be regarded as inevitable.[1] The Norman Conquest in 1066 merely hastened a process which had progressed farther on the continent than in England. The purpose of the castle was to protect the local seat of administrative authority, and during the early decades of English feudalism such protection was almost essential. The England of the Conqueror and his sons was not an orderly society with established courts and law that was readily enforced. It was a place where two cultures – three if one includes the Welsh – contended and where a very small force of immigrants maintained its authority by means of what, in present-day terminology, might be called terrorism.

There was thus a rash of fortified places. No one knows how many, since for most there is no documentation and for many the archaeological evidence is uncertain. At no time were there as many castles in England as during the first century of English feudalism. Thereafter their number gradually diminished. In this process two factors operated over most of England. On the one hand, from the early years of Henry II, the king clawed back some of the authority and jurisdiction which had, explicitly or implicitly, been delegated to the strong men in each local area. The process was neither continuous nor even, and was at times strenuously resisted. This resistance, right down to the fourteenth century, was most likely to take the shape of the defence of baronial castles against the forces of the king. However it may have been interpreted at a later date, the *Magna Carta* of 1215 was an assertion of baronial opposition to the encroachment of royal authority, and implicitly a claim by the barons to continue to build, inhabit and use their castles as they willed. Gradually, however, with the development of the king's courts and the broadening functions of sheriffs and, later, of justices of the peace, the castle in the sense of a protected home and seat of local authority lost its usefulness over much of England.

The other factor in the decline in the number of castles was the ever-increasing cost of building, maintaining and garrisoning them. Early earthwork castles called for little more than an army of unskilled labourers. But as masonry replaced wooden palisades, and towers, drawbridges and portcullises were introduced, so the cost of building mounted. Materials had to be bought and craftsmen hired, and the masonry castle priced itself out of the range of all except the king and the richest of the subjects. Even the maintenance of the older castles in good order became increasingly burdensome, and one after another they were abandoned to the weather, the vandal and the stone-robber.

The increasing cost of a castle was paralleled by the growing concentration of the nation's landed wealth in the hands of a diminishing number of magnates. Baronial families, in general, had but a short lease on life.[2] One after another they became extinct in the male line, and their possessions reverted to the crown or were carried by heiresses to other families. Contrived marriages might lead to a sudden accession of wealth, and, with a kind of inevitability, rich families grew richer and the poorer slipped unnoticed from the ranks of the baronage. The rich were enabled to build and enlarge castles consistent with their status; the poor had to be content with at most a protected home.

As a result of this concentration of wealth and privilege, a narrow class – the peerage – began to separate out from the broad mass of the baronage. They received writs of summons to Parliament and formed the nucleus of the House of Lords.[3] There were no more than some sixty peers before the end of the Middle Ages, and between them they controlled most of the baronial castles that remained inhabitable and in use. There were, of course, exceptions. Occasionally a knight benefited from 'the windfall profits of war', and built above his station, or a poor baron acquired lands by marriage. But such cases were few. Great castles in diminishing number, but of increasing splendour, belonged only to the king or to the magnates.

The later Middle Ages were 'an age of ambition'.[4] Everyone strove for wealth, but above all for rank and status, and, as rank without its outward symbols held little attraction, men also strove for the marks which made rank visible. Heraldry was refined to show gradations in status. Dress and diet emphasised social standing. The great lord was constantly surrounded by an entourage whose size, which may have run to hundreds, was a measure of his wealth and rank. In additon to servants, it included men-at-arms and knights and even lesser members of the aristocracy. His standing was enhanced if he was seen to have men of rank around him. But the foremost symbol of status was his castle.

Since possession of a castle was becoming more a badge of rank than a means of protection, it seemed all the more necessary to control the building of castles. The use of the royal prerogative to grant licences to crenellate was, in effect, a form of sumptuary legislation, like authorising forms of dress and access to certain foods. One cannot really pretend that this degree of control over castle-building was necessary or even desirable on military or strategic grounds. It was a means of distinguishing between those who exercised power and influence and those who did not. In this we may perhaps find a reason why so many sought a licence but never acted upon it. The possession of such a permission may itself have been regarded as a status symbol.[5]

If the castle was of little military significance in the fifteenth century, it was of none in the sixteenth. And yet, in its outward form – its gatehouse, towers and crenellations – the castle lived on. Its military features were incorporated into structures which could not possibly have had any military significance. By the end of the Middle Ages cathedral and monastic precincts were, more often than not, surrounded by a crenellated wall and entered by way of a gatehouse. And these adjuncts came to be adopted by schools, by colleges at Oxford and Cambridge and even by hospitals, indeed by any institution of corporate character. Many times in the course of human history the outward form of structures, ceremonies and institutions has been preserved long after they had themselves ceased to be functional, and the factors that had brought them into being had disappeared. Their preservation was not necessarily a case of conscious atavism. They had come to be associated with segments of society or with a particular social group, and to change or terminate them would be to denigrate the latter. So it was with the castle. From being a necessary accompaniment of a certain quasi-military status it had become an empty symbol, but nevertheless the object of ambition of every aspiring member of the upper classes. And to the newly ennobled or enriched it set a seal upon their new status.

The castle, furthermore, was integrated with other symbols of rank and status. Its gatehouse might be adorned with the heraldic achievements of its lord. Within its walls there was not only accommodation for a large retinue, but also chambers that were varied in quality and adjusted to the rank of those who used them.

Such castles were few in number because few could afford to build and maintain them. The king himself developed Windsor and Winchester and, in addition, held the Tower. A few castles were built *ab initio* to serve these ends, but most 'palace-castles', like Alnwick, Kenilworth, Plessey and Warwick, had been developed over many decades. They continued to be built in the sixteenth century, but the 'martial face', which even in the fifteenth had been merely a facade, was stripped away until by its end scarcely anything remained of it. The surveyors who inventoried the possessions of Edward Stafford, Duke of Buckingham, were uncertain whether to call his unfinished palace at Thornbury a castle or a house. Wolsey's Hampton Court and Henry VIII's Nonsuch were even less military, and Cecil's Hatfield and Thynne's Longleat exhibited only an extravagant domesticity.

The plan of the late medieval castle, with courtyard and gatehouse and inward-looking apartments, was perpetuated more in academic and charitable institutions than in the homes of the aristocracy. The latter acquired a symmetrical facade and, in order to obtain adequate floorspace, adopted a two-pile structure. The result was a Chatsworth, a Kedleston or a Holkham, from which every trace of castellation had been banished.

But castellation returned by the back door. In the grounds of the great houses of the later eighteenth century follies and artificial ruins began to appear to 'improve' the landscape. They were part of the romantic movement, but in the forms which they assumed they reverted to those of the medieval castle, as it was perceived in the late eighteenth and the nineteenth centuries.[6] Sham castles and battlemented towers were erected in conspicuous places. It was not long before the wheel of fashion came full circle. Homes began to be built in a castellated style, and grand mansions incorporated battlemented towers and arrow slits. They even styled themselves 'castle'.

The nineteenth-century revival of castellated forms, like the fifteenth-century castle of pretence, was rooted in the sociology of the period. It was one of the ways in which 'new' men became assimilated to the established aristocracy; it was a claim to be among the élite.

The decay of the traditional castle as the home and centre of administration of members of the landholding classes coincided with the emergence of a structure, different in function and ultimately different in form. This was the fort erected for coastal or frontier defence. Coastal castles built during the years following the Conquest were essentially feudal. They had been built by barons and were defended by those who owed military service to their lords. With the decay of the liens which had held feudal society together, it became necessary to find some other way of achieving the defence of the country. This was by means of forts, built, garrisoned and maintained by the king. No one owed service to them. The constable or governor was appointed by the crown, and he hired as many men as the Exchequer authorised him to do.

One of the first of such 'castles' was probably the tower at Rye (Sussex), ordered to be built by Henry III, and subsequently handed over for the local borough to maintain.[7] It stands above the cliff and the coastal marshes, and survives today as a tower — the Ypres Tower. Whether it was conceived as a refuge for the local population or as a strong point, able to command the seaward approaches to the town, is far from clear. That it was intended to help protect the south coast is apparent from its association in the records with Hastings Castle. Furthermore, some kind of tower appears to have been planned also at New Winchelsea, though whether it was ever built is uncertain.

Little more appears to have been done to strengthen the coastal defences of southern England before the middle of the fourteenth century. Porchester Castle was then strengthened,[8] Southampton Castle, which had been allowed to decay, was hastily repaired, and a 'new tower' built on the motte,[9] and, early in the next century, towers were built on each side of the harbour entrance at Portsmouth and a boom stretched between them.

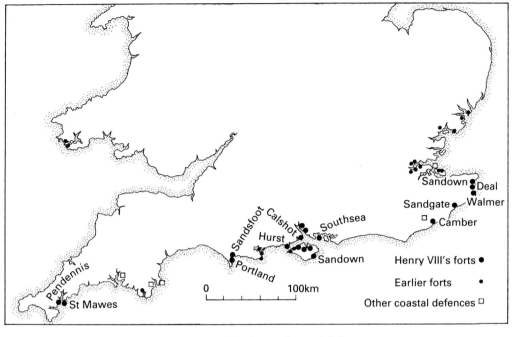

12.1 Henry VIII's scheme of coastal defence.

The frequency of French raids on the south coast led to the construction of forts to protect other harbours. In 1374 order was given to ensure the security of the harbour of Dartmouth, and a quarter of a century later licence was given to crenellate a building at the harbour entrance. Edward IV contributed to the cost of a boom to close it to hostile craft, and in 1481 the present Dartmouth Castle, on the west side of the harbour entrance, was begun, again with a substantial monetary grant from the king.[10] On the opposite shore and 500 metres distant, Kingswear Castle was built at about the same time.[11] Along the coast to the west, Plymouth was protected by a tower, Leland's 'strong castle quadrate', as well as by smaller blockhouses.[12]

Henry VIII planned to supplement the somewhat unsystematic defences of the south coast with a more carefully considered scheme of forts. In the late 1530s the danger of invasion by the forces of both Francis I of France and the German emperor was thought to have increased, and in 1539 the king put forward his scheme for protecting the coast. Artillery forts were planned at vulnerable points from the Humber to Cornwall. The first was begun in that year and, though the danger of invasion evaporated, work continued until they had been completed. Not all envisaged in the plan were actually built, but by 1547 no less than eighteen artillery forts had been erected from the Downs to Falmouth Harbour (Figure 12.1). Most were concentrated on the Straits of Dover, around the approaches to Portsmouth and Southampton, near Weymouth, and at the entrance to the Carrick Roads in Cornwall. In addition, minor forts were built on the Thames estuary and at the entrance to Poole Harbour.

Each fort was of distinctive plan.[13] Together they 'display variations on the same theme: burly, rounded, hollow, roofed bastions expanding outwards from a tall cylindrical keep and either concentrically or at least symmetrically clustered about it . . . Parapets are curved, embrasures widely splayed on the outside to allow guns to traverse a broad field of fire'.[14] Their design was a far cry from castles built only a half century earlier, and the contrast was not merely in design. They were a very different institution; they had no feudal overtones; they controlled in a legal sense no territory, and they attracted no services from their surrounding manors and parishes.[15] In a very few instances, as at Salcombe (Devon), Brownsea (Dorset) and Netley (Hampshire), local landed interests contributed to building them. Some towns, notably Plymouth and Yarmouth, strengthened their own defences, but overall the coastal defences were built and paid for by the crown. The king appointed their governors and paid their garrisons. The sheriff had no role in their administration, and if the newly created county official, the lord lieutenant, was occasionally involved, that was only because he had command of the local militia.

The coastal forts of Henry VIII and their predecessors at Dartmouth and Fowey do not mark the end of one tradition, that of the medieval castle. They are the starting-point of another, which was to run until the construction of Britain's coastal defences during the Second World War. It includes Elizabeth I's not inconsiderable contributions to coastal defence[16] at Upnor (Kent),[17] Carisbrooke[18] and Dover castles, and in the Channel Islands.[19] The sequence of coastal works was continued in the building of the Plymouth Citadel under Charles II, various minor works in the eighteenth century, the more comprehensive fortifications erected during the Napoleonic Wars and under Palmerston, and lastly the varied defences of 1939–45. By no stretch of the imagination can any of these works be called castles, though on occasion that term may have been applied to some of them.

If castles are regarded both as institutions and also as structural features, we thus have two different but overlapping traditions: that of the castle *sensu stricto*, and that of the fort. That the latter began more than a century before the former ended was not altogether coincidental. The castle *per se* had provided a kind of coastal defence from the early days of the Conquest until at least the end of the fourteenth century. That it continued to do so even after that is apparent from the additions made to Dover, Carisbrooke and other coastal castles. But, by and large, the castle proved inadequate for two major reasons. In the first place it was not built with artillery in mind, and, secondly, its maintenance and defence were never wholly divorced from the feudal structure of society. Control of it had been local, not national, and the national emergencies which arose in the sixteenth century called for general, not local or regional measures to deal with them.

NOTES

I CASTLES OF THE CONQUEST

1 Guillaume de Poitiers, ed. R. de Foreville, *Class Hist Fr* 23 (1952), II, 9
2 R. Glover, 'English Warfare in 1066', *EHR*, 67 (1952), 1–18
3 A pre-Conquest castle is claimed in *Carmen de Hastingae Proelio*, ed. C. Morton and H. Muntz, Oxford, 1972, ll. 605–6; R. A. Brown is more cautious: 'The Norman Conquest and the Genesis of English Castles', *Chât Gaill*, 3 (1969), 1–14
4 The topographical evidence given by William of Poitiers is suspect, and is contradicted by *William of Jumièges*, ed. J. Marx, Paris, 1914, pp. 135–6; see F. M. Stenton, *Anglo-Saxon England*, Oxford, 1971, p. 597
5 W. E. Kapelle, *The Norman Conquest of the North*, London, 1979, pp. 127–8
6 J. le Patourel, 'The Norman Colonization of Britain', *Settimane*, 16 (1969), 409–38
7 *Ibid.*, p. 420
8 J. C. Holt, 'The Introduction of Knight Service in England', *A-N St*, 6 (1984), 89–106
9 H. M. Chew, *The Ecclesiastical Tenants in Chief and Knight Service*, Oxford, 1932, pp. 3–10
10 J. le Patourel, 'Norman Colonization'
11 On the controversy regarding knight service, see: J. Gillingham, 'The Introduction of Knight Service into England', *A-N St*, 4 (1981), 53–64; J. O. Prestwich, 'Anglo-Norman Feudalism and the Problem of Continuity', *P & P*, 26 (1963), 39–57; S. Harvey, 'The Knight and the Knight's Fee in England', *P & P*, 49 (1970), 3–43; E. John, *Land Tenure in Early England*, Leicester, 1960, pp. 140–61
12 J. Yver, 'Les Châteaux forts en Normandie jusqu'au milieu du XIIᵉ siècle', *Bull Soc Ant Norm*, 53 (1955–6), 28–115
13 F. M. Stenton, 'Pre-Conquest Herefordshire', in *Preparatory to Anglo-Saxon England*, ed. D. M. Stenton, Oxford, 1970, pp. 193–202; J. H. Round, *Feudal England*, London, 1895, pp. 317–31
14 DB, i, 186a
15 A-S C, 137 (*sub* 1052)
16 Ordericus Vitalis, ed. M. Chibnall, IV, ii, 181
17 S. R. Blaylock, 'Exeter Castle Gatehouse: Architectural Survey, 1985', *Exeter Museums Archaeological Field Unit*, 1987
18 Ordericus Vitalis, IV, ii, 184
19 *An Inventory of the Historical Monuments of York*, vol. 2, *The Defences*, RCHM (England), 1972, pp. 59–89
20 Guillaume de Poitiers, II, 34
21 C. N. L. Brooke and G. Kier, *London 800–1216: The Shaping of a City*, London, 1975, pp. 30–42, 215–17
22 *Liber Eliensis*, ed. E. O. Blake, Camd Soc, 92 (1962), 194
23 Symeon of Durham, RS, II, 199–200
24 Guillaume de Poitiers, II, 35–6

25 J. Spurgeon, 'The Castles of Glamorgan: Some Sites and Theories of General Interest', *Chât Gaill*, 13 (1987), 203–26

26 D. C. Douglas, *William the Conqueror*, London, 1964, pp. 140–2, 215

27 Ordericus Vitalis, III, ii, 184

28 D. R. Cook, 'The Norman Military Revolution in England', *A-N St*, 2 (1978), 94–102; R. A. Brown, 'The Norman Conquest', *TrRHS*, 5th ser., 17 (1967), 109–30. See also M. Bennett, 'Wace and Warfare', *A-N St*, 11 (1988), 37–57

29 Pipe Rolls 20–22 Henry II, PRS, 21 and 25

30 Ordericus Vitalis II, 227, 229

31 Florence of Worcester, *Chronicon ex Chronicis*, ed. B. Thorpe, London, 1849, vol. II, p. 125

32 William of Malmesbury, *Historia Novella*, ed. K. R. Potter, London, 1955, p. 40

33 *Ibid.*, pp. 43–4.

34 H. W. C. Davis, 'The Anarchy of Stephen's Reign', *EHR*, 18 (1903), 630–41

35 J. H. Round, 'King Stephen and the Earl of Chester', *EHR*, 37 (1895), 87–91; H. A. Cronne, 'Ranulf de Gernons, Earl of Chester, 1129–1153', *TrRHS*, 4th ser., 20 (1937), 103–34; W. Farrer, *Honors and Knights' Fees*, vol. II, London, 1924, pp. 62–3. The text is in F. M. Stenton, *The First Century of English Feudalism*, Oxford, 1960, pp. 250–3, 286–8; J. W. Alexander, *Ranulf of Chester*, Athens, Ga, 1983

36 F. M. Stenton, *First Century*, p. 253

37 D. F. Renn, *Norman Castles in Britain*, London, 1968, p. 53

38 *Ibid.*, p. 253

39 *Gesta Regis Henrici Secundi*, RS, I, 68–9

40 H. G. Richardson, reviewing *The History of the King's Works*, *EHR*, 80 (1965), 553–6

41 H. G. Richardson and G. O. Sayles, *The Governance of Medieval England from the Conquest to Magna Carta*, Edinburgh, 1963, p. 71

42 *Documents Illustrative of the Social and Economic History of the Danelaw*, ed. F. M. Stenton, British Academy, 1920, no. 235, p. 167

43 'Extracts from the Chronicle or Cartulary of the Abbey of Meaux', *Col Top Gen*, 1 (1834), 9–13

44 *Historians of the Church of York*, RS, I, 302

45 *Middlesex*, RCHM, 1937, pp. 107–8, but see also *VCH, Middlesex*, 4 (1971) 107; H. Braun, 'Earliest Ruislip', *Tr Lond Middlx AS*, NS 7 (1937), 99–123; M. Morgan, *The English Lands of the Abbey of Bec*, Oxford, 1946, *passim*

46 G. Beresford, 'Goltho Manor, Lincolnshire: the Buildings and their Surrounding Defences', *A-S St*, 4 (1981), 13–36; *The Medieval Clayland Village: Excavations at Goltho and Barton Blount*, Soc Med Arch, Monograph 6, London, 1975, pp. 3–5; *Goltho: the Development of an Early Medieval Manor c. 850–1150*, London, 1987

47 *Charters of the Earldom of Hereford, 1095–1201*, ed. D. Walker, Camd Misc, 22, Camd Soc, 4th ser., I (1964), 1–75

48 *Gesta Stephani*, pp. 10–2

49 L. Alcock, 'Castle Tower, Penmaen: A Norman Ringwork in Glamorgan', *Ant Jl*, 46 (1966), 178–210; *Med Arch*, 5 (1961), 321; *Med Arch*, 6–7 (1962–3), 326

50 E. S. Armitage, *Early Norman Castles of the British Isles*, London, 1912, pp. 80–93

51 J. H. Round, 'The Castles of the Conquest', *Arch*, 58 (1903), 313–40

52 B. Hope-Taylor, 'The Excavation of a Motte at Abinger, Surrey,' *Arch Jl*, 107 (1950), 15–43; Hope-Taylor, 'Norman Castles', *Sci Am*, March, 1958, 42–8; J. Blair, 'William FitzAnsculf and the Abinger Motte', *Arch Jl*, 138 (1981), 146–8

53 Illustrated by Hope-Taylor, *Sci Am*, and now in the V. and A.

54 J. P. C. Kent, 'Excavations at the Motte and Bailey Castle of South Mimms, Herts, 1960–7', *Barnet S Bul*, 15 (1968)

55 VCH, *Middlesex*, vol. V, 1976, p. 282

56 S. E. Rigold, 'Totnes Castle: Recent Excavation', *Tr Dev A*, 86 (1954), 228–56

57 A. D. Saunders, 'Lydford Castle, Devon', *Med Arch*, 24 (1980), 123–86

58 M. W. Thompson, 'Excavations in Farnham Castle Keep, Surrey', *Chât Gaill*, 2 (1967), 100–5

59 M. W. Thompson, 'Motte Substructures', *Med Arch*, 5 (1961), 305–6

60 B. K. Davison, 'Early Earthwork Castles; A New Model', *Chât Gaill*, 3 (1969), 34–47

61 B. K. Davison, 'Aldingham', *Cur Arch*, 2 (1969–70) 23–4; *Med Arch*, 13 (1969), 258–9

62 *Med Arch*, 22 (1979), 263; 26 (1982), 225

63 A. Herrnbrodt, 'Der Husterknupp, eine niederrheinische Burganlage des frühen Mittelalters', *Bonn Jb*, 6 (1958), (Beihefte); Herrnbrodt 'Die Ausgrabung der Motte Burg Meer in Buderich bei Düsseldorf', *Chât Gaill*, 2 (1967), 62–72; M. Müller-Wille, 'Mittelalterliche Burghügel im nördlichen Rheinland', *Bonn Jb*, 16 (1966) (Beihefte)

64 M. Müller-Wille

65 H. J. Keuning, 'L'Habitat rural aux Pays-Bas', *Tijd Kon Ned Aards*, 55 (1938), 644–5; *Netherlands*, Geographical Handbook Series, NID, London, 1944, pp. 250–3

66 B. K. Davison, in *Chât Gaill*, 3 (1969), 37–47

67 L. Alcock, *Dinas Powys*, Cardiff, 1963, pp. 86–8

68 E. E. Evans, *The Personality of Ireland*, Cambridge, 1973, pp. 57–8; T. B. Barry, *The Archaeology of Medieval Ireland*, London, 1987, pp. 37–40

69 T. B. Barry, *Archaeology of Medieval Ireland*, p. 45; G. F. Barrett and B. J. Graham, 'Some Considerations concerning the Dating and Distribution of Ring-forts in Ireland', *Ulst Jl A*, 38 (1975), 33–45

70 M. W. Thompson, 'Motte Substructures'

71 A. D. Saunders, 'Lydford Castle'

72 B. K. Davison, in *Chât Gaill*, 3 (1969), 37–47

73 F. W. Maitland, *Domesday Book and Beyond*, Cambridge, 1897, p. 9

74 B. K. Davison, in *Som Dors NQ*, 28 (1961–7), 49–52; Davison, 'Castle Neroche: an Abandoned Norman Fortress', *Pr Som AS*, 116 (1971–2), 16–58

75 V. E. Nash-Williams, *The Roman Frontier in Wales*, Cardiff, 1969, pp. 111–12

76 P. Barker and R. Higham, *Hen Domen Montgomery*, RAI, London, 1982

77 A. D. Saunders, 'Launceston Castle', *Arch Jl*, 130 (1973), 251–4; 'Launceston Castle: An Interim Report', *Cornw Arch*, 3 (1964), 63–6; 'Excavations at Launceston Castle, 1970–76: Interim Report', *Cornw Arch*, 16 (1977), 129–37

78 J. Spurgeon, 'Castles in Glamorgan'

79 A-S C, 207 (*sub* 1137)

80 *Acta Sanctorum*, 3, 414

81 Barker and Higham, *Hen Domen*, pp. 51–9

82 *Manual of Field Engineering*, War Office, HMSO, 1899, p. 15; 1911 edn, p. 15

83 A distinction is commonly made between the 'tower-keep' and the 'hall-keep', the latter being lower and generally divided by a cross-wall

84 D. F. Renn, 'The Anglo-Norman Keep, 1066–1138', *JBAA*, 3rd ser., 22 (1959), 1–23

85 R. Allen Brown, 'Royal Castle-Building in England, 1154–1216', *EHR*, 70 (1955), 353–98

86 *The Tower of London: its Buildings and Institutions*, ed. J. Charlton, HMSO, 1978, p. 24

87 P. Crummy, *Aspects of Anglo-Saxon and Norman Colchester*, CBA Res Rept 39, 1981, p. 26

88 P. J. Drury, 'Aspects of the Origins and Development of Colchester Castle', *Arch Jl*, 139 (1982), 302–419

89 P. Bennett, S. S. Frere, S. Stow, 'Excavations at Canterbury Castle', in *The Archaeology of Canterbury*, vol. I, Maidstone, 1982; D. F. Renn, 'Canterbury Castle in the Early Middle Ages, in *ibid.*, pp. 70–5; *Med Arch*, 26 (1982), 187–8

90 D. F. Renn, 'The *Turris* de Penuesel: A Reappraisal and a Theory', *Suss Arch Collns*, 109 (1971), 55–64

91 J. G. Coad and A. D. F. Streeten, 'Excavations at Castle Acre Castle Norfolk, 1972–77,' *Arch J*, 139 (1982), 138–301; J. G. Coad, *Castle Acre Castle, Norfolk*, HMSO, 1984

92 W. H. Knowles, 'The Castle, Newcastle upon Tyne', *Arch Ael*, 4th ser., 2 (1926), 1–51; C. H. Hunter Blair, 'The Early Castles of Northumberland', *Arch Ael*, 4th ser., 22 (1944), 116–70. A document quoted in B. Harbottle and M. Ellison, 'An Excavation in the Castle Ditch, Newcastle upon Tyne, 1974–6', *Arch Ael*, 5th ser., 9 (1981), 75–250, mentions enclosures *super motam*, but *Med Arch*, 27 (1983), 206 refers only to a ringwork.

93 T. Darvill, 'Excavations on the Site of the Early Norman Castle at Gloucester, 1983–4', *Med Arch*, 32 (1988), 1–49

94 M. W. Thompson, *Farnham Castle*, HMSO, 1961

95 E. S. Armitage, *Early Norman Castles*, pp. 383–4

96 J. F. Verbruggen, 'Note sur le sens des mots Castrum, Castellum, et quelques autres expressions qui designent des fortifications', *Rv Belge PH*, 28 (1950), 147–55

97 J. H. Round, 'Tower and Castle' in *Geoffrey de Mandeville*, London, 1892, pp. 328–46

98 *Regesta*, III, no. 276 (1141), 102–3

99 i.e. Lantonia Secunda, to distinguish it from the original Llanthony in the Black Mountains

100 *Jordan of Fantosme's Chronicle*, ed. R. C. Johnston, Oxford, 1981, ll. 266 and 1418

101 Geoffrey Chaucer, *The House of Fame*, ll. 1185–6, p. 338

102 Sir Robert Bowes, *Book of the State of the Marches*, 1550, quoted in *A History of Northumberland*, vol. II, p. 209

103 C. C. Taylor, 'Cambridgeshire Earthwork Surveys: Motte and Bailey and Deserted Village, Castle Camps', *Pr Camb AS*, 64 (1972–3), 38–43; VCH, *Cambridgeshire*, vol. II, 1948, p. 21

104 M. Biddle, 'The Excavation of a Motte and Bailey Castle at Therfield, Hertfordshire', *JBAA*, 3rd ser., 27 (1964), 53–91

105 D. F. Renn, *Medieval Castles in Hertfordshire*, Chichester, 1971, pp. 21–2; *Hertfordshire*, RCHM, 1911, pp. 162–3

106 *Herefordshire*, RCHM, 1931, vol. I, pp. 181–4

107 P. Barker and R. Higham, *Hen Domen*, pp. 137–42

108 *Ibid.*, pp. 91–2

109 P. Barker, 'Hen Domen', *Cur Arch*, III, (1988), 137–42

2 THE CASTLE IN POLITICS AND WAR

1 Jean Yver, 'Les Châteux forts en Normandie jusqu'au milieu du XIIe siècle', *Bull Soc Ant Norm*, 53 (1955–6), 28–115

2 William of Jumièges, ed. Jean Marx, Paris, 1914, C. vii, i, pp. 115–16

3 Guillaume de Poitiers, ed. R. Foreville, *Class Hist Fr*, 1952, c. 8, (p. 19)

4 D. C. Douglas, *William the Conqueror*, London, 1964, pp. 141–2

5 J. Yver, 'Les Châteux forts', p. 57

6 The text is given in C. H. Haskins, *Norman Institutions*, Cambridge, Mass., 1918, pp. 281–4

7 Literally a stool or platform. It can only mean that the soil was lifted in stages, not in a single throw

8 *Recueil de textes relatifs à l'histoire de l'architecture*, ed. V. Mortet, Colln de Textes, 1911, vol. I, no. 80

9 Both Du Cange and Mortet translate *Propugnaculum* as 'hourd' or 'bretasche'.

10 Ordericus Vitalis, ed. M. Chibnall, II, 215

11 *Ibid.*

12 *Gesta Stephani*, ed. K. Potter, London, 1955, c. 15–16 (pp. 21–6)

13 Ordericus Vitalis, VI, 22–3

14 M. Chibnall, 'Robert of Bellême and the Castle of Tickhill', in *Droit privé et institutions*

régionales: études historiques offertes à Jean Yver, Rouen, 1976, pp. 151–6

15 *Leges Henrici Primi*, ed. L. J. Downer, Oxford, 1972, pp. 109–11

16 F. Liebermann, *Die Gesetze der Angelsachsen*, Halle, 1903, 1, p. 556

17 *The Medieval Latin Word List*, Oxford, 1934, gives *scannum* as a 'bank'; Du Cange as a 'platform'. It clearly has the same meaning as *scabellum*

18 *Gesta Stephani*, c. 49

19 *Ibid.*, c. 34

20 William of Malmesbury, *Historia Novella*, ed K. R. Potter, London, 1955, c. 468

21 *Ibid.*, c. 475; R. H. C. Davis, *King Stephen*, London, 1967, pp. 34–5

22 C. L. H. Coulson, Seignorial Fortresses in France in Relation to Public Policy, *c*. 864 to *c*. 1483, Doctoral thesis, University of London, 1972; 'Rendability and Castellation in Medieval France', *Chât Gaill*, 6 (1973), 59–67

23 *Florentii Wigorniensis Chronicon ex Chronicis* (Florence of Worcester), ed. B. Thorpe, London, 1849, p. 34

24 *Custodes in castellis strenuos viros collocavit*, Guillaume de Poitiers, II, 35

25 Florence of Worcester, II, 85; R. A. Brown, *Rochester Castle*, HMSO, 1969, pp. 10–11

26 J. H. Round, *Geoffrey de Mandeville: A Study of the Anarchy*, London, 1892, pp. 141–2; *Regesta*, III, no. 276 (pp. 102–3)

27 C. Lee Davis, 'The Norman Castle of South Mimms', *Tr Lond Mddlx AS*, NS 7 (1937), 464–71

28 J. H. Round, *Geoffrey de Mandeville*, p. 174; W. de Gray Birch, 'A Fasciculus of the Charters of Mathildis Empress of the Romans', *JBAA*, 31 (1875), 376–98

29 J. H. Round, *Geoffrey de Mandeville*, p. 174

30 Robert de Torigny, *Chronicles of the Reigns of Henry II, Stephen and Richard I*, RS, IV, 177

31 *Sicut cera a facie ignis*, William of Newburgh, *Chronicles of Stephen* etc., RS, I, 94

32 Annales de Wintonia, *Annales Monastici*, RS, II, 51

33 Henry of Huntingdon, RS, 280

34 *Gesta Regis Henrici Secundi* (Benedict of Peterborough), RS 49, I, 124, 126–7

35 S. Painter, 'English Castles in the Early Middle Ages: their Number, Location and Legal Position', *Spec*, 10 (1935), 321–32

36 D. Renn, 'The Demolition of the Keep at Bennington', *Ant Jl*, 41 (1961), 96–7

37 Pipe Roll, 23 Henry II, 144, PRS, 26, 1905

38 Annals of Dunstable, *Annales Monastici*, RS, III, 35

39 D. F. Renn, *Norman Castles in Britain*, London, 1968, p. 53

40 Pipe Roll, 26 Henry II, 53, PRS

41 Roger of Hoveden, RS, II, 105; Ralph de Diceto, RS, I, 414; *Gesta Regis Henrici Secundi* (Benedict of Peterborough), I, 124

42 Ralph de Diceto, I, 398, 404

43 Assize of Northampton, c. 8; W. Stubbs, *Select Charters*, p. 180

44 W. L. Warren, *Henry II*, London, 1973, p. 141

45 R. A. Brown, 'A List of Castles, 1154–1216', *EHR* (1959), 249–80

46 Sir Henry Ellis, *A General Introduction to Domesday Book*, London, 1833, vol. I, p. 180

47 J. F. A. Mason, 'The Rapes of Sussex and the Norman Conquest', *Suss Arch Collns*, 102 (1964), 68–93

48 J. F. A. Mason, *Willaim the First and the Sussex Rapes*, Historical Association, Hastings, 1966

49 C Docts Fr, I, no. 1130

50 DB, ii, 157, 163, 172

51 E. S. Armitage, *Early Norman Castles of the British Isles*, London, 1912, pp. 165–6

52 P. G. Stone, *Architectural Antiquities of the Isle of Wight*, London, 1891, pp. 72–5; *Book of Fees*, 2, 1242–93, 1301–6

53 J. F. A. Mason claims, *Suss Arch Collns*, 102, 68–93, that he had a castle at Saltwood, near Hythe

54 J. E. Lloyd, *A History of Wales*, London, 1911, vol. II, pp. 362–71

55 J. W. Alexander, 'The Alleged Palatines of Norman England', *Spec*, 56 (1981), 17–27; 'New Evidence on the Palatinate of Chester', *EHR*, 85 (1970), 715–29

56 J. F. A. Mason, 'Roger de Montgomery and his Sons', *TrRHS*, 5th ser., 13 (1963), 1–28

57 D. Walker, 'William FitzOsbern and the Norman Settlement in Herefordshire', *Tr Woolh FC*, 39 (1967), 402–12

58 W. E. Wightman, 'The Palatine Earldom of William FitzOsbern in Gloucestershire and Worcestershire', *EHR*, 77 (1962), 6–17

59 *Ibid.*

60 *L & P Hen VIII*, vol 5, no. 390; W. R. B. Robinson, 'The Marcher Lords of Wales 1525–1531', *Bd Celt St*, 26 (1974–6), 342–52

61 J. Meisel, *Barons of the Welsh Frontier: the Corbet, Pantulf and Fitz Warin Families 1066–1272*, Lincoln Neb., 1980, pp. 8–21

62 P. A. Barker, 'Caus Castle and Hawcock's Mount', *Arch Jl*, 138 (1981), 34

63 A. H. Anderson, 'Henry Lord Stafford and the Lordship of Caus', *Welsh H Rv*, 6 (1972), 1–15; T. Farmer, 'Castle and Barony of Caux', *Col Top Gen*, (1834), 228–33

64 DB, i, 185b

65 DB, i, 186a

66 DB, i, 254a

67 J. A. Tuck, 'Richard II and the Border Magnates', *North H*, 3 (1968), 27–52

68 W. E. Kapelle, *The Norman Conquest of the North*, London, 1979

69 Symeon of Durham, RS, II, 199–200

70 T. A. M. Bishop, 'The Norman Settlement of Yorkshire', in *Studies in Medieval History Presented to F. M. Powicke*, Oxford, 1948, pp. 1–14

71 *Ibid.*

72 William of Malmesbury, *De Gestis Pontificum*, RS 52, 208–9

73 E. Miller, 'The Background of Magna Carta', *EcHR*, 23 (1962), 78–83

74 G. W. S. Barrow, 'The Pattern of Lordship and Feudal Settlement in Cumbria', *Jl Med Hist*, I (1975), 117–38

75 J. E. A. Jollife, 'Northumbrian Institutions', *EHR*, 41 (1936), 1–42

76 J. C. Holt, *The Northerners: A Study of the Reign of King John*, Oxford, 1961, p. 41

77 J. le Patourel, 'The Norman Conquest of Yorkshire', *North H*, 6 (1971), 1–21

78 B. English, *The Lords of Holderness, 1086–1260*, Oxford, 1979, pp. 4–7

79 Chronica Monasterii de Melsa (Meux), RS 43, I, 89

80 *Early Yorkshire Charters*, III, nos. 1300, 1304, 1307

81 N. Denholm-Young, 'The Yorkshire Estates of Isabella de Fortibus', *Yorks AJ*, 31 (1934), 389–420

82 DB, i, 381a

83 W. Dugdale, *Monasticon Anglicanum*, ed. J. Caley, H. Ellis and B. Bandinel, London, 1825, vol. V, pp. 118–21; *Early Yorkshire Charters*, IV, no. 13

84 *Early Yorkshire Charters*, IV, 103; V, 1–3, 353–9

85 C Inq Misc, I, no. 519; *Early Yorkshire Charters*, V, 41–2

86 W. R. Powell, 'The Essex Fees of the Honour of Richmond', *Tr Ess AS*, I (1961–5), 179–89; S. J. Bailey, 'Five Hides in Abington of the Honour of Richmond', *Camb Law Jl* (1958), 189–98

87 G. V. Scammell, *Hugh du Puiset*, Cambridge, 1956, pp. 185–6

88 *Bolden Book*, ed. D. Austin, Chichester, 1982, pp. 6–7

89 J. Scammell, 'The Origin and Limitations of the Liberty of Durham', *EHR*, 81 (1966), 449–75

90 G. V. Scammell, *Hugh du Puiset*, pp. 43–4

91 *Ibid.*, p. 193

92 A. L. Poole, *From Domesday Book to Magna Carta*, Oxford, 1955, p. 275

93 C. H. Hunter Blair, 'The Early Castles of Northumberland', *Arch Ael*, 4th ser., 22 (1944), 116–70

94 L. Keen, 'The Umfravilles and the Barony of Prudhoe, Northumberland', *A-N St*, 5 (1982), 165–84

95 J. Tait, *Medieval Manchester and the Beginnings of Lancashire*, Manchester, 1904, pp. 152–3

96 E. S. Armitage, *Early Norman Castles*, pp. 183–4

97 *Ibid.*, pp. 129–30; DB, i, 332

98 S. Moorhouse, 'Excavations at Burton-in-Lonsdale', *Yorks AJ*, 43 (1971), 85–98; H. M. White, 'Excavations in Castle Hill, Burton-in-Lonsdale', *Antiq*, 41 (1905), 411–17.

99 M. Chibnall, *Anglo-Norman England 1066–1166*, Oxford, 1986, p. 52

100 A-S C, 172; J. Charlton, *Carlisle Castle*, HMSO, 1988

101 G. W. S. Barrow, 'The Pattern of Lordship . . . in Cumbria'

102 J. F. Curwen, ed., *Records Relating to the Barony of Kendale by William Farrer*, CWAS Rec Ser, 4 (1923)

103 W. E. Kapelle, *The Norman Conquest of the North*, p. 130

104 M. Chibnall, 'Military Service in Normandy before 1066', *A-N St*, 5 (1982), 65–77

105 *R B Exch*, ed. Hubert Hall, RS, 99

106 I. J. Saunders, *Feudal Military Service in England*, Oxford, 1956, pp. 47–8

107 E. Z. Tabuteau, 'Definitions of Feudal Military Obligations in Eleventh Century Normandy', in *On the Laws and Customs of England: Essays in Honor of Samuel E. Thorne*, Chapel Hill, N.C., 1981

108 *R B Exch*, 1, 212; H. M. Chew, *The Ecclesiastical Tenants-in-Chief and Knight Service*, Oxford, 1932, pp. 101–3

109 *R B Exch*, 1, 241–2

110 *The Charters of Norwich Cathedral Priory*, pt 2, ed. B. Dodwell, PRS, 44 (1985), 75, 79

111 J. H. Round, 'Castle-ward and Cornage', *The Commune of London and Other Studies*, London, 1899, pp. 278–88; *Arch Jl*, 59 (1902), 144–59

112 H. M. Chew, *Ecclesiastical Tenants-in-Chief*, p. 4

113 *Liber Eliensis*, pp. 252, 254

114 *Feudal Documents from the Abbey of Bury St Edmunds*, ed. D. C. Douglas, London, 1932, p. 83

115 *Registrum Antiquissimum*, I, ed. C. W. Foster, Lincs RS Soc (1931), no. 51, p. 35

116 *R B Exch*, 1, 271

117 *The Cartulary or Register of the Abbey of St Werburgh Chester*, ed. J. Tait, Cheth Soc, 79 (1920), 101–2; J. Tait, 'Knight Service in Cheshire', *EHR*, 57 (1942), 437–59

118 Quoted in C. H. Haskins, *Norman Institutions*, p. 9

119 Magna Carta, cap 29; Rot Lit Claus, I, 606; *R B Exch*, 2, 603–4

120 J. H. Round, 'The Origin of Belvoir Castle', *EHR*, 22 (1907), 508–10

121 *The Estate Records of the Hotot Family*, ed. E. King, Northts Rec Soc, 32 (1982), 37

122 *The Letters and Charters of Gilbert Foliot*, ed. Z. N. Brooke, A. Morey and C. N. L. Brooke, Cambridge, 1967, no. 310

123 *Sir Christopher Hatton's Book of Seals*, ed. L. C. Loyd and D. M. Stenton, Oxford, 1950, no. 24

124 *Ibid.*, no. 257

125 C Inq Misc, I 167–8

126 *Ibid.*, VII, 427; *R B Exch*, 2, 622–3; W. Budgen, 'Pevensey Castle Guard and Endlewick Rents', *Suss Arch Collns*, 76 (1935), 115–34

127 *The Chronicle of Jocelin of Brakelond*, ed H. E. Butler, London, pp. 28–9, 66–7

128 *R B Exch*, 717–23

129 J. H. Round, 'Castle Guard', 'Castle-ward and Cornage'

130 F. W. Hardman, 'Castle-guard Service at Dover Castle', *Arch Cant*, 49 (1938), 96–107

131 R. A. Brown, *Dover Castle*, HMSO, 1966

132 F. W. Hardman, 'Castle-guard Service'

133 S. Painter, 'Castle-Guard', *AmHR*, 40 (1934–5), 450–9

134 A. L. Poole, *Obligations of Society in the* XII *and* XIII *Centuries*, Oxford, 1946, p. 38

135 E. King, 'The Peterborough "Descriptio Militum" (Henry I)', *EHR*, 84 (1969), 84–101

136 *Plac Quo War*, 592

137 *Three Early Assize Rolls for the County of Northumberland*, Surt Soc, 88 (1891), 355–6

138 A. Ballard, 'Castle-Guard and Barons' Houses', *EHR*, 25 (1910), 712–15

139 *The Parliamentary Survey of the Duchy of Cornwall*, ed. N. J. G. Pounds, D C Rec Soc, 25 (1982), 74

140 E. G. Kimball, *Serjeanty Tenure in Medieval England*, Yale University Press, New Haven, Conn., 1936, p. 80; N. Neilson, *Customary Rents*, Oxford, 1910, *passim*

141 *Book of Fees*, pp. 74, 258, 699

142 W. V. Dumbreck, 'The Lowy of Tonbridge', *Arch Cant*, 72 (1958), 138–47

143 *The Domesday Monachorum of Christ Church, Canterbury*, ed. D. C. Douglas, London, 1944, p. 88

144 J. C. Ward, 'The Lowy of Tonbridge and the Lands of the Clare Family in Kent, 1066–1217', *Arch Cant*, 96 (1980), 119–31

145 *The Letters of Lanfranc, Archbishop of Canterbury*, ed. H. Clover and M. Gibson, 1979, no. 31

146 Florence of Worcester, II, 50

147 C. J. Spurgeon, 'The Castles of Montgomeryshire', *Montg Collns*, 59 (1965–6), 1–59

148 Florence of Worcester, II, 50

149 As at Bedford Castle, 1224; see M. F. Greenshields, 'The Siege of Bedford Castle', *Beds Mag* 4 (1954)

150 As at the siege of Exeter Castle, *Gesta Stephani*, c. 17

151 A list in D. R. Renn, 'Mottes: A Classification', *Ant*, 33 (1959), 106–12

152 *Dorset*, RCHM, 2, part 1, pp. 96–8

153 *A-S C*, 207; *The Chronicle of John of Worcester, 1118–1140*, ed J. R. H. Weaver, *Anecdota Oxoniensia*, Medieval and Modern Series, 13 (1908), 40

154 Henry of Huntingdon, p. 259

155 W. T. P. Short, *Collectanea Curiosa Antiqua Dumnonia, or an Essay on some Druidical Remains in Devon*, London, 1840, p. 21

156 *Gesta Stephani*, c. 15

157 H. W. C. Davis, 'The Anarchy of Stephen's Reign', *EHR*, 18 (1903), 630–41

158 C. F. Slade, 'Wallingford Castle in the Reign of Stephen', *Berks A J*, 58 (1960), 33–43

159 H. W. C. Davis, 'The Anarchy of Stephen's Reign'; disputed by A. L. Poole, *Domesday Book to Magna Carta*, p. 151

160 R. A. Stalley, 'A Twelfth Century Patron of Architecture: A Study of the buildings erected by Roger, Bishop of Salisbury', *JBAA*, 3rd ser., 34 (1971), 62–83

161 William of Malmesbury, *Historia Novella*, p. 24; *Magna Vita Sancti Hugonis*, ed. D. L. Douie and D. H. Farmer, Oxford, 1985, p. 131

162 H. Braun, 'Notes on Newark Castle', *Tr Thor Soc*, 39 (1935), 53–91

163 *Registrum Antiquissimum*, I, no. 51

164 *Ibid.*, no. 95; W. H. Hosford, 'The Manor of Sleaford in the Thirteenth Century', *Notts Med St*, 12 (1968), 21–39

165 P. J. Fasham, 'Excavations in Banbury, 1972', *Oxon*, 38 (1973), 312–38; K. A. Rodwell, 'Excavations on the Site of Banbury Castle', *Oxon*, 41 (1976), 90–147; VCH, *Oxfordshire*, vol. X, pp. 39–42 is in error.

166 M. Biddle, 'Wolvesey, the *Domus quasi palatium* of Henry de Blois in Winchester', *Chât Gaill*, 3 (1969), 28–36

167 A. W. Vivian-Neal and H. St George Gray, 'Materials for the History of Taunton Castle', *Pr*

Som AS, 86 (1941), 45–78; T. J. Hunt, 'Some 13th Century Building Accounts for Taunton Castle', *ibid.*, 115 (1971), 39–44

168 J. N. Hare, 'Bishop's Waltham Palace, Hampshire: William of Wykeham, Henry Beaufort and the Transformation of a Medieval Episcopal Palace', *Arch Jl*, 145 (1988), 222–54

169 E. H. Stone, *Devizes Castle: Its History and Romance*, Devizes, 1920, pp. 27–8

3 A PATTERN OF CASTLES

1 A. Harvey, *The Castles and Walled Towns of England*, London, 2nd edn, 1925, p. 3

2 J. H. Beeler, 'Castles and Strategy in Norman and Early Angevin England', *Spec*, 31 (1956), 581–601; *Warfare in England 1066–1189*, Ithaca, N.Y., 1966, *passim*

3 H. Braun, 'Hertfordshire Castles', *TrStAHAAS* (1938), 193–213

4 D. Hay, 'Booty in Border Warfare', *Tr Dugd Soc*, 31 (1954), 145–66

5 R. A. Brown, *English Medieval Castles*, London, 2nd edn, 1962, p. 189

6 F. Barlow, *The Feudal Kingdom of England 1042–1216*, London, 1961, p. 89

7 S. Painter, 'English Castles in the Early Middle Ages: their Number, Location and Legal Position', *Spec*, 10 (1935), 321–32

8 R. A. Brown, 'Framlingham Castle and Bigod, 1154–1216', *Pr Suff I A*, 25 (1949–51), 127–48; *Orford Castle*, HMSO, 1964, pp. 3–8

9 L. F. Chitty, 'Interim Notes on Subsidiary Castle Sites West of Shrewsbury', *Tr Shrop AS*, 53 (1949–50), 83–90

10 W. D. Walters, Royal Policy and English Castle Distribution, 1154–1216, M.A. thesis, Indiana University, 1968

11 *KW*, I, 21–3; Cardiff may perhaps be added to the list.

12 R. A. Brown, 'A List of Castles, 1154–1216', *EHR*, 74 (1959), 249–80

13 DB, i, 336b

14 H. C. Darby, *Domesday England*, Cambridge, 1977, pp. 289–320, 364–8

15 Subsequently moved to a site beyond the river and known as Barnwell

16 DB, i, 62b; W. H. St John Hope, *Windsor Castle: An Architectural History*, London, 1913, vol. I, pp. 1–3

17 J. le Patourel, 'The Norman Colonization of Britain', *Settimane* 16 (1969), 409–35

18 *Ibid.*, 412; R. S. Hoyt, *The Royal Demesne in English Constitutional History*, Ithaca, N.Y., 1950, pp. 81 ff

19 W. J. Corbett, 'The Development of the Duchy of Normandy and the Conquest of England', *Camb Med Hist*, 5 (1929), 481–553

20 B. K. Davison, 'Castle Neroche: An Abandoned Norman Fortress in South Somerset', *Pr Som AS*, 116 (1971–2), 16–58

21 R. Mortimer, 'The Beginnings of the Honour of Clare', *Battle Conf*, 3 (1980), 119–41

22 R. J. Ivens, 'Deddington Castle, Oxfordshire, and the English Honour of Odo of Bayeux', *Oxon*, 49 (1984), 101–19

23 F. M. Stenton, *Anglo-Saxon England*, Oxford, 1971 edn, p. 616

24 R. A. Brown, *Rochester Castle*, HMSO, 1969, pp. 5–7

25 R. J. Ivens, 'Deddington Castle, Oxfordshire: A Summary of Excavations 1977–1979', *S Midl Arch* (1983), 35–41

26 Charters of the Honour of Mowbray 1107–1191, ed. D. E. Greenway, British Academy, 1972, pp. xvii–lxi; T. S. Gololand, 'The Honour of Kirkby Malzeard and the Chase of Nidderdale', *Yorks AJ*, 33 (1938), 349–96

27 W. E. Wightman, *The Lacy Family in England and Normandy, 1066–1194*, Oxford, 1966

28 I. J. Saunders, *English Baronies*, Oxford, 1960, pp. 95–6

29 Florence of Worcester, RS, II, 106; *John of Worcester*, ed. J. R. H. Weaver, *Anecdota Oxoniensia*, vol XIII, Oxford, 1908, p. 55

30 R. A. Higham, 'Excavations at Okehampton Castle, Devon', part 1, *Pr Dev AS*, 35 (1977), 342

31 C Inq pm, II, no. 71; Saunders, *Feudal Military Service in England*, Oxford, 1956, pp. 30, 74, 93

32 DB i 105b

33 Bridestowe, Loxhore and Wembworthy; see R. Higham, 'Early Castles in Devon, 1068–1201', *Chât Gaill*, 9–10 (1982), 101–16

34 DB, i 934

35 J. le Patourel, 'Norman Barons', *Feudal Empires, Norman and Plantagenet*, London, 1984, pp. 3–31

36 J. H. Round, 'The Honour of Ongar', *Tr Ess AS*, NS 7 (1900), 142–52

37 K. B. McFarlane, 'The Rate of Extinction of Noble Families', in *The Nobility of Later Medieval England*, Oxford, 1973, pp. 172–6

38 W. Rees, 'The Mediaeval Lordship of Brecon', *Tr Cymm* (1915–16), 165–224

39 S. Painter, *Studies in the History of the English Feudal Baronage*, Johns Hopkins University Studies in History and Political Science, 61, no. 3, 1943, pp. 17–18

40 Bracton, *De Legibus*, II, 269

41 Their number was put by Painter at 'perhaps 1000 in 1146', *Studies in the History of the Baronage*, p. 48

42 Saunders, *English Baronies, passim*

43 N. Denholm-Young, 'Eudo Dapifer's Honour of Walbrook', in *Collected Papers on Medieval Subjects*, Oxford, 1946, pp. 154–61

44 J. H. Round, 'The Introduction of Knight Service into England', *EHR*, 6 (1891), 417–43

45 N. Denholm-Young, 'Feudal Society in the Thirteenth Century: the Knights', *Hist*, 29 (1944), 107–19; reprinted in *Collected Papers*, pp. 56–67

46 J. R. Morris, *The Welsh Wars of Edward I*, Oxford, 1901, pp. 35ff.

47 T. Rowley, *The Shropshire Landscape*, London, 1972, pp. 82–3

48 F. Barlow, *The Feudal Kingdom*, p. 90

49 E. S. Armitage, *Early Norman Castles of the British Isles*, London, 1912, p. 103

50 DB, i, 78b; *Testa de Nevill*, Rec Com, 164b

51 DB, i, 62b

52 DB, i, 238a

53 P. A. G. Clack and P. F. Gosling, eds., *Archaeology in the North*, Newcastle, 1976, pp. 189–90

54 H. Miles, 'Excavations at Rhuddlan, 1969–71: Interim Report', *Flint HS*, 25 (1971–2), 1–8

55 P. Barker and R. Higham, *Hen Domen Montgomery*, RAI, London, 1982, pp. 8–20

56 C. H. Houlder, 'Recent Excavations in Old Aberystwyth', *Cered*, 3 (1956–9), 114–17; R. A. Griffiths, 'The Three Castles at Aberystwyth', *Arch Camb*, 126 (1977), 74–87

57 W. M. l'Anson, 'The Castles of the North Riding', *Yorks AJ*, 22 (1913), 303–99; VCH, *Yorkshire*, vol. II, pp. 31–3

58 l'Anson, 'Castles of the North Riding'

59 E. J. Talbot and B. V. Field, 'The Excavation of Castell Madoc Ringwork, Lower Chapel, Breconshire', *Brych*, 12 (1966–7), 131–2

60 E. M. Jope and R. I. Threlfall, 'The Twelfth Century Castle at Ascot Doilly, Oxfordshire', *Ant Jl*, 39 (1959), 219–73; 'Excavations at the Twelfth Century Castle at Ascot D'Oilly', *Oxon*, 11–12 (1946–7), 165–7

61 J. N. L. Myres, 'Three Unrecognised Castle Mounds at Hamstead Marshall', *Tr Newb FC*, 6 (1930–3), 114–26

62 R. Payne-Gallwey, *The Crossbow*, London, 1903, pp. 20–1

63 H. C. Darby, *Domesday England*, Cambridge, 1977, pp. 90–1

4 THE ROYAL CASTLE AND PUBLIC ADMINISTRATION

1 R. A. Brown, 'A List of Castles, 1154–1216', *EHR*, 74 (1959), 249–80

2 *Ibid.*

3 A valuable analytical index to the published Pipe Rolls is in *Liber Memorialis*, PRS, NS 41, 1976

4 Based on R. A. Brown, 'Royal Castle-Building in England, 1154–1216', *EHR*, 70 (1955), 353–98

5 *KW*, II, 708–10

6 *Ibid.*, II, 830

7 R. A. Brown, *Orford Castle*, HMSO, 1964, pp. 9–19

8 A. L. Poole, *From Domesday Book to Magna Carta*, Oxford, 1955, pp. 335–8

9 *KW*, II, 783–4

10 The building accounts are printed in F. M. Powicke, *The Loss of Normandy, 1189–1204*, Manchester, revised edn, 1960, pp. 204–6

11 M. Biddle, 'Seasonal Festivals and Residence', *A-N St*, 8 (1985), 51–72

12 C Chart R, I, 209; Rot Lit Claus, I, 89b, 93b, 94b

13 For comparison, see R. A. Brown, *Orford Castle*, p. 11

14 *Histoire des Ducs de Normandie*, ed. F. Michel, Paris, 1840, pp. 174–5

15 *Roger of Wendover*, RS, III, 371

16 *Dorset*, RCHM, vol. II, part 1, pp. 57–78

17 R. R. Davies, 'Kings, Lords and Liberties in the March of Wales', *TrRHS*, 5th ser., 29 (1979), 41–61

18 *Cartulary or Register of the Abbey of St Werburgh Chester*, ed. J. Tait, Cheth Soc, NS 79 (1920), 101ff., c. 14

19 R. R. Davies, 'Kings, Lords and Liberties'

20 Cur Reg R, 1194–99, Rec Com, 1835, I, 426

21 J. G. Edwards, 'The Normans and the Welsh March', *Pr Brit Acad* (1956), 155–77

22 CPR, 1258–66, 281

23 William of Malmesbury, *De Gestis Pontificum*, RS 52, 208–9

24 E. Miller, 'The Background of Magna Carta', *EcHR*, 23 (1962–3), 72–83

25 J. C. Holt, *The Northerners: A Study in the Reign of King John*, Oxford, 1961

26 G. J. Turner, 'The Minority of Henry III', *TrRHS*, NS 18 (1904), 245–95; 3rd ser., 1 (1907), 205–62; Kate Norgate, *The Minority of Henry the Third*, London, 1912

27 C. Petit-Dutaillis, 'Une femme de guerre au XIIIᵉ siècle: Nicole de la Haie, gardienne du Château de Lincoln', in *Mélanges Julien Havet*, Paris, 1895, pp. 369–80; T. F. Tout, 'The Fair of Lincoln and the "Histoire de Guillaume le Maréchal"', *EHR*, 18 (1903), 240–65

28 CPR, 1272–81, 104

29 H. M. Colvin, 'Henry III' in *KW*, I, 110–19

30 R. J. Whitwell, 'The Revenue and Expenditure of England under Henry III', *EHR*, 18 (1903), 710–11

31 *KW*, I, 113

32 *Ibid.*

33 *KW*, II, 629–41; R. A. Brown, *Dover Castle*, pp. 7–10

34 A. J. Taylor, 'The Date of Clifford's Tower, York', *Arch Jl*, 91 (1955), 296–300

35 C Lib R, 1226–40, 453

36 *Ibid.*, 26

37 Tancred Borenius, 'The Cycle of Images in the Palaces and Castles of Henry III', *Jl Warbg Inst*, 6 (1943), 40–50

38 C Lib R, III, 32

39 R. S. Loomis, *The Arthurian Legends in Medieval Art*, London, 1938, pp. 25–6, 40–1

40 J. E. A. Jolliffe, *Angevin Kingship*, London, 1963, p. 140

41 W. Farrer, 'An Outline Itinerary of Henry I', *EHR*, 34 (1919), 303–82

42 R. W. Eyton, *Court, Household and Itinerary of King Henry II*, Dorchester, 1878

43 *The Itinerary of King Richard I*, ed. L. Landon, PRS, 1935

44 Rot Lit Pat, Introduction by T. Duffus Hardy, x ix ff. (unpaged)

45 CCR, I, 1227–31, 1

46 CCR, 1227–31, 453, 455, 507

47 CCR, 1231–4, 343, 65, 107

48 CCR, 1231–4, 249

49 CCR, 1264–8, 271

50 CCR, 1288–96, 392

51 CCR, 1279–88, 150

52 CCR, 1288–96, 451

53 CCR, 1288–96, 392

54 CCR, 1288–96, 391

55 CCR, 1288–96, 471; *Accounts of the Constables of Bristol Castle*, Brist R S, 34 (1982), xxv

56 H. Johnstone, 'The Wardrobe and Household of Henry, Son of Edward I', *Bull J R Lib*, 7 (1922–3), 384–420

57 As at Carmarthen and Llanbadarn, CCR, 1288–96, 426

58 Welsh hostages at Chester Castle were allowed 4d a day, which would have suggested a degree of comfort: CCR, 1288–96, 425

59 *Accounts of the Constables of Bristol Castle*, p. 77

60 *List of Sheriffs for England and Wales*, PRO, Lists and Indexes, IX, 1898

61 CCR, 1279–88, 463–4

62 C Lib R, 1240–45, 128, 191 when 100 marks were paid for keeping Chester, Beeston and Dyserth

63 CPR, 1232–47, 479

64 Gilbert Talbot claimed and got £100, spent in keeping Gloucester Castle, but not until his term of office was over: CCR, 1330–33, 270; see also *ibid.*, 243

65 CCR, 1307–13, 411

66 CPR, 1272–81, 299

67 CCR, 1307–13, 270

68 CPR, 1247–58, 447

69 *Ibid.*, 459

70 *Ibid.*, 162, 178, 336; also CPR, 1232–47, 100

71 CPR, 1225–32, 28

72 CPR, 1266–72, 343

73 CPR, 1247–58, 570

74 *Accounts of the Constables of Bristol Castle*, pp. 77–93

75 S. Bond, 'The Medieval Constables of Windsor Castle', *EHR*, 82 (1967), 225–49

76 R. A. Griffiths, *The Principality of Wales in the Later Middle Ages: The Structure and Personnel of Government*, vol. I, South Wales, *1277–1536*, Bd Celt St, 1972, pp. 193ff

76 J. C. Holt, 'Philip Mark and the Shrievalty of Nottinghamshire and Derbyshire in the Early Twelfth Century', *Tr Thor Soc*, 56 (1952), 8–24

77 C Lib R, 1251–60, *passim*; CCR, 1272–79, 16, 18, 34; *ibid.*, 1288–96, 19; *ibid.*, 1240–45, *passim*

78 C Lib R, 1240–45, 52

79 E. R. Stevenson, 'The Escheator', in *The English Government at Work, 1327–1336*, ed. W. A. Morris and J. R. Strayer, Boston, Mass., 1947, vol. II, pp. 109–67

80 M. Howell, *Regalian Right in Medieval England*, Univ Lond Hist Ser, 9 (1962)

81 *Ibid.*, p. 162

82 *Ibid.*, p. 163

83 W. A. Morris, *The Medieval English Sheriff to 1300*, Manchester, 1927, pp. 45–9; 'The Office of Sheriff in the Early Norman Period', *EHR*, 35 (1918), 145–75

84 J. Green, 'The Sheriffs of William the Conqueror', *A-N St*, 5 (1982), 129–45

85 W. A. Morris, 'The Sheriff and the Administrative System of Henry I', *EHR*, 37 (1922), 161–72; C. H. Walker, 'Sheriffs in the Pipe Roll of 31 Henry I', *EHR*, 37 (1922), 67–79

86 G. Templeman, 'The Sheriffs of Warwickshire in the Thirteenth Century', *Dugd Soc Occ Pap*, 7 (1948)

87 G. T. Lapsley, 'The Court, Record and Roll of the County in the Thirteenth Century', *Law Qt Rv*, 51 (1935), 299–325

88 T. F. Tout, 'The Welsh Shires: A Study in Constitutional History', *Y Cymm*, 9 (1888), 201–26

89 G. Templeman, 'The Sheriffs of Warwickshire'

90 'Wallingford', in *Historic Towns in Oxfordshire*, Oxfordshire Archaeological Unit, Survey 3, 1975, pp. 155–62

91 D. Baker et al., 'Excavations in Bedford 1967–1977', *Beds Arch Jl*, 13 (1979), 7–13

92 *Buckinghamshire, North*, RCHM, p. 16

93 *KW*, II, 682; W. Farrer, *Honors and Knights' Fees*, II, London, 1924, pp. 294–300

94 *KW*, II, 629

95 *Ibid.*, II, 616–24; *Dorset*, RCHM, II, pt 1, pp. 57–9

96 T. J. de Mazzinghi, 'Castle Church, with some Account of its Parish and Manor and of its Escheat tempore Henry VIII', *Staffs Collns*, 8 (1887); R. W. Eyton, *Domesday Studies: An Analysis and Digest of the Staffordshire Domesday*, London, 1881, pp. 20–2

97 E. S. Armitage, *Early Norman Castles of the British Isles*, London, 1912, pp. 211–16; *Med Arch*, 25 (1981), 202

98 C. H. Hunter Blair, 'The Sheriffs of Northumberland, part 1, 1076–1602', *Arch Ael*, 4th ser., 20 (1942), 11–90

99 J. Scammell, 'The Origin and Limitations of the Liberty of Durham', *EHR*, 81 (1966), 449–75

100 G. V. Scammell, *Hugh du Puiset Bishop of Durham*, Cambridge, 1956, pp. 42–4

101 G. W. S. Barrow, 'The Pattern of Lordship and Feudal Settlement in Cumbria', *Jl Med Hist*, 1 (1975), 117–38; *Records Relating to the Barony of Kendale by William Farrer*, ed. J. F. Curwen, CWAS Rec Ser, 4 (1923)

102 *List of Sheriffs*

103 J. Tait, *Medieval Manchester and the Beginnings of Lancashire*, Manchester, 1904, pp. 159–61

104 *List of Sheriffs*, p. 72

105 R. S. Somerville, *History of the Duchy of Lancaster*, London, 1953, pp. 1–11

106 W. A. Morris, 'The Office of Sheriff'; 'The Sheriffs and the Administrative System'; J. Gree, 'Sheriffs of the Conqueror'

107 William of Malmesbury, *De Gestis*, RS, 253

108 *Medieval Worcester: An Archaeological Framework*, ed. M. O. Carver, Worcs Arch Soc, 1980, pp. 55–8; P. Barker, 'The Origins of Worcester', *Tr Worcs AS*, 3rd ser., 2 (1968–9), 7–116

109 W. Page, *London: Its Origin and Early Development*, London, 1923, p. 81

110 *Calendar of Plea and Memoranda Rolls, 1323–64*, ed. A. H. Thomas, Cambridge, 1926, pp. 31, 73; *Calendar of the Letter Books of the City of London*, ed. R. R. Sharpe, *passim*

111 CPR, 1388–92, 389

112 CPR, 1247–58, 417, 504

113 CCR, 1223–27, 444–5

114 R. B. Pugh, *Imprisonment in Medieval England*, Cambridge, 1968, p. 64

115 CCR, 1242–7, 282–3; CPR, 1345–8, 345

116 CPR, 1258–66, 202

117 CCR, 1327–30, 158

118 C Lib R, 1245–51, 247

119 G. E. Woodbine, 'County Court Rolls and County Court Records', *Harv Law Rv*, 43 (1929–30), 1083–1110; C. H. Jenkinson and M. H. Mills, 'Rolls from a Sheriff's Office of the Fourteenth Century', *EHR*, 43 (1928), 21–32

120 *Liber Memorandorum Ecclesie de Bernewelle*, ed. J. W. Clark, Cambridge, 1907, p. 238; C Fine R, 1319–27, 276.7

121 For example, at Swansea Castle, CCR, 1323–27, 620

122 CPR, 1258–66, 384

123 CPR, 1225–32, 189

124 V. H. Galbraith, 'The Tower as an Exchequer Record Office in the Reign of Edward II', in *Essays in Medieval History Presented to Thomas Frederick Tout*, ed. A. G. Little and F. M. Powick, Manchester, 1925, pp. 231–47

125 *Guide to the Contents of the Public Record Office*, London, HMSO, 1963, vol. I, pp. 1–3; V. H. Galbraith, *An Introduction to the Use of the Public Records*, Oxford, 1934, pp. 35–52; CCR, 1360–64, 64; *ibid.*, 1422–29, 214

126 F. W. Maitland, *The Constitutional History of England*, Cambridge, 1908, p. 132

127 M. H. Mills, 'The Medieval Shire House', in *Studies Presented to Sir Hilary Jenkinson*, ed. V. Conway-Davies, Oxford, 1957, pp. 254–71

128 B. Cozens-Hardy, 'The Old Shirehouse at Norwich', *Norf Arch*, 35 (1970), 145–8

129 C. Inq Misc, III, no. 366

130 CCR, 1330–33, 252

131 *Bedfordshire Coroners' Rolls*, ed. R. F. Hunisett, Beds HRS, 41 (1960), no. 136

132 Cur Reg R, 2, 264

133 R. B. Pugh, *Imprisonment in Medieval England*, Cambridge, 1968, pp. 4–5, 57–86

134 R. B. Pugh, 'Medieval Sussex Prisons', *Suss Arch Collns*, 97 (1959), 69–81

135 The Sheriff of Wiltshire used Devizes and Marlborough as well as Sarum

136 *Wiltshire Gaol Delivery and Trailbaston Trials 1275–1306*, ed. R. B. Pugh, Wilts Rec Soc, 33 (1977), *passim*

137 Rot Parl, III, 441; *Ancient Petitions Relating to Northumberland*, ed. C. M. Fraser, Surt Soc, 176 (1961)

138 *Crime in East Anglia in the Fourteenth Century: Norfolk Gaol Delivery Rolls, 1307–1316*, ed. Barbara Hanawalt, Norf RS, 1976, no. 63

139 *Ibid.*, no. 146

140 *Select Cases from Coroners' Rolls*, Seld Soc, 9 (1895), 79–81

141 Welsh Assize Roll, 210, 3d a day was allowed with 2d for a servant

142 F. J. Field, 'The Carvings in the Entrance to Major MacIvor's Cell, Carlisle Castle', *TrCWAS*, NS 37 (1937), 13–23; J. Charlton, *Carlisle Castle*, HMSO, 1988, p. 8

143 *Welsh Assize Roll, 1277–1284*, ed. J. Conway Davies, Bd Celt St, *Law and History*, 7 (1940), 210

144 *Assize of Clarendon*, c. 7; Stubbs, *Select Charters*, p. 171

145 *Select Cases in the Court of King's Bench under Edward I*, vol. I, ed. G. O. Sayles, Seld Soc, 55 (1936), 126

146 VCH, *Yorkshire: City of York*, p. 523

147 Cur Reg R, VIII, 397; *Records of the Borough of Leicester*, ed. M. Bateson, London, 1899, vol. I, p. 368; *Leet Jurisdiction of the City of Norwich during the XIIIth and XIVth Centuries*, ed. W. Hudson, Seld Soc, 5 (1891), 11

148 C Inq pm, IV, 360

149 W. M. Palmer, *Cambridge Castle*, Cambridge, 1928, pp. 24–5

150 CCR, 1234–7, 189–91; *ibid.*, 546–53

151 Bracton, *De Legibus*, ed. Thorne and Woodbine, vol. II, pp. 61, 201–2

152 H. Jenkinson, 'Rolls from a Sheriff's Office'

153 J. G. Noppen, *Chapter House and Pyx Chamber*, HMSO, 1936; the term 'pyx' denotes a locked chest

154 J. E. A. Jolliffe, 'The Chamber and the Castle Treasures under King John', in *Studies in Medieval History Presented to Frederick Maurice Powicke*, ed. R. W. Hunt, W. A. Pantin and R. W. Southern, Oxford, 1948, pp. 117–42; Jolliffe, *Angevin Kingship*, pp. 250–5

155 Jolliffe, *Angevin Kingship*, p. 246

156 H. A. Harben, *A Dictionary of London*, London, 1918, p. 417

157 T. F. Reddaway, 'The King's Mint and Exchange in London', *EHR*, 82 (1967), 1–23

158 Alice Beardwood, 'The Royal Mints and Exchanges', in *The English Government at Work*, vol. 3, *Local Administration and Justice*, ed. W. H. Dunham, Cambridge, Mass., 1950, pp. 35–66

159 *Plac Quo War*, p. 660

5 THE CASTLE IN PEACE AND WAR

1 D. F. Renn, 'The Anglo-Norman Keep, 1066–1138', *JBAA*, 3rd ser., 22 (1959), 1–23; J. C. Perks, 'Newark Castle and the Great Tower', *Tr Thor Soc*, 43 (1939), 22–6

2 I. H. Jeayes, *Descriptive Catalogue of the Charters and Monuments in the Possession of . . . Lord Fitzhardinge at Berkeley Castle*, Bristol, 1892, no. 1

3 The author is deeply indebted to Dr Charles Coulson, whose *Handlist of English Royal Licences to Crenellate 1200–1578* (MS) has been invaluable

4 A. Oswald, 'Interim Report on Excavations at Weoley Castle', in *Essays in Honour of Philip B. Chatwin*, Oxford, 1962, pp. 61–85; C. A. Ralegh Radford, *Acton Burnell Castle*, HMSO, 1954

5 Rot Lit Claus, I, 379b

6 *Ibid.*, I, 459b

7 B. Harbottle and P. Salway, 'Nafferton Castle, Northumberland', *Arch Ael*, 4th ser., 38 (1960), 129–44; Harbottle, Salway and B. J. N. Edwards, 'Nafferton Castle, Second Report', *ibid.*, 39 (1961), 165–78

8 N. J. G. Pounds, Beverston Castle, *Arch Jl* (Supplmt), 145 (1988), 48–51

9 For example *situm castri de Benifeld* (Benefield) *et dimidiam virgatem terre*, Henry of Pytchley's *Book of Fees*, ed. W. T. Mellows, Northts R S, 2 (1924), 74

10 R. Grosvenor Bartelot, 'The Vanished Mediaeval Castles of Dorset', *Pr Dev AS*, 66 (1945), 65–75; *Dorset*, RCHM, vol. I, pp. 183–4

11 John Hutchins, *The History and Antiquities of the County of Dorset*, Westminster, 1861–74, vol. I, pp. 156–7; 260–3; *Dorset*, RCHM, vol. I, pp. 156–7

12 *Complete Peerage, passim*; E. Mason, 'Magnates, Curiales and the Wheel of Fortune', *Battle Conf*, 2 (1979), 118–40

13 'Calendar of Inquisitions Post Mortem', No. 2, ed. G. H. Fowler, *Beds HRS*, 19 (1937), nos. 116 and 150

14 *Annals of Dunstable*, RS 36, III, 66. In the same context an otherwise unknown castle at 'Lutune' is mentioned.

15 M. E. Wood, *Thirteenth Century Domestic Architecture in England*, *Arch Jl*, 105, Supplmt (1950), 64–9

16 *Medieval Moated Sites*, ed. F. A. Aberg, CBA Res Rept 17 (1978)

17 H. E. J. Le Patourel, in *Medieval Moated Sites*, pp. 21–8

18 H. E. J. Le Patourel, *The Moated Sites of Yorkshire*, Med Arch, Monographs, 5 (1973), pp. 17–18

19 B. K. Roberts, 'Moats and Mottes', *Med Arch*, 8 (1964), 219–22; F. V. Emery, 'Moated Settlements in England', *Geog*, 47 (1962) 378–88

20 P. N. Jones and D. Renn, 'The Military Effectiveness of Arrow Loops: Some Experiments at White Castle', *Chât Gaill*, 9–10 (1982), 445–56
21 *City of York*, vol. 2, *The Defences*, RCHM, 1972, p. 165
22 R. E. Oakeshott, *The Archaeology of Weapons*, London, 1960, pp. 293–4
23 R. Payne-Gallwey, *The Crossbow*, London, 1903, pp. 14–32
24 C Lib R, 1240–45, 144
25 R. Payne-Gallwey, *The Crossbow*
26 C Lib R, 1267–72, no. 1140
27 C Lib R, 1260–7, 273
28 CCR, 1256–9, 232
29 CCR, 1259–61, 245
30 CCR, 1268–72, 586
31 CCR, 1251–3, 163 and numerous other references in the Close Rolls
32 References to the making and despatch of crossbows are too numerous to cite; most are in the Close Rolls
33 CCR, 1264–8, 149
34 C Lib R, 1240–5, 258, and 1245–51, 258
35 C Lib R, 1245–51, 234
36 C Lib R, 1240–5, 122
37 CCR, 1237–42, 409
38 C. E. Hart, *Royal Forest*, Oxford, 1966, pp. 267–72
39 CCR, 1254–6, 260; also CCR 1264–8, 157, 160, when he was still at work there
40 C Lib R, 1245–51, 119, 287
41 C Lib R, 1245–51, 41, 185
42 C Lib R, 1260–7, 3, 112
43 C Lib R, 1240–5, 146
44 CCR, 1264–8, 149
45 C Lib R, 1240–5, 299; *ibid.*, 1245–51, 370 (Hereford); C Lib R, 1245–51, 370 (Chester); *Cheshire in the Pipe Rolls, 1158–1301*, ed. M.H. Mills and R. Stewart-Brown, L & C Rec Soc, 92 (1838), *passim*
46 C Lib R, 1260–7, 273: *fenestras volantes* at Winchester
47 Drawings in *Encyclopedia Britannica*, *sub* 'Engines of War'
48 C. Oman, *A History of the Art of War in the Middle Ages*, London, 1924
49 J. M. Kendall, 'The Siege of Berkhamsted Castle in 1216', *Ant Jl*, 3 (1923), 37–48
50 C Lib R, 1251–66, 248, 267
51 C Lib R, 1327–30, 411
52 C Lib R, 1338–40, 517
53 CPR, 1367–70, 205
54 C Lib R, 1245–51, 246
55 CCR, 1242–7, 219
56 C Lib R, 1260–7, 175
57 CCR, 1231–4, 352
58 CCR, 1307–13, 399
59 CPR, 1338–40, 442
60 CPR, 1350–4, 418
61 CPR, 1361–4, 42
62 CPR, 1340–3, 566
63 C Lib R, 1260–7, 294
64 CCR, 1272–9, 515
65 CCR, 1234–7, 65

66 CCR, 1323–7, 247

67 CCR, 1272–9, 316

68 C Lib R, 1251–60, 255

69 C Lib R, 1251–60, 106

70 J. M. Kendall, 'The Siege of Berkhamsted Castle'

71 C Lib R, 1240–5, 255

72 J. M. Kendall, 'The Siege of Berkhamsted Castle'

73 *Calendar of Ancient Correspondence concerning Wales*, ed. J. G. Edwards, Bd Celt St, vol. 2 (1935), section IV, 5 (p. 22)

74 C Lib R, 1240–5, 257

75 C Lib R, 1240–5, 287

76 C Lib R, 1267–72, nos. 365, 999, 1029, 1499

77 *Calendar of Ancient Correspondence*, IV, 90 (pp. 30–1)

78 Texts are given in K. Norgate, *The Minority of Henry III*, London, 1912, pp. 296–8. See also G. J. Turner, 'The Minority of Henry III', *TrRHS*, NS 18 (1904), 245–95; 3rd ser., 1 (1907), 205–62

79 Corpus Christi College Cambridge, MS 16 fo 60

80 A. L. Poole, *From Domesday Book to Magna Carta*, Oxford, 1955, p. 348

81 *KW*, II, 708–10

82 J. T. Appleby, *England without Richard, 1189–1199*, London, 1965, pp. 62–85

83 *The Chronicle of Richard of Devizes*, ed. J. T. Appleby, London, 1963, p. 34. The Treaty of Winchester is examined in App. F, pp. 90–8

84 Pipe Roll of 16 John, PRS, NS 35 (1959), *passim*, and for 17 John, PRS, 37 (1961)

85 W. Stubbs, *Select Charters*, 9th edn, Oxford, 1929, pp. 291–302, caps 29, 30 and 31

86 A. L. Poole, *From Domesday Book to Magna Carta*, p. 479

87 Walter of Coventry, RS 58, ii, 226–7

88 R. A. Brown, *Rochester Castle*, HMSO, 1969, pp. 12–15

89 Rot Lit Claus, 1, 238b

90 R. A. Brown, *Rochester Castle*, p. 13

91 *Liber Memorandorum Ecclesie de Bernewelle*, ed. J. W. Clark, Cambridge, 1907, pp. 59–60

92 See also P. K. Baillie Reynolds, *Kenilworth Castle*, HMSO, 1965, pp. 1–2

93 G. J. Turner, 'The Minority of Henry III', part 1, p. 258

94 *Ibid.*, p. 264

95 Notably in *L'Histoire de Guillaume le Maréchal*, ed. P. Meyes, vol. 2, Paris, 1844, esp. ll. 16467–16540, and *Histoire des Ducs de Normandie et des Rois d'Angleterre*, ed. Francisque Michel, Paris, 1840, pp. 193ff;

96 T. F. Tout, 'The Fair of Lincoln and the *Histoire de Guillaume le Maréchal*', *EHR*, 18 (1903), 240–65. The account in F. M. Powicke, *The Thirteenth Century*, Oxford, 1953, pp. 11–12, does not in archaeological terms make any sense. F. W. Brooks and F. Oakley, 'The Campaigns and Battle of Lincoln, 1217', *RPAS Lincs*, 36 (1921), 295–312

97 Roger of Wendover, RS 84, IV, 34–5

98 R. V. Turner, 'William de Forz, Count of Aumâle: an Early Thirteenth Century English Baron', *Proc Am Phil Soc*, 115 (1971), 221–49

99 Rot Lit Pat, 152

100 For the Castle Bytham affair see K. Norgate, *The Minority of Henry III*, pp. 163–7

101 Roger of Wendover, RS 84, IV, 67

102 *Royal Letters*, RS 27, 1, 100–1

103 CPR, 1216–25, 374

104 This was Norgate's opinion, *The Minority of Henry III*, pp. 190–1

105 Walter of Coventry, RS 58, II, 244

106 Radulph of Coggeshall, RS 66, 205
107 D. Baker, E. Baker et al., 'Excavations in Bedford, 1967–1977', *Beds Arch Jl*, 13 (1979), 7–64
108 Annals of Dunstable, RS 36, iii, 86–9
109 Rot Lit Claus, I, 608, 608b, 617, 617b
110 R. A. Brown, *English Medieval Castles*, London, 2nd edn, pp. 197, 160–3; also G. H. Fowler, 'Munitions in 1224', *Beds Rec Soc*, 5 (1920), 117–32
111 Rot Lit Claus, I, 632, 632b, 642, 655
112 *cum beschis et picoisis et trublis et alliis*, Rot Lit Claus, I, 655
113 *in recompencionem lapidum quos nobis habere fecerunt ad petrarias et mangunellos nostros*
114 R. F. Treharne, *The Baronial Plan of Reform, 1258–1263*, Manchester, 1932, pp. 74, 99, 189–92; *Documents of the Baronial Movement of Reform and Rebellion 1258–1267*, ed. R. E. Treharne and I. J. Sanders, Oxford, 1973; pp. 6–37; F. M. Powicke, *King Henry III and the Lord Edward*, Oxford, 1947, vol. I, pp. 411–55
115 VCH, *Warwickshire*, vol. I, p. 380; *KW*, II, 684; F. M. Powicke, *The Thirteenth Century*, p. 213; *King Henry III and the Lord Edward*, pp. 531–2
116 CPR, 1216–25, 417–20; the list is discussed in K. Norgate, *The Minority of Henry III*, n. 8, pp. 290–2
117 CPR, 1247–58, 637–9
118 CPR, 1247–58, 270
119 CPR, 1247–58, 538
120 CPR, 1258–66, 70–1, 163–4
121 CPR, 1258–66, 178–9
122 CPR, 1258–66, 266, 278
123 CPR, 1272–81, 9, 156, 162–3, 272
124 *Northamptonshire*, RCHM, vol. I, pp. 18–19
125 CCR, 1272–9, 34, 447; 1279–88, 2, 447; 1288–96, 19; C Lib R, 1226–40, 10; 1251–60, 27, 182
126 CPR, 1266–72, 410
127 CCR, 1279–88, 447
128 C Lib R, 1240–5, 94
129 C Lib R, 1240–5, 177
130 CPR, 1232–47, 31
131 CCR, 1288–96, 196
132 Rot Hundr, II, 236
133 *Ibid.*, II, 236
134 CCR, 1279–88, 463
135 Rot Hundr, II, 77
136 Pipe Roll of 10 Edward II, m 34, as quoted in R. M. Serjeantson, *The Castle of Northampton*, Northampton, 1908, pp. 30–1
137 CPR, 1258–66, 207
138 CCR, 1264–8, 176
139 For instance Dynevor and Llanbadarn in 1327: CCR, 1327–30, 129
140 Roll of Divers Accounts, ed. F. A. Cazel, PRS, NS 44 (1974–5), 46
141 C Lib R, 1260–7, 151
142 C Lib R, 1260–7, 135
143 CPR, 1258–66, 278
144 C Lib R, 1267–72, 889
145 CCR, 1272–9, 68
146 CPR, 1307–13, 400
147 C Lib R, 1267–72, 1304
148 C Fine R, 1307–19, 348, 378

149 C Mem R, 1326–7, nos. 1661, 2091, 2101–2, 2116
150 CCR, 1242–7, 50, 328, 373, 425
151 Magna Carta, caps. 30, 31
152 Rot Hundr, I, 46
153 *Ibid.*, I, 76
154 CCR, 1313–8, 535
155 CPR, 1247–58, 399
156 C Lib R, 1267–72, 425; *ibid.*, 1251–60, 320
157 C Lib R, 1240–5, 110
158 C Mem R, 1326–7, no 2101
159 CPR, 1307–13, 464; C Lib R, 1267–72, no. 2392
160 CCR, 1242–7, 377, 420, 509
161 CCR, 1247–51, 2
162 CCR, 1242–7, 341–2; C Lib R, 1245–51, 246
163 CCR, 1247–51, 345
164 C Lib R, 1240–5, 318
165 CCR, 1242–7, 303, 362; C Lib R, 1245–51, 25, 105
166 C Mem R, 1326–7, 1577
167 CPR, 1452–61, 247; for stores at Nottingham Castle, see CCR, 1296–1302, 61
168 CCR, 1237–42, 13
169 C Lib R, 1240–5, 48 (Lancaster); *ibid.*, 1245–51, 160 (Nottingham)
170 C Lib R, 1245–51, 28
171 C Lib R, 1245–51, 47
172 C Lib R, 1240–5, 32, 58, 89, 172
173 CCR, 1247–51, 145
174 CCR, 1234–7, 394
175 CCR, 1237–42, 38
176 CCR, 1342–7, 301
177 CCR, 1242–7, 303; *ibid.*, 1234–7, 31; C Lib R, 1245–51. 272; CCR, 1231–4, 94
178 E. M. Jope, and G. C. Dunning, 'The Use of Blue Slate for Roofing in Medieval England', *Ant Jl*, 34 (1954), 209–17
179 C Lib R, 1240–5, 265
180 CCR, 1234–7, 96–7, 309; also *Building Accounts of King Henry III*, ed. H. M. Colvin, Oxford, 1971, pp. 130–87
181 CCR, 1237–42, 85, 163
182 CCR, 1237–42, 79, 85, 91, 93
183 CCR, 1251–3, 84; 1254–6, 301
184 CCR, 1234–7, 96–7
185 CCR, 1237–42, 279, 371
186 E. Neaverson, *Mediaeval Castles in North Wales*, Liverpool, 1947
187 CCR, 1231–4, 101 (Exeter); *ibid.*, 1242–7, 327 (Chester)
188 CCR, 1237–42, 271; the lands were in the king's hands
189 C Lib R, 1240–5, 222
190 C Lib R, 1240–5, 162–3
191 C Lib R, 1226–40, 444
192 CCR, 1237–42, 132
193 CCR, 1237–42, 311 (Scarborough)
194 CCR, 1227–31, 136; 1251–3, 167; C Lib R, 1245–51, 190
195 The fother of about 19½ hundredweight was the common measure of lead
196 L. F. Salzman, 'The Property of the Earl of Arundel, 1397', *Suss Arch Collns*, 91 (1953), 32–52

197 CCR, 1242–7, 283
198 C Lib R, 1240–5, 74
199 CCR, 1237–42, 299
200 C Lib R, 1240–5, 53
201 CCR, 1237–42, 152

6 THE BARONIAL CASTLE

1 Sidney Painter, *Studies in the History of the English Feudal Barony*, Johns Hopkins Studies, 61, no. 3, Baltimore, Md., 1943
2 N. Denholm-Young, 'Eudo Dapifer's Honour of Walbrook', *Collected Papers on Medieval Subjects*, Oxford, 1946, pp. 154–61
3 Based on I. J. Sanders, *English Baronies*, Oxford, 1960
4 R. R. Davies, 'Kings, Lords and Liberties in the March of Wales', *TrRHS*, 5th ser., 29 (1979), 41–61
5 S. Painter, *English Feudal Barony*, pp. 20–2
6 *Ibid.*, p. 22
7 *Ibid.*, p. 48
8 *R B Exch*, RS, II, 737–45; dated to *temp* Henry III
9 *Ibid.*, II, 603–5
10 P. E. Curnow and M. W. Thompson, 'Excavations at Richard's Castle, 1962–1964', *JBAA*, 3rd ser., 32 (1969), 105–17
11 J. F. Baldwin, 'The Household Administration of Henry Lacy and Thomas of Lancaster', *EHR*, 42 (1927), 180–200
12 L. Fox, 'The Honor and Earldom of Leicester: Origin and Descent, 1066–1399', *EHR*, 54 (1939), 385–402
13 L. Fox, 'The Administration of the Honor of Leicester in the Fourteenth Century', *Tr Leic AS*, 20 (1938–9) 289–374
14 L. Fox 'Ministers' Accounts of the Honor of Leicester (1322–1324)', *ibid.*, 19 (1936–7), 199–273; 20 (1938–9), 77–158
15 Among them Brinklow, Lilbourne, Fillongley, Preston Capes
16 W. E. Wightman, *The Lacy Family in England and Normandy, 1066–1194*, Oxford, 1966
17 P. A Lyons, 'Two Compoti of the Lancashire and Cheshire Manors of Henry de Lacy, Earl of Lincoln', *Cheth Soc*, 112 (1884)
18 J. F. Baldwin, 'Household Administration'
19 *Ibid.*
20 P. A. Lyons, 'Two Compoti'
21 This would have been John de Lacy, eighth baron of Halton and first earl of Lincoln, who died in 1240
22 J. F. Baldwin, 'Household Administration'
23 *Ibid.*
24 W. E. Rhodes, 'Edmund, Earl of Lancaster', *EHR*, 10 (1895), 19–40, 209–37
25 F. W. Powicke, *Henry III and the Lord Edward*, Oxford, 1947, p. 523
26 R. Somerville, *History of the Duchy of Lancaster*, London, 1953, pp. 8–14
27 J. F. Baldwin, 'Household Administration'
28 J. C. Davies, *The Baronial Opposition to Edward II: Its Character and Policy*, London, 1918, pp. 25–50
29 M. McKisack, *The Fourteenth Century, 1307–1399*, Oxford, 1959, pp. 64–70
30 S. Armitage-Smith, *John of Gaunt*, Westminster, 1904, pp. 205–6
31 M. Coate, 'The Duchy of Cornwall: Its History and Administration', *TrRHS*, 4th ser., 10

(1927), 135–69; N. J. G. Pounds, *The Parliamentary Survey of the Duchy of Cornwall*, part 1, *Introduction*, D C Rec Soc, NS 25, 1982

32 *Ministers' Accounts of the Earldom of Cornwall, 1296–1297*, ed. L. M. Midgeley, part 2, Camd Soc, 3rd ser., 67, 1945

33 N. J. G. Pounds, 'The Duchy Palace at Lostwithiel, Cornwall', *Arch Jl*, 136 (1979), 203–17

34 P. L. Hull, *The Caption of Seisin of the Duchy of Cornwall (1337)*, D C Rec Soc, NS 17 (1971), xii–xxvi

35 M. Altschul, *A Baronial Family in Medieval England: the Clares 1217–1314*, Johns Hopkins Studies, 83, no. 2, 1965, pp. 222–5

36 N. Denholm-Young, *Seignorial Administration in England*, Oxford, 1937, pp. 14–18

37 C Inq pm, I, no. 54; III, no. 552; N. Denholm-Young, *Seignorial Administration*

38 N. Denholm-Young, *Seignorial Administration*, pp. 3–4

39 C Inq pm, III, no. 423

40 *Ibid.*, X, no. 45

41 *Ibid.*, IX, no. 198

42 *Ibid.*, IX, no. 177

43 *Ibid.*, X, no. 110

44 N. Denholm-Young, *Seignorial Administration*, p. 22

45 W. Rees, 'The Medieval Lordship of Brecon', *Tr Cymm* (1915–16), 165–224

46 J. B. Smith, 'The Lordship of Glamorgan', *Morg*, 2 (1958), 9–37; J. C. Davies, 'The Despenser War in Glamorgan', *TrRHS*, 3rd ser., 9 (1915), 21–64

47 N. Denholm-Young, *Seignorial Administration*, p. 22

48 P. A. Faulkner, 'Castle Planning in the Fourteenth Century', *Arch Jl*, 120 (1963), 215–35

49 *Dorset*, RCHM, vol. II, part 1, pp. 57–78

50 J. C. Perks, 'The Architectural History of Chepstow Castle during the Middle Ages', *TrBGAS*, 67 (1946–8), 307–46; *Chepstow Castle*, HMSO, 1967, pp. 14–20

51 C. N. Johns, *Caerphilly Castle*, HMSO, 1978, pp. 53–8 and *passim*

52 B. M. Morley, 'Aspects of Fourteenth Century Castle Design', in *Collectanea Historica: Essays in Memory of Stuart Rigold*, ed. A. Detsicas, Maidstone, 1981, pp. 85–92

53 CPR, 1232–47, 23; J. E. Doyle, *The Official Baronage of England 1066–1885*, London, 1886. vol. I, p. 25

54 CPR, 1232–47, 258

55 CPR, 1232–47, 426; 1266–72, 671; CCR, 1231–4, 546

56 CPR, 1301–7, 206; this relates to the motte and bailey which preceded Ralph Cromwell's brick tower

57 CPR, 1266–72, 291

58 C Misc Inq, VII, 1399–1422, 7

59 CPR, 1247–58, 51

60 CPR, 1232–47, 180, 244; CPR, 1247–58, 621

61 CCR, 1261–4, 1–2

62 CPR, 1266–72, 143

63 CPR, 1266–72, 305

64 CCR, 1237–42, 299

65 T. F. Tout, 'The Earldoms under Edward I', *TrRHS*, NS 8 (1894), 129–55; *Report on the Dignity of a Peer*, PP, 1826, First Rept, App. 1

66 T. F. Tout, 'The Earldoms under Edward I'

67 The Duchy of Cornwall was created in 1337 on the basis of the earldom left vacant by the death of John of Eltham, and was vested in the firstborn son of the monarch. It thus alternated between the crown and the Prince of Wales.

68 CPR, 1266–72, 67

69 CPR, 1247–58, 473
70 CPR, 1247–58, 621
71 CPR, 1247–58, 423; CPR, 1258–66, 428
72 CPR, 1258–66, 428
73 CPR, 1232–47, 31, 32
74 CPR, 1232–47, 490; also 26, 34
75 CPR, 1258–66, 211, 231
76 CPR, 1266–72, 246
77 CPR, 1301–7, 76
78 CPR, 1338–40, 216
79 D. Williams, 'Fortified Manor Houses', *LeicAHS*, 50 (1974–5), 1–16
80 C. Inq Misc, I, 239; CPR, 1216–25, 238
81 CCR, 1259–61, 283–4
82 CCR, 1261–4, 129–30
83 CCR, 1261–4, 250
84 CCR, 1227–31, 69; *tantum prosterni faciat quod muri illi remaneant altitudinis X pedum tantum*
85 CCR, 1231–4, 268–9; 1234–7, 213
86 CCR, 1234–7, 224
87 CCR, 1261–4, 278
88 CPR, 1258–66, 281
89 CCR, 1279–88, 170–1
90 CCR, 1237–42, 381
91 CCR, 1279–88, 342
92 C Chart R, 1257–1300, 304
93 CCR, 1231–4, 554
94 CCR, 1231–4, 546
95 CCR, 1259–61, 173
96 CCR, 1261–4, 1–2
97 *Ministers' Accounts for West Wales 1277–1306*, ed. Myvanwy Rhys, Cym Rec Soc, 13 (1936), 155
98 *Ibid.*, 3
99 *The Chancellor's Roll for 8 Richard I*, ed. D. M. Stenton, PRS, NS 7 (1930), 211
100 *The Accounts of the Ministers for the Lordships of Abergavenny, Grosmont and White Castle for the Year 1256–1257*, ed. A. J. Roderick and William Rees, part 3, SW Mon Rec Soc, 4 (1957), 5–29
101 S. Painter, *English Feudal Baronage*, p. 170
102 *Ibid.*, pp. 173–4
103 N. Denholm-Young, *Seignorial Administration*
104 M. Altschul, *Baronial Family*, p. 206
105 R. V. Turner, 'William de Forz, Count of Aumale: An Early Thirteenth Century English Baron', *Pr Am Phil Soc*, 115 (1971), 221–49
106 S. Painter, *English Feudal Baronage*, p. 174
107 J. M. W. Bean, *The Estates of the Percy Family 1416–1537*, Oxford, 1958, p. 33
108 E. Mason, 'The Resources of the Earldom of Warwick in the Thirteenth Century', *Midl H*, 3 (1975–6), 67–75
109 C. Ross, 'The Estates and Finances of Richard Beauchamp Earl of Warwick', *Dugd Soc Occ Pap*, 12 (1956)
110 E. Mason, 'Resources of the Earldom of Warwick'
111 H. L. Gray, 'Incomes from Land in England in 1436', *EHR*, 49 (1934), 607–39
112 T. B. Pugh and C. D. Ross, 'The English Baronage and the Income Tax of 1436', *BIHR*, 26 (1953), 1–28

113 S. Painter, *English Feudal Baronage*, p. 173

114 *Ibid.*, p. 173

115 R. A. Brown, 'A List of Castles'

116 D. G. MacLeod, 'Rayleigh Castle', *Ess Jl*, 5 (1970), 112–15

117 Ranulf Higden, *Polychronicon*, RS 41, viii, 198–200

118 *KW*, II, 559–60; M. H. Ridgway and D. J. C. King, 'Beeston Castle, Cheshire', *J Ches/NW AS*, 44 (1957), 1–23; *Beeston Castle*, HMSO, 1962

119 P. L. Drewett, 'Excavations at Hadleigh Castle, 1972: A Second Interim Report', *Ess Jl*, 8 (1973) 79–87; 'Excavations at Hadleigh Castle, Essex, 1971–1972', *JBAA*, 3rd ser., 38 (1975), 90–154; *KW*, II, 659–66

120 M. W. Thompson, 'The Origins of Bolingbroke Castle, Lincolnshire', *Med Arch*, 10 (1966), 152–8

121 P. L. Drewett and D. J. Freke, 'The Great Hall at Bolingbroke Castle, Lincolnshire', *Med Arch*, 18 (1974), 163–5

122 C. A. Ralegh Radford, 'Acton Burnell Castle', in *Studies in Building History*, ed. E. M. Jope, London, 1961, pp. 94–103; *Acton Burnell Castle*, HMSO, 1957; J. West, 'Acton Burnell Castle, Shropshire', in *Collectanea Historica*, ed. A. Detsicas, pp. 85–92

7 THE FRONTIER REGIONS OF MEDIEVAL ENGLAND

1 R. A. Brown, 'Royal Castle-Building in England, 1154–1216', *EHR*, 70 (1955), 353–98

2 Sir Charles Peers, *Porchester Castle Hampshire*, HMSO, 1933, p. 6

3 Barry Cunliffe, 'Excavations at Porchester Castle, III', *Res Repts Soc Ant*, 34 (1977), pp. 2–7; Colin Platt, *Medieval Southampton*, London, 1973, p. 13

4 R. A. Brown, 'Royal Castle-Building'

5 Sir Charles Peers, *Carisbrooke Castle, Isle of Wight*, HMSO, 1933

6 William Rees, *South Wales and the March 1284–1415*, Oxford, 1924, pp. 26–8

7 D. Walker, 'William FitzOsbern and the Norman Settlement in Herefordshire', *Tr Woolh FC*, 39 (1967), 402–12

8 D. Walker, 'The Norman Settlement in Wales', *Battle Conf*, 1 (1978), 131–43

9 Lynn Nelson, *The Normans in South Wales, 1070–1171*, Austin, Texas, 1966, pp. 8–13. On cantref and commote see J. E. Lloyd, *A History of Wales*, London, 1939, vol. I, pp. 300–8

10 G. R. J. Jones, 'Post-Roman Wales', in *The Agrarian History of England and Wales*, vol. I, part 2, Cambridge, 1972, pp. 283–382, esp. pp. 301–2

11 Ordericus Vitalis, II, 237

12 DB, i, 252

13 A-S C, 132, 151

14 *Anglesey*, RCHM(W), 1937, pp. 123–4

15 J. B. Smith, 'The Middle March in the Thirteenth Century', *Bd Celt St*, 24 (1970–2), 77–93

16 S. Walker, 'The Lordship of Builth', *Brych*, 20 (1982–3), 23–33

17 W. Rees, 'The Mediaeval Lordship of Brecon', *Tr Cymm* (1915–16), 165–224

18 *Annales Cambriae*, RS, 20

19 J. B. Smith, 'The Lordship of Glamorgan', *Morg*, 2 (1958), 9–37

20 L. D. Nicholl, *The Normans in Glamorgan, Gower and Kidweli*, Cardiff, 1936

21 *Ibid.*, p. xiii

22 R. R. Davies, 'Henry I and Wales', in *Studies in Medieval History Presented to R. H. C. Davis*, London, 1985, pp. 132–47

23 W. Rees, 'Gower and the March of Wales', *Arch Camb*, 110 (1961) 1–29

24 I. W. Rowlands, 'The Making of the March: Aspects of the Norman Settlement of Dyfed', *Battle Conf*, 3 (1980), 142–57

25 J. G. Edwards, 'The Normans and the Welsh March', *Pr Brit Acad* (1956), 155–77

26 Sir John Lloyd, *A History of Wales*, London, 1939, vol. II, p. 424
27 R. R. Davies, 'Kings, Lords and Liberties in the March of Wales, 1066–1272', *TrRHS*, 5th ser., 29 (1979), 41–61
28 Walker, 'Lordship of Builth'
29 R. W. Eyton, *Antiquities of Shropshire*, London, 1860, vol. X, pp. 228–35
30 Rot Parl, I, 206b–207
31 Rot Cur Reg, 1194–99, 1835, I, 426
32 W. Rees, *South Wales and the March*, pp. 42–70
33 *A Calendar of the Public Records Relating to Pembrokeshire*, ed. H. Owen, London, 1911, vol. I, p. 41
34 *Cartae et Alia Munimenta, quae ad Dominium de Glamorgancia pertinent*, ed. G. T. Clark, Cardiff, 1910, vol. II, no. 615 (pp. 649–51)
35 *Ibid.*, no. 321 (p. 320)
36 *Calendar of Ancient Correspondence Concerning Wales*, ed. J. G. Edwards, Cardiff, 1935, vol. XIX, no. 136 (p. 103)
37 *Ibid.*, vol. IV, no. 4 (p. 21)
38 *Ibid.*, vol. X, no. 95 (pp. 45–6)
39 *Ibid.*, vol. III, no. 154 (p. 17)
40 W. Rees, 'Gower and the March of Wales', *Arch Camb*, 110 (1961), 1–29
41 *Cartae et Alia Munimenta*, no. 1099 (p. 1459)
42 Inq pm, 1410, printed in G. T. Clark, *Cartae et Alia Munimenta*, no. 599, p. 1459
43 *Brut y Tywysogyon or Chronicle of the Princes: Red Book of Hergest Version*, trans. T. Jones, Bd Celt St, 16 (1955)
44 D. J. Cathcart King, *The Castle in England and Wales*, London, 1988, pp. 130–46
45 C. N. Johns, *Caerphilly Castle, Mid Glamorgan*, Cardiff, HMSO, 1978; W. Rees, *Caerphilly Castle, A History and Description*, 1937
46 *KW*, I, 295
47 C. H. Houlder, 'Recent Excavations in Old Aberystwyth', *Cered*, 3 (1956–9), 114–17
48 R. A. Griffiths, 'The Three Castles at Aberystwyth', *Arch Camb*, 126 (1977), 74–87
49 *Annales Cambriae*, RS 20, 108; J. E. Morris, *The Welsh Wars of Edward I*, Oxford, 1901, p. 154
50 A. J. Taylor, 'Master James of St George', *EHR*, 65 (1950), 433–57
51 *KW*, II, 625
52 T. Edwards, 'Dyserth Castle', *Arch Camb*, 6th ser., 12 (1912), 263–94
53 *Annales Cambriae*, RS 20, 101
54 J. H. Harvey, 'The Medieval Office of Works', *JBAA*, 3rd ser., 6 (1941), 20–87. For details see *Records of the Wardrobe and Household 1285–1286*, ed. B. F. Byerly and C. Ridder, HMSO, 1977; ditto *1286–1289* HMSO, 1986
55 A. J. Taylor, 'Castle-building in Wales in the later Thirteenth Century', in *Studies in Building History: Essays in Recognition of the Work of B. H. St J. O'Neil*, London, 1961, pp. 104–33
56 J. G. Edwards, 'The Building of Flint', *Flint HS*, 12 (1951), 5–20
57 A. J. Taylor, 'Castle-building in Wales'
58 D. J. C. King, 'Two Castles in Northern Powys: Dinas Bran and Caergwrle', *Arch Camb*, 123 (1974), 113–39
59 A. J. Taylor, 'The Earliest Reference to Works at Hope Castle', *Flint HS*, 22 (1965–6), 76–7
60 D. J. C. King, 'Two Castles in Northern Powys'
61 D. Pratt, 'The Medieval Borough of Holt', *Tr Denb HS*, 14 (1965), 9–74
62 *KW*, I, 335
63 *Survey of the Honour of Denbigh, 1334*, ed. P. Vinogradoff and Frank Morgan, Brit Acad, 1914
64 T. F. Tout, 'The Welsh Shires: A Study in Constitutional History', *Y Cymm*, 9 (1888), 201–26
65 A. J. Taylor, *Conway Castle and Town Walls*, HMSO, 1961
66 *KW*, I, 357–65

67 J. A. Steers, *The Coastline of England and Wales*, Cambridge, 1946, pp. 134–6
68 A. J. Taylor, *Caernarvon Castle*
69 *KW*, I, 370–1
70 R. E. M. Wheeler, *Segontium and the Roman Occupation of Wales*, London, 1923
71 J. E. Morris, *The Welsh Wars*, pp. 240–70
72 *Ibid.*, p. 253
73 *Anglesey*, RCHB(W), pp. 8–13
74 J. G. Edwards, 'Edward I's Castle-Building in Wales', *Pr Brit Acad*, 32 (1946), 15–81
75 E. Neaverson, *Mediaeval Castles in North Wales*, Liverpool, 1947, pp. 45–6
76 Based on J. G. Edwards, 'Edward I's Castle-Building'
77 *Calendar of Ancient Petitions relating to Wales*, ed. W. Rees, Bd Celt St, 28 (1975), 337
78 *Ibid.*, 223
79 In 1278 William de Valence appealed for money to pay workmen at Aberystwyth, since his supply was exhausted: Cal Anc Corr Wales, 169
80 M. Howell, *Regalian Right in Medieval England*, Univ Lond Hist Ser, 9 (1962), 162–4
81 J. G. Edwards, 'Edward I's Castle-Building'
82 A. J. Taylor, 'Castle-building in Wales'
83 J. G. Edwards, 'Edward I's Castle-Building'
84 F. M. Powicke, *The Thirteenth Century*, Oxford, 1953, pp. 435–6
85 A. J. Taylor, 'Master James of St George'
86 This is argued by A. J. Taylor, 'Castle-Building in Thirteenth Century Wales and Savoy', *Pr Brit Acad*, 63 (1977), 265–92; 'The Castle of St Georges d'Espéranche', *Ant Jl*, 33 (1953), 33–47
87 A. J. Taylor, 'The Date of Caernarvon Castle', *Ant*, 26 (1952), 25–34
88 G. W. S. Barrow, *The Kingdom of the Scots*, London, 1973, pp. 142–4
89 Simeon of Durham, RS, I, 140
90 G. W. S. Barrow, *The Kingdom of the Scots*, p. 155
91 G. W. S. Barrow, 'Northern English Society in the Twelfth and Thirteenth Centuries', *North H*, 4 (1969), 1–28
92 G. W. S. Barrow, *The Anglo-Norman Era in Scottish History*, Oxford, 1980
93 W. E. Kapelle, *The Norman Conquest of the North*, London, 1979, p. 194
94 I. J. Sanders, *English Baronies*, Oxford, 1960, pp. 127–8
95 G. W. S. Barrow, 'The Pattern of Lordship and Feudal Settlement in Cumbria', *Jl Med Hist*, 1 (1975), 117–38
96 W. E. Kapelle, *The Norman Conquest of the North*, p. 199
97 Quoted in C. H. Hunter Blair, 'Baronys and Knights of Northumberland 1166–1266', *Arch Ael*, 4th ser., 30 (1952), 1–54
98 Rot Lit Claus, I, 379b
99 *Ibid.*, I, 459b
100 J. F. Curnow, 'The Castles and Fortified Towers of Cumberland, Westmorland and Lancashire North of the Sands', *CWAAS*, extra ser., 13 (1913); N. Pevsner, *Buildings of England: Cumberland and Westmorland*, Harmondsworth, 1967, pp. 20–1
101 G. W. S. Barrow, *The Anglo-Norman Era*, pp. 21–2; F. M. Powicke, *The Thirteenth Century*, pp. 580–1
102 F. M. Powicke, *The Thirteenth Century*, p. 577
103 *Ibid.*, pp. 602–11
104 *Calendar of Documents relating to Scotland*, ed. J. Bain, vol. II, p. 1115
105 A. J. Taylor, 'Master James of St George' for the text of the king's instructions
106 *KW*, I, 413
107 On garrisons and expenditure in these castles see *Documents Illustrative of the History of Scotland*, ed. J. Stevenson, Edinburgh, 1870, 2 vols
108 *The Chronicle of Lanercost 1272–1346*, ed. H. Maxwell, Glasgow, 1913, p. 204

109 *Ibid.*, p. 223
110 *KW*, II, 819
111 *Roxburghshire*, RCHM(S), 1956, vol. II, pp. 407–11
112 *KW*, I, 420

8 CASTLE AND COMMUNITY

1 *Survey of the Honour of Denbigh 1334*, ed. P. Vinogradoff and F. Morgan, Brit Acad, Oxford, 1914
2 W. H. Walters, *The Edwardian Settlement of North Wales in its Administrative and Legal Aspects*, Cardiff, 1935, pp. 9 ff
3 J. W. F. Hill, *Medieval Lincoln*, Cambridge, 1948, pp. 82–106; J. W. F. Hill, 'Notes on Some Aspects of the Legal and Constitutional History of the City of Lincoln', *RP Ass Arch S 5*, 37 (1923–5), 177–232
4 *Acta Sanctorum*, III, 414
5 Lambert of Ardres, as quoted in E. S. Armitage, *Early Norman Castles*, pp. 89–90
6 *Essex*, RCHM, 1916, vol. I, pp. 51–7
7 P. Barker and R. Higham, *Hen Domen Montgomery*, RAI, London, 1982; and P. Barker, 'Hen Domen', *Curr Arch*, 111 (Sept. 1988). The latter offers a reconstruction of the buildings in the bailey
8 W. Horn, 'The Potential and Limitations of Radiocarbon Dating in the Middle Ages: the Art Historian's View', in *Scientific Methods in Medieval Archaeology*, Berkeley, Cal., 1970, pp. 23–87; N. W. Alcock and R. J. Buckley, 'Leicester Castle: The Great Hall', *Med Arch*, 31 (1987), 73–9
9 M. Biddle and B. Clayre, *Winchester Castle and the Great Hall*, Winchester, 1983, pp. 25–36
10 *KW*, II, 859
11 *Ancient Petitions Relating to Northumberland*, ed. C. M. Fraser, Surt Soc., 176 (1961), no. 79
12 R. A. Brown, *Castle Rising*, HMSO, 1978
13 C. A. Ralegh Radford, *Restormel Castle*, HMSO, 1935
14 M. W. Thompson, 'A Single-Aisled Hall at Conisborough Castle, Yorkshire', *Med Arch*, 12 (1968), 153
15 C. A. Ralegh Radford, *White Castle*, HMSO, 1962
16 Ralegh Radford, *Grosmont Castle*, HMSO, 1946. An almost identical transformation took place at Llawhaden Castle, Pembroke
17 *A Calendar of the Public Records Relating to Pembrokeshire*, ed. H. Owen, Soc Cymm, 1911, vol. I, p. 66
18 *Ibid.*, vol. 2, 1914, p. 77
19 *Ibid.*, vol. 3, 1918, p. 131
20 *Accounts of the Chamberlains and other Officers of the County of Chester 1301–1360*, ed. R. Stewart-Brown, L C Rec Soc, 59 (1910), 167
21 C Misc Inq, I, no. 153 (p. 54)
22 M. Wood, *The English Medieval House*, London, 1965, pp. 261–76
23 *Calendar of Ancient Correspondence Concerning Wales*, ed. J. G. Edwards, Bd Celt St, 2 (1935), III, no. 153 (p. 16)
24 *Accounts of the Chamberlains of Chester*, p. 235
25 *Ministers' Accounts for West Wales 1277 to 1306*, ed. M. Rhys, Cym Rec Soc, 13 (1936), 474
26 'Chepstow Assize Roll, 1415', in *The Marcher Lordships of South Wales 1415–1536: Select Documents*, ed. T. B. Pugh, Bd Celt St, 20 (1963), 75
27 Viscount Dillon and W. H. St John Hope, 'Inventory of the Goods and Chatels belonging to Thomas, Duke of Gloucester and seized in his Castle at Pleshey', *Arch Jl*, 54 (1897), 275–308

28 *Ancient Petitions relating to Northumberland*, ed. C. M. Fraser, Surt Soc, 176 (1961), 99

29 C Lib R, 1226–40, p. 310

30 *Ibid.*, 350

31 *Ibid.*, 310; 1245–51, 248

32 *Ibid.*, 1240–5, 102; This relates to the first Rhuddlan Castle which stood a short distance from the river

33 *Ibid.*, 1245–51, 116, 240

34 *Flintshire Ministers' Accounts 1301–28*, ed. A. Jones, Flint HS, 1913, 34

35 *Ministers' Accounts for the Lordships of Abergavenny, Grosmont, Skenfrith and White Castle*, ed. A. J. Roderick and W. Rees, SW Mon Rec Soc, II (1950), 67–125

36 Presumably that of St Mary Magdalene; see R. N. Hadcock, 'A Map of Mediaeval Northumberland and Durham', *Arch Ael*, 4th ser., 16 (1939)

37 CPR, 1391–6, 353; C Inq Misc, III, 979

38 *Accounts of the Chamberlains of Chester*, p. 219

39 CCR, 1242–7, 24

40 CCR, 1251–3, 429

41 C Lib R, 1251–60, 289

42 *KW*, I, 549–50

43 CCR, 1234–7, 274; 1256–9, 347; 1272–9, 269; 1288–96, 10

44 CCR, 1254–6, 121

45 CCR, 1272–9, 146, 164

46 C Inq Misc, II, no. 244; III, no. 366

47 *Regesta*, II, no. 569, p. 18

48 C Inq Misc, VI, 147

49 C Lib R, 1260–7, 94; CCR, 1237–42, 74

50 J. H. Johnson, 'The King's Wardrobe and Household', in *The English Government at Work*, ed. J. F. Willard and W. A. Morris, Cambridge, Mass., vol. I, 1940, pp. 206–49; C Inq Misc, IV, no. 375

51 *Calendar of Records, Pembrokeshire*, p. 104

52 C Lib R, 1245–51, 310

53 C Lib R, 1226–40, 321

54 C Lib R, 1240–5, 137

55 *Accounts of the Chamberlains of Chester*, p. 10

56 *Ministers' Accounts, West Wales*, p. 47

57 *The Account Roll of the Chamberlain of West Wales from Mich. 1301 to Mich. 1302*, ed. E. A. Lewis, Bd Celt St, II, part 1 (1923), 49–86

58 C Lib R, 1260–7, 91

59 Cambridge University Library, Palmer MSS, 240

60 Personal communication from Mr Guy Beresford

61 There was also a fortified mill at Beaumaris Castle

62 *Northamptonshire*, RCHM, vol. I, pp. 43–4

63 C Inq Misc, II, no. 1703; H. K. Bonney, *Fotheringhay*, 1821, pp. 29–30

64 C Inq Misc, II, 1703

65 C Inq Misc, III, no. 979

66 As at Scarborough, C Inq Misc, III, no. 435

67 CPR, 1272–81, 430

68 CPR, 1408–13, 52

69 CCR, 1242–7, 283

70 CCR, 1242–7, 415

71 CCR, 1354–60, 572

72 CCR, 1288–96, 25; CPR, 1330–4, 82

73 CPR, 1216–25, 287

74 CPR, 1391–6, 466

75 C Lib R, 1251–60, 504

76 *Accounts of the Chamberlains of Chester*, p. 241

77 *Marcher Lordships, Select Documents*, p. 163

78 CCR, 1313–18, 394

79 C Lib R, 1260–7, 28–9

80 C Inq Misc, II, no. 1381 (dated 1333)

81 C Inq pm I, 838

82 C Inq pm, I 813

83 *Regesta*, II, nos. 1363, 1366

84 *Ibid.*, no. 1606 (*c.* 1129)

85 *The Lancashire Pipe Rolls and Early Lancashire Charters*, ed. W. Farrer, Liverpool, 1902, p. 385

86 *Cartae et Alia Munimenta*, ed. G. T. Clark, Cardiff, 1910, vol. I, no. 129

87 *Ibid.*, no. 321

88 *Ibid.*, nos 919, 1050, 1051. Cf. no. 1293: *capitale mesuagium cum pertinenciis in le castell baillie in Kibouur* (perhaps the prehistoric earthwork of Cefn Cribwr, west of Bridgend)

89 C Inq Misc, II, no. 1795

90 CCR, 1237–42, 153

91 B. Ayers, *Excavations within the North-East Bailey of Norwich Castle 1979*, E Angl A R, 28 (1985), 3–6

92 *The Records of the City of Norwich*, ed. W. Hudson and J. C. Tingey, Norwich, 1906, vol. I, p. xlii

93 Bl Pr Reg, II, 60

94 C Inq Misc, III, no. 435

95 W. Farrer, *Lancashire Pipe Rolls*, Liverpool, 1902, p. 105

96 C Inq Misc, I, 96

97 C Fine R, 1319–27, 420

98 J. R. H. Moorman, 'Edward I at Lanercost Priory 1306–7', *EHR*, 67 (1952), 161–74

99 CCR, 1247–51, 340

100 CCR, 1279–88, 150

101 CCR, 1296–1302, 58

102 CCR, 1288–96, 425

103 CCR, 1307–13, 25

104 CCR, 1296–1302, 6

105 CCR, 1288–96, 392

106 CCR, 1478–85, 1065

107 CCR, 1468–76, 1423; 1461–8, 25

108 CCR, 1461–8, 113

109 CPR, 1391–6, 609

110 CPR, 1396–9, 552

111 CPR, 1391–6, 363

112 CPR, 1350–4, 443

113 CPR, 1364–7, 101; C Lib R, 1260–7, 82, 197

114 CPR, 1388–92, 36; CCR, 1251–3, 74

115 CCR, 1369–74, 342

116 CCR, 1478–85, 1283

117 C Lib R, 1245–51, 338; 1260–7, 174

118 *Accounts of the Chamberlains of Chester*, p. 6

119 *Ibid.*, pp. 42, 245

120 *Ibid.*, p. 141

121 *Ibid.*, pp. 181, 222

122 *Cartae et Alia Munimenta*, vol. v, no. 1836

123 C Inq Misc, IV, 391; V, 271

124 As at Haverford: *Calendar of Public Records, Pembrokeshire*, p. 66; *Lancashire Inquests, Extents and Feudal Aids* part 3, *1313–1355*, ed. W. Farrer, L & C Rec Soc, 70 (1915), 68

125 *Calendar of Public Records, Pembrokeshire*, p. 28

126 C Inq Misc, V, no. 113

127 C. Inq Misc, I, no. 953

128 As at Overton Castle, Cheshire: *Accounts of the Chamberlains of Chester*, p. 9; C Lib R, 1267–72, 533

129 CCR, 1227–31, 18

130 CCR, 1237–42, 281; the castle is on chalk, and it is surprising that the ditch was capable of holding water

131 CCR, 1237–42, 31

132 C Lib R, 1260–7, 190

133 CCR, 1237–42, 279; 1254–6, 90

134 CCR, 1259–61, 325; 1296–1302, 51; C Lib R, 1260–7, 128

135 CCR, 1296–1302, 535

136 *Ancient Petitions Relating to Northumberland*, pp. 176–7

137 *Lancashire Inquests and Extents*, p. 78

138 C Inq Misc, I, no. 1741

139 *Flintshire Ministers' Accounts 1301–1328*, Flint HS, 1913, 48; for comparable expenses at Rhuddlan, see *ibid.*, p. 17

140 C Inq pm, II, 813

141 C. E. Hart, *Royal Forest*, Oxford, 1966

142 CCR, 1251–3, 331

143 CCR, 1251–3, 306; C Inq Misc, I, 247

144 *rogum*, probably a lime kiln; CCR, 1256–9, 248

145 CCR, 1251–3, 167; *Accounts of the Constables of Bristol Castle*, ed. M. Sharp, Brist RS, 34 (1982), xlvii–liii

146 CCR, 1237–42, 56

147 CCR, 1237–42, 29, 40, 57, 96; 1247–51, 461

148 CCR, 1237–42, 39, 85, 159, 163, 279

149 CCR, 1237–42, 367

150 CPR, 1301–7, 362

151 CCR, 1247–58, 459; probably Alice Holt Forest was meant

152 C Inq Misc, II, no. 1649

153 C Inq Misc, I, p. 279

154 C Inq Misc, I, no. 1394

155 C Inq Misc, I, no. 998; Rot Hundr, II, 407, 452

156 CPR, 1388–92, 308–9; 1399–1401, 539

157 As at Rhuddlan in 1283; CCR, 1279–88, 216

158 As at Carlisle – £9..2..4 a year: *The Pipe Rolls of Cumberland and Westmorland*, ed. H. M. Parker, CWAAS, extra ser, 12 (1905), 197

159 CPR, 1396–9, 285; C Inq Misc, VI, no. 228; CPR, 1247–58, 99, where the castle was farmed for £50

160 *Calendar of the Public Records, Pembrokeshire*, vol. II, p. 7

161 As at Clun, Oswestry and Shrawardine: C Lib R, 1226–40, 458. For Shrawardine, here called 'Castell Philipp', see C Inq Misc, VI, no. 237

162 On this see M. Altschul, *A Baronial Family in Medieval England: the Clares, 1217–1314*, Johns Hopkins University Studies, 83, no. 2 (1965), 246–50

163 C Fine R, 1272–1307, 459

164 CPR, 1301–7, 76

165 CPR, 1247–58, 416

166 CPR, 1247–58, 417, 449

167 *Ancient Petitions relating to Northumberland*, nos 96, 108; *Three Early Assize Rolls for the County of Northumberland*, Surt Soc 88 (1891), p. 115; Rot Hundr, I, 110, 112

168 Rot Hundr, I, 111

169 Rot Hundr, II, 188

170 *Rolls of the Justices in Eyre for Yorkshire, 1218–19*, ed. D. M. Stenton, Seld Soc, pp. 209, 424; C Inq Misc, I, no. 1127

171 C Inq Misc, VI, 126

172 C Inq Misc, II, no. 112

173 *Select Cases in the Court of King's Bench under Edward I*, vol. I, ed. G. O. Sayles, Seld Soc, 55, 1936

174 CPR, 1258–66, 333

175 CPR, 1266–72, 245

176 CPR, 1385–9, 261, 263

177 For Builth: CPR, 1292–1301, 162; 1313–17, 322, 325. For Montgomery, CPR, 1317–21, 170

178 CPR, 1292–1301, 474

179 As at Halton Castle, Cheshire: *Two Compoti of the Lancashire and Cheshire Manors of Henry de Lacy*, ed. P. A. Lyons, Cheth Soc, 112 (1884), 144

180 *Select Cases in the Court of King's Bench*, vol. I, pp. 113, 114

181 *Crown Pleas of the Devon Eyre of 1238*, ed. H. Summerson, D C Rec Soc, 28 (1985), 41

182 Rot Hundr, I, 131

183 *Regesta*, I, no. 62; renewed by Henry II, *ibid.*, II, no. 1060

184 *Regesta*, II, no. 1382

185 *Buckinghamshire*, RCHM, vol. II, p. 17 (Little Missendon); pp. 324–5 (Bolebec)

186 *Calendar of the County Court, City Court and Eyre Rolls of Chester, 1259–1297*, ed. R. Stewart-Brown, Cheth Soc, NS 84 (1925), 55

187 'Two Estate Surveys of the Fitzalan Earls of Arundel', ed. M. Clough, *Tr Shrop AS*, 67 (1969), 68

188 C Inq Misc, IV, no. 147

189 *An Abstract of the Feet of Fines relating to the County of Sussex*, ed. L. F. Salzman, Suss Rec Soc, 7 (1908), 59–62

190 L. F. Salzman, 'Documents relating to Pevensey Castle', *Suss Arch Collns*, 49 (1906), 1–30; W. Budgen, 'Pevensey Castle Guard and Endlewick Rents', *Suss Arch Collns*, 76 (1935), 115–34

191 *Documents and Extracts illustrating the Honour of Dunster*, ed. Sir H. C. Maxwell-Lyte, Som Rec Soc, 33 (1917–8), 17; see also Cur Reg R, 15, 421

192 *Calendar of the Public Records, Pembrokeshire*, vol. I, *Lordship of Haverford*, p. 41; *Borough Customs*, ed. M. Bateson, vol. II, Seld Soc, 21 (1906), 161–6

193 *Ancient Petitions relating to Northumberland*, no. 183

194 CPR, 1388–92, 9; repeated with additions, 48

195 C Inq Misc, IV, no. 147

196 CPR, 1385–9, 160

197 CPR, 1381–5, 553

198 CPR, 1321–4, 288–9
199 CPR, 1350–4, 233
200 C Inq Misc, IV, no. 92
201 C Inq Misc, II, no. 1381
202 *Ancient Petitions relating to Northumberland*, no. 156
203 *Ibid.*, no. 22
204 W. D. Simpson, 'Dunstanburgh Castle', *Arch Ael*, 4th ser., 16 (1939), 31–42
205 Sir Robert Bowes, *Book of the State of the Marches* (1550) as quoted in W. D. Simpson, 'Dunstanburgh Castle', *Arch Ael*, 4th ser., 16 (1939), 31–42
206 C Inq Misc, VII, 141
207 C Inq Misc, VII, 273
208 CCR, 1323–7, 627
209 CCR, 1234–7, 424; 1253–4, 274–5
210 C Lib R, 1260–7, 188
211 C Lib R, 1260–7, 202
212 CCR, 1237–42, 210, 382–3, 442; C Lib R, 1240–5, 37; 1226–40, 433 446, 459
213 CCR, 1231–4, 101
214 C Lib R, 1245–51, 4
215 P. Crummy, *Aspects of Anglo-Saxon and Norman Colchester*, CBA Res Rept 39, 1981; P. J. Drury, 'Aspects of the Origin and Development of Colchester Castle', *Arch Jl*, 139 (1982), 302–419
216 Gloucester Cartulary, RS, I, 318. The Pipe Roll of 31 Henry I mentions £7..6..8 *in operationibus turris Gloec.* See also *Regesta*, II, no. 706; T. Darvill, 'Excavations on the Site of the Early Norman Castle at Gloucester, 1983–84', *Med Arch*, 32 (1988), 1–49
217 L. E. W. O. Fullbrook-Leggatt, 'Medieval Gloucester', *TrBGAS*, 66 (1945), 1–48. For an analogous case at Bourg l'Evèque in Normandy see C Docts Fr, vol. I, no. 1021. Other exchanges of land are mentioned above, p. 000
218 CPR, 1216–25, 29
219 CPR, 1232–47, 167
220 'Ministers' Accounts of the Honor of Leicester (1322–1324)', ed. Levi Fox, *Tr LeicAS*, 19 (1936–7), 199–273; 20 (1938–9), 77–158
221 C Lib R, 1245–51, 36
222 C Chart R, I, 434
223 CCR, 1296–1302, 261; *KW*, II, 716.17
224 C Inq Misc, III, no. 1016
225 *Ancient Petitions relating to Northumberland*, no. 181; C Inq Misc, II, 384–5
226 CPR, 1232–47, 39, 74
227 J. N. Langston, 'Priors of Lanthony by Gloucester', *TrBGAS*, 63 (1942), 1–144 (p. 52)
228 *The Marcher Lordships of South Wales: Select Documents*, p. 163
229 J. W. F. Hill, *Medieval Lincoln*, Cambridge, 1948
230 CPR, 1399–1401, 218
231 *The Red Paper Book of Colchester*, ed. W. Gurney Bentham, Colchester, 1902, p. 8
232 P. J. Drury, 'Aspects of the Origins of Colchester Castle'
233 CCR, 1343–6, 528
234 C Fine R, 1272–1307, 524
235 CCR, 1374–7, 532
236 *Lancashire Inquests and Extents*, part 3, p. 193
237 *Regesta*, II, no. 991
238 It probably lay outside the ramparts of the Anglo-Saxon burh, but inside the Roman; see *Medieval Worcester*, ed. M. O. H. Carver, *Tr Worcs AS*, 3rd Ser., 7 (1980), 55–8 and fig. 2

239 CPR, 1216–25, 46; 52

240 Rot Lit Claus, I, 335b; *The Cartulary of Worcester Cathedral Priory*, ed. J. Darlington, vol. I, PRS, 38, 174

241 *Ancient Petitions relating to Northumberland*, no. 51

242 Records of the City of Norwich, I, xlii

243 C Chart R, V, 421; confirmed, *ibid.*, VI, 145

244 F. R. Beechano, *Notes on Norwich Castle*, privately printed, 1888, pp. 15–17

245 Samuel Weston's Map of Chester, published by James Hunter, 1798

246 R. H. Morris, *Chester in the Plantagenet and Tudor Reigns*, privately printed, n.d., but *c*. 1895, pp. 107–9; *Calendar of Chester City Council Minutes 1603–1642*, ed. J. Groombridge, L & C Rec Soc, 106 (1956), ii–iii

247 C Chart R, VI, 155

248 CCR, 1429–35, 106

249 C Chart R, VI, 64

250 Records of Norwich, xlii

251 L. Fox, 'Ministers' Accounts of the Honor of Leicester'

252 C Lib R, 1226–40, 230

253 *City of York*, RCHM, vol. 2, *The Defences*, pp. 59–66

254 R. M. Serjeantson, *The Castle of Northampton*, Northampton, 1908; *An Inventory of Archaeological Sites and Churches in Northampton*, RCHM, 1985, pp. 47–50

255 R. A. Brown, *Rochester Castle*, HMSO, 1969, plan

256 *Regesta*, II, no. 1118

257 Rhuddlan may be a marginal case; see H. Miles, 'Excavations at Rhuddlan, 1969–71: Interim Report', *Flint HS*, 25 (1971–2), 1–8; A. J. Taylor, *Rhuddlan Castle*, HMSO, 1956

258 *Records of the Borough of Leicester*, ed. M. Bateson, vol. I, London, 1899, pp. 10–11; The Pipe Rolls of Cumberland and Westmorland 1222–1260, ed. F. H. M. Parker, *CWAAS*, extra ser. 12 (1905), *passim*

259 *The Welsh Assize Roll 1277–1284*, ed. J. C. Davies, Bd Celt St, 7, 1940, 180–1

260 This advantage cannot be quantified; see H. A. Cronne, *The Borough of Warwick in the Middle Ages*, Dugd Soc Occ Pap, 10 (1951), 13

261 *R B Exch*, II, 466; *Ancient Petitions relating to Northumberland*, ed. C. M. Fraser, Surt Soc, 176 (1961), no. 41, p. 56

262 *The Lancashire Pipe Rolls and Early Charters*, ed. W. Farrer, Liverpool, 1902, pp. 141–2

263 H. G. Richardson, *The English Jewry under Angevin Kings*, London, 1960, pp. 7–9

264 R. Davies, 'The Mediaeval Jews of York', *Yorks AJ*, 3 (1875), 147–97; M. Adler, 'Jews in Medieval England', Jew H S (1939), 127–73

265 C. Roth, 'Medieval Lincoln Jewry and its Synagogue', Jew H S (1934), 28

266 V. D. Lipman, 'The Jews of Medieval Norwich', Jew H S (1967), 17–18

267 S. Cohen, 'The Oxford Jewry in the Thirteenth Century', Jew H S, 13 (1936), 293–322

268 CPR, 1258–66, 320–1

269 M. Beresford, *New Towns of the Middle Ages*, London, 1967, pp. 125–9

270 DB, i, 248b

271 M. Bateson, 'The Laws of Breteuil', *EHR*, 15 (1900), 73–8, 302–18, 496–523, 754–7; 16 (1901), 92–110, 332–45; A. Ballard, 'The Law of Breteuil.', *EHR* 30 (1915), 646–58

272 E. A. Lewis, *Medieval Boroughs of Snowdonia*, London, 1912, pp. 152–7. Holt appears to have been the only exception: D. Pratt, 'The Medieval Borough of Holt', *Tr Denb HS*, 14 (1965), 9–74, but Holt was a baronial (de Warenne) borough

273 M. Bateson, 'The Laws of Breteuil'

274 *The Parliamentary Survey of the Duchy of Cornwall*, ed. N. J. G. Pounds, D C Rec Soc, part 2, NS 27

275 'The Caption of Seisin of the Duchy of Cornwall (1337)', ed. P. L. Hull, D C Rec Soc, 17 (1971), 119–20

9 CASTLE AND CHURCH

1 '. . . if a ceorl throve so that he had fully five hides of his own land, church and kitchen, bell-house and burh-gate, seat and special duty in the king's hall, then was he thenceforth of thegn-right worthy' (W. Stubbs, *Select Charters*, p. 88)
2 CCR, 1242–7, 24
3 CCR, 1234–7, 443
4 C Lib R, 1240–5, 104
5 C. A. Ralegh Radford, *Restormel Castle*, HMSO, 1965; S Toy, 'Round Castles of Cornwall', *Arch*, 83 (1933), 220–6
6 R. A. Brown, *Orford Castle Suffolk*, HMSO, 1964
7 C. H. Hartshorne, 'Conway Castle', *Arch Camb*, NS 17 (1854), 1–12
8 Sir Charles Peers, *Richmond Castle Yorkshire*, HMSO, 1953
9 J. H. Denton, *English Royal Free Chapels 1100–1300: A Constitutional Study*, Manchester 1970, p. 5
10 CCR, 1381–5, 321
11 CCR, 1242–7, 208, 225; timber from Rockingham Forest; roofing tiles from a collapsed stable: *ibid.*, 283
12 CCR, 1247–51, 321
13 C Lib R, 1240–45, 257
14 C Lib R, 1245–51, 192
15 C Lib R, 1245–51, 246
16 C Chart R, 1257–1300, 69; this is an *inspeximus* of an earlier charter
17 C Inq pm, VI, 759
18 CCR, 1360–4, 281
19 CCR, 1360–4, 160
20 CCR, Hen IV, vol. I, 163
21 CCR, 1364–8, 399
22 CPR, 1361–4, 344
23 CPR, 1272–81, 270
24 CCR, 1234–7, 428
25 CPR, 1416–22, 310
26 *Regesta*, III, no. 632; a confirmation by Queen Matilda of an earlier charter. Stephen further confirmed the grant, *ibid.*, no. 633.
27 C Chart R, 1300–26, 420
28 CCR, 1323–7, 95
29 *Regesta*, II, no. 1159. St Mary's was an Augustinian Priory
30 C Chart R, 1327–41, 10
31 *Regesta*, II, no. 1486; Stephen's confirmation, *Regesta* III, no. 435 mentions also the tithes belonging to the chapel
32 W. Dugdale, *Monasticon Anglicanum*, 1825 edn, vol. III, pp. 547–8
33 CCR, 1302–7, 26; CPR, 1377–81, 553
34 CCR, 1330–3, 356
35 CCR, 1349–54, 22, 72
36 CPR, 1348–50, 355. The advowson later passed into lay hands: C Inq pm, IX, 52. The 'old' castle is now represented by a degraded motte on the eastern edge of Basing
37 *Farleigh Hungerford Castle*, HMSO, 1989

38 T. J. Miles and A. D. Saunders, 'The Chantry Priests' House, at Farleigh Hungerford Castle', *Med Arch*, 19 (1975), 165–94

39 C Chart R, I, 109

40 J. McNulty, 'The Endowment of the Chapel of St Michael in Clitheroe Castle', *TrHSLC*, 91 (1939), 159–63; J. McNulty, 'Clitheroe Castle and its Chapel: their Origins', *TrHSLC*, 93 (1942), 45–53; W. Dugdale, *Monasticon Anglicanum*, edn of 1825, vol. V, p. 121

41 A. J. Taylor, 'Evidence for a pre-Conquest Origin for the Chapels in Hastings and Pevensey Castle', *Chât Gaill*, 3 (1969), 144–51

42 *Ibid.*; Sir Charles Peers, *Pevensey Castle*, HMSO, 1953

43 *Regesta*, III, no. 184

44 F. G. Heys, 'Excavations at Castle Green, 1960: A Lost Hereford Church', *TrW Woolh FC*, 36 (1958–60), 343–54

45 VCH, *Warwickshire*, vol. VIII, p. 532

46 J. Haslam, 'Parishes, Churches, Wards and Gates in Eastern London', in *Minsters and Parish Churches*, ed. J. Blair, Oxford, 1988, pp. 35–43

47 *Med Arch*, 8 (1964), 255–6. This corrects the plan given in *KW* II, 709

48 *The Tower of London: its Buildings and Institutions*, ed. J. Charlton, HMSO, 1978, p. 132

49 H. M. and J. Taylor, *Anglo-Saxon Architecture*, Cambridge, 1965, vol. I, pp. 214–17

50 *KW*, II, 629–41

51 C Lib R, 1251–60, 32. There were also bells in the chapel of Marlborough Castle, C Lib R, 1251–60, 62

52 CCR, 1377–81, 292; CCR, 1385–9, 56; CCR, 1392–6, 170; CCR, 1396–9, 9; CCR, Hen IV, I, 84, 152, 344

53 CPR, 1374–7, 407

54 C Inq pm, V, 533

55 C Inq pm, IX, 52

56 CPR, 1281–92, 495

57 *An Inventory of Early Chancery Proceedings concerning Wales*, ed. E. A. Lewis, Bd Celt St, 3 (1937), 249. This chapel received tithes from certain lands: R. W. Eyton, *Antiquities of Shropshire*, London, 1860, vol. X, p. 345

58 CPR, 1358–61, 511

59 W. Stubbs, *Select Charters*, pp. 450–2. The king reserved the right to waive the statute, and, in fact, made much use of this right: F. M. Powicke, *The Thirteenth Century*, Oxford, 1953, p. 325

60 *Documents Relating to the Priory of Penwortham*, ed. W. A. Hulton, Cheth Soc, 1853, I

61 E. S. Armitage, *The Early Norman Castles of the British Isles*, London, 1912, pp. 183–5

62 R. F. Butler, 'Brimpsfield Church History', *TrBGAS*, 81 (1962), 73–87; 82 (1963), 127–42

63 L. C. Lloyd, 'The Origin of the Family of Aubigny of Cainhoe', *Beds HRS*, 19 (1937), 101–9

64 J. Blair, 'Secular Minster Churches in Domesday Book', in *Domesday Book: A Reassessment*, ed. P. Sawyer, London, 1985, pp. 104–42

65 A. J. Taylor, 'Chapels in Hastings and Pevensey Castles'

66 Plan in C. Dawson, *History of Hastings Castle*, London, 1909, vol. I, p. 495

67 *Ibid.*, vol. I, p. 106

68 *Ibid.*, vol. I, p. 151

69 *Ibid.*, vol. I, p. 161

70 *BE: Sussex*, pp. 118–19

71 T. P. Hudson, 'The Origins of Steyning and Bramber', *South H*, 2 (1980), 11–29

72 DB, i, 253; J. A. Morris, 'Shrewsbury Castle: An Historical Sketch', *Tr Shrop AS*, 49 (1937), 97–118

73 CPR, 1247–58, 411; CPR, 1330–4, 58

74 W. G. D. Fletcher, 'The Church of St Michael within the Castle, Shrewsbury', *Tr Shrop AS*, 4th ser., 8 (1920–1), 254–9

75 J. F. A. Mason and P. A. Barker, 'The Norman Castle of Quatford', *Tr Shrop AS*, 57 (1961–4), 37–62; *Med Arch*, 5 (1961), 319

76 W. G. Clark-Maxwell and A. Hamilton Thompson, 'The College of St Mary Magdalene, Bridgnorth, with some Account of its Deans and Prebendaries', *Arch Jl*, 84 (1927), 1–87; A. Hamilton Thompson, 'Notes on Colleges of Secular Canons in England', *Arch Jl*, 74 (1917), 139–239

77 W. G. Clark-Maxwell, 'The Chantries of St Leonard's Church, Bridgnorth', *Tr Shrop AS*, 4th ser., 8 (1920–1), 209–45

78 R. Hughes, 'The Foundation of St Clement's in the Castle of Pontefract', *Yorks AJ*, 14 (1898), 147–57. This article corrects and elaborates the charters given in W. Dugdale, *Monasticon Anglicanum*, edn of 1825, vol. V, pp. 118–121

79 G. Tate, *The History of the Borough, Castle and Barony of Alnwick*, Alnwick, 1869, vol. II, pp. 66–8

80 L. Fox, *Leicester Castle*, Leicester, 1944, pp. 7–9

81 A. Hamilton Thompson, 'Notes on Colleges of Secular Canons'

82 CPR, Hen VI, I, 162

83 'Wallingford', in *Historic Towns in Oxfordshire*, ed. K. Rodwell, Oxfordshire Archaeological Unit, Survey 3, 1975, pp. 155–62; *Monasticon Anglicanum*, VI, 1330. An *inspeximus* is given in C Chart R, 1257–1300, 209, 269

84 CPR, 1361–4, 35; C Chart R, 1257–1300, 209; CPR, 1301–7, 197; CPR, 1361–4, 35; CPR, 1388–92, 4

85 CCR, 1441–7, 251

86 J. K. Hedges, *The History of Wallingford*, London, 1881, vol. II, pp. 285–90; CPR, 1388–92, 4

87 CPR, 1446–52, 80

88 Miss Haddon, 'Caistor Castle', *JBAA*, 36 (1880), 22–6

89 A. D. K. Hawkyard, 'Thornbury Castle', *TrBGAS*, 95 (1977), 51–8

90 C. H. Hunter Blair and H. L. Honeyman, *Warkworth Castle, Northumberland*, HMSO, 1974; *BE: Northumberland*, 1957, pp. 313–18; W. D. Simpson, 'Warkworth: A Castle of Livery and Maintenance', *Arch Ael*, 4th ser., 15 (1938), 115–36

91 CPR, 1391–6, 224; D. Knowles and R. N. Hadcock, *Medieval Religious Houses: England and Wales*, London, 1953, p. 355

92 CPR, 1399–1401, 344

93 CCR, Hen IV, IV, 317

94 R. Marks, 'The Glazing of the Collegiate Church of the Holy Trinity, Tattershall', *Arch*, 106 (1979), 133–56

95 C Lib R, 1240–5, 265; CCR, 1251–3, 306; W. H. St John Hope, *Windsor Castle: An Architectural History*, London, 1913

96 A. K. B. Roberts, *St George's Chapel Windsor Castle 1348–1416: A Study in Early Collegiate Administration*, Windsor, 1947, p. 4

97 *KW*, II, 872–4

98 D. Knoop and G. P. Jones, 'The Impressment of Masons for Windsor Castle, 1360–63', *Econ H*, 3 (1934–7), 350–61

99 *KW*, II, 874

100 Folding plan *in KW* II, Plans

101 W. H. St John Hope, *Windsor Castle*, London, 1913, vol. II, pp. 374–477

102 *The Vision of Piers Plowman*, B Text, passus 19, ll. 462–6

103 *The Tower of London*, ed. J. Charlton, pp. 46–51

104 *Essex*, vol. III, *North-East*, RCHM, pp. 51–4; P. J. Drury, 'Aspects of the Origins and Development of Colchester Castle', *Arch Jl*, 139 (1982), 302–419

105 W. H. Knowles, 'The Castle of Newcastle upon Tyne', *Arch Ael*, 4th ser., 2 (1926), 1–51

106 R. A. Brown, *Dover Castle*, HMSO, 1966

107 R. A. Brown, *Rochester Castle*, HMSO, 1969, pp. 42–3

108 R. A. Brown, *Orford Castle Suffolk*, HMSO, 1964, pp. 14–16

109 M. W. Thompson, *Conisbrough Castle*, HMSO, 1959, pp. 7–8

110 F. J. E. Raby and P. K. Baillie Reynolds, *Framlingham Castle*, HMSO, 1938. pp. 23–4

111 C. A. Ralegh Radford, *White Castle*, HMSO, 1962, pp. 10–11

112 C. A. Ralegh Radford, *Goodrich Castle*, HMSO, 1933, pp. 10–12

113 C Lib R, 1245–51, 13

114 C Lib R, 1245–51, 45

115 C Lib R, 1245–51, 204, 208

116 C Lib R, 1251–60, 57; that the two were independent is apparent from C Lib R, 1251–60, 47 and 307

117 C Lib R, 1245–51, 157

118 C Lib R, 1251–60, 95

119 *Pipe Roll, 26 Henry III*, Yale Historical Publications, 1918

120 C Lib R, 1267–72, no. 2431. On St Josse see CCR, 1234–7, 431

121 Pipe Roll, 26 Henry III, 258–9

122 C Lib R, 1240–5, 136, 181, 242; for the chapel in the bailey, see C Lib R, 1240–5, 161. The 100s. spent on the latter suggests two chaplains

123 CPR, 1354–8, 12

124 C Lib R, 1245–51, 20, 54, 88, 115, 193, 209, 263, 284, 309, 383

125 As at Winchester, C Lib R, 1267–72, 549, 610; for Nottingham, C Lib R, 1245–51, 93; for Northampton, C Lib R, 1245–51, 191

126 J. H. Parker, *Some Account of Domestic Architecture in England*, Oxford, 1859, vol i, pp. 181–2; N. J. G. Pounds, 'Beverston Castle', *Arch Jl*, 145 (1988), suppl. 48–51

127 C Lib R, 1245–51, 247

128 C Lib R, 1245–51, 358; C Lib R, 1267–72, 1095

129 CCR, 1251–3, 126; C Lib R, 1251–60, 62

130 A new missal for the new chapel in the Tower of Southampton Castle cost 40s.: C Lib R, 1251–60, 526

131 As at Dover, C Lib R, 1245–51, 122–3

132 CCR, 1313–8, 107, 142, 371 and numerous later references

133 C Inq pm, VIII, 474

134 Instances are too numerous to cite. It is the exceptions from 50s. that arouse interest

135 Bl Pr Reg, part 2, 1351–65, 75

136 *Ibid.*, 185

10 THE CHANGING ROLE OF THE CASTLE

1 J. C. Davies, 'The Despenser War in Glamorgan', *TrRHS*, 3rd ser., 9 (1915), 21–64

2 K. B. McFarlane, 'Bastard Feudalism', *BIHR*, 20 (1943–5), 161–80

3 B. D. Lyon, 'The Money Fief under the English Kings, 1066–1485', *EHR*, 66 (1951), 161–93

4 N. B. Lewis, 'The Organisation of Indentured Retainers in Fourteenth Century England', *TrRHS*, 4th ser., 27 (1945), 29–39

5 A. E. Prince, 'The Indenture System under Edward III', in *Historical Essays in Honour of James Tait*, ed. J. G. Edwards, V. H. Galbraith and E. F. Jacob, Manchester, 1933, pp. 283–97

6 T. B. Pugh, 'The Magnates, Knights and Gentry', in *Fifteenth Century England*, ed. S. B. Chrimes, C. D. Ross and R. A. Griffiths, Manchester, 1972, pp. 86–128

7 *Ibid.*

8 B. D. Lyon, 'The Money Fief'

9 K. B. McFarlane, *The Nobility of Later Medieval England*, Oxford, 1973

10 C. Oman, *A History of the Art of War in the Middle Ages*, London, 1924, vol. II, pp. 226-7; B. H. St J. O'Neil, *Castles and Cannon*, Oxford, 1960, p. 2. For a recent survey, see Andrew Saunders, *Fortress Britain*, London, 1989, pp. 15-21

11 *Documents Illustrative of the History of Scotland, 1286-1306*, ed. J. Stevenson, Edinburgh, 1870, vol. II, no. 639; J. Burtt, 'Extracts from the Pipe Roll of the Exchequer, 27 Edward III (1353), Relating to the Early Use of Guns and Gunpowder in the English Army', *Arch Jl*, 19 (1862), 68-75

12 The term 'cannon' derives from the Latin *canna*, a 'tube', and 'gun' from its mechanical predecessor, the mangonel

13 A. R. Hall, 'Military Technology', in C. Singer et al., *A History of Technology*, vol. II, 1956, pp. 695-730

14 P. Contamine, *War in the Middle Ages*, trans. M. Jones, Oxford, 1984, pp. 142-3

15 H. W. L. Hime, 'Our Earliest Cannon 1314-1346', *Pr R Art S*, 31 (1904-5), 489-94

16 T. F. Tout, 'Firearms in England in the Fourteenth Century', *EHR*, 26 (1911), 666-702

17 P. Contamine, *War in the Middle Ages*, pp. 200-1

18 CPR, 1476-85, 448, when William Nele, 'gunnoure', received a pension of 6d a day for 'making cannon within the Tower'; B. H. St John O'Neil, *Castles and Cannon*, p. 4

19 T. F. Tout, 'Firearms in England'; there was also a 'powder house' within the Tower, CPR, 1461-67, 23; 1476-85, 383

20 CPR, 1452-61, 20

21 CPR, 1399-1401, 99-100; 1401-5, 433, 504; 1452-61, 110

22 J. R. Kenyon, 'Early Artillery Fortifications in England and Wales: a Preliminary Survey and Reappraisal', *Arch Jl*, 138 (1981), 205-40

23 L. B. L., 'Cowling Castle', *Arch Cant*, 2 (1859), 95-102

24 J. R. Kenyon, 'Artillery and the Defences of Southampton c. 1360-1660', *Fort*, 3 (1977), 8-14

25 D. F. Renn, 'The Earliest Gunports in Britain?', *Arch Jl*, 225 (1968), 301-3

26 J. R. Kenyon, 'Early Gunports: A Gazetteer', *Fort*, 4 (1977), 4-6; A. M. T. Maxwell-Irving, 'Early Firearms and their Influence on the Military and Domestic Architecture of the Borders', *Proc SAS*, 103 (1970-1), 192-244

27 C. A. Ralegh Radford, *Tretower Court and Castle*, HMSO, 1969

28 C Docts Scotl, III, 1307-57, no. 1542

29 M. W. Thompson has gathered together John Leland's observations on the condition of castles in his day: *The Decline of the Castle*, Cambridge, 1987, App. 2, pp. 171-8

30 Leland, III, 107

31 Leland, I, 99

32 Leland, III, 18

33 R. Somerville, *History of the Duchy of Lancaster*, London, 1953, pp. 17-24; S. Armitage-Smith, *John of Gaunt*, London, 1904, pp. 216-18

34 S. Armitage-Smith, *John of Gaunt*, p. 218

35 *John of Gaunt's Register, 1379-1383*, ed. E. Lodge and R. Somerville, Camd Soc, 3rd ser., vols. 56 and 57, 1937

36 P. L. Drewett, 'Excavations at Hadleigh Castle, Essex, 1971-72', *JBAA*, 38 (1975), 90-154; J. Charlton, ed., *The Tower of London*, HMSO, 1978, folding plan

37 William of Worcester, *Itineraries*, ed. J. H. Harvey, Oxford, 1969, pp. 399-400

38 *KW*, I, 228-41

39 R. A. Brown, *Dover Castle*, HMSO, 1966, p. 9

40 *KW*, II, 783-92

41 CPR, 1377-81, 284

42 C. Platt, *Medieval Southampton: the Port and Trading Community, A.D. 1000-1600*, London, 1973, pp. 126-9; *KW*, II, 840-4

43 *Dorset*, RCHM, vol. II, part 1 (1970), pp. 57–64

44 *KW*, II, 778–9

45 There were, however, licences to crenellate the *towns* of Aberystwyth, Montgomery and Deganwy

46 J. Le Patourel, 'Fortified and Semi-fortified Manor Houses in Eastern and Northern England in the Later Middle Ages', in *La Maison Forte au Moyen Age*, ed. M. Bur, Paris, 1986, pp. 17–29

47 J. Charlton, *Brougham Castle*, HMSO, 1985

48 P. J. Leach, 'Excavations at Stoke-sub-Hamdon Castle, Somerset, 1976', *Pr Som AS*, 124 (1980), 61–76

49 J. Collinson

50 H. Brakspear, 'The Bishop's Palace, Sonning', *BBOAJ*, 22 (1916), 9–21

51 N. D. McGlashan and R. E. Sandell, 'The Bishop of Salisbury's House at his Manor of Potterne', *WAM*, 69 (1974), 85–96

52 VCH, *Sussex*, vol. IV, p. 134

53 N. Denholm-Young, *Seigneurial Administration in England*, Oxford, 1937, p. 22

54 C. Ross, 'The Estates and Finances of Richard Beauchamp, Earl of Warwick', *Dugd Soc Occ Pap*, 12 (1956), 8–9

55 J. F. Baldwin, 'The Household Administration of Henry Lacy and Thomas of Lancaster', *EHR*, 42 (1927), 180–200; L. Fox, 'Ministers' Accounts of the Honor of Leicester', *Tr Leic AS*, 19 (1936–7), 199–273; 20 (1938–9), 77–158

56 J. M. W. Bean, *The Estates of the Percy Family 1416–1537*, Oxford, 1958, p. 7

57 J. Le Patourel, in *La Maison Forte au Moyen Age*, pp. 17–29

58 B. A. Hanawalt, *Crime and Conflict in English Communities 1300–1348*, Cambridge, Mass., 1979, pp. 64–96

59 CPR, 1321–4, 157

60 CPR, 1327–30, 148

61 CPR, 1330–4, 236

62 CPR, 1374–7, 229

63 CPR, 1374–7, 217

64 CPR, 1381–5, 259

65 CPR, 1391–6, 357

66 CPR, 1391–6, 273, 552–3

67 CPR, 1401–5, 211

68 CPR, 1413–6, 65. This is an extremely high valuation

69 R. M. Clay, *The Mediaeval Hospitals of England*, London, 1909, *passim*

70 N. W. Alcock et al., Maxstoke Castle, Warwickshire', *Arch Jl*, 135 (1978), 195–233

71 A. Emery, *Dartington Hall*, Oxford, 1970 contains an extended discussion of these late 'castles', pp. 226–58

72 H. D. Barnes and W. D. Simpson, 'The Building Accounts of Caistor Castle, 1432–1435', *Norf Arch*, 30 (1952), 178–88

73 Barnes and Simpson, 'Caistor Castle', *Ant Jl*, 32 (1952), 35–51

74 Paston Letters, I, 427

75 C. Kerry, 'Codnor Castle and its Ancient Owners', *JlDerbAS*, 14 (1892), 16–33

76 CPR, 1381–5, 340

77 *Farleigh Hungerford Castle*, HMSO, 1983

78 Sir Charles Peers, *Kirby Muxloe Castle*, HMSO, 1957

79 S. E. Rigold, *Baconsthorpe Castle*, HMSO, 1966

80 A. Emery, 'Ralph Lord Cromwell's Manor at Wingfield (1439–1450): its Construction, Design and Influence', *Arch Jl*, 142 (1985), 276–339; M. W. Thompson, 'The Construction of the Manor at South Wingfield, Derbyshire', in *Problems in Economic and Social Archaeology*, ed. G. de G. Sieveking et al., London, 1976, pp. 417–38

81 A. Emery, *Dartington Hall* contains, pp. 226–37, a discussion of comparable semi-fortified palaces

82 A. D. K. Hawkyard, 'Thornbury Castle', *TrBGAS*, 95 (1877), 51–8

83 *L & P Hen VIII*, 506

84 W. D. Simpson, 'Dunstanburgh Castle', *Arch Ael*, 4th ser., 16 (1939), 31–42

85 D. J. C. King, *Llanstephan Castle Carmarthenshire*, HMSO, 1963

86 C. A. Ralegh Radford, *Kidwelly Castle*, HMSO, 1952

87 P. E. Curnow, 'The Tower House at Hopton Castle and its Affinities', in *Studies in Medieval History presented to R. Allen Brown*, ed. C. Harper-Bill, C. Holdsworth and J. L. Nelson, Woodbridge, 1989, pp. 81–102

88 J. West, 'Acton Burnell Castle, Shropshire', in *Collectanea Historica: Essays in Memory of Stuart Rigold*, Maidstone, 1981, pp. 85–92

89 W. D. Simpson, 'The Castles of Dudley and Ashby-de-la-Zouch', *Arch Jl*, 96 (1939), 142–58

90 *Med Arch*, 23 (1979), 262; 25 (1981), 202; 29 (1985), 198–9

91 S. E. Rigold, *Nunney Castle*, HMSO, 1957

92 W. D. Simpson, 'The Warkworth Donjon and its Architect', *Arch Ael*, 4th ser., 19 (1941), 93–103; W. D. Simpson 'Warkworth, a Castle of Livery and Maintenance', *Arch Ael*, 4th ser., 15 (1938), 115–36; C. H. Hunter Blair and H. L. Honeyman, *Warkworth Castle, Northumberland*, HMSO, 1954

93 B. M. Morley, *Hylton Castle, Tyne and Wear*, HMSO, 1979

94 R. B. Pugh and A. D. Saunders, *Old Wardour Castle, Wiltshire*, HMSO, 1968

95 *The Building Accounts of Tattershall Castle 1434–1472*, ed. W. D. Simpson, Lincs RS, 55, 1960

96 A. Hamilton Thompson, *Tattershall: the Manor, the Castle and the Church*, Lincoln, 1928, pp. 11–12

97 *Huntingdonshire*, RCHM, 1926, pp. 34–8

98 M. W. Thompson, 'The Date of "Fox's Tower", Farnham Castle, Surrey', *Surr Arch Collns*, 57 (1960), 85–92

99 A. J. Taylor, *Raglan Castle*, HMSO, 1950; A. Emery, 'The Development of Raglan Castle and Keeps in Late Medieval England', *Arch Jl*, 132 (1975), 151–86; J. R. Kenyon, *Raglan Castle*, HMSO, 1988

100 T. L. Jones, *Ashby de la Zouch Castle*, HMSO, 1953

101 'Indentures of Retinue with John of Gaunt, Duke of Lancaster, Enrolled in Chancery 1367–1399', ed. N. B. Lewis, Camd Misc, 22, Camd Soc, 4th ser., (1964), 77–112

102 *The Vision of Piers Plowman*, B Text, passus X, ll. 94–9

103 P. A. Faulkner, 'Castle Planning in the Fourteenth Century', *Arch Jl*, 120 (1963), 215–35

104 *Ibid.*, 227

105 F. R. H. Du Boulay, *An Age of Ambition*, London, 1970, p. 65

106 Rot Parl, III, 415

11 TOWER-HOUSE, PELE AND BASTLE

1 D. Pringle, 'A Group of Medieval Towers in Tuscania', *Pap BSR*, 42 (1974), 179–223; A. W. Lawrenc, 'Early Medieval Fortifications near Rome', *Pap BSR*, 32 (1964), 89–122; A. Settia, 'La casa forte urbana nell'Italia centrosettentrionale: Lo sviluppo di un modello', in *La Maison Forte au Moyen Age*, ed. M. Bur, Paris, 1986, pp. 325–30

2 Salimbene, *MGH*, 32, pp. 222

3 A. Settia, 'La casa forte'

4 J. K. Hyde, *Society and Politics in Medieval Italy: the Evolution of Civil Life, 1000–1350*, London, 1973

5 Its foundations have probably been found near Ludgate Circus; see *The Times*, 31 July, 1989

6 The castle known from Aga's engraving was a later construction on a different site.

7 The Eyre of London, 14 Edward II, ed. H. Cam, Seld Soc, 2 (1968–9), 170–3

8 Quoted in J. H. Round, *Geoffrey de Mandeville*, London, 1892, p. 89

9 *Calendar of the Letter Books of the City of London*, Book C, p. 143

10 *Ibid.*, Book H, p. 155

11 *Ibid.*, Book G, p. 24

12 CPR, 1338–40, 62

13 CPR, 1385–9, 42

14 CPR, 1292–1301, 30

15 CPR, 1391–6, 133

16 M. Biddle, 'Wolvesey: the *Domus quasi palatium* of Henry de Blois in Winchester', *Chât Gaill*, 3 (1969), 28–36

17 A. W. Goodman, *The Manor of Godbegot in the City of Winchester*, Winchester, 1923; B. Cunliffe, *Winchester Excavations 1949–60*, vol. I, Winchester, 1964, pp. 49ff

18 J. W. F. Hill, 'The Manor of Hungate or Beaumont Fee in the City of Lincoln', RPAS Lincs, 38 (1926–7), 175–208

19 *The Registrum Antiquissimum of the Cathedral Church of Lincoln*, ed. C. W. Foster, vol. I, Lincs RS, 1931, pp. 277–82

20 CPR, 1405–8, 3

21 D. F. Renn, 'The Castles of Rye and Winchelsea', *Arch Jl*, 136 (1979), 193–202

22 CPR, 1405–8, 3

23 M. Barley, *Houses and History*, London, 1986, pp. 116–17

24 *BE: Cumberland and Westmorland*, 1967, p. 21

25 P. Smith, *Houses of the Welsh Countryside*, RCAHM(W), 1975, p. 338

26 M. Barley, 'Nottinghamshire Medieval Manor Houses', *Nottm Med St*, 32 (1988), 167–75

27 M. Wood, *The English Medieval House*, London, 1965, pp. 166–75

28 M. Barley, 'Nottinghamshire Medieval Manor Houses'

29 *VAG Newsl*, no. 12, Jan. 1987

30 *The History of Lympne and its Castle*, privately printed and sold locally

31 *Dorset*, RCHM, vol. II, part 2, pp. 294–5 and Pl. 157

32 V. M. and F. J. Chesher, *The Cornishman's House*, Truro, 1968, p. 27

33 'Kyme Castle: the Tower', *Arch Jl*, 103 (1946), 189–90

34 T. P. Smith, 'Hussey Tower, Boston: A Late Medieval Tower-house of Brick', Lincs AHA, 14 (1979), 31–7

35 Pevsner dates them to c. 1510: *BE: Lincolnshire*, p. 633; Barley gives c. 1460 for Rochford Tower. This writer prefers the earlier date.

36 *Buckinghamshire, North*, RCHM, pp. 94–8

37 C. A. Markham, 'Astwell Castle in Northamptonshire', AASRP, 27 (1923–4), 308–15

38 *Cambridge*, RCHM, vol. II, pp. 381–2; M. Wood, *The English Medieval House*, p. 167

39 *Ibid.*, p. 171

40 *Ibid.*, pp. 22–3

41 P. J. Tester, 'The Ruined Buildings Adjoining Nurstead Court', *Arch Cant*, 98 (1982), 241–3

42 K. W. E. Gravett and D. F. Renn, 'The Tower of Stone Castle, Greenhithe', *Arch Cant*, 97 (1981), 312–18

43 M. Wood, *The English Medieval House*, pp. 166–7; E. C. Rouse, *Longthorpe Tower*, HMSO, 1964

44 *Ibid.*, pp. 8–19

45 P. Smith, *Houses of the Welsh Countryside*, p. 338

46 P. Smith and P. Hayes, 'Llyseurgain and the Tower', Flint HS, 22 (1965–6), 1–8

47 D. F. Renn, 'The Round Keeps of the Brecon Region'

48 M. Wood, *Thirteenth Century Domestic Architecture in England*, *Arch Jl*, 105, suppl vol., 1950, pp. 64–70; J. F. A. Mason, *Stokesay Castle*, official guide, n.d.

49 M. Wood, *Thirteenth Century Domestic Architecture*, pp. 70–2; *Shropshire*, BE, 1958, p. 200

50 P. Smith and P. Hayes, 'Llyseurgain'

51 Quoted in R. L. Storey, 'The North of England', in *Fifteenth Century England*, ed. S. B. Chrimes, C. D. Ross and R. A. Griffiths, Manchester, 1972, pp. 129–44

52 *Ibid.*

53 R. L. Storey, 'Disorders in Lancastrian Westmorland: Some Early Chancery Proceedings', *TrCWAAS*, NS 53 (1954), 69–80

54 *L & P Hen VIII*, 3, part 2, no. 3039

55 P. Ryder and J. Birch, 'Hellifield Peel – A North Yorkshire Tower-House', *Yorks AJ*, 55 (1983), 73–94

56 P. Dixon, 'Shielings and Bastles: A Reconsideration of Some Problems', *Arch Ael*, 4th ser., 50 (1972), 249–58; P. Dixon, 'Tower-houses, Pelehouses and Border Society', *Arch Jl*, 136 (1979) 240–52

57 *Roxburghshire*, HBMC(S), pp. 42–4

58 J. F. Curwen, *The Castles and Fortified Towers of Cumberland, Westmorland and Lancashire North of the Sands*, *TrCWAAS*, extra ser., 13 (1913), 173–87

59 G. Fairclough, 'Edlingham Castle: the Military and Domestic Development of a Northumbrian Manor: Excavations 1978–80: Interim Report', *Chât Gaill*, 9–10 (1982), 373–87; *Med Arch*, 23 (1979), 260–1; 24 (1980), 247–9; 25 (1981), 201–2

60 P. Borne and P. Dixon, 'Halton Castle Reconsidered', *Arch Ael*, 5th ser., 6 (1978), 131–9

61 J. Gibson, 'Featherstone Castle, Northumberland', *Arch Ael*, 4th ser., 2 (1926), 125–31

62 R. L. Story, 'The Manor of Burgh-by-Sands', *TrCWAAS*, 54 (1955), 119–30; R. Hogg, 'Excavation of the Fortified Manor House at Burgh-by-Sands', *ibid.*, 105–18

63 J. F. Curwen, *The Castles and Fortified Towers of Cumberland*, pp. 319–22

64 S. E. Rigold, 'Shank Castle, Cumberland', *TrCWAAS*, 54 (1955), 144–50

65 W. D. Simpson, 'Belsay Castle and the Scottish Tower-Houses', *Arch Ael*, 4th ser., 17 (1940), 75–84

66 L. Miller, 'Northumberland Pele Towers', *Arch Jl*, 133 (1976), 168–79

67 S. Cruden, *The Scottish Castle*, Edinburgh, 1960, pp. 100–43

68 P. Dixon, 'Towerhouses, Pelehouses and Border Society'

69 *Roxburghshire*, RCAM(S), 1956, pp. 42–5; *Selkirkshire*, RCAM(S), 1957, pp. 35–65

70 W. M. Mackenzie, *The Mediaeval Castle in Scotland*, London, 1927, pp. 202–4

71 C. Tabraham, 'Smailholm Tower: A Scottish Laird's Fortified Residence on the English Border', *Chât Gaill*, 13 (1987), 227–38

72 S. Cruden, *The Scottish Castle*, pp. 152–76

73 P. Dixon, 'Shielings and Bastles'; S. J. Watts, 'Tenant-right in Early Seventeenth Century Northumberland', *North H*, 6 (1971), 64–87

74 P. Dixon, 'Shielings and Bastles'

75 D. L. W. Tough, *The Last Years of a Frontier*, Oxford, 1928, pp. 87–92

76 G. E. P. Laws, *A Guide to Turton Tower*, Blackburn, 1983

77 Quoted in P. Campbell and P. Dixon, 'Two Fortified Houses in Haltwhistle', *Arch Ael*, 4th ser., 48 (1970), 169–81

78 P. Dixon, 'Towerhouses, Pelehouses and Border Society'

79 H. Ramm, R. W. McDowall and E. Mercer, *Shielings and Bastles*, HMSO, 1970

12 CONCLUSION

1 R. A. Brown, *Origins of English Feudalism*, London, 1973, pp. 82ff

2 K. B. McFarlane, 'The Wars of the Roses', *Pr Brit Acad*, 50 (1964), 87–119; McFarlane, *The Nobility of Later Medieval England*, Oxford, 1973, pp. 172–6

3 *Reports from the Lords Committees on the Dignity of a Peer of the Realm*, pp. 1826, vii and viii

4 F. R. H. Du Boulay, *An Age of Ambition*, London, 1970, pp. 61–79

5 C. Coulson, 'Structural Symmetry in Medieval Castle Architecture', *JBAA*, 132 (1979), 73–90;
   C. Coulson, 'Hierarchism in Conventual Crenellation: An Essay in the Sociology and
   Metaphysics of Medieval Fortification', *Med Arch*, 26 (1982), 69–100

6 M. W. Thompson, *The Decline of the Castle*, Cambridge, 1987, pp. 117–37

7 D. Renn, 'The Castles of Rye and Winchelsea', *Arch Jl*, 136 (1979), 193–202

8 *KW*, II, 787–92; for a survey of coastal defences at this time see A. Saunders, *Fortress Britain*,
   London, 1989, pp. 22–33

9 *KW*, II, 840–4

10 B. H. St J. O'Neil, *Dartmouth Castle*, HMSO, 1934

11 W. G. Hoskins, *Devon, A New Survey of England*, London, 1954, pp. 385, 421

12 *The Itinerary of John Leland*, ed. L. Toulmin Smith, vol. I, p. 214; *KW*, IV, 484–5

13 *KW*, IV, 415–606

14 J. R. Hale, 'The Defence of the Realm, 1485–1558', *KW*, IV, 367–401

15 At Falmouth the tenants of Sir John Killigrew were obligated to perform garrison duty, a curious
   feudal survival: Cal State P D, 1591–4, 152

16 Sir John Summerson, 'The Defence of the Realm under Elizabeth I', *KW*, IV, 402–14; K. J.
   Barton, reviewing *Castellarium Anglicanum*, *Arch Jl*, 141 (1984), 357–8

17 A. D. Saunders, *Upnor Castle (Kent)*, HMSO, 1967

18 C. R. Peers, *Carisbrooke Castle Isle of Wight*, HMSO, 1933

19 J. Le Patourel, *The Building of Castle Cornet, Guernsey, I Documents Relating to the Tudor
   Reconstruction*, Manchester, 1958

Index